# BOLIVIA:

# REVOLUTION AND THE POWER
# OF HISTORY IN THE PRESENT

# Bolivia:

# Revolution and the Power of History in the Present

## Essays

**James Dunkerley**

**British Library Cataloguing-in-Publication Data**
A catalogue record for this book is available
from the British Library

ISBN (paperback) 978-1-900039-81-9
ISBN (hardback)   978-1-900039-87-1

INSTITUTE FOR THE STUDY OF THE
**A M E R I C A S**
UNIVERSITY OF LONDON · SCHOOL OF ADVANCED STUDY

Institute for the Study of the Americas
31 Tavistock Square
London
WC1H 9HA

Telephone: 020 7862 8870
Fax: 020 7862 8886

Email: americas@sas.ac.uk
Web: www.americas.sas.ac.uk

# CONTENTS

# LIST OF TABLES

# Preface

The essays in this book were written over a period of nearly 30 years. With the exception of the opening piece on Evo Morales, they have not been substantially revised for the present book and so very much reflect the political and academic concerns prevailing at the time of their composition. At times, as in the survey of the 1980s, this involves a close and detailed narrative of matters that rarely figured in the news outside Bolivia, and when they did so, it was too often as noisy headlines pandering to hardy preconceptions if not outright prejudice.

The first chapter argues that one of the key obstacles facing the understanding of Bolivia by outsiders is that it is usually presented as a 'problem', whereas I believe that the affairs of the country are as complex and interesting as are those of, say, the US or Italy. They are simply consequential to fewer people, and often to the greater good of the human condition as a whole. This is not, of course, to say that Bolivia is 'good' by dint of being very poor or that it is somehow virtuous in that so many of its inhabitants are indigenous or mestizo. It is simply to object — on grounds of understandability as well as basic good manners — to the country and its people of all classes and convictions being used as a proxy for the political causes and sentimental ambitions of foreigners. There never will be any stopping of this, but it does need regular correction, not least in the form of cultural debate.

Students of Latin America have become wearily familiar with the cycles of boom and bust in attitudes towards the region held by the rest of the world. Very often, of course, these closely track the business cycle itself, with a 'missing decade' (the 1980s) preceding a buoyant phase of 'emerging markets' (the early 1990s) that gives way to a 'missing half decade', itself displaced by a return to growth in primary exports thought to herald a new phase of Chinese-led export expansion. Many such stories may be told through numbers, but they certainly do not lack powerful human consequences and can

determine not only the mood of a public era but also the temper of
the scholarship that it throws up. That is even more true of the
armed and radical politics of revolution and reaction that affected
much of South America and almost all of Central America in the
1970s and 1980s. Given that Latin America traded mostly with the
USA and itself, that Washington's writ ran very strong through the
Caribbean, and that the region shares strong cultural and institutional
experiences, it is not so surprising that we can trace certain conti-
nent-wide patterns of behaviour.

Yet, as vividly illustrated by, say, Peronism in Argentina, or the
political culture of Mexico, each country remains unique within that
wider unity. As elsewhere, this applies to Bolivia in both remarkable
and unremarkable ways, as I seek to demonstrate briefly in Chapter
3 with respect to the erratic 'transition' to liberal democratic institutionality. Yet events have increasingly shown that the country's
singularity modulates around not just its indigenous population and
culture but particularly around the interface between that population
and culture and a wider, outer ('globalised') political economy. That
economic system is certainly capable of delivering material progress
and even substantial welfare, but such transformations are often
associated with the loss of treasured value systems and ancient
modes of behaviour. Such an experience — wrenching and mes-
merising by turn — is no normal variation of the business cycle
over-determined by the world lottery in commodity prices. Equally,
it is not readily reducible to the left- and right-wing categories of
political culture that have hung on with remarkable resilience nearly
two decades after the end of the Cold War. If Gonzalo Sánchez de
Lozada's neo-liberal stabilisation of 1985 seemed to return the vex-
atious national economy firmly to the fold of the Washington
Consensus, the popular mobilisations from 2000 onwards succeeded
in showing how shallow were the civic roots of such a public policy.
Yet what I hope Chapter 1 illustrates is that such a contrarian experience was firmly rooted in local conditions and was only responsive
in a secondary manner to a more extensive, regional 'pink tide' of
governments critical of US policy. (Evo Morales would have 'happened' even if Hugo Chávez had not, but it is plain that President
Chávez has made Morales's job different, and generally easier.)

Most of the chapters collected here were written before I came, like many historians and social scientists, to a full appreciation of the deeper social currents at play — currents more readily recognisable to social anthropologists. Accordingly, much of the present material is concerned with the operation of ideas and institutions recognisable not just elsewhere in Latin America but even in North America and Europe. And these still matter: the conduct of elections free from fear and favours; the orderly distribution and management of public goods, particularly health and education; the defence of human rights and a culture of citizenship in which transparency, accountability and reciprocity are upheld at no significant prejudice to harmless particularities of culture and identity. At certain times and places, such phenomena might be seen as not just mundane but even as merely vestiges of a public order of pretence about to be swept away by powerful millennial forces.

Yet the great paradox of early twenty-first-century Bolivia is that the very sources of 'disorder' — the complicators of a smooth market civilisation — are often simply seeking to secure an equitable share of the very resources (and fair access to the systems) that they are disturbing. I have employed the term 'revolution' here more as a heuristic device — a means of reformulating a problem from a more creative perspective — than as a conclusive definition. However, as Sinclair Thomson and Forrest Hylton show in a study of wonderful range and fluency, whether taken in terms of state crisis or those of the restructuring of political power, the transformation of subjectivity or the possibility of a counter-revolution, there is a strong case that since 2000 Bolivia has been undergoing a revolutionary experience from which it will never return to the *status quo ante*.[1]

The chapters here have been arranged in receding chronological order — not, perhaps, how a standard work of history should proceed, but most of these pieces are more directly concerned with the present and the manner in which the past has been rearticulated within the present. Fuller context and a more regular narrative are given in two book-length studies written in the early 1980s, when the country seemed to be approaching a systemic collapse not so dissimilar to that of recent years and when the particularities of the military deserved attention.[2]

My interest in Bolivia began with an undergraduate dissertation that sought to explain why it was that Che Guevara's guerrillas were so readily defeated six years before. That task led naturally to a study of the Bolivian armed forces at a time when Latin American military establishments were widely unpopular and very difficult to study up close with an appropriate ethnography or serious institutional analysis. The experience was not always pleasant — my first fieldwork was conducted during the Banzer dictatorship, and I lacked the native wit, familiarity with local conditions or an intimate network of friends to stay out of trouble. I vividly recall a fellow postgraduate student at Oxford failing to recover either physically or psychologically from the experience of researching the Mataco people of the Chaco Boreal. Even in the present era of internet, cheap phone calls and a comprehensive 'shrinkage' of world space, such pressures on postgraduate researchers remain tough.

Moreover, it was only years later — when I was drafting the study of Francisco Burdett O'Connor (Chapter 7 of this volume) — that I finally clued up to the intellectual and existential ambivalences that had lured me into an otherwise inadvisable academic enterprise yielding what was by today's careerist standards an absolutely hopeless publications tally of one journal article in English (Chapter 6). As I quote René Zavaleta Mercado as saying in Chapter 1, Bolivia possesses either two armies or one profoundly schizophrenic military apparatus, on the one hand representative of a small, embattled but proud nation, and, on the other, trained and often viscerally predisposed to impose the *noche triste*, cutting down the multitude as if it were an atavistic enemy.

The earnest researches of 30 years ago benefited hugely from the help of senior scholars such as Gunnar Mendoza, Alberto Crespo Rodas and José Luis Roca, all of whom worked selflessly in the public sector and suffered periods of exile and censorship. From the first, I learnt that every researcher should always return the results of their investigations to the libraries and archives from which they have derived material (and often a well-paid northern career, effectively subsidised by very poor southern taxpayers). From the second, I acquired a measured appreciation of the metaphysical, which sometimes stopped at the telling of ghost stories but on one occasion threatened the exhumation of human remains and on another an earnest visit to an *adivinadora*, who threatened death by vomitous asphyxiation to the thief of a bracelet in the UMSA library reading room. And it was in the company of the third that I relearnt the merits of standing and shouting — entirely necessary in the face of brute force in July 1980, when the army of the *noche triste* staged a coup and expelled Dr Roca from the Embassy of Bolivia in Eaton Square, London. There was, though, some compensation in that the subsequent death threats from García Mesa's minions forced the ex-ambassador to take up an armour-plated research fellowship at the Institute of Latin American Studies.[3]

Although diplomatic ties between Great Britain and Bolivia were severed for over 50 years after 1854, strong British involvement in silver and tin mining contributed to a wider interest in the country, and this has endured. When I went to Oxford in the 1970s, a distinct group of 'Bolivianists' was emerging in the UK. It was headed by Laurence Whitehead, who seems to have acquired the brief from Raymond Carr, the historian of Spain and then Warden of St Antony's College who claims that his initial notes on the Revolution of 1952 were stolen at the check-in at Buenos Aires' Ezeiza airport. Some might think that such things happen only on the banks of the Isis and the Río de la Plata, but Laurence has subsequently spread the word on a world scale through a truly epic career of conference participation. I should also issue a very belated apology to another (by then non-Oxford) member of this group, Olivia Harris, for interrupting a political meeting held in November 1979 to protest against the coup of Alberto Natusch Busch. I did so, in rather Bolivian manner, because — the words echo woundingly to this day — she and the other participants were mere 'bourgeois reformists' who had either not seen or purposefully ignored the searing light of permanent revolution. It was only upon reading Olivia's collected essays that I fully understood the scale of my stupidity and the formidable nature of her own good humour. More recently, the long-awaited publication of *Qaraqara-Charca* — written with Tristan Platt and Therese Bouysse-Cassagne — has hugely enriched our understanding of social and political power in the southern Andes between the fifteenth and eighteenth centuries.[4]

I wish that I was just a little bit younger for all sorts of reasons, but not the least of these because I could have been more actively

researching the history of Bolivia in the company of exceptionally talented people — most of them women — who in recent years have
transformed our understanding of the country. No less than those
born in the 1920s and 1930s, these intellectuals born in the 1960s have
assumed civic responsibilities in directing public institutions, taking
charge of national and international associations as well as teaching for
a pittance. However — mostly in the guise of the Coordinadora de la
Historia — they have continued to conduct fine research and publish it
in an accessible and engaging manner. Rossana Barragán, Ana María
Lema, Seemin Qayum, María Luisa Soux, and Esther Aillón are just a
few of those whose labours have placed Bolivian historiography far
higher than might be expected given the paucity of local resources.[5]

Almost every passage in the pages that follow was drafted with the
direct support of the Institute of Latin American Studies (ILAS) and
its successor the Institute for the Study of the Americas (ISA), both of
the University of London, where I have worked with only very short
interruptions since 1981. Both at 'the Institute', as I write still located
in Tavistock Square, and at Queen Mary, located with greater assurance
still on the Mile End Road, I have benefited from thoroughly benign
bosses and some of the most talented colleagues you could wish for.
Oxford might be an ancient university town but London is a great one
and remains so after the collegiate carve-up of the 1990s. Sometimes,
when I witness the professoriat's prodigious capacity for complaint, I
am put in mind of the *bloqueos* of Achacachi or a miners' congress in,
say, Huanuni, where the plangent rhetoric, fluidity of manoeuvre, and
infinite righteousness combine in an intoxicating cocktail. The orange
glow of the 24/7 world city morphs into the frozen shadows of the
Andean alleyways, and parallax settles accounts with those who would
essentialise the exotic or deliver us only dichotomies.

### Notes

1   *Revolutionary Horizons: Popular Struggle in Bolivia* (New York and
    London, 2007).
2   *Rebellion in the Veins. Political Struggle in Bolivia, 1952–1982*
    (London, 1984); *Orígenes del poder militar. Historia del ejército boli-
    viano, 1879–1935* (La Paz, 1988).

3    Alberto Crespo Rodas, *Recuerdo Crepuscular* (La Paz, 2002); José
     Luis Roca, *Bolivia después de la capitalización* (La Paz, 2000).
4    *To Make the Earth Bear Fruit: Ethnographic Essays on Fertility, Work and
     Gender in Highland Bolivia* (London, 2000); *Qaraqara-Charca. Mallku,
     inka y rey en la provincial de Charcas (Siglos XV–XVIII)* (La Paz, 2006).
5    A. Lema (ed.), *Bosquejo del estado en que se halla la riqueza nacional
     de Bolivia con resultados, presentado al examen de la nación por un alde-
     ano hijo de ella. Año de 1830* (La Paz, 1994); R. Barragán, D. Cajías,
     S. Qayum (eds.), *El Siglo XIX. Bolivia y América Latina* (La Paz,
     1997); D. Cajías, M. Cajías, C. Johnson, I. Villegas (eds.), *Visiones
     de fin de siglo. Bolivia y América Latina en el siglo XX*, (La Paz, 2001).

# ACKNOWLEDGEMENTS

All chapters originally appeared under their present titles. Chapter 1 was first published (in significantly shorter form) as 'Evo Morales, the Two Bolivias and the Third Bolivian Revolution', in the *Journal of Latin American Studies*, vol. 39, no. 1, February 2007. It appears here by kind permission of Cambridge University Press. Chapter 2 originally appeared as Occasional Paper no. 16, Institute of Latin American Studies (ILAS), University of London, 1998. Chapter 3 was first published as ILAS Research Paper, no. 22, 1990. Chapter 4 originally appeared as ILAS Occasional Paper no. 2, 1992. Chapter 5 was first published in Merilee S. Grindle and Pilar Domingo (eds.), *Proclaiming Revolution. Bolivia in Comparative Perspective,* David Rockefeller Center for Latin American Studies, Harvard University and Institute of Latin American Studies, University of London, 2003. Chapter 6 first appeared in the *Bulletin of Latin American Research*, vol. 1, no. 1, October 1981. Chapter 7 was originally published as ILAS Occasional Paper no. 22, 1999.

Thanks are due to all these publishers and editors for their intellectual and commercial collegiality.

# 1

## Evo Morales, Álvaro García Linera and the Third Bolivian Revolution

### The 'Problem' of Bolivia

> In the world there are large and small countries, rich countries and poor countries, but we are equal in one thing which is our right to dignity and sovereignty.
>
> Evo Morales, Inaugural speech,
> 22 January 2006

Lacking size in all but territory and imagination, Bolivia is indisputably a 'small country'. At the start of the twenty-first century her population falls just short of 9 million people and the GDP a little shy of $8 billion. Statistically, these figures roll out a GDP per capita of around $900, but Bolivia is a country that is really, not just averagely, poor — 35 per cent of its population (2,966,000 people) are completely indigent, subsisting on an income of less than $1 per day.[1] The first strategic plan issued by the government of Movimiento al Socialismo (MAS) headed by Evo Morales had as its markedly modest objective the reduction of the proportion of acutely poor to 27 per cent of all Bolivians within five years; the supposed Jacobins of the Andes hoped merely to diminish the pecuniary advantage of the richest tenth of Bolivians from 25 to 16 times the income of the bottom decile.[2]

This is stark stuff and never to be despised, but it is surely easy enough to understand. Very poor people, after all, are widely held to conduct bleak but essentially uncomplicated lives. The regnant ideas of our day postulate elementary remedies, in which a due dose of clear thinking, political will and decent behaviour will provide at least some deliverance from economic prostration. Smith, Condorcet and Paine had 'an end to poverty' firmly within their conceptual compass (as 'common sense') in the 1780s, and 200 years later the indefatigable Jeffrey Sachs (not yet backed by Bono) was instructing the government in La Paz to the same end.[3]

Accordingly, considerable indulgence was initially extended by the 'big' 'chancelleries of the world to the rather bumptious Morales and his entirely inexperienced cabinet comprised of indigenous activists (of all ages), sixty-something left-wingers from the 1970s, and forty-something radical intellectuals from the 1990s. Although protocol could so readily have been dispensed with, George W. Bush did make a congratulatory telephone call despite Evo having described himself as 'Washington's worst nightmare'. Even after the new government had (re)nationalised the hydrocarbons industry, halted the mandatory eradication of coca, and hosted three visits by Hugo Chávez in six months, the United States expressed little more than tight-lipped irritation.[4]

The nationalisation of gas — conspicuously conducted as a military operation to great media fanfare — was described by a normally sympathetic source as 'almost infantile'.[5] When, nearly a hundred years earlier, Alcides Arguedas published *Pueblo Enfermo*, a bravura historical essay of racially-powered pessimism, José Enrique Rodó suggested to him that a better title would be *Pueblo Niño* because Bolivia's ills, like those of Latin America as a whole, were transitory in their nature.[6] In 2005, after half a decade of civil strikes and blockades of roads (*bloqueos*) with five different presidents seeking to manage the seemingly hapless affairs of the republic, the British ambassador to a neighbouring country asked me in genuine anguish, 'why don't they just grow up?' Perhaps we should add adolescence to smallness and poverty as an exculpatory variable? After all, nearly half of the population is under 20 years of age and, with a life expectancy of 63, relatively few Bolivians are making claims on the country's precarious pension system — a fiscal fabrication at the heart of the 1990s privatisation ('capitalisation') experiment.

There are, in fact, evidence-based and plausible explanations for such phenomena. These range from accounts based on geographical determinism to those of historical revisionism, which we will consider shortly. Nevertheless, understanding the country today is far from easy, even if we simply wish to comprehend the apparent disavowal of modernity by many of its citizens and their failure to thrive according to Enlightenment postulates of 'progress'. As *The Economist* commented in July 2004, 'Bolivia is not for beginners'.[7] In recent years this defiance of the zeitgeist has been most energetically expressed through a kind of retentive mercantilism or telluric protectionism, with an effort to withhold the second-largest reserves of natural gas in South America from external forces deemed to be the direct heirs and successors of Iberian imperialists and Anglo neo-colonialists who, from the 1540s onwards, pillaged the mineral wealth of what was Kollasuyo, then Charcas, then Alto Peru, and from 1825 the Republic of Bolivia.[8] What might be termed 'the Potosí syndrome' could well be historically justified and economically reasonable, but it is also at the heart of the 'paranoid style' in Bolivian public life, with all 'the qualities of heated exaggeration, suspiciousness, and ... feeling of persecution' described by Richard Hofstadter for the USA.[9]

The indigenous features of this phenomenon are the most perplexing for those of an upbringing dominated by European rationalism. Less than half the population today regularly communicates in the languages of Aymara, Quechua and Guaraní, but in the 2001 census some 62 per cent of respondents identified themselves as 'indigenous', and in the 800,000-strong city of El Alto, situated right above La Paz, that figure rises to 75 per cent.[10] One of the leading popular organisations of recent years is the Confederación Nacional de Ayllus y Marcas del Qullasuyo (Conamaq). Conamaq is younger than the class-based peasant union, Confederación Sindical Única de Trabajadores Campesinos de Bolivia (CSUTCB), which emerged from the radicalism the late 1970s and the 1980s, and yet Conamaq congregates pre-colonial social organisations under a title that raises a question about the very existence of Bolivia. The banner of this movement is the *wiphala*, a flag of 49 squares of the seven colours of the rainbow, with the reds representing the *Mallkus* (literally 'Condors') or indigenous authorities. In a recent internet poll 48 per cent of 10,000 respondents supported the incorporation of the *wiphala* as a formal patriotic symbol of Bolivia. Given that 80 per cent of Bolivians have no telephone, let alone an internet connection, this suggests a significant degree of syncretism and cultural hybridity. It would certainly be at odds with the views of the most prominent *Mallku* of the present, Felipe Quispe of Achacachi, for whom, on some days, Kollasuyo is a separate utopian state,

> where there are no traitors, nor poor or rich, and we live in the same condition, without the political revenge that always comes with racism, because we don't want to replace white mestizo racism with that of the Indian.[11]

On other days Quispe, who was jailed for five years in the 1990s for guerrilla activity, has felt able to call upon the indigenous poor to,

> rise up in arms, hunt down and judge the bosses … burn the houses of the rich and starve out the cities that oppress and exploit us … only that which is native is good; the rest is rubbish.[12]

Such sentiments are assuredly at the radical end of the spectrum, and they only find resonance at times of crisis. Quispe's Movimiento Indio Pachakuti (MIP) won barely 6 per cent of the vote in the 2002 elections and just over 2 per cent in those of 2005. Yet Bolivia has been precisely in a state of crisis for the better part of a decade, so maybe the Aymara voters of the northern *altiplano* (Andean plain) sensibly do not vote for an organisation that is not essentially interested in the politics of voting. In all events, when Quispe declares an 'irreversible retirement' from political life because of his community obligations ('me toca cargar el chicote comunal'), one wonders. After all: 'I never imagined that the enemy of the Indian was the Indian himself.' Quispe disdains Evo Morales (*un sindicatero*) and sees vice-president Álvaro García Linera as a traitor to the old Ejército Guerrillero Tupaj Katari (EGTK). He and his like will always be on the far wings of institutionalised politics, but when political life is collectivised by mass action in the *altiplano* theirs is an inescapable presence.[13]

What will truly be irreversible is a self-confident indigenous presence in the management of broad parts of public life. Indeed, this has been in evidence since 2002, when the MAS won over a fifth of the national vote, securing a presence in congress that was, if anything, less conspicuous with regard to programme than to clothing and language — 'Ñoqapis munani parlayta' ('I too want to speak').[14] García Linera may have been over-ambitious in talking of 'four civilisations' existing within the space that is today Bolivia, but civilisations do not always trade under the same sign. Equally, Orlando Patterson surely has a point when he observes that 'identity politics often trump common sense', and it is the trumping that one remembers.[15] For Fernando Molina, a leading liberal critic of both Evo Morales and the traditional political class that he has displaced from office, the conflict of recent years has been underpinned by, 'a very active mass presence, culturally resistant to any involvement in a common project with those who do not share the same identity'.[16] Molina sees such a politics of refusal as underpinning a culture of *immobilism*, a deep and abiding obstinacy. On the other hand, a recent remarkable work of Aymara history in the early modern period by a group of European scholars reveals a far richer material and ideational culture, many cosmological and political motifs of which are still recognisable in our own day.[17]

A key part of that culture is what I would term 'rogatory', including a range of behaviours from formalist supplication to demanding with menaces, the practice of which may be as ethically satisfying as it is practically rewarding. Not everything is what it sounds to be in such a moral economy, which can move in and out of the Eurocentric 'rational repertoire' and which, as we will see, is nowhere near as immutable as some fondly believe and proclaim.

Another, allied, factor complicating the analysis of Bolivia since 2000 is that after 13 years of what Álvaro García Linera has termed 'popular slumber', there was an extraordinary acceleration in the pace of mass political activity.[18] Table 1.1 is long enough as it stands, but it still covers only the 'headline' occurrences in the making of Bolivia's current revolution. We may now, in 2007, begin to understand these events as a process — in some kind of a sequence — and so discern a pattern of continuity. Yet the country's reputation in academic analysis as well as newspaper lore is of the reverse — of discontinuity and repeated interruption of the prescribed performative pulse of a liberal democratic regime. In the old days it was the coup d'état that was the primary form of rupture, the instances being counted so assiduously as if the calculus might, through rational ordering, tame the kind of exasperation we have already noted. (The *Guinness Book of Records* has tallied 157 coups between 1825 and 1982; Jean-Pierre Lavaud has worked out that of the 73 presidents over that period, 33 held office for less than a year; and nobody has laboured more industriously over the enumeration of executive misadventure than Carlos Mesa, who himself held the presidency for a statistically respectable 20 months.)[19]

## Table 1.1: The Bolivian Revolution, 2000–2006

| | **2000** |
|---|---|
| Jan. | Coalition for Defence of Water and Life (*Coordinadora*) calls general strike in Cochabamba over water rates of newly privatised 'Aguas de Tunari'; government promises review. |
| Feb. | Renewed strikes over water supply and ownership in Cochabamba; military deployed, 175 injured. |
| April | Blockade (*bloqueo*) of regional roads and 10-hour civil strike in Cochabamba forces revocation of privatisation of water; state of siege in rural La Paz over *campesino* and *cocalero* protests; Felipe Quispe detained; two shot dead before CSUTCB signs truce. |
| June | March of lowland indigenous peoples for 'Land, Territories and Natural Resources'. |
| Sept. | Widespread *bloqueos* as *cocaleros* oppose new military posts in Chapare and teachers demand 50 per cent pay rise; CSUTCB halts talks; three protesters shot dead by army in Huarina. |
| Oct. | Banzer government formally accepts 50 CSUTCB demands; Quispe sets up MIP political party. |
| Nov. | Five killed in military removal of *bloqueos* in Chapare. |
| Dec. | Government declares 'Coca Cero' policy. |
| | **2001** |
| April | Quispe formally 'expels' Evo Morales from the CSUTCB. |
| May | Failure of Church-sponsored 'Second National Dialogue' over policies for privatisation and poverty reduction. |

| July | Two weeks of *bloqueos* in *altiplano* where some 'liberated territories' are declared. |
|---|---|
| August | Ailing Banzer, elected in 1997, replaced by vice-president Jorge ('Tuto') Quiroga; new agreement signed with CSUTCB and *cocaleros*. |
| Nov. | Nine killed in Chapare in clashes between police and *cocaleros*. |

## 2002

| Jan. | Evo Morales expelled from congress for alleged complicity in death of police officers in Chapare clashes. |
|---|---|
| Feb. | Quispe leads renewed *altiplano bloqueos*; three-week *bloqueo* in Chapare. |
| March | Quispe adopts electoralist strategy. |
| June | General elections narrowly won by Gonzalo Sánchez de Lozada and the MNR; US Ambassador Manuel Rocha warns against vote for Morales and MAS; Sánchez de Lozada forms 'Megacoalición' controlled by traditional forces; Evo Morales returns to congress. |
| August | US approves Andean Preferential Tariff (ATPDEA), reducing tariffs on many products upon condition of coca eradication. |
| Dec. | In the face of opposition, government declares suspension of eradication campaign but refuses to discuss any topic with MAS other than coca. |

## 2003

| Jan. | US envoy Otto Reich threatens aid cut if obligatory eradication not resumed; 12 *cocaleros* killed in repression of Chapare *bloqueo*; IMF requires reduction in budget deficit. |
|---|---|
| Feb. | Riots and widespread looting in La Paz over introduction of 12.5 per cent income tax designed to cut budget deficit; 29 shot dead and 205 injured as army clashes with mutineering police units; government withdraws tax. |

| | |
|---|---|
| June | 'Estado Mayor del Pueblo' established under Quispe's aegis to oppose proposed gas pipeline to Chile. |
| Sept. | Quispe leads hunger strike in El Alto over arrest of *altiplano* indigenous leader for imposing customary law on rustlers; six shot dead by troops at Warisata, near Quispe's home. |
| Oct. | Sánchez de Lozada overthrown after three uninterrupted weeks of *bloqueos*, and 11-day general strike over the gas question; 69 deaths in El Alto as a result of military operations to break 'siege' of La Paz, the centre of the conflict; vice-president Carlos Mesa, opposed to the repression, assumes presidency; coca eradication suspended. |

## 2004

| | |
|---|---|
| Jan. | Mesa challenges Chilean government at Inter-American Summit in Monterrey over Bolivia's land-locked status; government refuses pact with political parties in congress and promises new hydrocarbons law. |
| Feb. | Fifteen articles of the Constitution amended to permit the initiation of legislation by citizens, the holding of referendums and the establishment of a constituent assembly. |
| April | Without congressional approval, Mesa convokes a referendum over gas, proposing questions over increased state control and taxes, and the use of the gas issue in negotiations with Chile; opposition from 'Media Luna' departments headed by Santa Cruz and Tarija, which want enhanced 'autonomy', the COB trade union confederation and the FEJUVE (Federation of Neighbourhood Councils) of El Alto. |
| May | Clashes between government and party-dominated congress lead to renewed crisis; Morales calls for moderation over gas issue, supporting Mesa government and planned referendum. |
| June | Striking teachers kidnap minister of education; government refuses to include existing gas contracts in referendum. |

July    Referendum, held without major incident, approves national ownership of gas production at well head; Morales resumes attacks on Mesa administration; Filemón Escobar expelled from MAS.

Oct.    Santa Cruz threatens unilateral implementation of departmental 'autonomy' unless government calls binding referendum on the issue; congress votes for impeachment of Sánchez de Lozada and cabinet for 'genocide' in October 2003.

Nov.    Mesa accepts MAS call to halt coca eradication.

Dec.    MAS performs unevenly in first municipal elections to include citizen groups.

---

### 2005

---

Jan.    Petrol price rises required by IMF provoke strikes and *bloqueos* in altiplano; autonomist forces in Santa Cruz present 500,000-signature petition for referendum; occupation of prefecture of Santa Cruz and further direct action threatened; El Alto FEJUVE demands removal of 'Aguas de Illimani' and trial of Sánchez de Lozada; Mesa reiterates disavowal of repression in fierce denunciation of polarised forces; Morales calls Mesa 'principal enemy' of Bolivia; reduces attacks when government secures congressional support (*transversales*) from across the party spectrum.

Feb.    Government concedes direct election of prefects, proposes combined elections of constituent assembly and prefects with referendum over departmental autonomy.

March   Congress divided over relative and absolute tax/royalty levels proposed in new hydrocarbons law; civic strikes and *bloqueos* in El Alto over privatised water spread nationally; Mesa resigns, attacking opposition leadership on television; Morales and Quispe form radical 'Pact of Unity'; Mesa resignation withdrawn.

| | |
|---|---|
| April | The 76 hydrocarbons contracts signed under Decree 24806 ruled unconstitutional because not ratified by congress. |
| May | Congress approves new hydrocarbons law with 32 per cent profit tax and 18 per cent royalty; Mesa 'observes' law in effective blanket veto; relations with congress ruptured; MST land occupation in Santa Cruz; government calls emergency summit; Evo Morales booed in public. |
| June | Argentina and Brazil send envoys to seek political solution; military high command ratifies support for the democratic process; eight of the country's nine departments closed by *bloqueos* in demand of full nationalisation of gas and elections for a constituent assembly; Mesa resigns; peasants and miners blockade Sucre, preventing congressional leadership controlling presidential succession; Eduardo Rodríguez, president of the supreme court, assumes presidency and calls elections for December. |
| Dec. | MAS and Evo Morales win landslide victory in national elections. |

## 2006

| | |
|---|---|
| Jan. | Having undertaken a nine-country international tour, Morales assumes office amidst high expectations but in tranquil conditions. |
| May | Immediately following a visit by President Morales to Cuba, government declares 'nationalisation' of the hydrocarbons sector in unannounced military operation. |
| July | MAS wins constituent elections but fails to secure two-thirds majority. |
| August | 'Nationalisation' of hydrocarbons suspended because of financial weakness of YPFB, the state corporation; continued conflict in assembly over majority requirements. |
| Sept. | Petrobras continues to refuse gas price rises; replacement of Andrés Soliz Rada, responsible for gas nationalisation. |

Few can seriously dispute this empirical record or question its corrosive effect. However, from 2000 onwards it is the *bloqueo*, not the coup, that is the primary mechanism of 'disorder'. Notwithstanding the massacre of October 2003, it is the masses, not the armed forces, who are the principal authors. The exasperation caused abroad is, therefore, greater still. By March 2005, with social conflicts running at over 400 a year, even Carlos Toranzo, one of the calmest and wisest political commentators, was driven to write a column under the title 'Demandas legítimas':

> We demand the replacement of Aguas de Illimani by a social water company funded by the money that we demand from the World Bank and other international agencies … We demand that the fares of buses, micro-buses, provincial and departmental transport are frozen for 30 years so that the Government can demonstrate that it really has a genuine strategy for the sector. We demand the expulsion of the US embassy, of the European embassies and all the international organisations, of Coca Cola, Pepsi and Papaya Salvietti, because they are contaminated by Italians, so that we can begin a process of genuine national development.[20]

What is notable about this outburst is that it is the only time that I can recall in over 30 years that Toranzo has been found amongst the serried ranks of experts who habitually confuse cause with effect, taking the coups and *bloqueos* as the essence of the problem, rather than its expression.

We would do well to recall de Tocqueville's conviction that, 'The remedy for the vices of the army is not to be found in the army itself, but in the country'.[21] That might be thought to be explaining away a state institution with a bland social determinism that cannot so readily be applied to wide sectors of society as a whole. However, René Zavaleta Mercado, who opened his study of the political crisis of 1979–1980 with de Tocqueville's quote, postulates the existence of two distinct Bolivian armies, the first of which reflects the nationalist tradition:

> this is the army that must *feel* those aspects of the nation that existed before the nation or that lie behind its particularism, such as the properties of the earth and the corporatist vision of the world.

This is the army that occupied the San Alberto gas field on 1 May 2006, Colonel Rodríguez's FCTC troops so upsetting Petrobras executives but attracting great popular support, even from Santa Cruz, where the fact that this was territory defended against Paraguay in the Chaco War (1932–1935) momentarily overrode all other disputes.

The second of Zavaleta's armies is more widely recognisable:

> ... the classical army, the essential reason for which is the fear of the *noche triste*. The function of this army is to resist the siege of the Indians ... that atavism known as Tupaj Katari.[22]

Here we encounter the armed forces of October 2003, when some 70 civilians were shot down precisely in order to break the 'siege' of La Paz from (and by) El Alto through the withholding of oil supplies.

If such a dialectic can exist for the military, then, why not for the rural and urban poor? They, after all, denominated the social conflict of early 2000 over Aguas de Tunari in Cochabamba as 'the Water War' and the *bloqueos* of October 2003 as 'the Gas War'. Oscar Oliveira's memoir of the former struggle is a *testimonio* in truly heroic voice. Álvaro García Linera, who may not have entirely shaken off the Central American guerrilla influences of his youth or some nostalgia for the EGTK, identifies the establishment by Quispe of an Estado Mayor del Pueblo in June 2003 as a vital moment in the passage of events between February, when the army and the police shot more at each other than at civilians, and October, when the soldiers attacked the citizenry directly. And in that *noche triste* García Linera is clear that it was precisely the deaths suffered that ruptured the 'docility of the masses', making a qualitative difference between a partly symbolic and a fully physical conflict.[23]

The overthrow of Gonzalo Sánchez de Lozada and what García Linera terms 'the neo-liberal-patrimonial state' did not, though, take the form of direct armed attack on the institutions of that state, either in October 2003 or in December 2005. Rather, it has two symbolic moments. The first was at midnight on 16 October 2003, at the village of Patacamaya, some 109 kilometres from La Paz, when a colonel and miner embraced, and the army allowed 58 trucks of workers through to the seat of government to demand the removal of the president (who resigned immediately upon hearing this news).

The second took place at the end of the 2005 election campaign, when Evo Morales, accused by his leading opponent Jorge 'Tuto' Quiroga of preferring the *wiphala* to the flag of the republic, kissed the Bolivian tricolour, declaring that he had sworn allegiance to the flag every day as a conscript, while Quiroga had never submitted to any military service.[24] 'Bolivia is conflict,' Zavaleta once wrote, but it is not always presented to us in predictable form.

Photo 1.1: The conscript Evo Morales on sentry duty in the presidential palace, late 1970s [from P. Stefanoni and H. Do Alto, *Evo Morales. De la coca al palacio* (La Paz, 2006).

Events such as these did not appear in the foreign press, and they would scarcely promote 'the story' that newspapers must perforce tell, explain, and editorialise over. The simplifications inevitably required by such a narrative do, in their own way, also complicate the academic understanding of the present crisis since we are faced with a series of necessary-but-insufficient accounts often written in high register in order to win an audience and hold a line. This is just as true of veteran commentators as of eager stringers:

> When foreigners take an interest in Bolivia's natural resources, fortunes are made by the few and the mass of Bolivians stay hungry. It was like that with the Spanish when tens of thousands of Quechua and Aymara died working the great silver mountain at Potosí to fund the Spanish empire. It was like that under the military dictatorships and now, they have discovered, it is like that under elected governments too.[25]

And the paradigm of untrammelled exploitation is matched by another of uncomplicated struggle:

> In 2000 something remarkable happened. The Bolivian people rose up and expelled Bechtel from the country, keeping the water under democratic control. Over the past week the Bolivian people have risen again. They want to be allowed to grow coca without American interference, including — yes — for the huge global market in recreational drugs.[26]

Richard Gott has known Bolivia longer and understands it better than any other foreign journalist, so he adds a final, subordinate note of caution, but he still endorses the same image:

> One of the most significant events in 500 years of Latin American history will take place in Bolivia on Sunday when Evo Morales, an Aymara Indian, is inducted as president ... Morales's victory is just a symptom of economic breakdown and age-old repression. It also fulfils a prophecy made by Fidel Castro, who claimed the Andes would become the Americas' Sierra Maestra — the Cuban mountains that harboured black and Indian rebels over the centuries ... False dawns are common in Latin American history, but the

strength of the radical tide suggests that this time it will not be dammed, still less reversed.[27]

Hold on. This is Bolivia. If we are listening to the left, then we should expect to find the ultras closing fast on their tail, admonitory energies and inexhaustible corrective capacity directed less at the class enemy than the doctrinally insufficient. Here they come, in the not unfamiliar shape of Professor James Petras:

> Once again in Bolivia we have a popular leader elected to power. Once again we have an army of uncritical left cheer-leaders, ignorant of significant facts and policy changes over the last five years … with the exception of Chávez, the presence of Indians in high places did not lead to the passage of any progressive measures in basically neo-liberal regimes … the exuberant left and sectors of the far right (especially in the U.S. and Bolivia) evoke a scenario in which a radical leftist Indian president, responding to the great majority of poor Bolivians, will transform Bolivia from a white oligarchic-imperialist dominated country … An alternative scenario, the one I hold, sees Morales as a moderate social liberal … He will not nationalize petrol or gas MNCs.[28]

The decrying of delusion and treason was ever thus. Most folk abroad pleased at the election of Evo Morales will still have understood it in the terms used by Hilton, Hari and Gott — that is, through a model of dichotomous relations: international neoliberals v. exploited nationals; whites v. Indians; oligarchs v. subalterns; global models v. local experiences, etc. Yet when voiced so starkly, the difficulties do begin to emerge. Sinclair Thomson and Forrest Hylton, as radical in outlook as they are knowledgeable about Bolivia, register a discreet warning:

> we should avoid treating the crisis simply as a local effect of a predictable trans-national phenomenon. We should not take either 'neoliberalism' or 'globalisation' as an autonomous agent that inevitably generates its own grave-diggers … [29]

Thomson and Hylton are here picking up on an evident weakness of the left when it indiscriminately deploys the term 'neo-liberal model' as if that were everywhere a beast of self-evident characteristics — something that Fernando Molina has tellingly criticised as the

comfortable use of a rhetorical category to evade analytical responsibility.[30] Roberto Laserna asks what, precisely, the 'model' is
supposed to be in Bolivia — the 1985 stabilisation plan (Decree
21060), the political pacts, or maybe just the privatisations of the
1990s? He notes laconically that poverty, ethnic discrimination,
violence against women and children, and environmental degrada-
tion were all integral to Bolivian life before 1985. In the same vein,
Felipe Mansilla protests that it is thoroughly misguided to associate
all Andean morality with collectivism and reciprocity and all
European values as enshrined in possessive individualism.[31]

It is, nonetheless, hard to arrive at a more fairly weighted and
nuanced appraisal when so much of the local political discourse as
well as the international depiction rotates about the idea of 'two
Bolivias'. This, as Thomson and Hylton point out, is an image that
Quispe successfully projected beyond radical Aymara circles to civil
society as a whole.[32] Nowhere has the bipolarity been seized on with
more enthusiasm than in Santa Cruz and Tarija — the oil- and gas-
producing departments of 'the east', where there has been an
aggressive repudiation of the highland 'west's' suspicions about the
outside world and any export strategy. After the overthrow of
Gonzalo Sánchez de Lozada in October 2003, Roberto Ruiz, president of the Comité Cívico of Tarija, made it clear that 'the Gas War'
was seen by some as a distinctly pyrrhic victory:

> Bolivians have two options. One is to carry on thinking that
> we'll always be ripped off, so it's best not to do any deal at all
> in order that in 20 years' time we can enjoy the doubtful satis-
> faction of saying that nobody tricked us. We'll be in the same
> pitiful poverty, staring at ourselves like flies but, to be sure,
> unfleeced. The other option is to be proactive, establish clear
> rules and demand compliance to ensure that the black history
> is not repeated ... [33]

What is presented in Tarija as a choice, albeit a tough one, is
declaimed in Santa Cruz as an already settled state:

> The two Bolivias ... that which wants a relation with the
> wider world, which wants to improve economically, and that
> which wants the 500 years, the Bolivia of failure.[34]

Even before October 2003 nobody could plausibly claim that the gas question was a simple matter in commercial terms. Moreover, it would not have been so even if the proposition of exporting to the Pacific had been viable in 1990 (when Law 1494 introduced shared risk contracts between YPFB and private companies as well as a profits tax) or 1996 (when Law 1689 'capitalised' YPFB, radically reducing its reserved operating and regulatory powers, which were effectively thrown into the market-place) or 1997 (when two days before Sánchez de Losada left office for the first time, Decree 24604 greatly eased the contractual conditions for foreign firms). This has always been a highly complex area of commercial calculation as well as public policy. If there were some on the left who really believed that YPFB could be seamlessly transformed by edict into some kind of mega-*ayllu*, they discovered in August 2006 just how complicated it was to secure sufficient working capital to allow the company to operate with minimal efficiency (a little under $2 billion) and buy back the shares that had been 'sold' in 1997, let alone negotiate new export prices with neighbouring markets, or conduct professional audits of the foreign companies, or negotiate new operating contracts with them. And none of this addressed the issue of the payment of state pensions, the funds for which had been derived from YPFB's initial 'capitalisation'. The whole matter was, as *The Economist* rightly put it, 'a business dispute caught up in a social revolution', and few on a left disproportionately opposed to capitalist enterprise in the hydrocarbons sector (including, of course, state companies such as Petrobras) were concerned to bother themselves with the technical terms of that dispute.[35]

Equally, not many on the right and the commercial circuit — and certainly those within what must be deemed the very clumsy local management of the TNCs — seemed to have grasped just how much their high-risk, expensive and vulnerable business had become politicised, how deeply unpopular they had become in the valleys and the *altiplano*, and how a stubbornness on the part of the highland population might eventually translate into a much more rigorous fiscal climate and competitive pricing structure. The political paradox revealed from mid-2003 onwards is that a 'two Bolivias' strategy of the type promoted by Santa Cruz and the other departments of the *media luna* (ranged in an arc from Tarija in the south, through Santa Cruz, to Beni and Pando in the north) placed the TNCs at greater risk.

The conservative prospectus in all this has been most pugnaciously promulgated by the novelist Mario Vargas Llosa. In his syndicated newspaper column, Vargas Llosa has focused on the figure of Evo Morales, whose popularity is only explicable through 'that death drive that, according to Freud, is in dispute with the erotic in the depths of the human personality over its direction ...'[36] Once Morales was elected, Vargas Llosa took the fight to the likes of Richard Gott, predicting that the new president's 'dress-down signature style' of striped jumpers and leather jackets with textile trim would rapidly become the sartorial preference of *bien pensant* European and North American camp-followers. (That, happily, has proved to be just as poor a prediction as that proffered by Petras with regard to nationalisation.) Much more consequentially, Vargas Llosa effectively accused those circles of a form of racism:

> To pose the problem of Latin America in terms of race, as is done by the demagogues [Chávez, Morales, Humala] is incredibly irresponsible. It is the same as the stupid and interested prejudices against the Indians of those Latin Americans who believe that they are white ... besides, strictly speaking, Señor Evo Morales is no Indian ... [37]

Here, one senses, Vargas Llosa was attempting both to puncture the socio-moral pretensions of the left — *The Economist* likewise referred off-handedly to Morales as a 'mestizo trade union leader' — and move away from a 'two Bolivias' strategy wedded to further polarisation and likely to promote secession.[38] The response was delivered with remarkable pithiness by José Luis Roca, a rare supporter of both renationalising YPFB and departmental autonomy:

> Vargas Llosa denies that Evo is an Indian, arguing that he was only born into a 'poor indigenous family', although he does him the favour of admitting that he was 'as a child a llamaherd'. According to Vargas Llosian logic, Evo is not indigenous despite having indigenous parents.

Roca then slips into the second person from which to wound with a quick stab of Occam's razor:

In your article, you say that this 'racial purity, if indeed it
exists, is now confined to minorities so insignificant that they
don't even figure in the statistics'. But in the next line you
yourself claim, 'rather than being racial, the notions of Indian
and white are cultural and are impregnated with economic
and social meaning'. Very well, Fonchito … why don't you
apply this correct conceptualisation yourself and admit that
Bolivia at least has an overwhelming indigenous, not
'mestizo', majority …?[39]

This, of course, is polemic, but it touches on a vital issue. Evo
Morales was raised as a child speaking only Aymara, which was one
reason why he did not flourish at school in Argentina, where his
father was a migrant worker. He now speaks the language of his
childhood with halting confidence and will not talk publicly in it
without notes. After 20 years in the Chapare region of Cochabamba,
his Quechua is more practised and fluent but, like millions of
Bolivians, his first language is now Spanish, simply because it has to
be. What he chooses to identify with — what he promotes
consciously and actively, regardless of his personal trajectory,
language, clothing and social habits — are precisely those economic
and social meanings of ethnicity noted by Vargas Llosa.[40]

It is, however, one thing to request a certain consistency in
defining a social construction of race and another thing, quite
distinct, to reach an understanding of those processes through which
this takes place with all the inconsistency and idiosyncrasy of which
every society is capable.[41] Here the observer of contemporary
Bolivia faces a further problem: for a while there almost appeared to
be 'two Bolivias' within the very government itself, both deep in
uncharted territory. One, gruffly pledged to the unadumbrated
vulgate and, quick in temper, stands in scorn of any bookishness. It
was obliged to learn quickly how to anticipate responses that it had
never itself experienced. The other, with a formidable appetite for
the deployment of critical theory in political analysis, assumed office
having exhaustively narrated, interpreted and deconstructed that
selfsame passage. It has since been compelled to drop all footnotes,
quite a few syllables, and even some airs.

The first group is led not by Evo Morales, part of whose personal
industriousness involves a concern with new ideas, even if he is an

unschooled and instinctively incurious man.[42] Rather, it is headed by Foreign Minister David Choquehuanca, who proudly announced upon taking office that he had not read a book for 16 years and did not seem of a mind to start now that he had a new job. In fact, despite initially ordaining that the language of Bolivian diplomacy would be Aymara, asking for non-diplomats to be nominated for ambassadorial posts, and suggesting that schoolchildren would be better off with coca instead of milk in the morning because it contains more calcium, Choquehuanca's militant anti-intellectualism was a mix of ludic bravado and disconcertedness at the unknown demands of office. Since this was true for almost all 16 ministers, 40 vice-ministers and 120 directors general — the Bolivian executive is as 'small' as the country itself — some playful provocation was broadly cathartic.[43] Certainly, for Abel Mamani, leader of the campaign against Aguas de Illimani in El Alto, appointment to a newly created ministry of water represented an immediate translation from opposition activism to responsibility for national policy, with the effect of stilling a voice of regular complaint but irregular proposal.

Another current, of older radical professionals, such as Carlos Villegas, in charge first of development strategy and then hydrocarbons, and Nila Heredia at health, had already held prominent positions in the public sector and widely respected for their technical accomplishments. But when in his inaugural speech Morales expressed a respect for 'middle-class intellectuals', he was identifying in barely coded fashion the small but busy group around his vice-president, Álvaro García Linera, an indefatigable explainer of what he is doing, why he is right and — now he is engaged in real politics — why other people are wrong.[44]

At one level this is a complete boon for commentators — intellectuals who occupy public office are unusually prey to charges of hypocrisy as they scale speedily down from the heights where theory and sheer high-mindedness inevitably locate them, but apart from the tell-tale loquaciousness of the guild, they bequeath plenty of evidence of 'where they come from'. However, the present group is not so easy to 'map' because its scholarly commitments are very sophisticated and take in a range of influences from post-structuralist theory (Raúl Prada, leading the MAS contingent in the

constituent assembly)[45] to the often difficult and allusive work of
René Zavaleta Mercado (Luis Tapia),[46] and, in the case of García
Linera himself, to sources as different as E.P. Thompson (to whom
we shall return) and Jürgen Habermas (to whom we shall not).

García Linera is, as Pedro Shimose wryly notes, so gargantuan a
reader that he readily neutralises the back-biting bibliophobia of
*Canciller* Choquehuanca. This is a man who claims to have read 960
books during three of his years in jail (pretty much one a day), and
who now possesses a library of 10,000 titles. Irrepressibly curious
about the lacunae in Marx's published work in Spanish, he travelled
to Amsterdam to consult the original manuscript texts on India and
China — 'peoples without history'— and you feel that he really did
read *Das Kapital* in the windswept prison of Chonchocoro
(1992–1997) whilst on the outside Sánchez de Lozada sought to
'capitalise' Bolivia. It was, in truth, not a good idea to try to blow up
George Shultz when the secretary of state made a visit to La Paz, but
the inertial, dogmatic currents of *altiplano* Stalinism and Trotskyism
have an unenviably long record of provoking such exasperated
adventurism. Like Vargas Llosa, García Linera was raised in
Cochabamba and travelled abroad when young — he has a Mexican
degree in mathematics. His militancy in the EGTK could almost
make him a figure in the Peruvian novelist's brilliant tirade against
Sendero Luminoso, *La Historia de Mayta*. He certainly has set his
sights on asserting an alternative voice:

> There's the great challenge — to uphold the long tradition of
> the Latin American and Bolivian intellectual and break with
> that false, germ-ridden ideology of the Vargas Llosa type.[47]

García Linera's writings are too theoretically infused and sinuous in
style to be given here an appraisal of the depth they deserve. I will pick
up just one central motif — the reconstitution between 1986 and 2000
of a self-consciously working class movement into a variegated but
distinctively *plebeian* mass — as part of a more general proposition: that
Evo Morales stood, in January 2006, at the head of a third Bolivian
Revolution. If that revolution is indeed usefully seen as being plebeian
in nature and political expression, then, as García's critics argue, it is also
the product of a political economy that is *ch'enko* (entangled/thicket-

like/messy) and so can neither disown the liberal institutionality integral to its evolution nor avoid embracing collectivist practices.

## The Challenges of History

> In order to commemorate our forebears through your office,
> Señor Presidente del Congreso Nacional, I request a minute's
> silence for Manko Inka, Tupaj Katari, Tupac Amaru, Bartolina
> Sisa. Zárate Willka, Atihuaiqui Tumpa, Andrés Ibáñez, Che
> Guevara, Marcelo Quiroga Santa Cruz, Luis Espinal and many of
> my fallen brothers ...
>
> Evo Morales, inaugural speech

President Morales possesses an uncertain sense of moment — even
amidst his natural constituency he can often strike a wrong note
through excessive extemporisation. However, at his inauguration in
congress he was at pains to make a critique of the past of Bolivia,
which he compared to South Africa and explicitly described as 'colonial', without ever talking of 'revolution'. The preferred term used by
MAS is 'refoundation', which might be no less comprehensive but
has a much more constructive ring to it.[48] However, Evo requested
silence to commemorate names integrally associated with local revolutionary tradition, and within weeks, at the convocation of the
constituent assembly, he declared, 'This is where the democratic and
cultural revolution begins'.[49] As we have seen, the long-suffering
*Economist* reckoned the MAS victory amounted to a revolution, and
it is no surprise that *The Guardian* should also employ the term.[50] For
Carlos Toranzo, who could barely be described as sympathetic to the
strategy of the *bloqueo* so constantly employed from 2000 onwards,
the electoral triumph of December 2005 was,

> historic ... nothing other than a democratic revolution,
> conducted through the means of suffrage, according to the
> mechanisms of representative democracy and not by means
> of street violence.[51]

Yet very few elections are widely accepted as being 'revolutionary' so
soon after they occur, and even then (say, Great Britain in 1945 or
Argentina in 1946) this is a relative deployment of a term that, like

'democracy', has had its cutting edge whittled down by the tyranny of popular usage. Rarely do we find 'revolution' or 'democracy' employed in fine-grained academic analysis without the interposition of adjectives. Thus, Fernando Mayorga resisted the combination to describe the removal of Sánchez de Losada in October 2003:

> The idea of a revolution is the least pertinent here because the outcome of the October crisis has been expressed within a constitutional context, although it is undeniable that perceptions and prejudices about politics, culture and the economy have been substantially modified for the bulk of the population.[52]

At that stage Álvaro García Linera declared Bolivia to have entered a 'revolutionary epoch', which he characterised as,

> reiterated waves of social uprisings … which are separated by relative periods of stability, but which at each step, question or force the modification of … the general structure of political domination.[53]

We might usefully pause here to register the characterisation of social scientists, many of whom take their bearings from Theda Skocpol:

> Social revolutions are rapid, basic transformations of a society's state and class structures; and they are accompanied and in part carried through by class-based revolts from below. Social revolutions are set apart from other sorts of conflicts and transformative processes above all by the combination of two coincidences: the coincidence of societal structural change with class upheaval; and the coincidence of political with social transformation. In contrast, rebellions, even when successful, may involve the revolt of subordinate classes — but they do not eventuate in structural change.[54]

One could quibble over the weighting of 'eventuate' — after all, Zhou Enlai was only stretching a point in the 1970s when he said it was 'too soon to tell' what the historical significance of the French Revolution might be. However, the key elements are surely speed and scope of consequence, as noted by Jeff Goodwin:

> … revolutions entail not only mass mobilisation and regime change, but also more or less rapid and fundamental social,

economic and/or cultural change during or soon after the
struggle for power. (What counts as 'rapid and fundamental'
change, however, is a matter of degree, and the line between
it and slower and less basic change can be difficult to draw in
practice.)[55]

That is the line we must draw here. The speed is problematic since
we can only plot a regularity of popular mobilisation from January
2000, Sánchez de Lozada is overthrown in October 2003, and
Morales voted into power in December 2005 — a process that lasted
nearly six years without a single 'defining moment'.

The scope of consequences is also problematic since Goodwin's
'regime change' is generally understood in the style of Mark
Kishlansky — 'a rapid and unexpected rejection of one form of
government for another'.[56]  Yet in January 2006 Morales assumed
office according to all the same regulations and protocols that
obtained for Gonzalo Sánchez de Lozada, Carlos Mesa and Eduardo
Rodríguez before him. It is true that the previous day he had under-
gone a separate 'indigenous' inauguration at Tiahuanaku, but he did
not there promise a parallel programme; he gave a shorter, more
popular speech but made the same rhetorical points in an essentially
complementary and symbolic undertaking. The *form* of government
had not changed, and although Morales and MAS firmly proposed
that it should and would be altered, that process would take place
through the prescribed form of a constituent assembly. This,
together with the fulsome electoral victory in December 2005,
enables Toranzo to identify precisely a 'democratic revolution', but
according to Fernando Mayorga's logic the very element of formal
democracy diminishes the revolutionary character, and on the tight
definition provided by Goodwin we would need to see, at the very
least, substantially more economic and social change than was
witnessed through most of 2006. Certainly, we are still a very long
way from the *pachakuti* (both a 'revolution' in nature and a millennial
experience) desired by Félix Patzi, minister of education and the
most instinctively radical of Evo Morales's first cabinet:

> To speak of cyclical history is to remove oneself from
> modern, progressive civilization; it is to speak of another
> type of society, where neither reason nor the optimal use of

time are the key elements any more. On the contrary, it will
be individuals who control time. It is what I call human
happiness in opposition to slavery.[57]

Is it, then, at all sensible to talk of a 'revolution' that was at least six
years in the making and that had yet to deliver, in the form of materi-
ally implemented public policy, striking changes in the human
condition? This may, indeed, be tantamount to a promotion of rhetoric
and popular ambition over substantive and lasting change. Yet the first
years of the twenty-first century have continually upheld the images,
expectations and behavioural patterns associated with the urgency and
emergency of revolution. It is plain that a revolution is widely *felt* to be
underway. Many — let us say one million of the 1.5 million who voted
for MAS in 2005 — want it to succeed through adroit fulfilment of the
definitional requirements we have just considered; others recognise it as
itself being *ch'enko* — a veritable mess that needs to be muddled
through and sorted, but through retention of *both* democratic form
and social change; yet others — certainly not a few, maybe a million
too — wish to detain, restrict and even reverse it.

The Bolivian experience shares with other recent radical episodes
a *combination* of mass mobilisation and mass media. This was most
vividly exemplified during the presidency of Carlos Mesa, an experienced television presenter who repeatedly made resort to the
cameras and public appeals in highly charged discursive efforts to
resolve the *empate catastófico* caused by the highland *bloqueos* and the
civic mobilisation for autonomy by the *media luna*. At no stage that I
can recall in the last six years have television stations throughout the
country been closed down other than by common or garden
*apagones*. *Pace* Gil Scott-Heron, the revolution has been televised.
Indeed, because the events of the epoch — the elections and constitutional formalities as much as the mobilisations and repression —
have been piped into almost every electrified home in the country,
we need to take care in assessing the impact of such imagery. For, as
a result of the mass media, a process that might, by the lights of
sharp academic definition, not be at all comparable with 1789, 1917
or 1959 could still be construed as being precisely so by those
watching it closely and constantly. Of course, a revolution thought,
imagined or willed does not a revolution make (at least not to my

mostly structuralist mind), but this daily exposure to aural and visual recordings of the recent past does serve to transform the lived sense of time (the speed of events) and to affect the demand-delivery gap (either through *novela*-induced reveries or *denuncia*-enhanced impatience) and so the scope of 'change'.

We should take care but not worry. The social science criteria are simply unmeetable in the present or foreseeable future. Zhou Enlai is right for Bolivia too. We do, though, know that what has occurred has amounted to far more than the deployment of the 'weapons of the weak', as described by James Scott:

> the prosaic but constant struggle between the peasantry and those who seek to extract labor, food, taxes, rents and interest from them ... forms of class struggle ... [that] require little or no coordination or planning; they make use of implicit understandings and informal networks; they often represent a form of individual self-help; they typically avoid any direct, symbolic confrontation with authority.[58]

Equally, the very collectivist qualities of the conflicts of 2000–2006, the notable absence of a vanguard political party and the continued fragilities of MAS all suggest that, whatever has been happening, Bolivia might yet escape what Octavio Paz believed to be 'the logic of revolutions':

> The most cursory glance at the history of modern revolutions, from the 17th century to the 20th century (England, France, Mexico, Russia, China) shows that in all of them, without exception, from the very first days of the movement, groups possessed of greater initiative and talent for organisation than the majority, and armed with a doctrine, make their appearance. These groups very soon separate themselves from the multitudes. In the beginning they listen to and follow the multitudes; later they guide them; later still they represent them, and eventually they supplant them.[59]

The idea that the present experience constitutes a *third* Bolivian revolution is by no means original. Adolfo Gilly, who still has enough of the Trotskyist about him to be demanding of quantitative as well as qualitative criteria, has described it as such.[60] So have Forrest Hylton

and Sinclair Thomson who, like Gilly, identify the first in the upris-
ings of 1780–1782 (led, amongst others, by Tupaj Katari, whose
movement was linked to the Cuzco-centred insurrection of José
Gabriel Tupac Amaru), and the second in the 'National Revolution'
opened by the armed rising of 9–11 April 1952 and led by the MNR
until its overthrow by the military in November 1964.

I agree that the present process is quite distinguishable from that
of '1952', which can now almost be thought a cause of 2000–2006
by virtue of its insufficiencies. However, even in a rather shallow
numbers game, I have reservations about the inclusion of the Tupaj
Katari rebellion within any category identified as 'Bolivia'. That it
might be is entirely understandable in terms of popular exposition,
but we need to tread cautiously in the area of longitudinal analogy,
popular imagery and the invocation of the past. However sentimen-
tally forceful and intellectually beguiling, that concatenation glosses
over the fact that Bolívar was not born until two years after the
uprising, that Bolivia would not come into being for almost another
45 years, and, as Thomson himself has shown in a superlative essay,
there has been very little historiographical energy expended in the
cause of linking 1781 with the establishment of the republic in 1825:

> Within revolutionary nationalist discourse, it was the creole
> independence movement that generated most historical
> attention. 1781, by contrast, was much more difficult to
> accommodate within nationalist memory and teleology …
> The severed head of Tupaj Katari can find no convenient
> niche in the nationalist pantheon … 1781 stands for antago-
> nism and a parting of the ways between creole elites and the
> indigenous majority.[61]

It may even be excessive to say that 1781 was a revolt to restore
Kollasuyo that fed — eventually and with many extra elements —
into the invention of Bolivia.

Moreover, in his detailed deconstruction of the late eighteenth
century movement, Thomson argues that the war around La Paz was
not,

> the result of atavistic impulses on the part of Indian insur-
> gents, nor of other putatively pre-political sorts of
> anti-colonial nativism, peasant utopianism, or subaltern class

fury. What came to be seen by elites at the time and thereafter as 'race war' in La Paz emerged most immediately from conjunctural political conflicts, especially the failure of the Indian-creole alliance.[62]

Forty years later the creoles would act alone, albeit with the support of popular guerrilla forces, until the royalists were defeated by an invading patriot army headed by a Venezuelan (Bolívar) and a Colombian (Sucre).[63] Bolívar initially resented and resisted the invention of a new republic by the local creoles led by Casimiro Olañeta, but once reconciled to it (whether by the flattering nomenclature or through recognition of a formidable localist sentiment amongst the elite), he wrote a constitution which distinguished between 'Bolivians' ('All those born in the territory of the Republic'; Article 10.1) and 'Citizens' (amongst the requirements for which were 'To know how to read and write' and 'To have some employment ... without subjection to another person'; Article 13.3 and 4).[64] This is why Evo Morales and MAS now want to 'refound' Bolivia. Their programme is for the full and enduring reversal of that foundational distinction, which was only formally abolished after the Revolution of 1952. In that regard, at least, Hugo Chávez is helping to unpick the work of his hero.

Yet, set aside the issue of 'Bolivianness' and the parallels between 1781 and 2000–2006 are striking. Of course, the 1781 siege was of a walled town some ten blocks wide and six deep, reliant for its defence on holding the bridges over the Rivers Choqueyapu and Mejahuira — watercourses that have long since been built over in the modern city centre — as well as the surrender to the rebel forces of the then outlying church of San Francisco, now the central site of mass demonstrations. Equally, the eighteenth-century conflict was fully military in character, with no quarter spared on either side. Nicholas Robins estimates that a third of the town's population, some 10,000 people, died, mostly of starvation. A very large number of the attacking forces, which plainly served in communally organised shifts, as in recent years, were killed in frequent assaults.[65] In the 1780s El Alto was not a settlement of any size but it still formed the physical and psychological skyline. Spanish accounts of the siege relate the impact of Tupaj Katari's descents from the *altiplano*, usually in a red jacket though on one occasion in April the self-styled viceroy made a striking appearance adorned in gilded armour with a brooch of the sun on his chest, in the style of the Inka — not exactly the sartorial equivalent of Evo's jumper but also not without some iconographic similarity.[66]

In 1781 the besieging forces were unable to deprive La Paz of water as effectively as those of 2000–2005 could withhold supplies of petrol and fuel oil. Yet for Félix Patzi the *bloqueadores* of September and October 2000 instilled a great fear derived directly from a 'memory' of 1781:

> Everybody asked to go to the city, so that the centre of the dominant bureaucracy and aristocracy could be besieged. All this revived the memory of the siege of La Paz undertaken by Tupaj Katari in 1781. Until that moment nobody had believed that the indigenous were capable of reviving a struggle that had occurred over 200 years ago, and much worse as a contemporary form of struggle, capable of overthrowing the dominant system…The middle class employed in the state bureaucracy and private sector did not hold back; during the conflict it organised marches of white scarves demanding pacification … they ended up reciting '*Padre nuestro*' and '*Diós te Salve María*' as at the time of the siege … the women who joined these marches were creatures of white complexion, with skirts and high-heels, who, you could see from miles away, practised certain rules of endogamy in their marital relations because, when they passed, and the young people of dark skin flirted with them, they glared back at them; you could see in their faces a repudiation and scorn of the Indian.[67]

If, as E.P. Thompson reminds us, the labouring poor of eighteenth-century England left very few documents, fewer still remain to provide us with clues as to the thoughts and actions of humble folk in the eighteenth century Andes.[68] Today, though, the TV and radio provide constant documentary dissemination, so the way 1781 is 'remembered' is played out before our eyes, and it obviously does not exclude racist behaviour by the subaltern classes. The ribald remarks directed at the outraged creole ladies in 2000 had, by June 2005, been replaced by much more overtly aggressive activity. In the mobilisation that brought down the Mesa government there was widespread shouting of abuse between marchers and onlookers and scattered physical attacks by the protesters, according to *La Razón* particularly against men wearing ties.[69] Félix Patzi, ever the *enragé*, would have felt little sympathy for the 'pastiche' radicalism of the feminist group Mujeres Creando, whose marvellously provocative behaviour meant that they only escaped a prolonged beating by dint of intervention by the riot police, who in 'normal circumstances' might themselves have relished the chance to be the aggressors.[70]

From my perspective, the most remarkable aspect of all this is how *little* violence occurred in 2000–2006, given the scale of the popular mobilisation, the material and ideological interests at stake, and the strength of the historical tributaries flowing into such social antagonism. If we add the approximately 70 *cocaleros* killed since the restoration of constitutional government in 1982 to the equal number shot down in what might be termed the '25th Vendémiaire of Gonzalo Sánchez de Lozada' during October 2003, and the 30 killed in February 2003, plus the casualties on both 'sides' of lesser clashes, the total certainly does not exceed 300 lives lost — around the same number of casualties as in 1952 and far fewer than in 1781. This might be explained by the 'schizophrenic' character of the military or by the smallness of the police force, but recalling de Tocqueville, it surely has more to do with the fact that society — or, for those who can see 'two Bolivias', societies — did not, at some elemental level, *want* a civil war as a repetition of the 1780s.[71] That prolonged campaign of social and political 'nullification' through strike and *bloqueo* which so exasperated so many could very well be welcomed in retrospect as an extended and elaborate exercise in evading something far more tragic.[72] Tupaj Katari deployed some, rather inefficient, siege catapults as well as the sling and lance that were the arms of his infantry and, yes, cavalry, but the rebels eschewed the regular use of firearms. Even with their fractured identities and limited ordnance, the contemporary security forces could have inflicted a hugely greater toll than any in the past.

The first Bolivian revolution rarely threatened to take such a course. I would date it from 16 July 1809, when Pedro Domingo Murillo issued a proclamation denouncing three centuries of despotism and the fact that the creole elite suffered 'a form of exile in the bosom of our own land'. This revolution did not end with the arrival of the Patriot army under Sucre, or with Bolívar's fleeting visit later in 1825. I would see it as closing at the Battle of Ingavi, in November 1841, when independence from Peru was finally guaranteed and a creole republic based on the Audiencia de Charcas was given precedence over both the old viceregal limits of Peru and the market links between La Paz, Arequipa and Tacna.[73]

It is something of a paradox that the emblematic figure of this revolution is Andrés de Santa Cruz y Calahumana, who championed the ill-starred Peru–Bolivia Confederation (1836–1839). However, Santa Cruz, a mestizo with family origins in Huarina, education in Cuzco and strong early royalist affiliations, managed the young state with remarkable effectiveness. He upheld the alliance with the indigenous elite that Sinclair Thomson sees as having ruptured in 1781, and he displayed an assurance about the wider world that derived as much from Hispanic universalism as from a long and peripatetic military career. Registered at birth as Spanish but dismissed as *el indio jetón* by a Peruvian oligarchy aghast at his pretensions, Santa Cruz was sufficiently respectful of indigenous culture and *cholo* interests — he was far more protectionist than Bolívar — to consolidate the republic's foundation. His remains, repatriated from France by the military in 1965, are ceremoniously protected beside the presidential palace, and Evo Morales is the first Bolivian head of state to be decorated with a collar in Santa Cruz's name.[74]

The second revolution — that of April 1952 led by the MNR — possesses its own mausoleum. It contains the ashes of Colonel Germán Busch, the driving force behind the first nationalisation of oil in 1937. Another occupant is General Juan José Torres, army commander in 1969, when Gulf Oil was nationalised, and president in 1971 when the establishment of the radical Asamblea Popular provoked Hugo Banzer's coup that definitively ended the political process begun nearly 20 years earlier.[75] Before too long the MNR — a party which owed its origins to the Chaco War and its political schooling to the Constituent Assembly of 1938 — would revert to the operational 'default' of a military alliance, now backing Banzer's dictatorship of the *noche triste*. For Fernando Molina, Evo Morales and MAS are taking Bolivia back to the 'revolutionary nationalism of the 1950s',

when, in another paradox, it was the tin companies that were nationalised and the oil industry opened up to market forces.

Photo 1.2: Marshal Andrés de Santa Cruz y Calahuamana, c. 1860
(Collection of A. Santa Cruz, La Paz).

For Morales himself, the MNR regime was a shadow exercise, a kind of mestizo manoeuvre whereby land was distributed, but not in Santa Cruz, and the masses enfranchised, but with votes as tradable items in a strictly regulated market. The MNR leadership was a tie-wearing fraternity, for a while invigilated at the left by the FSTMB miners' union, itself influenced by anarcho-syndicalist and Trotskyist currents. That relation, however, barely touched the countryside and was largely played out as a parochial Cold War exchange. According to Jaime Paz Zamora (long-time leader of the MIR), his party was founded in 1971 in an effort to uphold the 'authentically popular' inheritance of 1952 and to adjust it to an era in which the promotion of democratic freedoms was now paramount.[76] It could be said that such an *entronque histórico* with the early MNR has now been taken up much more effectively by the MAS, which, in direct opposition to the late MNR, is seeking to revive not just the core features of 1952–1964 — nationalisation of the commanding heights of the economy, agrarian reform, formal democracy — but also other elements of the longer revolutionary process of 1937–1971. Amongst these we might mention the Constituent Assembly of 1938, the *Congreso Indigenal* of 1945, and the experience of rural organisation and struggle in the 1940s that has only recently been retrieved by scholars.[77]

That more recent historical legacy is sufficiently idiosyncratic to complicate any idea of Bolivian politics simply internalising and reflecting a regional tide of radical populism.[78] The influences beyond the physical frontiers of the republic are indeed vitally important. It is impossible to understand the period 2000–2006 without consideration of IMF pressure over the budget deficit, the international price of oil, or US pressure over coca. It is, moreover, very hard to imagine the initial months of the MAS taking the course they did without Cuban and Venezuelan support, which was far more critical than anything Perón did for the MNR in the 1950s. At the same time, the paucity of academic attention to the regional impact of the Argentine crisis of 2001–2003 badly needs redressing.[79] Nevertheless, even for a state so small and weak that it can usefully be tutored by Venezuela, these external factors have not been determinate, nor are they likely to endure in their present form. What, on the other hand, will make or break the current political process is the government's capacity to respond to the

peculiarly combustible social admixture of the ancient and the
modern captured in the term *ch'enko* and reflected in frequent allusion by García Linera and others to the term 'plebeian'.

Photo 1.3: Provisional president Hernán Siles Zuazo, protected by *miliciano*,
April 1952 (from *Album de la revolución*, La Paz, 2006).

## Forward with the Usable Past?

> How is it possible that since 6 August 1825 no natural
> resource has been industrialised in our country? Why is it that
> only primary materials are exported? For how long is Bolivia
> going to continue as an exporter of primary materials?

> Evo Morales, Inaugural speech

The response of Roberto Laserna (echoed by Fernando Molina) to
this question would be that Bolivia is divided not so much into two but
three parts. Yet these are still negatively correlated with each other to
produce an *empate catastrófico* similar to that between the 'two Bolivias'.
One quarter of the population lives in 'modern Bolivia', operates
according to a mindset of instrumental rationality and can at least
formulate universalist projects. However, this sector lacks the intellectual and material resources to realise those projects. As a result, it is
culturally inclined to be averse to risk and engage in rent-seeking
behaviour; its average household income is $491 per month, and a
third of this sector is classified as poor. A second group, of around
35 per cent of the population, operates within an informal economy
of essentially family-based activity, often migratory in character and
including an urban element. Extremely vulnerable to market disruption of cash-flow and social shocks to a favours-based system of rents,
this sector can rarely accumulate capital and often devotes its savings
to conspicuous consumption in carnival-based activity derived from
the provincial cultures to which it still belongs. It has an average
monthly household income of $299 and half of its members live in
poverty. Finally, there exist some 3.5 million people, 40 per cent of the
Bolivian population, within a 'natural economy' dominated by cultivation for subsistence. This is the group which most contributes to the
poverty levels with which we opened. For Fernando Molina, following
Arguedas, it has to be delinked from the more dynamic sectors,

> because its existence is predicated on the persistence of the
> past ... a group that defines itself by racial and cultural
> means, by what they *are*, and not by what they have a right to
> be (citizens) nor what they do or propose to do.[80]

For Laserna, the market reforms from 1985 did produce growth and change but only in the market-related circuit:

> It is clear that the stagnant sectors of the economy, which are composed by the natural and familiar economies, were and remain really successful in resisting the discipline and logic of the market. There are millions of *campesinos* and informal workers who use the market and at the same time block its expansion ... this is the structural *ch'enko*.[81]

From such a perspective — notwithstanding its almost equally negative appraisal of the political elite — it is not the neo-liberal reforms but the traditional, autochthonous society of Bolivia that lies behind its backwardness. Molina, in particular, criticises Evo Morales and Álvaro García because their strategy for breaking up the *ch'enko* is through a strong state and 'finishing' the 'incomplete' revolution of 1952. That might produce some expansion, or 'democratisation', of clientelist behaviour, but it will also fortify the culture in which natural resources are viewed as a gift to be distributed:

> ... 99 per cent of the MAS programme is a project for the industrialisation of a backward economy under the control of a 'strong state' that will eliminate undesirable elements and the constant conflicts of interest created by the private sector.[82]

Yet Molina admits that MAS is quite incapable of imposing itself, either by technology or by force, on the majority. Moreover, it will not get rid of the institutions of liberal democracy because it was precisely through them that it eventually came to power, even if it succeeded by other, direct means in stopping first policies and all government by forces that it opposed. Molina also sees clearly that by 2000 most Bolivians were exhausted by the loud claims and poor performance of liberalism, despite it paying tribute to local culture by denominating its privatisations as 'capitalisations', as if the property it was selling remained in the public sector, and by coupling it with genuinely popular and redistributive decentralisation.[83] Here, curiously, there is some common ground with García Linera:

> The MAS is in no sense seeking to form a socialist government. It is not viable because socialism is built on the basis of a strongly organised working class ... socialism is not

constructed on the basis of a family economy, which is what dominates in Bolivia, but on large industry ... What is the model for Bolivia? A strong state, and that is capitalism ... It isn't even a mixed system ... What I do as a Marxist is evaluate the actual potential for development in a society.[84]

### Table 1.2: Bolivian Labour-Force, 2004

| | |
|---|---|
| Agriculture | 1,625,581 |
| Hydrocarbons | 11,772 |
| Mining | 59,686 |
| Manufacturing | 493,315 |
| Construction | 136,145 |
| Commerce | 605,590 |
| Transport | 182,539 |
| Communications | 17,987 |
| Financial services | 31,352 |
| Public administration | 35,923 |
| Other services | 470,407 |
| Total | 3,770,299 |

**Source:** CEDLA estimates in *Pulso*, 245, 30.iv-6.v.04

Table 1.2 shows only very broad categories of work, and so on one reading it might be thought to make a case against both Molina and García Linera, but most of the manufacturing jobs are small-scale and workshop-related, just as the large number of service workers are generally linked to the domestic economy. We might also note the very few jobs in the hydrocarbons sector, from which so much is expected over the coming period, making an economic strategy 'beyond gas' imperative. These figures yield an open unemployment rate of 14 per cent (330,000 people) against a Latin American average of 11 per cent. A hundred thousand of the jobs in manufacturing were attributable to the ATPDEA treaty that suspended US tariffs in exchange for eradication of coca crops and was due to expire at the end of 2006; they were, then, extremely vulnerable.

A policy team working for UNDP has developed a diagnosis that is less pessimistic but somewhat similar to that of Fernando Molina. It extracts from three principal obstacles — 'diversificación sin especialización'; 'solidarios, pero solitarios'; and 'institucionalidad para algunos pocos' — a blue-print for a pluralist 'popular Bolivian economy', albeit with quite sober expectations as to the degree of complementarity between family — and firm-based production and the degree of institutional support for individual initiative.[85] Perhaps the fact that García Linera was accompanied on his first trip to renegotiate ATPDEA by Javier Hurtado, the radical head of the Irupana organic foods firm, signalled a more perspicacious approach to economic policy than many outside anticipated after the precipitate nationalisation of gas, but the lobby of the US Congress proved to be distinctly disappointing.[86] In any event, García Linera's references to 'Andean and Amazonian capitalism' increased markedly over the first months of the government.

Let me draw to a close by making a three-stage discursive manoeuvre of my own: first, by taking up the analytical revision that has attended 'class politics' over the recent period; next, by seeking to prise the *ch'enko* from an entirely deterministic association in an evocation of eighteenth-century England; and finally, by suggesting a refreshment of an analytical palate that depicts *plebiscitarian democracy* so narrowly and with scant regard to its ancient origins.

Although he died before the present political cycle had begun, René Zavaleta identified many of its latent features in his analysis of the crisis of 1979–1980. Instead of the term *ch'enko*, he used the phrase 'formación abigarrada' (multicoloured formation) to describe Bolivia,

> because you find in her economic stages (those of common taxonomic usage) placed upon each other without very much interaction at all, so whilst feudalism belongs to one culture and capitalism to another, here they are still appearing in the same space, one country being feudal and another capitalist … Who, then, would be so bold as to say that this heterogeneous combination might end up with a uniform matrix of power? … The only shared time for these forms is the general crisis which affects them … [87]

For Zavaleta the substantive social democracy of 1952 lay in the distribution of land, which provided some linkage between the two modes of production as well as between the collectivity and the individual: '... land is not just Pachamama. Holding a plot of land is the requirement of personal independence.'[88] This is a theme that García Linera is careful to uphold, as in his description of the *Coordinadora* that led the Cochabamba 'Water War' in 2000:

> If it does from the outset possess organisational forms that might be classified as of a traditional type, because they are founded on pre- or non-mercantile logics of access to land, water or public resources ... personal and group adherence to the movement is still voluntary and in the style of modern social movements.[89]

Likewise, García Linera distinguishes between 'the mob' (*muchedumbre*), which 'combines individualities without any affiliation or dependency other than the euphoria of immediate action' and 'the multitude', which 'articulates autonomous organisational structures of the subaltern classes'. For García Linera the rioting of February 2003 was mob action, the *bloqueos* of October the work of 'the multitude'. Although he never quite makes the claims for it as expansively as do Hardt and Negri, the vice-president of Bolivia sees 'the multitude' as providing a lot more than 'the wisdom of crowds'.[90] It is a social form that can inject public creativity into the peculiar socio-economic *ch'enko* that is Bolivia, compensating for the historical solitude of individuals stranded in the wrong mode of production as well as for classes denied any role in development. Plainly, García Linera's 'multitude' does not limit itself to a liberal democratic *modus operandi*, but its overall tendency must be towards pluralism and democratic pacts. At the end of the 1970s Zavaleta noted that, 'The working class ... had learned in its moment of class isolation that the only way it could be itself was by means of the democratic pact.'[91] García Linera's article of faith a quarter of a century later is that such a transformative self-recognition applies no less to those in the 'natural' and 'familiar' economies. The present article is itself now too far gone for any psephology, but the electoral signs from 2002 onwards would tend to support him.

What, then, is the 'disorder' about? Here the lack of historical sedimentation noted by Zavaleta is complicated by at least one further important element. That is the *reversal* of 'normal' historical evolution in the collapse of the tin mining industry in the 1980s, deindustrialisation in an only very partially industrialised society throwing 'modern' wage workers back into social circuits associated with other historical epochs. Their legacy of proletarian organisation, enforced engagement in agriculture, and modern market rationality have all combined to make coca production not just a means of survival but also a symbol of 'tradition' and a highly politicised issue. Little wonder that MAS is fragmented or that Evo Morales so frequently shifted his position in opposition, especially when the local actors were so emphatically joined by the North Americans, for whom all this appeared to be a cut-and-dried issue of morality and legality, and who paid good money to have the police and army sort it out for them.

Although, as we have seen, Washington was initially circumspect with the Morales government, within a few months it showed signs of regression over the single most important issue for Evo Morales — an issue over which he is able (reluctantly) to negotiate but cannot be seen by his home constituency to resile. After his speech to the UN General Assembly in September 2006, *The New York Times* finally registered, with some sense of astonishment, a matter that had long stood as common sense in Bolivia:

> … he's right to complain about American imperialists criminal-izing a substance that's been used for centuries in the Andes. If gringos are abusing a product made from coca leaves, that's a problem for America to deal with at home … America makes plenty of things that are bad for foreigners' health — fatty Big Macs, sugary Cokes, deadly Marlboros — but we'd never let foreigners tell us what to make and not make. The Saudis can fight alcoholism by forbidding the sale of Jack Daniels, but we'd think they were crazy if they ordered us to eradicate fields of barley in Tennessee.[92]

Here, then, the irrationality and obtuseness so conducive to conflict and violence are not Bolivian at all, but imposed on that people by foreigners who, as so often, first think they know best and then complain about the consequences.

Then there is the more straightforward anachronism in the continued existence of a plebeian culture to which we are unaccustomed because it is now virtually extinct in 'the north' where 200 years ago it prevailed quite extensively:

> the brief, bawdy, violent, colourful, kaleidoscope, picaresque
> world of pre-industrial society, when anything from a third to
> a half of the population lived not only on the subsistence line
> but outside and sometimes against the law … In their concep-
> tion of democracy, their attitude to leadership, property,
> social morality, their idea of unity and correspondence, their
> suspicion of the 'respectable' … their continuous expectation
> of betrayal, above all in their feeling for equality and craving
> for recognised manhood, sans-culottes and artisans are so
> similar that they sometimes seem identical. The differences in
> tone and temper — quite radical — can be explained by the
> brute distinction between a situation which was revolutionary
> and one which was not.[93]

In such a world, as Edward Thompson notes, 'some customs were of recent invention, and were in truth claims to new rights' — an eminently usable past and not one petrifying people, 'immobilising' them without rhyme or reason.[94]

This sense of a plebeian *condition*, rather than any sharper ideological character, might best be grasped through a combination of naturalism and political behaviour. Roger Ekirch calls plebeians 'masters by night', and Thompson notes, 'It is exactly in a rural society, where any open, identified resistance to the ruling power may result in instant retaliation … that one tends to find the acts of darkness.'[95] That might not be a world so far away from the one to which Evo Morales referred in his inaugural speech, noting that electricity had only reached his home school in 2003, or from the one of Felipe Quispe, who, for all that he is a militant 'child of the sun', still ensured that military activity in Achacachi was prepared under cover of night.

We might equally find a shared prominence of public festivities, dance and the carnival in poor societies dominated by the seasonal cycle and attached to spectacle:

> Many weeks of heavy labour and scanty diet were compen-
> sated for by the expectation (or reminiscence) of those
> occasions, when food and drink were abundant, courtship
> and every kind of social intercourse flourished, and the hard-
> ship of life was forgotten.[96]

In the same vein, the contemporary life of the city of Oruro circulates comprehensively about Carnival, and the non-celebratory life of La Paz is brought to a halt by the day-long parades of El Gran Poder and the Entrada Universitaria. Even the highly cerebral Álvaro García Linera so respects the importance of pageantry that, in the midst of the preparations for the Constituent Assembly, he flew all the way from Washington to Los Angeles to attend the finals of the Miss Universe competition and boost the morale of Desirée Durán, whose considerable charms had elevated her to the final ten contestants before she experienced the inevitable defeat. The vice-president's labours in this regard reanimated a polemic that is ardently conducted on an annual basis in Bolivia but long surpassed in Europe (less so in the USA). In 2006 Oscar Unzueta explained why such tradition retains unusual vitality:

> These events are important for the countries of the third world because they are a form of escaping invisibility, of taking the world stage without needing scientific resources or a major sporting apparatus, as in the Nobel prizes or the World Cup or the Olympics.[97]

Albeit sometimes expressed with a patina of post-modernity, such phenomena surely constitute what Max Weber called 'the authority of the 'eternal yesterday' … of the mores sanctified through the unimaginably ancient recognition and habitual orientation to conform'.[98] The other two legitimations of domination on which Weber lays stress are the legal and the charismatic, this latter being a gift of grace held by individual warlords, prophets or 'plebiscitarian rulers':

> Plebiscitary democracy — the most important type of leadership-democracy — is in its genuine sense a kind of charismatic authority which conceals itself under the *form* of a legitimacy which is derived from the will of the ruled and only sustained by them.[99]

In this vein, 'plebiscitary' has become one of those familiar adjectives interposed before 'democracy', most often to denote a form of populism where the rule of law is practically but not formally subordinated to the executive power, which habitually feigns constitutionalism and displays a palimpsest of the multitude in the holding of plebiscites. Hugo Chávez and Tony Blair have been depicted in such manner.[100]

Evo Morales manifestly is not Hugo Chávez, and Weber's tripartite model needs some adjustment to work for the case of Bolivia. It may be that Morales, who won his popularity not because he was outstanding but precisely because he was representative of 'normality', can still achieve charismatic status through 'charismatic acts'. He has cut his salary, abstained from alcohol, worked absurdly long hours, and shared the presidential residence with members of his cabinet. All this clearly expresses Weber's 'politics as a vocation'. But the plebiscitary character of the leadership-mass relation is distinctly bottom-up, being directed by the *cocaleros, juntas vecinales*, unions and sundry *Coordinadoras*. That is why Evo Morales so regularly 'flip-flopped' in policy. Indeed, at his inauguration speech in Tiahuanaku he felt obliged to uphold this familiar feature of opposition politics as he moved to occupy the position of ruler:

> I want to ask you, with much respect to our indigenous authorities, our organisations, our *amautas* (wise ones): control me, and, if I cannot advance, you push me on, sisters and brothers ... Correct me all the time; it is possible that I might make mistakes, I can make mistakes, we all make mistakes, but I will never betray the struggle of the Bolivian people ...[101]

Here we have much less a demand for ratification than a request for checks and balances. That, S.E. Finer argues, was the fundamental quality of the original *plebis scitum*, won through two 'secessions' (little less than *bloqueos*) of 494 and 287 BC by the plebeians of the early Roman Republic. On the second occasion these led to the *Lex Hortensia*, whereby the *concilium plebis* could, irrespective of the Senate, vote a resolution into law with a 'binding quality over the entire community ... definitively acknowledged'.[102] Those powers were also limited — the organised plebeians themselves lacked formal judicial power or the right to vote on peace and war — just as in their contemporary form — under the *de facto*, half-written 'mixed constitution' of 2000–2006 — they have similarly proved to be.

I think, then, that the recent Bolivian experience may from this perspective also be usefully understood as 'plebeian' in nature. The Constituent Assembly, in early session when these words were

written in September 2006, has already shown strong signs of
counter-testing the classical traditions of patricians and plebeians,
reflecting the simple but vital point made by Trevor Smith for the
UK of the 1960s: 'consensus, whether real or imagined is ultimately
prejudicial to democracy whose main foundation is organized
conflict'.[103] If that sounds just too rowdy and pious for the present
circumstances, it might be noted that it was not until MAS came into
office that any Bolivian government had a coherent policy, with real
support from the office of the presidency, to save the 22,000 infants
who die needlessly each year from malnutrition. Now, under
'Desnutrición Cero' — a policy reliant upon the combination of clinical skills and popular organisation — this invisible tragedy is finally
being confronted. Democracy may cost lives, but it saves them too.

## Notes

1   G. Gray (ed.), *La economía más allá del gas,* 2nd ed. (La Paz, 2005), p. 258.
2   *Bolivia digna, soberana y productiva para vivir bien* (La Paz, 2006).
3   G. Stedman-Jones, *An End to Poverty? A Historical Debate* (London,
    2004); E. Rothschild, *Economic Sentiments. Adam Smith, Condorcet and the
    Enlightenment* (Cambridge, Mass., 2001); J. Sachs, *The End of Poverty.
    How We Can Make It Happen* (Harmondsworth, 2005).
4   Given the importance attached to the coca question by Washington,
    the fact that in the first quarter of 2006 only 743 hectares of crop had
    been eradicated, as against 6,000 in 2005, makes it all the more remark-
    able that the US 'Drug Czar' John Walters should simply declare that
    the anti-drug campaign was 'not like before. We need better work.' *La
    Razón,* 27 June 2006. This is an important topic to which we must
    return, but it is worth registering here the much less-noticed US with-
    drawal of support for Bolivia's elite anti-terrorism force, the FCTC, on
    the grounds that its commander, Colonel Rory Rodríguez, was a MAS
    sympathiser. At a ceremony to mark the twenty-first anniversary of
    the formal foundation of the city of El Alto, President Morales
    declared this to be 'blackmail'. *La Razón,* 8 March 2006; *New York
    Times,* 6 March 2006. In the days following Venezuela offered to
    provide training to the FCTC. Aircraft of the Fuerza Aerea
    Venezolana are almost as frequently to be seen at Bolivia's airports as
    were the Hercules of the USAF in previous times. The increased mili-

tary presence of Venezuela was duly noted by *The Economist*, 8 July 2006, which either idly neglected or purposefully avoided any reference to prior North American assumptions as to rights of overseeing Bolivia's security from abroad.

5    Council on Hemispheric Affairs, Washington, Memorandum, 6 May 2006.

6    Quoted in H.C.F. Mansilla, *El carácter conservador de la nación boliviana* (Santa Cruz, 2004), p. 14.

7    *The Economist*, 17 July 2004.

8    Mexican president Vicente Fox, irritated by Morales' invitation of Subcomandante Marcos to his inauguration, unwittingly identified this Bolivian preparedness — even appetite — for repudiating the common commercial nexus: 'The new government has apparently said that Bolivia's gas will not be exported, so there's nothing to say. They're going to consume it there, or perhaps they'll eat it; perhaps they will.' *La Razón*, 11 January 2006.

9    *The Paranoid Style in American Politics* (New York, 1965), pp. 3, 5.

10   F. Hylton and S. Thomson, 'The Chequered Rainbow', *New Left Review*, vol. 35 (2005), p. 44.

11   *La Razón*, 25 Feb. 2005. In 2002 only 2.2 per cent of Bolivians used the internet, but there is ample anecdotal evidence of subsequent growth — Google has an Aymara translation facility, and the speed of general technological change was such that by 2004 there were three times more mobile phones than telephone landlines. *La Razón*, 14 Feb. 2005.

12   Quoted in Julio Cotler, 'Bolivia, Ecuador and Peru 2003–2004: A Storm in the Andes', Real Instituto Elcano, Madrid, 12 Jan. 2006. In 1990 Quispe wrote, 'the war of Tupaj Katari from 1781 to 1783 was not a total and definitive defeat, but there has been a tactical retreat from the city to our communities', *Tupaj Katari. Vive y vuelve . . . carajo!*, 2nd ed. (La Paz, 1990), pp. ix–x.

13   *Pulso*, 345, 28 April–4 May 2006. When the moral philosopher Kathryn Pyne Addelson declares that, 'it is in collective action that time and world are created', she expresses as an interpretation what in recent years has been lived as a material reality in Bolivia. *Moral Passages. Toward a Collectivist Moral Theory* (New Cork, 1994), p. xi.

14   *El Diario*, 30 Feb. 2002.

15   'Democracia multicultural y comunitaria', *T'inkazos*, La Paz, 17 Nov. 2004, pp. 70–1. Orlando Patterson, 'Ordinary Liberty: What Americans Really Mean by Freedom and its Implications', Lecture, London, June 2006.

16   *Evo Morales y el retorno de la izquierda nacionalista* (La Paz, 2006), p. 19.
17   T. Platt, T. Bouysse-Cassagne, O. Harris with T. Saignes, *Qaraqara-Charka. Mallku, inka y rey en la provincia de Charcas (Siglos XV–XVII)* (La Paz, 2006).
18   *La Razón*, 4 March 2005.
19   J-P. Lavaud, *L'instabilité politique de L'Amérique Latine: le cas de Bolivie* (Paris, 1991), p. 19; C. Mesa Gisbert, *Presidentes de Bolivia. Entre urnas y fusiles* (La Paz, 2003). It is a little disappointing to see how little has changed since I wrote over two decades ago,

> The newspapers trot out the mathematics of disorder — all of it fifth-hand and incorrect — but do not pose the question that if disorder is so prevalent, might it not be order itself? Could there not be a system in the chaos? Should it not be understood less as interruption than continuity?

James Dunkerley, *Rebellion in the Veins. Political Struggle in Bolivia, 1952–1982* (London, 1984), p. xi.
20   *La Razón*, 12 March 2005. The conflict statistics are from *Pulso*, 290, 24–31 March 2005. According to Gregorio Lanza, the optimistically entitled Director de Prevención de Conflictos, there were 1,800 agreements reached between state and civil society bodies under Sánchez de Losada and 5,400 under Mesa. *La Razón*, 16 Jan. 2005.
21   *Democracy in America* (1835) (New York, 1990), II, p. 269.
22   'Las masas en noviembre', in R. Zavaleta Mercado (ed.) *Bolivia Hoy* (Mexico, 1983), p. 51. 'Of course, the army, like any other corporation, belongs in the first place to its own history' (p. 50). Hence, according to General Antezana, 'It is necessary to reaffirm the permanent and traditional character of the Armed Forces in time and in history.' *La Razón*, 31 Jan. 2005. It is also probably for this reason that former Major Juan Ramón Quintana, minister of the presidency from January 2006, could declare that, 'the Bolivian army is one of the most popular in the world', *Pulso*, 274, 19–25 Sept. 2004.
23   *El Juguete Rabioso*, 26 Oct. 2003, 'La crisis del estado y las sublevaciones indígeno-plebeyas', in A. García Linera, R. Prada and L. Tapia, *Memorias de Octubre* (La Paz, 2004), pp. 51–8; O. Oliveira, in collaboration with T. Lewis, *Cochabamba! Water War in Bolivia* (Cambridge, Mass., 2004). For Zavaleta, 'War, in effect, is a crisis, and as such it exercises an unusual or extraordinary trans-subjective effect. Politics and commerce are similar in this but on a perennial basis.' *Lo nacional-popular en Bolivia* (Mexico, 1986), p. 239. According to the Israeli general Dan Halutz, victory is a matter of 'consciousness', not terri-

tory won, *The Economist*, 26 Aug. 2006. We could go further back with Roger Caillois, to see declarations of war as themselves reflecting and creating a suspension of normal social boundaries, 'Der Mensch und das Heilige', 1988, quoted in W. Schivelbusch, *The Culture of Defeat. On National Trauma, Mourning and Recovery* (London, 2003), p. 297. My own sense of all three 'wars' — water, gas and the long guerrilla campaign over coca — is that they were declared *ex post facto* as explicit markers for heroic physical struggle and as an implicit declaration of victory in a national culture averse to triumphalism.

24  *La Razón*, 18 March 2003; 14 December 2005.

25  Isabel Hilton, *The Guardian*, 21 Oct. 2003

26  Johann Hari, *The Independent*, 9 March 2005.

27  *The Guardian*, 20 Jan 2006.

28  'The Bankers Can Rest Easy. Evo Morales: All Growl, No Claws?', 4 Jan. 2006, Cislac Digest, no. 433, sent via LATAM-INFO, 11 Jan. 2006. Since Petras's bolshevism was for years practised in Binghamton, many matters must be indulged. Professors are properly required to profess, which includes issuing injunctions about precision and accuracy. But in the light of his withering comments above, Professor Petras might consider having words with his copy-editor (and his conscience) over J. Petras and H. Vellmeyer, *Social Movements and State Power. Argentina, Brazil, Bolivia, Ecuador,* (London, 2005), in Chapter 5 of which there are multiple errors of fact, misattributions of nomenclature, and a general sense of inaccuracy simultaneously conducive to and subversive of the overall hectoring tone.

29  'The Chequered Rainbow', p. 41. For a radical account that is unusually well-informed, see B. Kohl and L. Farthing, *Impasse in Bolivia. Neoliberal Hegemony and Popular Resistance* (London, 2006). For a variety of stimulating academic accounts, see S. Lazar and J.A. McNeish (eds.), 'The Millions Return? Democracy in Bolivia at the Start of the Twenty-First Century', *Bulletin of Latin American Research*, vol. 25, no. 2 (2006).

30  *Evo Morales y el retorno*, pp. 98ff.

31  *Pulso*, 250, 4–10 Feb. 2004.

32  'Chequered Rainbow', p. 50.

33  *Pulso*, 224, 21–7 Sept. 2003.

34  *El Nuevo Día*, 24 Dec. 2003, quoted in *T'inkazos*, 16, May 2004, pp. 17–18. At the mass meeting, 'Cabildo', of 28 January 2005, Rubén Costas, the leader of the Santa Cruz autonomy movement, declared, 'We want to be part of the community of nations with the dignity sought by Bolívar, so that abroad they don't think we're nothing but *cocaleros*'. *La Razón*, 29 Jan. 2005.

35  *The Economist*, 23 April 2005.

36  'Voluntad de Morir', *El País*, Madrid, 29 May 2005.

37  'Raza, botas y nacionalismo', *La Razón*, 15 Jan. 2006.

38  *The Economist*, 15 April 2006.

39  'El día en que se jodió Vargas Llosa', *La Razón*, 18 Jan. 2006. This general theme is well discussed in R. Albro, 'The Indigenous in the Plural in Bolivian Oppositional Politics', *Bulletin of Latin American Research*, vol. 24, no. 4 (2005).

40  *La Razón*, 15 June 2006. Morales was a little embarrassed on a visit to Quito by his lack of facility in the local Quechua dialect, which is quite distinct to that in Cochabamba.

41  'It is difficult to measure that *inter-subjectivity* that underlies what we call irradiation, and in any case it is not the measuring that has given us the fact. At the end of the day, the most important aspect of knowledge is the collective response to that knowledge'. R. Zavaleta, 'Forma clase y forma multitud', *Bolivia Hoy*, p. 231.

42  There is as yet no full biography of Morales. Very few personal details are given in Molina's study, despite its title. A useful condensed account of his personal experience, as well as an excellent survey of the period 2000 to 2006, is given in P. Stefanoni and H. Do Alto, *Evo Morales. De la coca al palacio. Una oportunidad para la izquierda indígena* (La Paz, 2006). Much useful information and insight are provided by Martín Sivak, the biographer of Banzer, in 'Evo sin suéter', *Gatopardo*, Buenos Aires, March 2006, and 'Un viaje con Evo Morales', *Playboy*, Argentine edition, August 2006.

43  'And why, exactly, Aymara? To discuss, in Aymara, with "Brother" Hugo Chávez? To rave against the system? To recover the sea along the lines of "¡Que se rinda tu abuela, carajo!" To compare Andean and US technologies? To have fun with the NGOs? To gas away with the Spaniards?' Pedro Shimose, 'Bibliófilos y bibliófobos', *La Razón*, 11 April 2006.

44  Compare:

> In social theory, the 'truths', the evidence, the legitimations are cultural caprices resulting from the historical trajectory of the structure and the operation of the intellectual field, of its processes of accumulation, verification and internal competence that have enshrined a certain mode of understanding, investigating and naming the world.

'¿Qué es la democracia?', in A. García Linera, R. Gutiérrez, R. Prada, L. Tapia, *Pluriverso. Teoría política boliviana* (La Paz, 2001), p. 81.

with

> No *tibilín* (little twit), no little Red Riding Hood, no Tuto, can reverse the nationalisation of hydrocarbons ... Podemos would benefit from a little reading, a little visiting of *barrios* and communities, a bath in the reality of the people's needs, that would improve their speeches a bit.

(*La Razón*, 20.vi.06) or 'We have beaten the anti-nation, the anti-history, the iniquity that is Podemos'. (*Pulso*, 329, 22–29 Dec. 2005).

45      What is the relation between writing and politics? We can certainly talk of political writing; this is trivial. There is more reward in talking about the politics of writing. This addresses the strategies inherent to the field of writing, to the design of possibilities of the trace in so many configurations of force, displacements of power, fields of intensity, feelings, depictions and literary empowerments.

('Genealogía política' in A. García Linera *et al.*, *Pluriverso*, p. 13) There is evidence that both Prada's perspective and his style were decompressed by the crisis, and particularly by October 2003, allowing him to address a more immediately recognisable 'genealogy':

> The grandfathers fought in the Chaco War, the fathers in the Revolution of 1952 or they were in the militia in the ill-fated period of the revolution. Now, the grandchildren, the children have risen up again, against the modern oligarchy. The call to defend our gas is the unifying element; the nation is seeking to be reborn.

'Política de las multitudes', in A. García Linera *et al.*, *Memorias de octubre*, p. 109. Prada's writing, like that of all the members of the 'Comuna'/'Muela del Diablo' group, often takes the form of long, sometimes reworked essays in joint collections. The best single example of his work is *Largo octubre. Genealogía de los movimientos sociales* (La Paz, 2004).

46   *La producción del conocimiento local. Historia y política en la obra de René Zavaleta* (La Paz, 2002); *La velocidad del pluralismo. Ensayo sobre tiempo y democracia* (La Paz, 2002). For Fernando Molina, Tapia's work is only coherent within its own closed world,

> political poetry ... entirely lacking in empirical content ... none of the opinion polls throughout this entire period have indicated that the dispossessed see the political crisis as an opportunity to 'reduce the spaces of domination' ...

*Pulso*, 263, 3–9 Sept. 2004. Molina considers Zavaleta to have promulgated a quite ordinary Marxism and nationalism in 'unusually brilliant paragraphs'. His own plangent positivist prose never flatters to deceive, so when confronted by activities neither measurable nor comprehendible in their own terms, he resorts to Pascal: 'Le coeur a ses raisons, que la raison ne connait point', *Evo Morales y el retorno*, p. 72. Tapia still works at the CIDES research centre of La Paz's public San Andrés University, but his close intellectual associate Fabián Yaksic was appointed vice-minister of decentralisation. F. Yaksic and L. Tapia, *Bolivia. Modernizaciones empobrecidoras* (La Paz, 1997).

47  *Pagina 12*, Buenos Aires, 10 April 2006. García Linera's former partner Raquel Gutiérrez wrote both with him and on her own: 'La forma multitud de la política de las necesidades vitales', in A. García Linera, R. Gutiérrez, R. Prada, L. Tapia, *El retorno de la Bolivia plebeya* (La Paz, 2000); 'La coordinadora de defensa del agua y de la vida', in García Linera *et al.*, *Tiempos de rebelión* (La Paz, 2001).

48       We want to refound the country, politics, democracy with our
         own hands: *campesinos*, workers, professionals, businessmen,
         different ethnic groups and indigenous peoples, all united, a
         country for us, for all. Political life is a right to all and not just for
         a few. It is not practised exclusively through the vote at elections.
         It is a daily practice, incarnate in the opinion, viewpoint, demands
         and campaigns of all and any individual and collectivity.
    Comunicado del Movimiento al Socialismo, 13 Oct. 2003, in *Observatorio Social de América Latina*, IV: 12 (Buenos Aires, 2004), p. 72. Immediately prior to assuming office Morales had visited South Africa as part of a nine-country tour that greatly enhanced his international profile. Bolivia subsequently established an embassy in Pretoria. In his speech the new president noted that it was 'scarcely 50 years ago' that indigenous people were banned from the central squares of La Paz, but he made no mention of the 1952 revolution, which ended that prohibition and made it 'difficult to uphold the thesis of apartheid', C. Toranzo, *Rostros de la democracia: una mirada mestiza* (La Paz, 2006), p. 19.

49  *La Razón*, 6 March 2006.

50  *The Guardian*, 3 May 2006.

51  *Rostros de la democracia*, p. 15.

52  *Juguete Rabioso*, 26 Oct. 2003. In the same interview Jorge Komadina said, 'The idea of a revolution is associated with the rapid and violent transformation of a state form and social order. So it is obvious that the present conjuncture does not fit that definition.'

53  *Juguete Rabioso*, 26 Oct. 2003

54  *States and Social Revolutions*, Cambridge 1979, p. 4.

55  *No Other Way Out. States and Revolutionary Movements, 1945–1991* (Cambridge, 2001), p. 9.

56  'Ironed Corpses Clattering in the Wind', *London Review of Books*, 17 Aug. 2006.

57  *Pulso*, 244, 23–29 April 2004. See also, F. Patzi Paco, 'Rebelión indígena contra la colonialidad y la transnacionalización de la economía: triunfos y vicisitudes del movimiento indígena desde 2000 a 2003', in F. Hylton, F. Patzi, S. Serulnikov and S. Thomson, *Ya es otro tiempo el presente. Cuatro momentos de insurgencia indígena* (La Paz, 2003).

58  *Weapons of the Weak. Everyday Forms of Peasant Resistance* (Yale, 1985), p. xvi.

59  'The Contaminations of Contingency', in *One Earth, Four or Five Worlds* (London, 1985), p. 192.

60  *La Jornada*, Mexico, 26 Jan. 2006.

61  'Revolutionary Memory in Bolivia: Anticolonial and National Projects from 1781 to 1952', in M. Grindle and P. Domingo (eds.), *Proclaiming Revolution. Bolivia in Comparative Perspective* (Cambridge, Mass. and London, 2003), pp. 130, 119. Félix Patzi, who consistently relegates the precise character of the *Q'ara* state, sees the period from 2000 as 'the third historical movement of indigenous rebellion' after Katari in 1781 and Zárate Willka in 1899. 'Rebelión indígena', in *Ya es otro tiempo*, p. 277.

62  *We Alone Will Rule. Native Andean Politics in the Age of Insurgency* (Madison, 2002), pp. 271–72. Forrest Hylton has made a similar critique of the historiography of the 1899 movement headed by Pablo Zárate, '*El temible willka*', for which he can find no hard evidence of racist motives by the insurgents, only attributions by their enemies (and some historians). 'El federalismo insurgente: una aproximación a Juan Lero, los comunarios y la Guerra Federal', *T'inkazos*, 16, 2004. Although he is critical of some of her work, Hilton's approach is close to that of Marta Irurozqui: 'The Sound of the Pututos: Politicisation and Indigenous Rebellion in Bolivia, 1826–1921', *JLAS*, vol. 32, no. 1 (2000). For a rather different perspective, see Nicholas Robins, *Native Insurgencies and the Genocidal Impulse in the Americas* (Bloomington, 2005).

63  J.L. Roca, *1809. La revolución de la Audiencia de Charcas en Chuquisaca y en La Paz* (La Paz, 1998); G. Mendoza (ed.), *José Santos Vargas. Diario de un comandante de la independencia americana, 1814–1825* (Mexico, 1982); R. Arze, *Participación popular en la independencia de Bolivia*, (La Paz, 1979).

64   'The Bolivian Constitution (1826)', in *El Libertador. Writings of Simón Bolívar* (New York, 2003), p. 65.

65   *Native Insurgencies*, p. 50.

66   M.E. del Valle de Siles (ed.), *Francisco Tadeo Diez de Medina. Diario del cerco de La Paz, 1781* (La Paz, 1981), p. 120; *Testimonios del cerco de La Paz. El campo contra la ciudad, 1781* (La Paz, 1980), p. 86.

67   'Rebelión indígena', in *Ya es otro tiempo*, pp. 215–6; 219–20. La Paz has only eight exit roads, and the three that do not pass through El Alto do not provide a route beyond surrounding valleys.

68   'The Patricians and the Plebs', in *Customs in Common* (Harmondsworth, 1993), p. 18.

69   *La Razón*, 3 July 2005.

70        In Europe ... there have emerged *postmodern* social movements, such as the movements of women, ecologists, homosexuals, etc. ... in Bolivia the middle class and certain intellectual circles previously affiliated with the left are not analysing their own condition because of their *pastiche* behaviour ... the only option is to imitate what comes from outside.

       'Rebelión indígena', in *Ya es otro tiempo*, p. 202. María Galindo, the driving force behind Mujeres Creando and author of the slogan 'Indias, putas, lesbianas juntas revueltas y hermanadas', is fully Patzi's match in the hard-fought contest to be Bolivia's lippiest iconoclast:

       Evo is beautiful, his skin is coffee like cacao, his political record is of demonstrations and yet more demonstrations, and his anti-imperialism is today by far the most important thing. That he might be an irresponsible father who pays nothing to his family and up to today has refused to recognise his daughter has had, still has, and will have no importance, none at all. What's more, it makes him all the more 'authentic', especially because Evo is not Eva and has no story to tell about his body, his desires and his defects.

       'No saldrá Eva de la costilla de Evo', circulated by email, 15 Feb. 2006.

71   The entire Bolivian police force numbers less than 22,000; in La Paz only 350 officers are assigned to special security duties. *La Razón*, 7 Sept. 2003.

72   I am here deliberately using the term most effectively adopted by John C. Calhoun from Jefferson, who in 1798 stated that it was the 'natural right' of a state in response to a federal act deemed to be unconstitutional. In his Fort Hill address of 1831, Calhoun declared,

This right of interposition, thus solemnly asserted by the State of Virginia, be called what it may — State-right, veto, nullification, or by any other name — I conceive to be the fundamental principle of our system.

R. Lence (ed.), *Union and Liberty. The Political Philosophy of John C. Calhoun* (Indianapolis, 1992), p. 371. The resolute defence of this principle over the issue of slavery (after Calhoun's death in 1850) led, of course, to one of the bloodiest civil wars in human history.

73    Upper Peru belongs by right to the Río de la Plata; in fact to Spain; by wish of its own people, who want a separate state, to independence; and by claim to Peru, who previously owned and wants it now ... To give it to the Río de la Plata would be to deliver it into anarchy. To give it to Peru would be to violate the international law which we have established. To create a new republic, as the inhabitants demand, would be an innovation which I do not care to undertake, for only an American assembly can decide that.

Bolívar, Lima, to Santander, 18 Feb. 1825, quoted in J. Lynch, *Simón Bolívar. A Life* (London, 2006), p. 199. The Argentine claim was aggressively pressed by Rosas but beaten back at the Battle of Montenegro in August 1838 by the military skill of Otto Braun, born in Kessel, and Francisco Burdett O'Connor, born in Cork.

74    C. Méndez, 'Incas Sí, Indios No: Notes on Peruvian Creole Nationalism and Its Contemporary Crisis', *JLAS*, vol. 28, no.1 (1996). I am most grateful to Natalia Sobrevilla, preparing a new biography of Santa Cruz, for the information on the registry of his birth.

75    Busch committed suicide at the age of 35 in 1939, apparently over his failure to enforce a decree requiring mining companies to hold all their gold and foreign exchange with the Banco Central — a kind of nationalisation. Personally beating up the elderly Alcides Arguedas, Busch was evidently as passionate as he was romantic, but the only authentic *noche triste* he inflicted was that when he blew out his brains with a Colt revolver. James Dunkerley, *Political Suicide in Latin America* (London, 1992). Torres was executed in Buenos Aires in 1976, apparently at the behest of Banzer and under the remit of 'Operation Condor', M. Sivak, *El asesinato de Juan José Torres* (Buenos Aires, 1997). The civilian leaders of 1952 do not lie in the mausoleum. Hernán Siles Zuazo, the brave and civilised man who led the April uprising, has a modest headstone in the Cementerio Jardín in Obrajes.

76 Interview, *El Picacho*, Tarija, 22 July 2006.

77 R. Barragán and J.L. Roca, *Regiones y poder constituyente en Bolivia* (La Paz, 2005); L. Gotkowitz, 'Revisiting the Rural Roots of the Revolution', and B. Larson, 'Capturing Indian Bodies, Hearths and Minds', in Grindle and Domingo, *Proclaiming Revolution*; L. Gotkowitz, *A Revolution for Our Rights: Indigenous Struggle for Land and Justice in Bolivia, 1880–1952* (Duke, forthcoming).

78 See, for instance, Jorge Castañeda, 'Latin America's Left Turn', *Foreign Affairs*, vol. 85, no. 3 (2006); *The Economist*, 15 April 2006, both of which in their distinctive prose distinguish between 'traditional populism and a modern, social democratic left', but while Castañeda unhesitatingly describes Evo Morales as a 'skilful and irresponsible populist', the sages of St James's withhold terminal judgement.

79 In October 2003 Fernando Mayorga remarked that whilst the slogan in Argentina had been 'Que se vayan todos', in Bolivia it had been 'Que se vaya uno' (Sánchez de Lozada). Over the next two years the former sentiment came to prevail. *El Juguete Rabioso*, 26 Oct. 2003.

80 *Evo Morales y el retorno*, p. 18.

81 Interview with Miguel Gómez Balboa, www.geocities.com/laserna. The term might, in this connotation, incorporate two phonetically similar Quechua verbs — *ch'in kay* (to be silent) and *ch'anqay* (to throw stones, which is the favoured means of the *bloqueo*).

82 *Evo Morales y el retorno*, p. 125.

83 *Evo Morales y el retorno*, pp. 60, 80.

84 Quoted in *Evo Morales y el retorno*, p. 126; *El Juguete Rabioso*, 18 Oct. 2006.

85 Gray, *La Economía más allá del gas*. The other four models assessed by the UNDP teams are: 'informalidad y ejército industrial de reserva; la subsunción o subordinación; microempresas; distrito industrial, clusters, y aglomeraciones productivas'.

86 Before the team left for Washington in July 2006, the president bade it farewell with a dawn *milluchada*, a burnt offering to Pachamama, at which the presiding *yatiri* (native priest) foresaw trouble pending. It did not wait long — the vice-president's US visa was refused, forcing Ambassador David Greenlee to hold the American Airlines flight at Viru Viru airport in Santa Cruz until the paperwork was sorted out, the mission transferred in a military plane from El Alto, and embarked on the commercial flight for Miami. There are surely several morals in this story.

87 'Masas en noviembre', *Bolivia hoy*, pp. 17, 19.

88   'Masas en noviembre', p. 40.

89   *Pulso*, 185, 21–27 Feb. 2003. For an analysis of the 'Water War' that exposes the limits of rational utilitarianism, see A. Nickson and C. Vargas, 'The Limitations of Water Regulation: The Failure of the Cochabamba Concession in Bolivia', *Bulletin of Latin American Research*, vol. 21, no. 1 (2002).

90   Hardt and Negri see 'the multitude as "all those who work under the rule of capital and thus potentially as the class of those who refuse the rule of capital"', *Multitude* (Harmondsworth, 2005), p. 106. In his critique of this position Malcolm Bull provides a useful historical *tour d'horizon* of theories of the masses and mass action, maintaining that 'from Cicero onwards, it was axiomatic that only when unified into a people could a multitude become a political agent', *New Left Review*, vol. 35 (2005), p. 38. J. Surowiecki, *The Wisdom of Crowds. Why the Many are Smarter than the Few* (New York, 2004).

91   'Masas en noviembre', in *Bolivia hoy*, p. 49.

92   John Tierney, 'Reading the Coca Leaves', *The New York Times*, 23 Sept. 2006.

93   G.A. Williams, *Artisans and Sans-Culottes* (London, 1968), p. 5.

94   *Customs in Common*, p. xiii.

95   *Customs in Common*, p. 66; R. Ekirch, *At Day's Close. A History of Nighttime* (London, 2005), p. 221.

96   *Customs in Common*, p. 51.

97   *La Razón*, 30 July 2006. This is not really my specialist field, but I would say that Miss Durán's style is very much that of Raquel Welch, also a *cruceña*, updated to the conditions of the early twenty-first century — Desirée is 19 and 5'10" tall but also training to be a petroleum engineer. Unkind tongues suggested that Don Álvaro might not have gone to watch Miss Durán in the style of a mathematician or even a human geographer:

> In last year's vice-presidential debates he was asked by the moderators — one suspects that this was not a neutral question — whether he had ever engaged in 'homosexual relations'. 'Not yet,' he answered nonchalantly. The nation gasped.

A. Guillermoprieto, 'The New Bolivia II', *New York Review of Books*, 21 Oct. 2006, p. 68.

98   'Politics as a Vocation', in H. Gerth and C. Wright Mills (eds.), *From Max Weber. Essays in Sociology* (London, 1948), pp. 78–79.

99   'Witschaft und Gesellschaft', quoted in D. Beetham, *Max Weber and the Theory of Modern Politics*, 2nd ed. (Cambridge, 1985), p. 266.

100 For general discussions, see P. Tamás', Socialism, Capitalism and Modernity', *Journal of Democracy*, vol. 3, no. 3 (1992); D. Collier and S. Levitsky, 'Democracy "With Adjectives". Conceptual Innovation in Comparative Research', Dept. Political Science, University of California, Berkeley, Working Paper 230, Aug. 1996; P. Mair, 'Partyless Democracy', *New Left Review*, vol. 2 (2000).

101 Quoted in Stefanoni and Do Alto, *Evo Morales*, pp. 157–58.

102 S.E. Finer, *The History of Government from the Earliest Times*, I (Oxford, 1997), p. 399. On 15 August 1805 Simón Bolívar made his vow to secure the emancipation of Spanish America at Rome's Monte Sacro, where Sicinius had led the protest of the plebeians in 494

103 *Anti-Politics* (London, 1972), p. 20.

# 2

# The 1997 Bolivian Election in Historical Perspective

The poll of 1 June 1997 in Bolivia might, perhaps, be thought outstanding only for its result — the constitutional election to the presidency of a man, General Hugo Banzer Suárez, who had taken that office by bloody coup 26 years earlier and held it for seven years as a dictator. Yet Banzer's election and the strong position of his party, Acción Democrática Nacionalista (ADN), in the congressional poll and its subsequent formation of a *megacoalición* (ADN/CONDEPA/MIR/UCS) may be seen as expressions of a wider 'consolidation' of the institutions of liberal democracy in Bolivia, marking an important shift away from the post-war pattern of corporatist politics 'by ultimatum'. That pattern had reached its peak in 1980–1985 with, first, the anarchic and drug-related dictatorship of General Luis García Mesa (1980–1981) and, then, the weak constitutional administration of the Unión Democrática y Popular (UDP, 1982–1985), which fell prey to syndicalist and radical demands which it could neither meet nor suppress. The poll in 1997 was the fourth national election to be held according to constitutional order since 1985, when the UDP had been obliged to leave office a year early. As a result, the election could be said to confirm a new pattern of political behaviour whereby conservative and populist forces negotiate electoral and administrative pacts and coalitions without facing stringent constraints from other domestic political forces. Yet neither Banzer nor his several allies in the *megacoalición* which took office in August 1997 were extravagant in their celebration or claims of achievement — a sobriety echoed by most commentators, if not the university Trotskyists who cosily issued a call for armed insurrection to oust 'the fascists' from power.

That call to arms jarred particularly in the context of the exhumation of the remains of Ernesto Che Guevara and six of his guerrilla comrades to be returned to Cuba on 12 July 1997, just a few weeks

short of the thirtieth anniversary of their execution. The youth of
the contemporary radical left seemed blind to the popular rejection of
the politics of violence, despite a dozen years of strict neo-liberal policies, fiscal parsimony, and only modest success in reforming a
centralised and patrimonialist state, in which corruption was widespread, if not endemic. Indeed, the smooth operation of the election
and the lack of conflict attending both its result and Banzer's inauguration are all the more remarkable given the instability and violence that
had prevailed for several years previously in neighbouring Peru and the
fact that Bolivia's own indigenous communities have never been properly included within the culture or institutions of a liberal state which
still exhibits a marked racism. Although no administration since 1985
has been able to avoid suspending the constitution under states of siege,
in order to restrict popular protests at the high social cost of deflation,
those mobilisations have not endured or grown. No serious guerrilla
force has taken root since the days of Guevara, the once powerful trade
union confederation (Central Obrera Boliviana, COB) is divided and
disoriented, and the legal left is but a shadow of its former self. Taken
together with Banzer's past and the high profile of entrepreneurs in his
government, this scenario would seem to suggest an uncomplicated
victory of the right, but that victory is certainly complicated, in terms of
ideology as well as institutions.

## The Electoral System

Elections have been held intermittently in Bolivia since the 1840s, but
they did not become meaningful in terms of the competitive allocation
of office until the 1880s, and the urban masses only became actively
engaged in the holding of polls from the 1920s. During the 1930s and
1940s military governments subordinated — but did not entirely eliminate — electoral contests, which could still affect local structures of
power and influence in the towns and mines. However, the restriction
of the vote to those who could read and write effectively disenfranchised the rural population, which accounted for the great majority of
the inhabitants of the Republic. As can be seen from Table 2.1, the
election of May 1951 — the last before the revolution of April 1952
— excited the active participation of less than 130,000 people: a 38 per

cent abstention rate by registered voters when these constituted a tiny segment of the total population.

This level of participation was in keeping with a social system in which urban trams hauled platforms behind them on which to carry those wearing indigenous dress, and in which free personal service of a servile nature was still common on the manorial estates of the Andean *altiplano* and valleys. The extent to which the 1952 revolution altered the 'formal political nation' can also be seen from Table 2.2, which shows the geographical distribution of the electorate following the introduction of universal suffrage by the Movimiento Nacionalista Revolucionario (MNR) when it took power through the revolution. (Table 2.2 also shows the decline by the 1990s of the old mining and agricultural centres in the southern Andean region of the country and the contemporary concentration of social power in the triangle of La Paz–Cochabamba–Santa Cruz.)

## Table 2.1: Electoral Participation, 1951–1989

|      | Population | Potential voters | Registered | Votes cast | Abstentions (%) |
|------|------------|------------------|------------|------------|-----------------|
| 1951 | 3,019,031  |                  | 204,649    | 126,123    | 38.4            |
| 1956 | 3,250,000  |                  | 1,119,047  | 955,349    | 14.6            |
| 1966 | 3,748,000  |                  | 1,270,611  | 1,099,994  | 13.4            |
| 1978 | 4,850,000  |                  | 1,922,556  | 1,971,968  | +2.6            |
| 1979 | 5,253,623  |                  | 1,876,920  | 1,693,233  | 9.8             |
| 1980 | 5,570,109  | 2,525,000        | 2,004,284  | 1,489,484  | 25.9            |
| 1985 | 6,429,226  | 2,931,123        | 2,108,457  | 1,728,365  | 18.0            |
| 1989 | 7,125,000  | 3,191,000        | 2,136,560  | 1,573,790  | 26.3            |

**Source:** J. Lazarte, *Revista de Estudios Políticos*, no. 74, October– December 1991. Annex. 3

### Table 2.2: Eligible Voters by Department, 1951–1997

| Department | 1951 | 1956 | 1966 | 1997 |
|---|---|---|---|---|
| La Paz | 72,512 | 260,443 | 436,049 | 1,068,900 |
| Cochabamba | 36,834 | 203,407 | 270,622 | 527,100 |
| Santa Cruz | 25,981 | 94,940 | 138,236 | 733,600 |
| Chuquisaca | 15,233 | 57,002 | 97,434 | 196,700 |
| Oruro | 26,116 | 62,485 | 79,057 | 172,200 |
| Potosi | 41,161 | 125,059 | 151,074 | 251,800 |
| Tarija | 16,281 | 29,563 | 44,406 | 157,400 |
| Beni | 10,093 | 15,385 | 40,474 | 132,800 |
| Pando | 2,009 | 3,046 | 8,4081 | 19,200 |
| Total | 246,220 | 851,330 | 1,341,433 | 3,259,700 |

**Source:** C. Mesa, *Entre urnas y fusiles*; Corte Nacional Electoral.

Although the first poll under universal suffrage — that of 1956 — may be used as a point of comparison for voter eligibility and participation, it scarcely offers us a useful, or even valid, reference point in comparing precise results or party performance. The same may be said of the elections of 1960 and 1964, which were similarly held under the revolutionary hegemony of the MNR, when competition was far from free and fair. This was particularly true in 1964, with the party splitting internally at the same time as it won a proportion of the vote almost on a Soviet scale (see Table 2.3)

### Table 2.3: 'Pre-Transition' Election Results (% Vote; Major Parties Only)

|        | 1951 | 1956 | 1960 | 1964 | 1966 | 1978 | 1979 | 1980 |
|--------|------|------|------|------|------|------|------|------|
| MNR    | 42.9 | 82.3 | 74.5 | 85.9 |      | 10.8 | 31.1 | 20.2 |
| ASD    | 32.1 |      |      |      |      |      |      |      |
| FSB    | 10.5 | 13.7 | 8.0  | –    | 12.5 |      |      |      |
| PL     | 5.2  |      |      |      |      |      |      |      |
| PIR    | 5 3  |      |      |      |      |      |      |      |
| MNRA   |      |      | 14.1 |      | 8.6  |      |      |      |
| FRB    |      |      |      |      | 61.6 |      |      |      |
| PDC    |      |      |      |      |      | 8.5  |      |      |
| UDP    |      |      |      |      |      | 24.6 | 31.2 | 38.7 |
| ADN    |      |      |      |      |      |      | 12.9 | 16.8 |
| PS-1   |      |      |      |      |      |      | 4.2  | 8.7  |
| Blank  |      | 1.5  | 1.2  | 5.7  | 5.8  | 1.8  | 3.2  | 11.2 |
| Null   |      | 1.1  | 1.2  | 6.5  | 2.4  | 0.9  | 10.0 | 6.3  |

**Sources:** Mesa; Corte Nacional Electoral.

Yet, just as the victory of the British Labour Party in May 1997 cannot usefully be compared with any poll prior to that of 1929 if both participation and results are taken as variables, so in Bolivia not a single poll before 1979 —15 years after the collapse of the MNR's 'National Revolution' — properly stands the test of comparison.

This is because the succession of military regimes that followed the MNR (see Table 2.4) either excluded the opposition and sharply restricted election campaigns (as in 1966) or simply fixed the results (as in 1978, a fact clearly shown by the 'excess voters' identified in Table 2.1). Nonetheless, in both 1979 and 1980 the MNR still retained the support of a considerable sector of the population, albeit at a level well short of a majority or one allowing the formation of a single-party administration (Table 2.3). Moreover, given that at the time of the polls of 1979 and 1980 the UDP was still strongly identified with the left wing of the MNR, one could argue that the revolutionary party of the 1950s continued to enjoy an 'historical primacy' but was no longer able to translate this into coherent ideological advantage or electoral victory. This, however, is something of a theoretical observation since the coups staged in 1979 and 1980 overthrew the election results of those years.

As a consequence of those interventions and the dictatorships they set up, we cannot talk of any election before 1985 being 'fully democratic' in the combined terms of participation, free competition, fair result and full social acceptance of that result. For this reason I have identified all earlier elections as 'pre-transition'. The watershed is certainly partial in terms of popular participation and party competition, but it is important when these are taken within the context of institutional continuity. One could certainly argue that the transition begins before 1985 — for instance, with Banzer's overthrow in 1978 — but it is only at that point that the transition became a profound process. Equally, one may wish to describe the position prevailing in 1997 less as 'democratic' than as 'polyarchic' on the grounds that there has not yet been a transformation from institutional continuity to a culture and popular expectation of pluralist behaviour within civil and political society.

Within this evolution the poll of 1997 incorporated the result of disparate efforts to settle on electoral arrangements which would prove socially fair as well as institutionally efficient. To some degree, as in 1986 and 1991, changes in electoral law were the outcome of pragmatic — even opportunist — political trade-offs; these should not be treated as emanating from disinterested 'statecraft'. On the other hand,

### Table 2.4: Bolivian Governments, 1951–1985

| | |
|---|---|
| 1951 | M. Urriolagoitia (PURS) |
| 1951–1952 | H. Ballivián (military) |
| 1952–1956 | V. Paz Estenssoro (MNR) |
| 1956–1960 | H. Siles Zuazo (MNR) |
| 1960–1964 | V. Paz Estenssoro (MNR) |
| 1964 | V. Paz Estenssoro (MNR) |
| 1964–1969 | R. Barrientos (military) |
| 1969 | L. Siles Salinas (PDC) |
| 1969–1970 | A. Ovando (military) |
| 1970–1971 | J.J. Torres (military) |
| 1971–1978 | H. Banzer (military) |
| 1978 | J. Pereda (military) |
| 1978–1979 | D. Padilla (military) |
| 1979 | W. Guevara (PRA/MNR) |
| 1979 | A. Natusch Busch (military) |
| 1979–1980 | L. Gueiler (PRIN/MNR) |
| 1980–1981 | L. García Mesa (military) |
| 1981 | Military junta |
| 1981 | C. Torrelio (military) |
| 1982 | G. Vildoso (military) |
| 1982–1985 | H. Siles Zuazo (UDP/MNRI) |

the electoral system put in place over the three years before the 1997 poll was generally the consequence of informed debate over constitutional reform and the relative merits of 'presidentialist' and 'parliamentary' political systems in the post-authoritarian era. Although the MNR had firm control over the executive and legislature, there was broad agreement that the electoral changes it introduced would address the difficulties of the proportional representation systems previously used: up until 1986, the D'Hondt formula, which could reward a party that won less than 1.5 per cent of the vote with up to three seats in the 130-strong lower house; thereafter, the St Laigue system, more favourable to larger political formations. The new system is very similar to that currently used in Germany and known in Europe as the 'additional member' mechanism, whereby half the deputies are elected from a party list *plurinomina* and half as individual candidates for constituencies *(uninominal)*. Under the law of 2 August 1996, article 60 of the constitution was amended to divide Bolivia's 424,000 square kilometres — slightly less than the size of France, Germany and Great Britain combined — into 68 constituencies in an effort to match rising localist sentiment, to curb some of the patronage power of the central party apparatchiks, and to enhance constituency affiliation and responsiveness as a factor in parliamentary behaviour.

As can be seen from Tables 2.5 and 2.6, this new system did not greatly alter the result of the poll in terms of the pattern of the vote from 1985 onwards (the 1997 results given in Table 2.5 are those for the plurinominal vote, which enables comparison with earlier polls). However, as an individual variable for the allocation of seats it was of some consequence (Table 2.7) since it enabled uninominal candidates of more regionally focused parties, such as CONDEPA in La Paz, to benefit from the strength of their slate as well as permitting celebrated individuals to buck the weakness of any party slate with which they were attached (Juan del Granado, the prosecutor of General García Mesa in La Paz for the MBL, Evo Morales, the leader of the coca growers' movement for IU in Cochabamba). Table 2.8 shows the geographical distribution of the plurinominal vote for the different parties.

## Table 2.5: National Elections, 1985–1997: Vote

| Party/Front | 1985 | 1989 | 1993 | 1997 |
|---|---|---|---|---|
| MNR | 456,704 (26.4%) | 363,113 (23.1%) | 585,837 (36%) | 396,235 (18.2%) |
| AP | | | 346,865 (21%) | |
| AND | 493,735 (28.6%) | 357,298 (22.7%) | | 485,705 (22.3%) |
| MIR | 153,143 (8.9%) | 309,033 (19.6%) | | 365,005 (16.8%) |
| CONDEPA | | 173,459 (11.2%) | 235,427 (14%) | 373,528 (17.2%) |
| UCS | | | 226,826 (14%) | 350,730 (16.1%) |
| MBL | | | 88,260 (5%) | 67,244 (3.1%) |
| IU | 10,072 (0.7%) | 113,509 (7.2%) | 16,137 (0.9%) | 80,806 (3.7%) |
| PS-1 | 38,786 (2.2%) | 39,763 (2.8%) | | |
| Total | 1,728,363 | 1,573,790 | 1,731,309 | 2,177,171 |
| Sitting: | Siles (UDP) | V. Paz (MNR) | J.Paz (AP/MIR) | Sánchez (MNR) |
| Elected: | V. Paz (94) | J. Paz (97) | Sánchez (97) | Banzer |
| Loser: | Banzer (51) | Sánchez (50) | Palenque (16) | (unopposed) |
| Pact/Coal.: | MNR/ AND | MIR/ AND | MNR/ MBUUCS | Megacoalión |

**Note:** Figures in brackets after names of elected and losing candidates refer to the number of votes cast in congress for each candidate in the vote for the presidency.

**Table 2.6: Elections, 1985–1997: Seats (130 Deputies; 27 Senators)**

| Party/Front | 1985 | 1989 | 1993 | 1997 |
|---|---|---|---|---|
| MNR | 59 | 49 | 69 | 30 |
| AND | 51 | 46 | | 43 |
| AP (MIR/ADN) | | | 43 | |
| MIR | 16 | 41 | | 30 |
| UCS | | | 21 | 23 |
| CONDEPA | | 10 | 14 | 22 |
| MBL | | | 7 | 5 |
| PS-1 | 5 | | | |
| IU | | 11 | | 4 |
| Eje | | | 1 | |
| Arbol | | | 1 | |
| Others | 26 | | 1 | |

**Source:** Corte Nacional Electoral.

This new, two-tier system operated with remarkable smoothness on polling day, the large majority of the electorate completing both the plurinominal upper half of the ballot paper for president, senators and slate-based deputies as well as the lower uninominal section. The efficient logistical preparation of the poll was notable, including the allocation of a mobile phone to urban electoral stations and extensive distribution of clear preparatory guides to the new system. It is, however, hard to comment with authority on the degree of 'tactical voting' indulged in by the electorate. In part this is because the system was completely untried in 1997, and in part it derives from the fact that the voters were generally unaware that, since the 1960s, no single party had won the 50 per cent of the vote required by the constitution to enable it to take power directly. Consequently, as stipulated by the constitution, the new congress would elect the president from the front-runners, thereby placing a premium on the pre- and post-election pacts that will be discussed shortly. In 1997 there was a general anti-MNR sentiment amongst the populist and conservative parties as well as on the left, but there was no pre-poll public agreement to form a coalition. As a result, the electorate could reasonably vote against the MNR in the expectation that this would probably change the government but not necessarily to the advantage of their preferred party, even if they voted for slate- and constituency-based candidates from the same organisation. Equally, it should be noted that the composition of the senate is calculated by yet another system, by which the winning party takes two of the three seats for each of the country's nine departments and the second-runner receives the remaining one. It defies belief that even the most psephologically sophisticated electorate could have calculated the probabilities of these three routes to the legislature (congressional *plurinominal*, congressional *uninominal*, senatorial) in addition to those of undeclared post-poll pacts whilst retaining the option of delivering a *voto de castigo* against the incumbent regime and, perhaps, reserving a separate vote for a favoured individual. In sum, it seems reasonable to suggest that the electorate simply voted according to general experience and proclivity with its calculations being no more detailed than those allowed by a broad estimation of the popularity of the alternatives.

Two other changes in the system deserve mention and may yet acquire more than formal importance. The first is the extension of the presidential term from four to five years. This is in keeping with a general Latin American pattern of extending executive mandates, either in themselves or — most recently and controversially in Peru and Argentina — by enabling the serving of successive terms. In

### Table 2.7: CONDEPA/MBL/IU: Slate and Constituency Votes

|  |  |  | Condepa | MBL | IU |
|---|---|---|---|---|---|
| La Paz | pl. |  | 289,175 | 13,146 | 9,113 |
|  | uni. |  | 228,086 | 38,969 | 11,430 |
| Santa Cruz | pl. |  | 11,233 | 12,170 | 2,521 |
|  | uni. |  | 9,915 | 24,328 | 873 |
| Chuquisaca | pl. |  | 12,249 | 16,378 | 2,257 |
|  | uni. |  | 6,870 | 23,759 | 5,869 |
| Cochabamba | pl. |  | 13,115 | 8,155 | 59,036 |
|  | uni. |  | 9,164 | 12,087 | 54,416 |
| Oruro | pl. |  | 24,596 | 1,987 | 960 |
|  | uni. |  | 18,257 | 5,277 | 3,214 |
| Potosí | pl. |  | 17,706 | 8,258 | 3,864 |
|  | uni. |  | 12,489 | 11,427 | 3,733 |
| Tarija | pl. |  | 3,774 | 4,503 | 655 |
|  | uni. |  | 2,933 | 11,185 | 585 |
| Beni | pl. |  | 1,321 | 2,196 | 134 |
|  | uni. |  | 1,167 | 2,572 | 879 |
| Pando | pl. |  | 359 | 451 | 55 |
|  | uni. |  | 957 | 491 | 2 |

**Source:** Corte Nacional Electoral.

Bolivia the question of re-election is not likely to become such an issue, partly because of the coalition nature of all governments over the last 12 years, but also simply because no government in that period ever succeeded in getting itself re-elected. It is, however, possible that Gonzalo Sánchez de Lozada, who left the presidency in 1997 — having previously lost the polls of 1989 and 1993 — could return as a strong candidate for the MNR in 2002. Since Sánchez de Lozada — popularly known as 'Goni' — was a leading architect of the 1985 economic stabilisation plan which has so strategically underpinned the political transition, his presence has become one of the most notable features of public life. However, it should be stressed that he neither seeks a 'populist' niche of the type created by Fujimori and Menem nor, indeed, does he possess great interest in the type of 'charismatic' politics so often counter-poised to the administration of neo-liberal policies.

Secondly, reforms to the constitution required that at least 30 per cent of all candidates in the 1997 poll be women. This unusual experiment in affirmative action proved relatively uncontroversial, perhaps because it did not result in any significant shift in the gender balance of representatives. Eventually, women accounted for 31 per cent of all candidates, 13 being elected to the 157-strong legislature (10 as plurinominal candidates: two as uninominals, and one senator). If the stand-bys (*suplentes*) for successful candidates are counted, a total of 34 were elected (all these coming from the party lists but not gaining enough votes to gain a seat under the quota assigned to their party). In 1989, 14 out of 157 legislators (or 7 per cent) were women; in 1993 the number was 12 (with four *suplentes*). At present 135 out of 1,625 municipal councillors are women although in some cities, such as Sucre, women are a clear majority of voters. Local elections were held in 1987 for the first time since 1949 and then at two-yearly intervals, every other contest falling in the year of the national election but being held six months later, as in 1993 and 1997, which will serve as the first real test of the new system of local government discussed below.

### Table 2.8: 1997 Presidential Election (% Slate vote by Department) (Not Rounded)

|            | ADN  | MNR  | MIR  | UCS  | CON  |
|------------|------|------|------|------|------|
| La Paz     | 20.3 | 12.9 | 11.1 | 9.7  | 37.5 |
| Santa Cruz | 24.9 | 24.2 | 16.0 | 25.9 | 2.2  |
| Beni       | 32.7 | 32.5 | 8.6  | 18.5 | 1.4  |
| Pando      | 38.3 | 26.9 | 15.9 | 9.9  | 3.2  |
| Oruro      | 21.9 | 15.6 | 17.5 | 15.0 | 20.5 |
| Potosi     | 19.6 | 16.7 | 21.8 | 14.9 | 10.9 |
| Cochabamba | 23.7 | 11.7 | 19.9 | 16.2 | 4.3  |
| Chuquisaca | 20.8 | 18.2 | 19.7 | 14.0 | 9.4  |
| Tarija     | 10.7 | 26.5 | 41.9 | 9.6  | 3.0  |
| National   | 22.3 | 18.2 | 16.8 | 16.1 | 17.2 |
|            | MBL  | IU   | VS   | Eje  | PDB  |
| La Paz     | 1.9  | 1.3  | 1.8  | 0.6  | 0.4  |
| Santa Cruz | 1.9  | 0.4  | 1.5  | 0.4  | 0.6  |
| Beni       | 2.3  | 1.0  | 0.2  | 0.1  | 0.1  |
| Pando      | 2.8  | 0.4  | 0.2  | 0.3  | 0.1  |
| Oruro      | 1.7  | 1.8  | 1.8  | 0.5  | 0.4  |
| Potosi     | 3.6  | 2.1  | 1.0  | 2.9  | 0.5  |
| Cochabamba | 2.2  | 15.9 | 1.0  | 0.4  | 0.6  |
| Chuquisaca | 9.5  | 1.4  | 1.1  | 0.8  | 0.4  |
| Tarija     | 3.7  | 0.5  | 0.4  | 0.5  | 0.1  |
| National   | 3.1  | 3.7  | 1.4  | 0.8  | 0.5  |

ADN — Acción Democrática Nacionalista; CONDEPA — Conciencia de Patria; Eje Pachakuti; IU — Izquierda Unida; MBL — Movimiento Bolivia Libre; MIR — Movimiento de la Izquierda Revolucionaria; MNR — Movimiento Nacionalista Revolucionario; PDB — Partido Democrático Boliviano; UCS — Unión Cívica de Solidaridad; VS — Vanguardia Socialista.
**Source:** Corte Nacional Electoral.

Finally, in this regard it is worth making a brief comparative comment. I have chosen to do this with reference to the systems pertaining to the British Isles, but not simply because both the Irish republic and the UK held general elections within weeks of that in Bolivia. There is a broader sense in which the study of Latin American politics is stymied by comparisons being limited to the region or to those extra-continental states deemed to be undergoing a similar political experience (for example, in terms of transition from authoritarianism, Spain and Portugal in the 1970s and Eastern Europe in the 1990s). Yet the debate over the British electoral system has sharpened markedly over the last decade, to the extent that the Scottish Assembly approved by referendum in 1997 will be elected according to the additional member system, combining party lists and Westminster constituency MPs. Furthermore, had the Labour Party not won such a resounding victory, its leadership on 1 May might have been obliged to succumb to the significant lobby for the introduction of proportional representation in the UK as a whole. Table 2.9 shows what the effect of the main electoral systems would have been on the composition of the House of Commons.

### Table 2.9: UK General Election of May 1997: Actual and Simulated Results

| Party | First past post | Alternative | STV | Additional members |
|-------|-----------------|-------------|-----|--------------------|
| Conservative | 165 | 88 | 189 | 207 |
| Labour | 419 | 452 | 346 | 303 |
| Liberal Democrat | 46 | 90 | 87 | 111 |
| Others | 29 | 29 | 37 | 38 |

(Alternative: second preference votes by constituency; STV: single transferable vote in large, multi-member constituencies; additional members: 50 per cent MPs chosen from party-list and 50 per cent from single-member constituencies).
**Source:** *Economist*, 20 September 1997..

**Table 2.10: Ireland: General Election Results 1951–1997
(% First Preference Votes; Dail)**

| | Fianna Fail | | Fine Gael | | Labour | | Sinn Fein | | Progressive Democrats | |
|---|---|---|---|---|---|---|---|---|---|---|
| | % | Seats | % | Seats | % | Seats | % | Seats | % | Seats |
| 1951 | 46.3 | 69 | 25.8 | 40 | 11.4 | 16 | | | | |
| 1954 | 43.4 | 65 | 32.0 | 50 | 12.1 | 19 | 0.2 | 2 | | |
| 1957 | 48.3 | 78 | 26.6 | 40 | 9.1 | 12 | 5.4 | 4 | | |
| 1961 | 43.8 | 70 | 32.0 | 47 | 11.7 | 16 | 3.0 | 0 | | |
| 1965 | 47.7 | 72 | 34.1 | 47 | 15.4 | 22 | | | | |
| 1969 | 44.6 | 75 | 33.3 | 50 | 16.6 | 18 | | | | |
| 1973 | 46.2 | 69 | 35.1 | 54 | 13.7 | 19 | | | | |
| 1977 | 50.6 | 84 | 30.6 | 43 | 11.6 | 17 | | | | |
| 1981 | 45.3 | 78 | 36.5 | 65 | 9.9 | 15 | | | | |
| 1982 (Feb.) | 47.3 | 81 | 37.3 | 63 | 9.1 | 15 | | | | |
| 1982 (Nov.) | 45.2 | 75 | 39.2 | 70 | 9.4 | 16 | | | | |
| 1987 | 44.2 | 81 | 27.1 | 51 | 6.5 | 12 | 1.9 | 0 | 11.9 | 14 |
| 1989 | 44.2 | 77 | 29.3 | 55 | 9.5 | 15 | 1.2 | 0 | 5.5 | 6 |
| 1992 | 39.1 | 68 | 24.5 | 45 | 19.3 | 33 | 1.6 | 0 | 4.7 | 10 |
| 1997 | 39.3 | 77 | 27.9 | 54 | 10.4 | 17 | 2.5 | 1 | 4.7 | 4 |

**Others:**

| | |
|---|---|
| Greens: | 1987 0.4% (0) |
| | 1989 1.5% (I) |
| | 1992 1.4% (1) |
| | 1997 2.8% (2) |
| Democratic Left | 1992 2.8% (6) |
| | 1997 2.5% (4) |

**Source:** Richard Sinnott, *Irish Voters Decide*, Manchester University Press, 1995.

Equally, whilst the Irish adoption of the single transferable vote (STV) for popular elections to the most powerful chamber of the legislature (the Dail) is far from unique in Europe, it possesses a greater comparability with Bolivia than most. Ireland only experienced her revolution three decades earlier, the absence of subsequent military intervention allowing a prolonged competition between large and generally conservative movements, Fianna Fail and Fine Gael, to which the contemporary leaderships of the ADN and MNR might aspire. In the same way, both the MIR and the MBL might see in the Irish Labour Party an example of an influential junior coalition role although in 1997 Dick Spring's party was punished for its pragmatic alliance with Fine Gael only slightly less severely than was Antonio Aranibar's MBL for backing the MNR in 1993–1997. What is clear from the recent Irish experience is that the small parties have failed to make an impact on the position of the traditional movements to the same degree as have the new populist formations in Bolivia. However, this might well not last if the remarkable health of the Irish economy in the 1990s starts to fail — a fact so obvious that it should remind us that electoral systems may indeed matter but, ultimately, they merely translate decisions determined in a world made up of different measurements and estimations.

## Parties and Blocs 1985–1996

As can be discerned from Tables 2.3 and 2.4, the MNR was the dominant party in the political landscape of 'pre-transition' Bolivia: between 1952 and 1985 only one (very short) civilian government was headed by a president who was not a serving or past member of the party. If, as has sometimes been argued, the Bolivian party system is 'inchoate', this must have more to do with the fragmentation than the institutional longevity of its core political movement.

Nevertheless, the return to prominence of the MNR after 1985 cannot be explained simply by its long-standing bedrock of support so much as by its capacity to exploit this in response to the economic and social crises presided over by the UDP coalition between 1982 and 1985. The key element in this regard was the *movimientista* jilting of expansionist and corporatist policies associated with the 1952 revolution and its imposition of a severe deflationary programme through Decreto Supremo 21060, introduced by president Víctor Paz

Estenssoro on 29 August 1985, less than a month after coming to power. That measure succeeded in driving down the hyperinflation that had prevailed under the military dictatorships and the UDP and, despite sporadic popular opposition and mobilisation, the decree continued to operate as a constant in macroeconomic policy under all governments thereafter. This continuity has been partly due to the fact that the programme was initially designed and later implemented by non-members of the MNR, such as Juan Cariaga and Juan Antonio Morales. It also resulted from the decision of the ADN — which had publicly campaigned for this policy in the 1985 elections whereas the MNR had been distinctly pusillanimous about it — to accept with good grace the purloining of its programme as well as to support the Paz administration under a formal agreement known as the 'Pacto por la Democracia'. This might be deemed the single most important instance of elite consensus in the Bolivian transition; it certainly enabled the government to withstand the extended popular reaction against the stabilisation plan and the collapse of the tin price at the end of the year. It is doubtful whether the administration could have survived either pressure had the unions grouped in the COB not already over-reached themselves in contest with the UDP, but the experience of conservative collaboration from late 1985 onwards was itself very important.

Under Víctor Paz the MNR effectively reversed the economic policies of 1952–1956 with which the president had once been so intimately associated. It is highly unlikely that Hugo Banzer could have achieved this, if congress had recognised his heading of the 1985 poll and elected him to the presidency on the grounds of his modest yet perceptible victory in the popular vote (Table 2.5). Banzer was not seen as a 'monetarist' in the Pinochet mould, but he was still identified with military rule, and he possessed few links with other parties with which to build an alliance; in August 1985 only the ADN congressmen voted for him (Table 2.6). As an elder statesman and the erstwhile compañero of Hernan Setes Zuazo, the outgoing UDP president, Víctor Paz combined association with a radical past, unparalleled experience, and 'imperial' style that enabled him to pick up the votes of the many small parties which won seats in this first truly post-dictatorial poll. Such a 'super-presidentialism' befitted a man in his eighth decade, and it has been depicted as the magisterial

manner of closing a career of 50 years. It was, though, more consequential than that. In the first place, Paz was the only figure in the
political landscape to whom Banzer could at that moment defer with
grace whilst retaining his political capital; Paz's presence allowed
Banzer to lose the presidential run-off in style and yet hold the legal
right together. Secondly, although the vagaries of the electoral
system had given the MNR a lead over the ADN in terms of seats,
the *movimientistas* did not seek — and could barely hope — to repeat
the run-off vote throughout a four-year term.

Instead, they sided with the ADN to form an unassailable majority
in congress over the very parties who had just voted for Paz; this
alliance guaranteed the passage of virtually all legislation through
congress (Table 2.6). Thirdly, as a result of these factors, Paz was able
to hand day-to-day management of economic policy to his finance
minister Gonzalo Sánchez de Lozada, who scarcely needed to worry
himself with the problems of parliamentary alliances or sustaining
popularity as he piloted through Bolivia's remarkable stabilisation and
sought, with much less success, to fire up its desultory growth.

The combination of a strong ideological and parliamentary conservative alliance, the presidency in the hands of a 'father of the nation'
figure, and a highly able and confident manager of the economy was
certainly felicitous for the implementation of public policy. Indeed, it
may have saved Bolivia from becoming authentically 'inchoate' as the
majority of its population suffered wretchedly under the impact of
deflation, the collapse of the tin industry, the far from perfect rules of
competition in *narcotráfico*, and the initially weak poverty alleviation
programmes. Yet the strengths of this truly transitional administration
spawned a backlash as well as encouraging hubris within the MNR,
which predictably put Sánchez de Lozada up as its presidential candidate, and unpredictably broke off the Pacto por la Democracia prior
to the poll of 1989. We still lack a detailed and authoritative explanation for this move, but all the indications are that, having benefited so
handsomely from coalition politics, the MNR seriously misconstrued
the reasons for this, mistakenly assumed that it would be rewarded by
the voters for reducing inflation and could therefore jettison the
ADN and move behind the electoral pendulum to the centre. Under
the circumstances, it is remarkable that the party was not more
severely punished at the 1989 poll, and although it lost both the pres-

idency and a congressional majority, it was able to constitute a vocal opposition and retain many appointments in the state sector, particularly the senior ranks of the judiciary.

However, in 1989 the defeat of the MNR was less notable than the manner in which the new administration was formed — an experience which gave rise to the popular story that, on visiting the shrine of the Virgin of Urkupiña, Sánchez de Lozada asked that he might be granted his wish to win the election, Jaime Paz Zamora that he be made president, and General Banzer that he be allowed to run the country, and all three had their wishes fully realised. As can be seen from Table 2.5, the MNR headed the poll, just ahead of the ADN, with a considerable improvement in the vote of Paz Zamora's Movimiento de la Izquierda Revolucionaria (MIR), a centrist movement which had quit the UDP government as soon as it entered crisis, despite the fact that Paz Zamora was vice-president of the Republic. No longer at the head of the poll, now plainly unable to ally with the MNR, and with the smaller parties located firmly on the left of the spectrum, Banzer played kingmaker by backing Paz Zamora, the third-placed candidate, to be president. Despite the closeness of the MIR's result to those of the front-running parties, this decision aroused acute controversy over the legitimacy of the congressional vote for the presidency, and the constitution was later amended to restrict the run-off to the two candidates leading the popular poll.

Banzer, whilst punishing his erstwhile allies for their fair-weather friendship, refused to enter into another formal agreement. Nonetheless, the loose Acuerdo Patriótico (AP) between the ADN and the MIR lasted up until and through the poll of 1993, and its strong parliamentary majority fortified the image of a benevolent ex-dictator generously backing a party formed 18 years before precisely in order to overthrow his regime. Again, coalition politics had contrived to throw up a strangely complementary pairing — this time in terms of generation and partisan reconciliation. The AP would not seriously tamper with the macro-economic strategy established in 1985 whilst it strove to project a more balanced approach to stabilisation and a more relaxed, modern and 'inclusive' style of government.

The fact that this failed to consolidate over the following four years owes a good deal to the role of the MIR, which was the junior party of the alliance despite holding the presidency. With its roots in radical Christian Democracy and the insecurely radical urban middle classes of the late 1960s, the MIR had never been tempted for long to dwell within the hard, 'Leninist' left of Bolivia that had such a rigorous programmatic pedigree, proletarian constituency and unsated appetite for sectarianism. Its role as a 'bridge-party' of the centre, able to operate flexibly with the populist derivations of the old MNR and the orthodox left rooted in the unions had made the MIR a vital element in the UDP and, arguably, delivered victory to that coalition in 1980. Now, though, the MIR sought to hold both the centre ground and power by blocking with the right. The tensions caused by this shift had already split the party in 1986 between a pragmatic officialist wing and a 'principled' group under the leadership of Antonio Aranibar that went on to form the Movimiento Bolivia Libre (MBL). Three years later, with its vote doubled and supported by the ADN, the MIR seemed to have extracted maximum advantage from its relocation in the political spectrum. However, it is telling that the MBL (which fought the 1989 poll as part of the left-wing pact Izquierda Unida) began to describe itself as *trigo limpio* — a phrase which artfully differentiated it from the rising reputation for placemanship and corruption acquired by the Paz Zamora faction, now distributing the offices and favours of the state with an energy exclusive to those who have never previously availed themselves of the rewards of the patrimonialist circuit.

This sense of corrosion in a still incipient, fragile system was hardened by a serious dispute between the legislature (controlled by the AP) and the supreme court (dominated by the MNR) that came to involve impeachment of the justices of the court and a dangerous stalemate over interpretation of the constitution, blocking much government business. The fact that the result of the elections and political manoeuvres could so readily destabilise ostensibly non-partisan institutions of the state was both generally disruptive and a specific warning to the MNR that, just as it could not expect to win elections outright or make and break alliances at will, nor could it simply transfer the tasks of opposition to those sections of the state apparatus that it happened to control with an indifferent or neutral effect on the constitutional order as a whole. The eventual solution of this crisis in May 1991 included the exchange of a new electoral law for retention of the justices in their posts. But, as might be expected, this did not presage the comprehensive reform of the judicial system advocated by modernisers from all parties (including the MNR's René Blattmann, who managed to introduce some important changes in custodial policy and sentencing procedure in the 1993–1997 government).[9]

Both official placemanship and the crisis over the supreme court revealed the extent of drug interests in the political parties and the state, the question of *narcotráfico* returning to the top of both domestic and diplomatic agendas after a relatively low profile in the mid-1980s (despite the fact that receipts from cocaine had readily entered the banking system and palpably palliated the impact of structural adjustment). In this respect it is important to recall that Jaime Paz Zamora and the AP administration took office in August 1989, on the very cusp of the collapse of the Soviet bloc, and that this government would witness the collapse of communism in the company of the Bush administration in the United States, which sought to implement a comprehensive anti-drug campaign in the western hemisphere. The prior preparedness of the Paz Estenssoro government formally to collaborate with high-profile interdiction operations — such as 'Blast Furnace' in 1986 — that involved deployment of US forces on Bolivian soil had given the MIR what seemed to be a low-cost nationalist platform, from which it continued to proclaim in office that 'coca is not cocaine'. This was a popular enough motif at home, and it played well with those sections of the international community convinced that Washington was seeking to shift to the south the economic, social and political costs of its antidrug campaign by emphasising the problems of supply over those of demand. However, Paz Zamora misjudged a balance of forces that was, indeed, exceptionally mercurial. In addition to the wider international instability, including the de-escalation of the Central American civil wars that had so preoccupied Washington, his cabinet had to make sense of the unprecedentedly violent intromission of the cartels into Colombian politics; the extensive operations of Sendero Luminoso in neighbouring Peru; and the emergence there of Alberto Fujimori as a regional political figure of maverick qualities but critical importance for La Paz. Even with the invasion of Panama at the end of the year, it is not difficult to imagine how, in such a scenario, a policy of avowed autonomy towards the US might commend itself, especially if conducted in harness with collaboration in practice.

## Table 2.11: Drugs and US Aid

*Anti-drug Operations, Bolivia 1991–1997*

| Detained/ destroyed | 1991 | 1992 | 1993 | 1994 | 1995 | 1996 |
|---|---|---|---|---|---|---|
| Processing plants | 1,386 | 1,052 | 938 | 1,613 | 2,131 | 1,660 |
| Distillation vats | 2,531 | 1,913 | | MOM | 3,077 | 2,819 |
| Persons | 1,047 | 1,226 | 1,376 | 2,634 | 2,494 | 2,585 |
| Cocaine base (tons) | 9.48 | 10.19 | 9.51 | R.R2 | 9.5 | 10.0 |

**Source:** FELCN .

*Coca Cultivation and Eradication*

| Year | Cultivated (est. hectares) | Eradicated (hectares) |
|---|---|---|
| 1986 | 25,800 | |
| 1987 | 30,646 | |
| 1988 | 38,400 | |
| 1989 | 41,816 | |
| 1990 | 44,462 | |
| 1991 | 39,086 | |
| 1992 | 36,746 | |
| 1993 | 35,500 | 2,400 |
| 1994 | 35,000 | 2,240 |
| 1995 | 30,000 | 5,492 |
| 1996 | 25,000 | 7,575 |

1997–1998 target set by US — 7,000 hectares by May 1998 — agreed by *cocaleros*, 2 September 1997.
**Source:** *Presencia*, 20 July 1997.

*US Aid to Bolivia ($m)*

|                 | 1993 | 1994  | 1995 | 1996 |
|-----------------|------|-------|------|------|
| Economic support | 59.5 | 31.0  | 16.7 | 15.0 |
| Development     | 26.9 | 19.8  | 30.0 | 28.2 |
| Food aid        | 43.2 | 36.0  | 19.9 | 21.3 |
| Total           |      | 129.6 | 86.8 | 66.6 |

**Source:** USAID.

Although drug scandals over the last decade have involved members of all the main parties together with the police, armed forces and judiciary, Washington's attention focused on the MIR, particularly once combined pressure from the embassy and press forced interior minister Guillermo Capobianco from office in March 1991. After the MIR left government in 1993, the party's number two, Oscar Eid, was jailed for four years for protecting traffickers, and Washington refused to issue visas to either Jaime Paz Zamora himself or to Carlos Saavedra, a senior minister in the outgoing government and effectively Eid's replacement in the party hierarchy. This probably did the MIR little harm in the 1997 poll since it enabled the party to make a positive virtue out of its necessary distance from the US, but it has further complicated an already critical aspect of public policy for several years. As can be seen from Table 2.11, interdiction operations and reduction of the cocales were maintained under the Paz Zamora government with roughly the same results as those registered by its predecessor and successor. These have been distinctly modest in the sense that between 1986 and 1996 the overall area under coca has been reduced little, if at all. But given that Bolivia is, in Washington's estimation, the world's second largest producer of coca and cocaine — and that cultivation of the former nearly doubled over the period — the expenditure of some $200 million in eradication and interdiction might be said to have yielded some success.

A significant degree of compliance with Washington was always necessary for the simple reason that the US accounts for over 30 per cent of Bolivia's foreign trade. However, the prominence under the Clinton administration of the policy of 'decertification', whereby disbursement of US aid is conditional upon local acceptance and realisation of eradication targets, has sharpened the relationship, not least because World Bank loans — and much private investment — would also be put in jeopardy. As Table 2.11 shows, under the Sánchez de Lozada government Bolivia received a diminishing amount of aid from the US, largely as a result of economic recovery. However, the most vulnerable funds — those for development — have not reduced and could have been frozen or withdrawn had the administration in La Paz not been so warmly disposed towards Washington and generally able to deliver compliance on the part of the most reluctant *cocaleros*, who have replaced the miners as the most vocal and independent sector of the populace. It is telling that, once it had issued a 10-point 'ethical charter', the first public challenge faced by the Banzer government in 1997 was to extract from Evo Morales and the coca growers of the Chapare an agreement to meet the US-ordained targets. Indeed, the initial weeks of the Banzer government reflected in raw form the exigencies of fiscal policy imposed by external conditionality — vice-president Quiroga had almost immediately to attend the Hong Kong conference of the IMF and World Bank. This increasingly familiar 'globalised' scenario, however, included much less violence than in Colombia or even Peru or Mexico. The Bolivian experience of *narcotráfico* has at no stage involved guerrilla groups, and it has rarely thrown up producers or traders whose operations consistently depend upon violent activity. Interdiction on the scale indicated in Table 2.11 has inevitably involved loss of life, and the specialist anti-drug forces have regularly been accused of human rights violations (under the 1993–1997 government 22 people died, 105 were wounded and 2,002 were detained in public order operations). Yet the dichotomy between corruption and violence is as false as it is simplistic, and the ideological and institutional trajectory of national politics from 1985 onwards cannot be seen in isolation from — or as simply parallel to — the character of the local drug economy, especially its connections with the semi-legal cultivation of the coca leaf that directly underpins the subsistence of tens of thousands of poor people. The national election of 1993 reflected this state of affairs in confirming the serious nature of the challenge to the traditional parties from two new movements of strong 'populist' vocation and style: Conciencia de Patria (CONDEPA) led by ex-folk musician and La Paz television proprietor Carlos Palenque, who had polled well in 1989, and the Unión Cívica de Solidaridad (UCS), set up by the *Cochabambino* beer magnate Max Fernández, who was equally of humble origin. Although CONDEPA began its existence as an urbanised Aymara movement focused on the poorest sectors of El Alto and La Paz, whilst the UCS was less regionally restricted and appeared to gain more success in the provinces, both parties had clearly emerged and developed in response to the deflationary climate and restructuring begun by DS 21060. Headed by charismatic figures, driven by loose rhetoric and sharp expression of complaint, invoking threats to community and cultural values, dependent upon the reputation of being as well as representing 'outsiders', these movements sought national as well as local office but rarely propounded precise policies that might form the basis of a platform for government. Indeed, although much interesting analysis has been devoted to their ambiguous origins, declamatory discourse and contradictory impact on cultural identity, it is possible to view both organisations as vehicles for a machine politics run by a new entrepreneurial sector of *mestizo* background.

In 1993 each of the populist parties won nearly a quarter of a million votes (14 per cent of the turnout), in part at the expense of the AP coalition — which could only muster half of the votes that the ADN and MIR had won by running separately in 1989 (Table 2.5) — but also partly by swallowing up the support of the small, radical, regional and personalist parties. These had secured 26 seats in the 1985 congress and were now all but eliminated from the scene by a 'catch all' oppositional offensive which eschewed traditional ideology and yet did not sacrifice rhetorical energy to the pursuit of state position, thereby expanding an already formidable capacity to deliver clientelist favours. The 'professional' politicos had little difficulty in disparaging Palenque's reliance upon the 'culture of complaint' stoked up by his TV programme '*Tribuna libre del pueblo*', and they could plausibly doubt the solidity of support for Fernández based upon liberal distribution of free beer. Yet the 1993 poll clearly established popular proclivity for these options — whatever the degree of protest this entailed — and that of 1997 would confirm their presence on the scene, notwithstanding the recent death of both leaders and the involvement of both parties in government (CONDEPA in the municipal administration of El Alto and La Paz; UCS in the national coalition led by the MNR).

If the 1993 election result required the conservatives to negotiate with the new populist organisations, it also indicated a recurrent tendency on the part of the electorate to punish the incumbent administration, this time more severely than it had the MNR in 1989 (repeating this result in the local elections of December 1993 — see Table 2.12). On that basis Gonzalo Sánchez de Lozada readily won both the highest popular vote and the congressional run-off, in which Banzer did not even figure. However, the *movimientistas* had learnt the lessons of 1989, and they went to some lengths to construct a coalition which would include not only the centre-left MBL (not itself engaged in a pragmatic pirouette of a type it once scorned so severely) but also the UCS, which lacked any track record or ideological basis for rejecting the lure of office, and, as vice-president, Víctor Hugo Cárdenas Conde, who headed the Movimiento Revolucionario Tupaj Katari de Liberación (MRTKL). This last appointment was seemingly a very generous sop to the rather stiff but talented and honourable Aymara intellectual who held a very modest constituency in the northern *altiplano*. However, it transpired to be one of Sánchez de Lozada's more inspired gambles in that Cárdenas, with an awkward combination of idealism and realpolitik, single-mindedly promoted the idea of a multi-ethnic state through the representation of indigenous identity, this form of 'cultural politics' proving remarkably popular at home and abroad. The impact on hard policy was slight in the extreme — as Cárdenas's initial supporters were quick to point out — but the longer-term influence could be much more consequential, forming a piece with Bolivia's avoidance of the type of social disintegration and violence witnessed in Peru.

### The Sánchez de Lozada Administration

The MNR needed to form a coalition in 1993 in order to control both houses of congress. In the event, it assembled an alliance which mustered 97 of the 157 seats at stake — more than the number needed for amending the constitution, which would be required if Sánchez de Lozada was to realise his ambitious programme of reforms, the 'plan de todos'. This had initially seemed little more than flamboyant campaign rhetoric, but 'Goni's' reputation as an innovative *técnico* easily outstripped that of Banzer or Jaime Paz, whose coalition had become mired in 'sleaze' and inertial tinkering with the earlier MNR programme. Moreover, one should not under-estimate the degree to which the decision by Cárdenas and Aranibar (separately) to cross the traditional ideological divide both encour-aged a popular view of the new administration as a post-Cold War government and gave Sánchez de Lozada himself the resolve to pursue his own programme with non-partisan energy. In the event, neither of these minor coalition allies salvaged much from the expe-rience of 1993–1997 if this is measured narrowly in zero-sum, partisan terms: the MRTKL was unable even to stand in 1997, and the MBL was severely chastised by the voters. By contrast, the UCS, which was the least creative and disciplined member of the govern-ment, escaped the backlash entirely, perhaps because it was so 'semidetached' that it never became associated with a programme that went well beyond DS 21060 in dismantling the institutional and macroeconomic legacy of the 1952 revolution.

The two axes of the 'plan de todos' lay in administrative decentral-isation and privatisation, but both were designed with greater attention to mass 'participation' than most policies of this type, now familiar in the subcontinent because of their popularity with the large multilateral organisations, particularly the World Bank. Although neither policy had been fully implemented by 1997, the electorate had clearly regis-tered their initial impact. In the case of the Ley de participación popular of April 1994 there had been a significant distribution of fiscal revenue from the central state to the 311 Organizaciones Territoriales de Base (OTBs) established across the country to admin-ister health, education and other local services. In 1990 Bolivia's total municipal budget had been $22 million; by 1996 it was over $150 million — more than 30 per cent of total public expenditure. Between

1994 and 1995 municipal expenditure per capita rose from $11.20 to $41.10, but it should be noted that a full 46 per cent of the population was concentrated in just seven municipalities. The establishment of *comités de vigilancia* was supposed to give local support for the statutory restriction of spending on wages to 10 per cent of each OTB's budget as well as to provide more general oversight. To the inevitable incidence of poor organisation in the transfer of services and 'windfall' exploitation of confusion and change by local caudillos and crooks, one should add the no less predictable conflicts over resources both within and between OTBs. It is as yet difficult to gain a firm sense of the impact on local structures and dynamics of power.

Government propaganda was often highly exaggerated. Many communities did certainly receive income for the first time, and others now managed enhanced resources, but, by the same token, their new duties implied a far greater expenditure. The electoral outturn of this root and branch alteration of the country's local government was not sensibly predictable beyond the early success registered by the parties of the governing coalition in the December 1995 local poll as a result of a huge publicity campaign (Table 2.12).

Sánchez de Lozada dubbed his government's privatisation policy one of 'capitalisation' (Law 1544 of March 1994), insisting that the sale of 50 per cent of the stock of public companies, together with transfer of full managerial powers to the private sector, was essential in order to overhaul inefficient entities. This sale was depicted as being a necessary complement to the stabilisation policy of a decade earlier in renovating the legacy of 1952. By the time of the poll nine companies had been sold for a total of $1.7 billion (not all of which was in liquid form). These included the national airline, Lloyd Aereo Boliviano (to the Brazilian VASP); ENTEL, the weak but potentially very profitable telecommunications company (to the Italian STET, which was soon subject to regulatory fines); and two sales that aroused controversy on the grounds of national security — the national railway company to the Chilean Cruz Blanca corporation (which immediately closed down the Sucre–Potosí branch line) and YPFB's oil and gas distribution branch (at $263 million, worth around 30 per cent of the company's total value) to ENRON–Shell. The prior performance of many of these companies was sufficiently poor to limit popular protest within a society generally sympathetic to the idea of public ownership. Moreover, the rise of new foreign investment from $35 million in 1990 to $520 million in 1996 lessened the impact of charges that Sánchez de Lozada, himself a wealthy entrepreneur, was stripping the state of assets on behalf of the business community.

### Table 2.12: Municipal Elections, 1993 and 1995

| Party | 1993 | | 1995 | |
|---|---|---|---|---|
| | % | Concejales | % | Concejales |
| ADN–PDC | 7.8 | 262 | 11.4 | 233 |
| ASD | 1.8 | 10 | – | – |
| CONDEPA | 19.6 | 323 | 15.5 | 131 |
| EJE | 0.6 | 15 | 1.8 | 25 |
| FRI | 2.2 | 17 | 3.1 | 27 |
| FSB | 2.1 | 10 | – | – |
| IU | 0.8 | 8 | 3.0 | 58 |
| MBL | 11.7 | 213 | 13.3 | 216 |
| MIR | 9.4 | 245 | 9.3 | 138 |
| MKN | – | – | 0.2 | 4 |
| MNR | 34.9 | 1,330 | 21.3 | 478 |
| MPP | – | – | 1.9 | 8 |
| MRTKL | 0.2 | 2 | 1.2 | 33 |
| UCS | 8.4 | 372 | 17.5 | 231 |
| VR-9 | 0.2 | 3 | 0.5 | 2 |
| Total votes | 1,119,854 | | 1,716,007 | |
| Null/void | 70,042 | | 89,625 | |
| Registered | 2,231,945 | | 2,840,492 | |
| Abstentions (%) | 47 | | 36 | |

If this policy was both more predictable and controversial than 'popular participation', there can be little doubt about the novelty (and strong electoral potential) of the government's proposals for the use of the receipts of privatisation — distribution to the public in the form of pensions. This required a considerable logistical undertaking since the central Bolivian state had previously run only one very modest pension system — for the veterans of the Chaco War against Paraguay (1932–1935), now covering only 8,603 *beneméritos* and 13,571 widows (subject to unusual assessment in case of matrimony on fraudulent grounds by *cazabenemeritos*). In the event, the reorganisation of pension funds (AFPs) proved to be more restrictive for savers than even the much-vaunted Chilean system since membership of one of the two private systems in La Paz, Santa Cruz and Cochabamba and the one reserved for the rest of the country was obligatorily assigned (although mandatory levels of contribution could be enhanced in all). The closure of some substantial professional schemes was not accompanied with full guarantees for their transferred assets, and it was fiercely resisted by, for instance, the national medical association, which witnessed serious problems in public sector clinical provision as a result of the attendant amalgamation of professionally associated hospitals and clinics. The military, by contrast, quickly accepted the proposals but appears not to have grasped the full consequences of closure and amalgamation — something that may be subject to review in the wake of Banzer's election.

By far the greatest attention was focused on the payment of a pension (Bono de Solidaridad — Bonosol: a sunny enough term to throw a shadow over any affinity with the Mexican public works system set up by Carlos Salinas) to those over 65 years of age. The plan was to pay the equivalent of $248 to some 300,000 pensioners in 1997. This, it should be stressed, represented a considerable sum to many inhabitants of a country with such a low average income (some $800 per head). Indeed, the promise soon flushed out many new 'citizens'; there were 614,000 more registered voters in 1997 than in 1993, including two men of 93 and 107 years in the La Paz town of Ancoraimes who had never previously acquired any documentation from the state. With its capacity for simple registration under pressure — let alone its actuarial skills — the state managed to pay pensions to only 150,000 people by the time of the poll, and substantial doubts remained as to the capacity of the AFPs to meet early expectations despite the fact that they had overnight become some of the most powerful and protected bodies within the national economy. On the other hand, efforts within the MNR to exploit the Bonosol for party ends were largely contained, and Banzer was able to identify himself closely enough with a system the details of which he criticised — for example, by promising to lower the rural retirement age to 55 — so as not to lose electoral advantage.

As with the other main planks of government policy, the brief record of the pension reform was not so poor in either conception or execution to suggest that the administration would be seriously penalised by the voters. There were understandable doubts concerning manipulation of unfamiliar systems and institutions — a response equally elicited by new agrarian reform legislation. In the past, such statutes have proved highly and justifiably controversial, especially in the *altiplano* and valleys, but the new law appeared to be wholly favourable to community and small-owner interests in its abolition of low-level taxation, the guarantees given to collective title, and the privileges advanced to the communities in terms of allocation of public lands. Nevertheless, the statute was treated in many sectors as being a contemporary expression of a free-market lineage stretching back to Bolívar's Trujillo decree, Melgarejo's piratical expropriations of 1866, and the decisive Ley de ex-vinculación of 1884. Certainly, either the MNR's authorship nor the support of Victor Hugo Cárdenas led to a widespread conviction that the law was a simple development or improvement on the agrarian reform of August 1953.

Perhaps in all these cases the imbrication of public and private spheres — the admixture of community and individual interest — was indeed recognised, being viewed as both potentially efficient and equitable, but it was not yet trusted to work. It has been observed that Sánchez de Lozada could be seen more as a 'legislator' than a 'governor', but even had he and his government expended more effort on the tasks of reassurance as opposed to celebration, it may be doubted whether they would have greatly soothed a popular disquiet which, as in 1985–1989, had less to do with rational calculation than a more profound insecurity.

Something of the same reaction may be found in the voters' response to general economic performance, which was formally solid enough to give grounds for the 'feel-good factor' that has so attracted Anglo-Saxon psephologists in recent years. As might be expected, given his experience as finance minister for Víctor Paz Estenssoro, 'Goni' kept inflation under tight control, obtaining an average of 10 per cent over 1993–1996 and a level of 8 per cent — the lowest in 20 years — over the 12 months prior to the poll. At 3.9 per cent the rate of economic growth was less impressive, especially with the population expanding at 2.4 per cent. However, as we have seen, investment was quite healthy in terms of Bolivia's distinctly modest record in the past, and recent export performance was relatively satisfactory — $1.2 billion in 1996 with decreased volume but increased value in minerals and reduced sales of some non-traditional products (coffee, vegetable oil, artisanal produce) matched by increases in others (soya, Brazil nuts, wood). Moreover, confirmation of substantial reserves of natural gas (up to 9 trillion cubic feet) available from 1999 was capped by the signing of a 22-year contract to supply Brazil with gas worth up to $500 million a year through a 3,150 km pipeline under construction between Rio Grande and Puerto Súarez.

These, of course, were big and generally distant issues, often learnt about from the mass media rather than sensed directly in daily life. On the street and in popular consciousness the image and experience of 'progress and modernity' were far more ambiguous. This can be seen in the manifestation of the market-as-modern-retailing, with the establishment in La Paz of a string of new or expanded supermarkets — Ketal, Hypermaxi, Zatt, Bonanza. By mid-1997 these had captured some 15 per cent of urban grocery sales but not on the classic grounds of the economies of scale and loss-leaders, their prices failing to undercut those of the traditional street and covered markets across a range of 32 basic necessities, and being markedly higher on prime cuts of meat. It is unlikely that higher standards of hygiene account for this market-share, which probably owes more to the pleasurable sensation of supermarket shopping, even if that currently constitutes an 'event' based on novelty or becomes part of a more differentiated strategy of buying by consumers. There are still millions of dollars tied up in highly profitable *cholo* wholesale and

retail enterprises in the streets and alley ways in the north of the city
and El Alto; Bolivia is very far from adopting 'mall culture' even if its
most affluent suburbs may embrace the idea and institute their own
mini-versions of it. However, the process is more advanced in Santa
Cruz, and McDonald's decision to establish a restaurant in the
capital cannot be seen as $2 million lightly expended in a society
dedicated at all levels to traditional heavy lunches. In the same vein,
the growth of the telecommunications sector by over 11 per cent in
the last two years — compared with the general rate of 4 per cent
— is, as elsewhere, to a large extent accounted for by *cellular* phones.
Increased use of personal computers amongst the urban middle
class, together with rapid rises in the rate of connection to the
internet in both private and public spheres, suggest that this is a
strong complementary source of expansion and a possible conduit
for the poorest nation in South America to short-cut some of the
arduous routes out of 'underdevelopment'.

The need to escape that condition is underlined by its very
extremity. In 1996, as we have noted, the average per capita income
in Bolivia was $800 per annum; life expectancy stood at 60 years, and
the official infant mortality rate at 75 deaths per 1,000 live births. The
fact that 38 per cent of children under five are malnourished indicates the principal reason for such an appalling statistic. Basic
sanitation, control of diarrhoea, promotion of breast feeding, and
access to paediatric care are low-cost essentials for child survival —
especially in the first 12 months of life — but these remain largely
dependent upon foreign aid and NGOs. The public health system is,
in fact, more disorganised than it is subverted by malfeasance, but
the level of corruption, clientelism and favouritism is seen as high
throughout the state as a whole. In 1997 the company Transparency
International ranked Bolivia as the thirty-sixth worst case of corruption in the world (Nigeria coming last in fifty-fourth position). The
methodology employed in this exercise was criticised as being clumsy
and 'subjective', but the ranking of Chile at half Bolivia's level does
not strike one as a travesty, and objections to the league table from
La Paz were not unreservedly fortified by the simultaneous
announcement by the local police that they had broken a major car-
ring operated out of the navy offices by one Captain Clever Alcoba.

In fact, even within the legal sphere, attention to the division of the spoils remains sharp enough to suggest only a very slight reduction in patrimonialist practices. Following Banzer's victory the press reported that his allocation of the senior offices of state had resulted in the ADN receiving 54.14 per cent of the ministries and CONDEPA 14.28 per cent. At one level this is no more than a contemporary expression of Bourbon punctiliousness, but it does also suggest an instinctive suspension of belief in public service.

One recent instance of the retrograde nature of partial 'modernity' can be seen in the case of five members of the small Uru-murato ethnic group who were arrested in August 1994 for hunting birds protected by law in their traditional grounds of Lake Poopó. Held in jail for a year without trial, they were eventually released on bail, but after three years had received no sentence from Judge Ana Rosa Quiroga; during this period one of those held, a 78-year-old man, had died — 'of fright' according to his co-defendants, who were freshly charged with 'ecological crimes' in September 1997. An equal sense of the pertinence of the past could be found in the limited success of the arms amnesty offered to the Laime people of the north of Potosí by the local prefect in the week before the election. Although the authorities celebrated the hand-over of several modern weapons by the community, this was the third such agreement in two years and seemed most unlikely to pacify a region which had experienced violent land disputes throughout the colonial and republican eras. There was certainly nothing in the new agrarian legislation that offered relief on that score. On the other hand, the continuing cultural and economic power of the Entrada del Gran Poder in La Paz, and the rise to prominence in recent years of the Entrada Universitaria, represent confident and energetic expressions of indigenous tradition, no less impressive for the inclusion of Afro-Bolivian rhythms or the participation of young white women pirouetting in baroque *minipolleras*. The idea of a 'pluri-multi-ethnic state' still languishes in the imagination of intellectuals bailed from detention in a Cold War mind-set, but civil society is increasingly proud of its non-hispanic culture, which is now sufficiently integrated into the mainstream to lose the tag of 'folklore' and foment an appreciable market. Even the notoriously Europhile and

circumspect middle class of Santiago de Chile expressed admiration
at the passage down their alameda of a large contingent of Bolivian
dancers in 1995, and in the last few years La Paz tailors have become
an essential element in the economy of the Rio carnival. This was the
backdrop to CONDEPA's electoral success, as it was to the smooth
integration of Víctor Hugo Cárdenas into the MNR government of
1993–1997. It is also surely an important contributory factor to the
absence of a racially charged violence that could rock the dominant
market and state (sometimes described as 'Americanised' because of
their integration into the wider US circuit but better understood as
being 'European', rather than indigenous, in origin).

## The 1997 Campaign

The election campaign of 1997 enveloped and expressed these
powerfully contradictory features as well as the more explicit display
of party and personal conduct. The fact that the UCS leader Max
Fernández died in an air crash in 1996 and CONDEPA's Carlos
Palenque expired of a heart attack in the midst of the campaign
could well account for the high vote of those parties in the June poll,
just as it might explain any subsequent decline and extinction. It is
unlikely, however, that the general 'style' of these parties will disap-
pear from the national scene, regardless of the success experienced
by the Fernández and Palenque children in handling the inherited
vitalicio leadership of their parents' organisations.

The continued salience of the MIR in electoral calculations was
underscored by its ability to bisect the vote of CONDEPA and the
UCS. The MIR's 21-point programme opened with an appeal for
'confidence in ourselves', and it ended with the slogan, 'Solutions —
yes; experiments — no', which is arguably in contradiction with the
first point but unarguably rhetoric of the most vapid type. This characteristic feature of the MIR's politics was to some degree offset by
thinly veiled nationalist sniping at the US, and the party did not have
to concern itself greatly with radical challenges. The representative
of the orthodox left, Juan de la Cruz of Izquierda Unida,
campaigned on the grounds that Bolivia is a state without a nation;
that it needs to be socialised; and that the only way to rid it of

corruption is to throw out the entire current system. His most detailed proposal was that parliamentary business should be conducted in indigenous languages — not itself a very novel idea and equally unappealing when so few parliamentarians were bilingual or even understood Aymara, Quechua or Guaraní. The precise prescriptions of Leninism had been removed from the socialist prospectus, but their rectilinear clumsiness was retained and simply given a graft of autochthonous allusion. The left appeared anachronistic and conservative rather than radical and innovative; its diagnosis of the country's ills was exceptionally broad, and it lacked precise propositions which might give it a more than denunciatory presence. Its only success lay in the election of individuals, such as Evo Morales and Juan del Granado, who had a record of strong personal conduct in opposition.

Nevertheless, it is the case that, between them, the MBL and IU won over a quarter of the vote polled by the MNR, which received slightly more votes in absolute terms than in 1989 but a much reduced proportion of the total ballot. This was a decisive defeat for the *movimientistas*, whose following almost fell to that of the second-string parties — CONDEPA, MIR and UCS. The MNR clearly suffered from the now predictable 'pendulum-effect', whereby the outgoing administration is conclusively repudiated, as well as from direct distrust of the economic and administrative reforms, and possibly, through this, some recycled aversion to the social cost of stabilisation a dozen years earlier. In addition, the party's original presidential candidate, René Blattmann, was precipitately replaced by the more traditional figure of Juan Carlos Durán, who was a competent minister and dependable campaigner but always looked as if he was loyally leading the party into a period of opposition.

The scale of the MNR's defeat in the popular vote was magnified by the manner in which this was converted into seats; it would seem to have suffered disproportionately from the introduction of the additional member system. Equally, it is easy to exaggerate the dimensions of the victory won by Hugo Batizer and the ADN, who were only narrowly ahead in a system that privileges marginal advantage as much as it compels coalitions. Furthermore, the ADN is so close to the MNR in ideological terms that it was possible for the electorate simul-

taneously to vote against the MNR and to retain its economic model.
Finally, of course, whilst the populist movements could amass considerable support, theirs remained a largely expressive politics, lacking both the programmatic coherence and administrative expertise to sustain a serious challenge for government. They still required the catalyst of an orthodox state manager in order to win ministries, and, as has been suggested, it is far from clear whether, after the death of their leaders, they can maintain momentum. Should one of them fail, it is doubtful that the other would automatically reap the benefit. The 'populist moment' may not have disappeared, but one potent electoral manifestation of it could well have passed.

These factors place the AND's victory in context, but that party itself depended heavily on the figure of Hugo Banzer Suárez, and he overcame several important personal obstacles to win the presidency. The first of these concerned the rise in nationalist sentiment that has for some time tracked the debate over *narcotráfico*, and which was particularly stoked up by the regional 'Copa de América' soccer championship held between the poll and the inauguration (Bolivia eventually being beaten into second place by Brazil despite great hopes of repeating the famous home victory by the 1963 national side). As a traditionally pro-US soldier trained in Argentina, and as a man who had warmly embraced General Pinochet at Chavaña in 1975 in an abortive effort to open discussion of Bolivia's most important and contentious boundary dispute, Banzer was vulnerable on this front. His position was not assisted by the decision of Peru — at fierce odds over its border with Ecuador — to withdraw completely from all disputation over its southern border resulting from Chile's victory of the War of the Pacific (1879–1884). This decision prompted the emergence in Bolivia of the popular saying, 'Never trust Chilean honour, Peruvian fraternity, or Bolivian justice', a sentiment which might not have stuck long in popular consciousness were it not for the high profile of the Chilean companies in the privatisation market.

Reflexive patriotism found fuller expression still as a result of Bill Clinton's decision to lift the 20-year old US ban on advanced weaponry to the southern cone countries, which prompted fears of a regional arms race. The threat of renewed tension between Chile and Argentina, together with the revelation that Chile had planted hundreds of thousands of landmines along its northern borders, must, of course, be seen in a post-Malvinas, as well as a (partially) post-dictatorial and post-communist scenario. The difference between the Bolivian military budget of $149 million and Chile's of $1,970 million amounts to far more than the cost of a proper navy; even under authoritarian regimes the Bolivian armed forces have never held or seriously aspired to the resources and status of those in Chile. It is widely accepted that access to the sea by retrieval (or exchange) of sovereign territory can only be gained through diplomatic initiative. This very recognition could have pumped up the rhetorical atmosphere from mid-1997, but the *froideur* of pronouncements — civilian and military alike — from Santiago might well have had something to do with Banzer's apparent agreement in 1978 with the Argentine high command to permit offensive operations across Bolivian territory into that of Chile. Whatever the case, and even if the new president's early waspish exchanges with the ex-leftists directing foreign policy in the Frei government stemmed directly from his electoral needs, there is reason to doubt whether the two countries will seriously seek to restore diplomatic relations in the short term.

The more publicised and serious challenge faced by Banzer was that he authorised the killing of scores of people and violated the human rights of thousands under the de facto regime of 1971–1978 — acts for which he remained unpunished, the strong implication being that he retained a vocation for dictatorship. This latter point was not weakened by the fact that Banzer himself never disputed the general existence of repressive activity and the suppression of civil liberties in the 1970s and had made no expression of atonement or apology for them; he openly argued that they had been justified by the circumstances of the time. However, he was evidently able to persuade nearly half a million voters that they could support him as a leader in a democratic system. Moreover, there are strong reasons for supposing that he was supported by the bulk of this constituency precisely as a democratic leader — that is, in terms rather distinct from those of his own result in 1985 or the support given to Generals Ríos Montt in Guatemala and Pinochet in Chile.

In the first place, the Bolivian political scenario in 1971, when Banzer took power, was undeniably one of social polarisation, polit-

ical insurgency and the widespread collapse of law and order. His
coup was amongst the most violent in national history, but it was not
manifestly so because of his personal leadership. The subsequent
regime could plausibly be presented as 'of its time', and was —
unlike Pinochet's — generally less murderous and restrictive than the
coup which opened it. Moreover, Banzer was thrown out of office
by his own peers, and was not subsequently seen as representing a
consensus of either the officer corps or conservative opinion.
However, it is more important that his regime was followed by the
anarchic dictatorships of 1980–1982, which exhibited a greater
proclivity for delinquency than ideology and which went some
appreciable way to suppressing the memory of anterior tyranny.
Nothing like this, of course, happened in Chile, where Pinochet
imposed himself upon the succeeding regime by constitutional fiat,
whereas in Guatemala, the regime of Mejía Víctores could afford to
be milder than that of Ríos Montt and understood the transition to
civilian rule as an essential counter-insurgency measure.

Thirdly, Banzer's conduct in the post-dictatorial era was exemplary.
In 1982 he had accepted the reintroduction of the 1967 constitution
and the restoration of the 1980 election victory of the UDP (which
contained ministers from the Communist Party) and, as we have seen,
he acquiesced in his 1985 loss of the congressional run-off despite
winning the popular poll. In 1989 he fulfilled a minority role in government with sobriety, and even if he seemed to have decided to go into
retirement, his conduct in opposition under the MNR administration of
1993–1997 gave no cause for concern. These democratic *bona fides* had
been won through a combination of high- and low-profile roles, in and
out of office, but they had been accumulated very largely through the
acceptance of disappointment and defeat.

At the same time, it should be noted that General Banzer had been
subjected to an energetic and detailed impeachment by the radical
leader of the PS-1, Marcelo Quiroga Santa Cruz, who was assassinated
in García Mesa's coup of July 1980. The staging of that indictment,
together with the failure of the governments of 1978–1980 to proceed
against the ex-president in the courts, seems to have bled off a portion
of the earlier popular demand for a settlement of accounts and punishment. It stands in marked contrast to the treatment of García Mesa,

who was jailed for 30 years for political crimes committed before, during and after the 1980 coup. The fact that, shortly after coming to office, president Banzer authorised an official investigation into the killing of Marcelo Quiroga Santa Cruz and the whereabouts of his remains could be seen as a theatrical flourish and a further low-cost display of the general's lack of animus. Nevertheless, it is worth noting that at the time the sentiment was circulating quite widely that Banzer, having lost both his sons in accidents, had now paid a personal price for his own actions, whatever he said about the past and however genuine his avowed dedication to the rule of law.

In short, Banzer may not have been liked or even respected, but he was no longer extensively distrusted or hated. It was almost as if, by osmosis, the Bolivian electorate discerned that to be a democrat it was not necessary to share ideas or values, or even to have a pleasant past; the sole requisite is that one accept all the rules of the game. Very often these self-same rules require — formally or practically — a settlement of accounts over past conduct; however, in Bolivia they were not applied to Banzer in this manner, and there is little expectation that they will be. Banzer's election belies the notion that liberal democracy requires a consensual rewriting of history; there are absolutely no guarantees that it will lead to any greater social convergence (or *concertación*). It should, instead, be viewed as the outcome of a series of tough, pragmatic decisions by a political society at least as mature in its calculations as some supposedly more sophisticated electorates.

### Che Guevara and the Importance of Historical Memory

During the late 1970s, after the death of General Franco, a poster of Ernesto Che Guevara circulated in Spain on which the 'classic' heroic portrait by Alberto Díaz Korda was accompanied by a slogan: 'I shall return, but not as a poster'. This proclamation carries a strong echo of the last words attributed to Tupaj Amaru, executed by the Spaniards for leading the rebellion of 1781–1783: 'I may die, but I shall return as millions'. The idea of a *pachakuti* — a total cycle, renewal, even millennium — has particular resonance in the southern Andes, where it lies at the centre of a cosmovision and goes well beyond the notion of redemptive reincarnation of fallen heroes. These slogans were posthumously assigned to both men as supposed self-fulfilling prophesies, and if they possess a certain unsettling power in our day of quantifiable certainties, it is because they have not proved to be wholly false. The great insurgent leader from Cuzco had his name appropriated by the Uruguayan guerrillas of the 1960s and those of Peru in the 1980s whilst Che, of course, has never ceased to be present as more than an icon. Moreover, when he did finally return in material form through the uncovering of his skeleton near Vallegrande in July 1997, there was even a certain diminution in the power of that poster image. Discovery, return to Cuba and eventual re-interment in a pharaonic mausoleum at Santa Clara — the site of his greatest military victory — provided the kind of private relief and settlement of accounts so ardently sought by the relatives of those who have been 'disappeared' in recent decades in Latin America. Yet it also brought the public Guevara down from the sphere of myth, where many had been more than happy to keep him.

The fact that the discovery of Guevara's bones stemmed from the researches of a biographer rushing to meet a deadline that would enable publication before the thirtieth anniversary of his execution throws light on the forensic power of the contemporary chronicle. At the same time, however, the story of the exhumation occluded reappraisal of the life itself, the commemoration prompting celebration of a man who was heroic in the cause of a collectivist anti-heroism. This paradox did not stand alone; the response to the discovery of Che's remains excited commentary that was generally disconcerting in that — rather like that attending the death of Princess Diana two months later — it revolved around the symbolism of exemplary or sacrificial spirits, wherein rationality stands at less than a premium. Earlier debates over the more prosaic contradictions of his life — those of an Argentine youth in the post-war years; of a Franciscan lover of the good life; of the 'straight-talker' locked into a world of conspiracy — were now subsumed into this grander theme. However, the incongruity of the pulsating commodification of such an ascetic egalitarian did not seem to be drawing to a close, even in the desultory effort to create a tourist industry around the makeshift shrine at La Higuera and the sites of the bloody skirmishes around it.

In the event, most dignitaries of the continental and international left shunned the activities organised at Vallegrande, preferring to attend the large concerts and ceremonials organised in Buenos Aires and Santiago de Chile as well as Havana. It is understandable, in simple logistical terms, why a man so dedicated to rural guerrilla warfare and who died in the countryside should be celebrated in large cities; there is no real anomaly in the 'otherness' of heroism. Equally, one should not be surprised that amidst all the reflections and analysis there was little consideration of what Guevara meant for Bolivia itself, now nearly reduced to that spot on the globe where an internationalist coincidentally happened to meet his destiny. This is not the place for a full discussion of the character of the anniversary of Che's death, still less the substance of his life, but a few brief points can be made from the perspective of Bolivia and the elections held there a few weeks before his exhumation.

There is now strong evidence to suggest that Guevara had only gone to Bolivia in late 1966 as a step in a planned combative return to his Argentine homeland. It is also unlikely that his choice of this neighbouring country as a guerrilla site relied wholly on the advice of Régis Debray, even if his consultant's *normalien* assurance would have then seemed much less the construction of an *idiot savant* than it does today. Che had already been in Bolivia himself, on tour 13 years earlier as a recently qualified doctor and before he had acquired the radicalism that crystallised the following year in his witnessing the overthrow of the Arbenz regime in Guatemala. There is, however, some of his developing attitude in a letter written to his father at the end of July 1953, just before the introduction of the agrarian reform which at the time provided a sharp sense of the weakness of the state but would later prove to be a critical dyke against social radicalism:

> I am a little disillusioned about not being able to stay here because this is a very interesting country and it is living through a particularly effervescent moment. On the 2nd of August the agrarian reform goes through, and fracas and fights are expected throughout the country. We have seen incredible processions of armed people with Mausers and Tommy-guns, which they shoot off for the hell of it. Every day shots can be heard and there are wounded and dead as a result.

> The government shows a near-total inability to retain or lead
> the peasant masses and miners, but these respond to a certain
> degree, and there is no doubt that in the event of an armed
> revolt by the Falange ... they will be on the side of the MNR.
> Human life has little importance here, and it is given and taken
> without great to-do. All of this makes this a profoundly inter-
> esting situation to the neutral observer.

In the light of this, it is tempting to read much into Che's visit, on
the day of the agrarian reform, to the Bolsa Negra mine outside La
Paz. The miners had, quite naturally, taken the day off work to go to
town and participate in the celebrations with campesino contingents
(the reform was formally signed by Víctor Paz at Ucureña,
Cochabamba). Having toured the silent shafts of Bolsa Negra, Che
passed the returning miners on his way back to the city, again being
impressed by the explosions of dynamite and discharge of guns. It
strikes one as particularly odd that during his month in the country the
young Argentine should have contrived to miss both the agrarian
reform celebrations and the extraordinary experience of Bolivia's
proletariat in its Andean engagement. Indeed, this failed rendezvous
might be interpreted as reflecting less a proclivity to favour the rural
over the urban than a general clumsiness when it came to 'being there'.
Certainly, in 1966–1967 Guevara categorically misjudged the mood,
social resource and political capacity of both rural and industrial
working people. In itself this probably did not cost him his life, but the
lack of sensitivity and sobriety in assessing local detail always meant
that escape was the best outcome awaiting the guerrillas.

By 1997 the social constituency (the 'big motor') that Che's foco
(the 'little motor') was intended to ignite had been scattered by a
comprehensive deindustrialisation and the dismantling of the corporatist institutions of the 1950s. The miners are now numbered in
their hundreds, the confused COB is split over the degree of collaboration it should offer the new Banzer government, and Mario
Monje, the communist leader who once disputed Che's appropriation of the radical vanguard in Bolivia, lives out an isolated old age
on the outskirts of Moscow. Yet the overall picture is far from clear.
Banzer's insistent refusal in public to treat Guevara's endeavour as
anything more than a red invasion appeared backward-looking and

ungenerous; it was not widely echoed, even in conservative circles. Nor did the government's ostentatious listing of the 54 soldiers and civilians killed by the guerrillas and declared heroes in 1967 strike a chord of anything but sadness. In keeping with the nature of Banzer's own election a few weeks earlier, there was a marked lack of adversarialism in the political atmosphere (in November Fidel Castro did not hesitate to stand next to Banzer for the photo-call at the Seventh Ibero-American summit in Venezuela). A similar mood appears to have prevailed in Buenos Aires and Santiago; an epoch had passed, and if Che was returning, it was not as an exemplar of a precise form of insurgency but as the embodiment of higher values and ideals.

In Vallegrande and the village of La Higuera, where he was shot, Che is evidently more than a celebrity. Elsewhere in the country he might be said no longer to be an 'outsider', a source of embarrassment (or pride) in that he was killed in Bolivia. Perhaps Banzer's observations found scant response because Guevara was now seen less as an internationalist fighting against global reaction in a local setting than as somebody who had misconstrued the nature of nationalism in Bolivia — who had made a specific mistake in interpreting the country. In this he might almost be described as truer to his origins as an Argentine than to his mature convictions as a communist. Furthermore, one gains the sense from a longer historical perspective that, whilst the 1966–1967 guerrilla movement never came to pose a serious threat of ideological conquest, it did raise fears of dismemberment of a type wearily familiar to a populace well schooled about the reduction of their national territory through wars — that of the Pacific (1879–1884), in Acre (1899–1901) and in the Chaco (1932–1935) — in addition to cut-price sales to Chile and Brazil by the likes of president Melgarejo. These experiences have been the traumatic testing-grounds for any logic that might lie behind the existence of a country deemed by some — not least Chilean generals and US diplomats — to have nurtured too many problems to be worthy of existence. This existence may have been upheld on the simple grounds that no neighbour has historically sought outright conquest and merely opted for maximum annexation of land with lowest social intake, but the state now confronts a new challenge in the integration of regional markets, particularly through Mercosur, of which Bolivia is an associate member.

These circumstances go some way to explaining why so much controversy should be aroused in the weeks around the 1997 election by the publication of a work of amateur history, *La mesa coja* by Javier Mendoza. Making extensive use of the notes of his father, the great archivist Gunnar Mendoza, the author proposed that one of the founding documents of the nation — the 1809 proclamation of the Junta Tuitiva in La Paz — was not, in fact, signed or even composed by the members of that body, as had widely been believed for 150 years. Rather, according to Mendoza's methodological mix of strong documentary deduction and psychological induction, that document was a later 'creation forgery', and the real original derived from dissident jurists and priests in Chuquisaca (Sucre), who had far greater need and desire to form a state independent of Peru and the Viceroyality of La Plata than did the merchants of La Paz. In effect, Mendoza was revindicating the place of Sucre as the capital of the nation, impugning *paceño* claims to have promoted the birth of the nation, and reviving a debate which was widely thought moribund because it had no contemporary relevance.

The exchanges over this issue combined a ferocious abandonment of common sense by traditionalist politicians with a pained reservation on the part of professional historians, for whom Mendoza's approach was too glib by half. But all participants passed without comment over the critical point that — whoever might have been responsible for the start of the independence struggle — it was completed by a Colombian (Sucre) assisted by two Irishmen (O'Leary and O'Connor), a German (Braun) and an Englishman (Miller) in the execution of a strategic plan drawn up by a Venezuelan (Bolívar). This internationalist presence at the very origin of the state has always been the source of some ambivalence. However, modern nationalists may find some solace in a sentiment expressed by Bolívar to Santander in a letter of October 1825, on his first and only visit to the country just named after him: 'If Brazil invades, I will fight as a Bolivian — a name I had before I was born.'

Simón Bolívar accepted the existence of Bolivia, and probably for better cause than on account of it bearing his name, and he did so despite the fact that its establishment created another obstacle to his federalist design for the subcontinent — an objective and idiom so similar to those of Guevara. Moreover, it could be argued that Bolívar's secular, militarist republicanism savoured very much of that practised by Che 135 years later. Neither man would surely have much difficulty in interpreting the election of 1997 in the terms of their day. For Bolívar, Banzer's election does not quite vindicate his 1826 'Message to the Assembly of Bolivia', but it could be recognised as the intervention of a caudillo to sort out the *política criolla* of the lawyers and harness their disputations to the higher needs of the nation. For Che, the campaign would surely have amounted to little more than the squabbles of temporising liberals at the service of US imperialism as they extinguished the depleted legitimacy won in 1952. However, one suspects that neither man would fully grasp how and why many Bolivians could both concur with these assessments and yet still place such a politics above the emphatic pursuit of utopia to which these two historic 'extra-Bolivians ' were pledged.

## Notes

1    I have discussed this pattern in *Rebellion in the Veins. Political Struggle in Bolivia*, 1952–1982 (London, 1984).

2    See, for example, Laurence Whitehead (1981), 'Miners as voters: The Electoral Process in Bolivia's Mining Camps', *Journal of Latin American Studies*, vol. 13, no. 2, pp. 313–46.

3    Robert A. Dahl, *Polyarchy: Participation and Opposition* (New Haven, 1971); Laurence Whitehead, 'Bolivia's Failed Democratisation, 1977–80', in G. O'Donnell, P. Schmitter and L. Whitehead (eds.), *Transitions from Authoritarian Rule: Latin America* (Baltimore, 1986).

4    *La Razón*, 29 May 1997.

5    The principal lobby in this regard was Charter 88. For a detailed appraisal, see Patrick Dunleavy, Helen Margetts, Brendan O'Duffy and Stuart Weir *Making Votes Count* (University of Essex: Democratic Audit, paper no. 11, 1997). Bolivia still lacks a comprehensive psephological study. The polls of 1979, 1980, 1985 and 1989 are surveyed from the perspective of party results in Salvador Romero Ballivian *Geografía electoral de Bolivia* (La Paz, 1993). A broad summary of all results may be found in Carlos Mesa Gisbert, *Presidentes de Bolivia. Entre urnas y fusiles* (La Paz, 1990).

6    Slightly different figures are given in Dunleavy *et al.*, *Making Votes Count*.
7    This argument is made by S. Mainwaring and T. Scully (eds.), *Building Democratic Institutions. Party Systems in Latin America* (Stanford, 1995), the editors drawing largely on that volume's chapter on Bolivia by Eduardo A. Gamarra and James M. Malloy, who themselves describe the system as patrimonialist.
8    This anecdote is recounted in a most useful analysis of recent Bolivian political developments: Eduardo A. Gamarra, 'Hybrid Presidentialism and Democratization: The Case of Bolivia', in Scott Mainwaring and Matthew Soberg Shugart (eds.), *Presidentialism and Democracy in Latin America* (Cambridge, 1997).
9    For a full account of this crisis and the wider political and institutional landscape, see María del Pilar Domingo Villegas, 'Democracy in the Making? Political Parties and Political Institutions in Bolivia, 1985–1991' (D.Phil. thesis, University of Oxford, 1993).
10   The best analysis of the political consequences of the cocaine trade is Hugo Rodas Morales, *Huanchaca: modelo político-empresarial de la cocaína en Bolivia* (La Paz, 1997).
11   On 16 August 1997 the new administration issued an injunction to its members, supporters and civil servants including the following: 1. Strict adhesion to the law; 2. Respect for the citizen; 3. Correct use of state property (no private use of public vehicles or cellular phones; no use of sirens except by the vehicles of the president and vice-president); 4. Austerity; 5. Discipline; 6. Sobriety; 7. Sense of self-criticism; 8. Sense of modesty; 9. Democratic collegiality with opponents; 10. Honesty (*La Razón*, 17 Aug. 1997).
12   *Presencia*, 16 Feb. 1997.
13   Fernando Mayorga, *Max Fernández. La política del silencio* (La Paz, 1991); Fernando Mayorga, *Discurso y política en Bolivia* (La Paz, 1993); Carlos F. Toranzo Roca and Mario Arrieta Abdalla, *Nueva derecha y desproletización en Bolivia* (La Paz, 1989); Hugo San Martin, *El palenquismo* (La Paz, 1991); Joaquin Saravia and Godofredo Sandoval, Jach'a Uru: *La esperanza de un pueblo? Carlos Palenque, RTP y los sectores populares urbanos de La Paz* (La Paz, 1991); Rafael Archondo, *Compadres al micrófono: la resurrección metropolitana del ayllu* (La Paz, 1991); Roberto Laserna, *Productores de democracia* (Cochabamba, 1992); J. Antonio Mayorga, *Gonismo. Discurso y poder* (Cochabamba, 1996); Carlos Blanco Cazas and Godofredo Sandoval, *La alcaldia de La Paz. Entre populistas, modernistas y culturalistas, 1985-1993* (La Paz, 1993).

14  Santa Cruz (13%); La Paz (12%); Cochabamba (7%); El Alto (7%); Oruro (3%); Sucre (2.5%); Tarija (2%).

15  A. Solís Rada, *La fortuna del presidente* (La Paz, 1997).

16  By early 1997 the state had contrived to identify 1,176 *cazabeneméritos* of between 17 and 50 years of age. At that stage the youngest veteran of the Chaco War would have been 77 (*Hoy,* 9 March 1997). Whilst a very poor state must certainly guard against inadmissible claims on its slight resources, one feels distinctly uneasy about this particularly rigorous audit, and it is to be hoped that both younger women and elderly gentlemen derived happiness and security from even the prospect of union.

17  *Última Hora,* 20 April 1997.

18  As the AFPs went into operation the need for regulation of the financial sector was starkly illustrated by the revelation that the country's Fondos de Vivienda (building associations or co-operatives) had not been obliged to maintain proper accounts before 1993 despite holding an estimated $130 million. *Presencia,* 11 Sept. 1997.

19  *Última Hora,* 18 May 1997; *Presencia,* 16 June 1997.

20  Eduardo Gamarra, 'Goni's Unsung Swansong', *Hemisphere,* Miami, April 1997.

21  *Presencia,* 20 and 26 July 1997.

22  *Presencia,* 21 June; 11 Sept. 1997.

23  *La Razón,* 31 Aug. 1997.

24  *Presencia,* 2 and 3 Sept. 1997.

25  Banzer's slogan of 'Pan, techo, trabajo' might sound rather corporatist, but it is a good deal less so than the 'Paz, orden, trabajo' motif he deployed 20 years earlier and which was reminiscent of the Petain/Laval refrain, 'Travail, famille, patrie'. In any event the ADN slogan was much snappier than that dreamt up by the MNR's spin-doctors: 'Soluciones de verdad! Para una cosecha generosa'.

26  Jon Lee Anderson, *Che Guevara. A Revolutionary Life* (London, 1997).

27  Regis Debray, *Revolution in the Revolution?* (London, 1968).

28  Quoted in Anderson, *Che Guevara,* p. 104.

29  Javier Mendoza Pizarro, *La mesa coja. Historia de la proclama de la Junta Tuitiva del 16 de Julio de 1809* (La Paz and Sucre, 1997).

30  Bolivar, Potosí, 21 Oct. 1825, to Santander, see H. Bierck and V. Lecuna (eds.) *Selected Writings of Bolivar II* (New York, 1951), p. 543.

# 3

# Political Transition and Economic Stabilisation: Bolivia, 1982–1989

## Introduction

For many Bolivians there was more than a touch of irony in the fact that at the inauguration of Carlos Saúl Menem as president of Argentina in July 1989 so much attention — for once respectful and inquiring — should be paid to one of their number, present as a guest of honour. The man in question, Gonzalo Sánchez de Lozada, was treated as little less than a Delphic oracle by Julio Alsogaray, Menem's economic adviser, Nicaraguan president Daniel Ortega and the local media, all anxious to learn how this ex-minister of planning and prospective president had contrived to cut Bolivia's inflation rate from 15,000 per cent to 16 per cent in the space of two years without provoking food riots or a widespread collapse of social order. Many in La Paz had good cause to wince at 'Goni's' casual injunction — rendered in a thick accent bred of a youth spent in North America — that the only stabilisation plan worth its salt was one accompanied by a state of siege, under which recalcitrant trade unionists could be packed off to Patagonia for a while. Although this observation derived directly from the Bolivian experience, it scarcely modulated with the discourse of democracy accompanying the first handover between elected presidents in Argentina in more than 60 years. Nonetheless, whatever their political colours, those Bolivians who had witnessed the role of the Argentine military advisers in the coup of July 1980 and knew of the failure of their rich neighbour to pay the millions of dollars it owed for imports of natural gas were inclined to indulge the sly rumours that Menem had asked Sánchez de Lozada to be his economy minister and another Bolivian guest, Hugo Banzer Suárez — ex-dictator and also a challenger for the presidency — to be chief of police.

The cultural aspects of such badinage should not be disregarded, but beneath them lies the important fact that the political economy of Bolivia was no longer being treated abroad as a hopeless 'basket case' administered through corporatist politics that shifted between military authoritarianism and a syndicalist-led 'populism'.[1] In fact, many of the features that underpinned this perception remained intact after both the return to constitutional government in October 1982 and the election of the Movimiento Nacionalista Revolucionario (MNR) in July 1985. Equally, it should be said that recent foreign attention to the Bolivian economy has not been matched by an interest in the country's politics.[2] Indeed, long-standing presumptions have been only partially dislocated since, in both economic and political fields, Bolivia has continued to manifest extreme experiences since 1982.

Apart from the fact that the country remains the poorest in mainland America, it has suffered from both the greatest inflation and the most severe deflationary policies witnessed in the continent since the early 1970s. At the same time, the first two civilian governments since the collapse of dictatorship served in their own ways to uphold — and even encourage — the image of a bi-polar model of politics, albeit within the broad parameters of the rule of law. (The first time — it might be added — since the mid-1940s, when the last stage of the government of Gualberto Villarroel (1943–1946) and the first of that led by Enrique Hertzog (1947–1949) witnessed respectively 'populist' and 'authoritarian' policies applied under fragile but discernible constitutional conditions.)

In many respects, 'redemocratisation' in Boliva has been associated less with the institutional tasks of establishing a constitutional polity than with the expression of starkly contrasting social and economic policies. On the one hand, the coalition government of the Unión Democrática y Popular (UDP; 1982–1985) led by Hernán Siles Zuazo may be viewed as typically 'populist' in that its essential thrust was towards deficit financing, acquiescence in labour demands, radical rhetoric and a notable respect for human rights. On the other, the MNR government led by Víctor Paz Estenssoro (1985–1989) responded to an extraordinary economic crisis exacerbated — but by no means generated — by the UDP with an exceptionally severe and orthodox adjustment programme, alliance with Banzer's right-wing Acción Democrática Nacionalista (ADN), disregard for the *fuero sindical,* and a clear disposition to reduce the state, encourage private capital, and collaborate with the international status quo on issues such as the debt (in a formally heterodox but practically conformist manner) and the cocaine trade, or *narcotráfico* (on a formally conformist but practically heterodox basis).

The sense of an essential modal continuity with the pre-dictatorial era was sustained by the enduring dominance of political life by an 'historical' party — the right-(Paz) and left-(Siles) wings of the MNR — although such a pattern is also visible elsewhere, with the partial and complicated exceptions of Brazil and Ecuador. However, in the Bolivian case this sense was peculiarly enhanced by the fact that the two post-dictatorial presidents were themselves the principal architects of the state born of the 1952 revolution (Paz being president in 1952–1956 and 1960–1964, Siles in 1956–1960). Indeed, although the passage of time and changing circumstances determined that they could no longer conduct themselves as they had 20 or 30 years earlier — a fact most evident in the need to form coalitions and leave the more energetic aspects of *caudillismo* to subalterns of a younger generation — the cyclical features of political life were underscored in a profoundly paradoxical fashion in that Paz, who had nationalised the tin mines, introduced an agrarian reform, and applied highly inflationary policies in the first years of the revolution, now sought to dismember the state mining corporation (Comibol), announced a substantial adjustment to the agrarian reform, and conducted a rigorously deflationary economic policy. Siles, by contrast, had initially been associated with the MNR's conservative wing, and in 1956–1957 entered into a decisive conflict with the trade unions grouped in the Central Obrera Boliviana (COB) precisely by applying an orthodox stabilisation plan that cut real wages, increased unemployment and reduced state expenditure to the requirements of the IMF and Washington. The fact that he strenuously resisted taking such a course in the early 1980s was widely perceived as emanating not just from a commitment to 'populism' but also from a personal refusal to relive the extreme bitterness of the mid-1950s. These reversals of prior practice were not, in fact, as simple as depicted, but they did throw into sharp relief the trajectory

of individual personalities so that even in the 1989 election dominated by figures of the 1970s (Banzer and Jaime Paz Zamora of the
Movimiento de la Izquierda Revolucionaria (MIR)), and the 1980s
(Sánchez de Lozada and Carlos Palenque of Conciencia de Patria
(CONDEPA)), it was easy to underestimate the degree to which
Bolivian politics had changed.

The general lack of interest in discovering the degree of balance
between, on the one hand, Bolivia as *part of* the regional experience
of redemocratisation and a manifestation of that experience *in
extremis* (the relationship unity/diversity), and, on the other, the
persistence of the old/'traditional' and the emergence of the new/
'modern' (the relationship continuity/rupture) cannot properly be
rectified here. However, it should be noted at the outset that, while
this chapter does not pretend to deal in detail with economic
management,[3] the coca and cocaine economies[4] or the travails of the
left — all critical issues in the post-dictatorial era — none of these
phenomena lacks features that run counter to received beliefs and
that confuse easy paradigms.[5]

With respect to the economy, it is evident that, in addition to
notable failures to spur growth under both administrations, after 1985
the state sector was simply diminished rather than overhauled; agriculture was largely ignored and excluded from fiscal reform for purely
political reasons (the 'traditional' *movimientistas* over-ruling the 'modern'
technocrats), and with the exception of a few instances of cooperativisation (most notably municipal telephone systems) and asset-stripping
(the sale of Comibol's reserves of unprocessed ore), privatisation
remained a pious hope. Similarly, following a constant pattern since
1952, efforts to encourage new private investment produced insignificant results beyond recycling an increased proportion of narcodollars
through formal channels. The social cost of both hyperinflation under
the UDP and stabilisation under the MNR was exceptionally high; the
latter altered its form but certainly did not reduce its impact.

In terms of coca and cocaine the record of the last decade is similarly mixed. Whilst there have been indisputably major shifts in the
patterns of production, population and labour in certain regions
(Cochabamba, Santa Cruz and the Beni), and the officially sanctioned circulation of narcodollars has contributed significantly to

mitigating the effects of the depression, there was no escalation of mafia-led violence on the scale witnessed in Colombia or, under rather different political and productive conditions, Peru. Equally, *narcotráfico* is not only based on legal cultivation of coca (in all areas until late July 1989; legally, only in the Yungas of La Paz thereafter), but it has also failed to produce distinct cartels. Rather, insofar as the capital flight of the 1970s and early 1980s has been reversed, its assets have been recirculated through established structures and activities. In the same vein, it has deepened rather than extended previous systems of kinship–patronage and corruption, building on existing modes of illegal practice in the armed forces, police and leading political parties in a relatively 'unpartisan' fashion. The legacy of the open association of the military regime of 1980–1982 with the cocaine trade has been a pattern of discreet infiltration — not the much-vaunted 'takeover' — and, with several honourable exceptions, a response to US pressure that follows the logic of *'obedezco pero no cumplo'* rather than decisive action. Although between 1984 and 1987 the US changed the emphasis of its policy from halting trade in cocaine to reducing production of coca, the terms it demanded of La Paz on both counts could not possibly have been met without destroying both the constitutional order and the economy — a fact clearly understood, if never admitted, in the US embassy.

Finally, debate over the defeat of the left has frequently suffered from the *schadenfreude* of disillusioned fellow travellers and closet reactionaries. Both they and the honest celebrants of the collapse of radicalism may properly identify this in the left's own terms — the structures and discourses derived from 1917 and 1952 — yet these must also be assessed in the light of the weaknesses of the right and those features of the new conservative order that have preserved the need for (and incidence of) popular mobilisation at the same time as they have altered its forms. Although the defeat of traditional radicalism was given a definitive character first by the association of *both* the COB and the parties of the left with the chaos of the UDP period, and then by the effective dismemberment of the miners' union (FSTMB) following the 1985 tin crash, the moral authority of the left has been far less damaged than has its social project. An apparently minor compensation that might be deemed intrinsic to such a decisive setback in terms of power-politics, this is in fact a matter of considerable consequence in a country where the state imbricates closely with civil society, where the left has a minimal tradition of violence, and where the left's failings were seen (with some justification) to result from it being 'out of date' in its methods rather than wrong in its ideas.

Thus, after 1985, the right exercised the political power given it by the electorate with both flair and decision, but it failed to establish hegemony; at best it won acquiescence, which is a necessary but insufficient condition for hegemony. At the same time, it signally failed to institutionalise either the fragile consitutional order or its own domination. 'Concertación' proceeded by pacts, yet these pacts depended upon a division of the administrative spoils of the state between parties that had very diverse histories but minimal ideological differences.

The failures of the left between 1982 and 1985 provided the right — including the MIR — with neither the necessity nor the incentive to engage in any compromise beyond cabinet alliances. This certainly enabled the deflationary programme to be imposed without great difficulty, yet by the time of the 1989 election campaign the contradictions of such an unchallenged dominion had been laid fully bare. Not only was the 1985 MNR–ADN 'Pacto por la Democracia' broken on the premise — in the words of MNR Foreign Minister Guillermo Bedregal — that 'pacts are made to be broken', but the right also found itself engaged in a three-way internecine conflict resulting in a so-called *triple empate* (very roughly a quarter of the votes for each of the ADN, MNR and MIR) that could only be managed by electoral malpractice and a 12-week circus of offers and counter-offers over the spoils of state in an effort to secure the presidency through a vote in congress. This process involved a suborning of the judiciary that paralleled the extraordinarily prolonged and inefficient 'trial' of the leading figures of the 1980–1982 dictatorship, most particularly General García Mesa, who happily absconded in the middle of deliberations. In short, the final months of the 1985–1989 MNR administration witnessed an outbreak of *politiquería* of such proportions that the right came close to losing its already tenuous claim to uphold constitutionalism, whatever its successes on the economic front. The majority of the left stood paralysed before this scenario, but a three-week hunger strike by two young radical leaders — Roger Cortez (Partido Socialista-1; PS-1) and Víctor Hugo Cárdenas (Movimiento Revolucionario Tupaj Katari de Liberación Nacional; MRTKL) — in protest at the fraudulent cancellation of 14 election results (including their own, but also those of all other parties bar the MIR, which was the principal force 'managing' the 1986 election law it had sponsored in congress) — not only drew widespread sympathy but also signalled the potential for a radical renaissance within the constitutionalist framework.

This preliminary qualification to a broadly held view of the primary qualities of the transition to constitutional government highlights the importance of those aspects of politics that are not immediately competitive and relate to what we might call the moral economy of public conduct.[6] On such a non-partisan plane the Bolivian experience of transition proves more complex and fragile than many care to admit. Seven years after it had been installed, the critical issue with regard to the consolidation of parliamentary democracy was whether this could be ensured through the dominance of forces that had little to do with its initial restoration and which were content to maximise the advantages of their economic policies without attending to the institutional and ideological fissures bequeathed by the collapse of the traditions of 1952. The administrations of Siles and Víctor Paz were largely able to camouflage this structural weakness (one of the few characteristics that they shared), but it remained far from certain that a third regime, bereft of a historical discourse and the privilege of catharsis provided by initial bouts of redistribution or deflation, would prove capable of ensuring stability within or without the parameters of the 1967 constitution — which was, after all, the product of a military regime.

It is, of course, entirely plausible to view the prospects for the 'Gobierno de Unidad y Convergencia' headed by Jaime Paz Zamora and dominated by the ADN in a much more favourable light. It may be argued that the decision of General Hugo Banzer to withdraw his challenge for the presidency twice in four years justified the ADN's claim to be a paragon of democratic virtue. Equally, the final realisation of the longstanding slogan 'Jaime Presidente' can be seen as vindicated both in terms of the MIR's claim to represent a new

generation of political actors and its capacity to abandon the imped-
imenta of its erstwhile radicalism. (The claim was not without some
foundation, although it was often forgotten that Paz was over 50
when he donned the presidential sash; the capacity was irrefutable
but cost the division of the party.) Collaboration between what were
normally viewed as the traditional right-wing and social democratic
forces in the national political spectrum could also be presented as a
mature strategic decision to introduce a modicum of flexibility into the
austere economic policies incarnated in Decree 21060 of August 1985
without permitting a wholesale rush into inflation. Finally, a broader
apologia for the formation of such an administration may be based on
the fact that, although its component parties came second and, by
some margin, third in the election of May 1989, their combined vote
was within 5,000 of the maximum achieved by any two candidates and
did not, therefore, represent a significant abuse of the 'popular will'.

Against such a view, it is worth noting the extraordinary incoherence
of the Paz Zamora regime, composed of parties whose origins — in
'neo-Marxism' and military dictatorship respectively — were not just
polarised but had led to proscription and blood-letting over two
decades. The absence of any significant accord prior to that signed two
days before the congressional election of the president suggested that
while such differences might have been radically reduced over the years,
they had finally been papered over for the purposes of obtaining office
rather than as result of a more profound ideological convergence. In
this regard, the strident electoral campaign of the MNR, and particularly Sánchez de Lozada, provided a more persuasive case for an
'exclusionary alliance', indicating the limited political space available to
the dominant bloc and the acrobatics required to operate within it at the
same time as maintaining the pretence of competition. (In practice,
personalism accounted for almost all of the competitive spirit of the
affair, the high profile given by the MNR to 'Goni' permitting the MIR-
Nueva Mayoría fully to exploit its dependence on the figure of Jaime
Paz and thereby hustle into the background any lingering vestiges of
social democratic ideology.)

In short, the 1989 poll obliged the right to take its differences
into government. Yet for many — perhaps a majority — of those

who voted for the MIR and the ADN, the purpose of their ballot was precisely to exclude the other from office. Moreover, this sentiment was strongly echoed within the rank and file of both parties whilst recompense in the forms of jobs and favours — *pegas* — was naturally reduced by the alliance despite the creation of two new ministries. At the same time, a bedraggled left could view with some relief the prospects provided by a fusion of 'opportunists' and 'authoritarians' that combined (misguided) popular fears of a return to the economic policies of the UDP (with which the MIR was still associated) and the political system of the Banzer dictatorship (with which the ADN, as a 'vertical', if not personalist, organisation was even more closely associated).

Although superstition is by no means the first victim of modernity or a negligible factor in politics, it is perhaps a touch sour to note that when, during the congressional debate of 4 August 1989 to elect the new president, ex-deputy Víctor Hugo Cárdenas sought to support his rejection of the rigged results of the May poll with a quote from the scriptures, it was discovered that the Bible upon which the new members of the legislature had sworn their oath was, in fact, a missal in Latin, unintelligible to all. At the time, this incident provoked some levity, but as the notably inferior contributions from the floor dragged on until seven the next morning there was comment in the *barra* that the next four years would be based as much on ignorance as on blind faith.

## Background

Discussion of political transitions — broadly understood here to signify changes of governmental system — cannot be limited to factors of conjuncture and agency, although these are the most apparent constituents of a phenomenon in which elements of rupture are more pronounced than those of continuity. This is especially true of Bolivia, where, as has already been inferred, modern politics can be described as a 'continuity of ruptures'. Some sense of this may be gleaned from Table 3.1.

## Table 3.1: Bolivian Governments, 1952–1982

| | |
|---|---|
| 1952–1956 Víctor Paz Estenssoro | April 1952 National Revolution; popular (MNR) mobilisation; major mines nationalised; agrarian reform; rule by decree; rightist opponentsrepressed; inflation. |
| 1956–1960 Hernán Siles Zuazo (MNR) | 'Semi-open' election; deflation; army rebuilt; right and left opposition harassed; centralist control of MNR; COB in retreat. |
| 1960–1964 Víctor Paz Estenssoro | 'Semi-open' election; economic (MNR) stability; COB subordinate; MNR divisions grow; army role increases; left harassed. |
| 1964 Víctor Paz Estenssoro | 'Semi-open' election; MNR splits; (MNR) army becomes main political arbiter. |
| 1964–1969 René Barrientos Ortuiio | Coup, followed by repression of COB (military) and left; military-campesino pact; economic stability with opening to foreign capital; 1967 constitution; controlled congress; short-lived guerrilla; massacres in mines. |
| 1969  Luis Adolfo Siles Salinas | Vice-presidential succession after (PDC) death of Barrientos; effective military rule. |
| 1969–1970 Alfredo Ovando Candia | Coup; 'nationalist' military rule with (military) mixed cabinet; short-lived guerrilla; left recovers in conditions of semi-legality. |
| 1970–1971 Juan José Torres (military) | Coup; 'left nationalist' military rule; COB-dominated asamblea popular; political polarisation. |
| 1971–1978 Hugo Banzer Suárez | Coup; right-wing authoritarianism; (military) military alliance with MNR (Paz) and FSB to 1974; 1974–1948 'institutionalist' |

| | |
|---|---|
| | regime under personalist control; COB and left repressed; collapse of military campesino pact; economic growth; progressive indebtedness. |
| 1978 Juan Pereda Asbún (military) | Fraudulent election followed by coup; weakened dictatorship. |
| 1978–1979 David Padilla Arancibia | Coup; 'benign dictatorship' by army (military) constitutionalists. |
| 1979 Walter Guevara Arce | Elected by congress after failure of Siles (PRA/MNR) (31.22 per cent) and Paz (31.13 per cent) to secure victory in poll; weakened executive. |
| 1979 Alberto Natusch Busch | Coup; 16-day dictatorship defeated by (military) worker, congressional and US opposition. |
| 1979–1980 Lidia Gueiler Tejada | Appointed by congress; weakened (PRIN/MNR) executive; attempts at deflation. |
| 1980–1981 Luis García Mesa (military) | Coup, following UDP victory in elections; left repressed; AND militants serve rightist dictatorship tarnished by support from narcotráfico |
| 1981 Military junta | Coup, following US and military opposition to García Mesa and Interior Minister Luis Arce Gómez; left remains repressed; military divided. |
| 1981 Celso Torrelio Villa (military) | Internal coup; army hardliners retain power but adjust policies to US demands. |
| 1982 Guido Vildoso Calderón | Institutional agreement; hardliners lose (military) power to 'transitionalists'; curbs on COB lifted; economic crisis deepens. |

A number of very broad points signalled by the table and relevant to an understanding of developments after 1982 deserve further emphasis.

1.   Governmental stability was not primarily associated with constitutionalism, still less with the holding of elections.

Insofar as such an association can be stipulated, it applies only to the period 1899–1930 under the *ancien régime* of the Liberal and Republican Parties, during the domination of the tin oligarchy, prior to the introduction of universal suffrage and with exceptionally insecure terms of competition.

From 1956 the MNR presided over a full and formal constitutional apparatus. However, this was heavily manipulated, coexisted with important mechanisms of 'popular'/party control (militias; secret police; expanded syndicalist *fueros*), and reflected — even encouraged — political instability from 1960 onwards.

The *banzerato* of 1971–1978 was profoundly anti-democratic in character and, in line with similar regimes in the Southern Cone, postulated a direct relationship between stability and the absence of political competition and civil liberties.

2.   Constitutionalism was broadly viewed as intrinsically weak, highly vulnerable to alternative means of expressing corporate interests, and more of a mechanism of truce/transition than continuity. It was not closely identified with the interests of any social class.

After 1964 the *fuero sindical* had been suppressed under dictatorships but also respected by some military regimes, notably Torres but also Padilla, and was not intimately associated with a full division of powers. The union movement had historically gained most under 'Bonapartist' regimes (Busch, Villarroel, MNR, Torres). Similarly, the right had flourished under authoritarianism (1946–1951; 1964–1969; 1971–1978) and found itself critically divided in 'open' elections (1951; 1960; 1964).

As a result, civilian conservatives were accustomed to 'knock on the barracks door' and service military regimes whilst many on the left continued to place hopes in 'progressive' officers right up to the early 1980s. Outside of the COB leadership — vulnerable but divided over this issue since 1964 — the Communist Party (PCB) and MIR were the most prone to this option, particularly in 1979–1981.

The first election since 1951 for which the result was not, for various reasons, a foregone conclusion, was that of 1979. In this respect, the most important feature of constitutionalism was greatly diminished in the popular eye.

Such a trajectory meant that it was not just extremist political actors but broad sectors of civil society that harboured substantial doubts as to the value of constitutionalism in modulating antagonistic social programmes for any significant period of time. It was identified with stalemate, not consensus; it lacked hegemony.

3.   By the late 1970s the political legacy of 1952 had become dissipated to the degree that no single electoral front could secure a victory in terms of its identification with the revolution. At the same time, both the right and the left lacked the ability to break from minority electoral status on their own. As a result, party alignments remained very fluid and dominated by pragmatism.

From 1978 to 1983 this process revolved around three insecure nuclei:

a) on the right, Banzer's ADN, the most constant formation but still prone to militarist overtures and limited in its popular appeal by both its conservatism and the authoritarian past of its leader;

b) on the centre-right, Víctor Paz's MNR, bolstered by its association with 1952 (particularly in the *campo*) yet limited by Paz's erstwhile collaboration with Banzer; and a significant right-wing current still amenable to cooperation with the military; alliance with Oscar Zamora's 'Maoist'

PCB–ML counteracted these tendencies to a strictly minimal degree and after 1979 was of greater regional than ideological importance (Zamora, like the Paz family, is from Tarija; in 1989 he backed the MIR–NM and became minister of labour);

c) on the left, Siles's MNRI, which compensated for a lesser inheritance from the revolutionary era with its progressive stance from the early 1970s. However, the party was less disciplined and emphatically led than the MNR, and depended heavily upon its alliance with both the 'modern' left (MIR) and that of more orthodox hue (PCB), which alienated other important radical currents (particularly the PS-1) and made the front the least stable of all, reliant on tactical as well as conviction voting by many members of the COB.

It was not until 1982 that these currents were able to operate with significant independence from the officer corps. They failed to establish any viable coalition government before October of that year and at no stage between 1979 and 1989 did an electoral front win a clear mandate at the polls.

As a consequence, exceptionally fluid terms of competition aggravated ideological differences to spur organisational division, a multiplicity of tactical alliances, and a progressive erosion of political affinities constructed over three decades.

4. The military remained critically divided between 1978 and 1982.

A number of factors are evident here: antipathy to Banzer's personalist rule; the endurance of a subordinate 'progressive Bonapartism' (derived not only from the 1930s and 1940s but also from the influence of the MNR and the impact of the Velasco regime in Peru); and the competitive influences of, particularly, Argentina (anti-communism) and the US (*anti-narcotráfico*).

5. Syndicalism continued to exercise considerable popular authority.

Although the COB leadership consistently desisted from
pursuing the central objective of its 1970 programme to establish a popular, socialist democracy, the rank and file were
centrally responsible for mass opposition to militarism
between 1977 and 1982. This not only enhanced the COB's
legitimacy but also heightened that of direct action although it
was now in significant contradiction with the end — constitutional government — to which it was employed.

The anti-dictatorial struggle was, therefore, not only
conducted along traditional corporatist lines, it also enlivened
expectations of economic and political reorganisation that
were singularly at odds with the objectives and capabilities of
the major political parties.

6.      The violation of human rights and culture of violence
        followed a pattern distinct from that elsewhere in the Southern
        Cone (except Paraguay).

The left had a very marginal history and culture of violence;
guerrillism was insignificant as a factor either in generating dictatorial government in the first place or in overthrowing it. Whilst
appreciable, the level of terror under Banzer was notably lower
than that in Chile or Argentina. That under García Mesa was
temporarily of a comparable level but occurred after two years
of struggle, without US support and amidst extreme military
division over paramilitary activity organised by Argentine
'experts' and foreign fascists. Active resistance continued
throughout and fear was not systematised.

As a result, constitutionalism was not as closely associated as
elsewhere with either a 'setting of scores' or 'peace at any
price'. This was a two-edged sword. On the one hand, it facilitated military acquiescence in transition through the
scapegoating of very few individuals (excluding Banzer —
unsuccessfully charged in congress in 1979 — and Garcia
Mesa's associates bar members of the cabinet). On the other,
it reduced the cathartic and consensual qualities of civilian
administration in the immediate post-dictatorial period.

7.  The chronological pattern of 'redemocratisation' was at variance with that elsewhere.

Pressure from Washington and mass mobilisation from late 1977 produced what was, in regional terms, an early experience of transition, without a graduated *apertura* or support from neighbouring states (except Peruvian neutrality). Recidivist militarism thereby gained critical external support, notably from Argentina. The left, by contrast, was in a position to be spurred by the example of the Nicaraguan revolution (notably in November 1979).

The eventual inauguration of Siles in October 1982 more closely fits the regional pattern, but it should be noted that he entered office having won elections held in 1980 on a platform ill-suited to the new political and economic conditions. Unlike the pattern elsewhere (but not in Ecuador), the left took office before the right, which actively sought such an outcome once militarism was clearly doomed.

8.  The role of Washington was important but not decisive.

Under Carter, pressure on the military was forthright and spurred reactionary nationalism. However, conservative expectations of fulsome support from Reagan were dashed by the cocaine issue, which obliged continued policies of containment despite the relative strength of the left.

This combination had the effect of curbing left-wing nationalism and enabled the US to maintain a relatively low profile, relying less on 'intervention' than on 'benign non-collaboration'. Both before and after 1982 the effect was eventually decisive but slow to emerge.

9.  The military regimes did not attempt to introduce a neo-liberal economic model.

Despite fierce efforts to suppress wage costs, occasional endeavours at privatisation, (unrewarding) concessions to foreign capital and general adhesion (up to 1978) to IMF directives, the military maintained the MNR's statist approach. Its constituency was upheld through reapportioning the surpluses, contracts and loans accumulated through the post-52 public sector exchange rate policies favourable to agri-business and proscriptions of trade unions.

This pattern was facilitated by the price and loan boom of the mid-1970s, which terminated in the midst of the transition. Restoration of civilian government occurred within weeks of the 1982 debt crisis and after 24 months of extensive pillaging of public finances (through both old-fashioned larceny and the raising of dubious loans).

Economic and political 'logics' were therefore, as elsewhere, 'out of sequence'. Yet Bolivia was partly distinctive in that no major orthodox deflationary offensive had been attempted prior to redemocratisation; this option thus remained pending. (A broadly similar position obtained in Peru in 1980, but under much more favourable circumstances; even in 1989 the Paraguayan economy remained singular enough not to admit to ready comparison; one might argue about the degree of 'shock' inflicted by Martínez de Hoz in Argentina, but if it was more modulated than in Chile it was certainly more concerted than any policy hitherto essayed in Bolivia.)

10. The period of transition itself witnessed no significant 'new social movements' to which its success might be attributed.

It is the case that the *campesino* movement acquired unprecedented weight and independent organisational form in the CSUTCB in 1979, but this development upheld in more radical form many of the 'traditions' of the *altiplano,* restoring some of the diminished influence of the rural majority. It did not represent a major shift in socio-economic structures, and neither did it produce a decisive realignment of political power or patronage; radical expectations for this were soon dimmed by the MNR's resurgent electoral appeal and the latent anti-communism of *katarismo.*

The issue of formal, national political power was decided between 1977 and 1982 very much in terms of established forces and discourses. It was only after 1983–1984 that the parameters of collective identity and organisation — in both town and countryside — began to register significant change. However, it should be noted that (a) the growth of the 1970s had expanded the urban middle class, providing Banzer with a constituency, primarily at the expense of the MNR, and (b) the germs of economic change — *narcotráfico* and weakness in the mining sector — were already quite evident in the early 1980s, and both played a part in the transition, even if at that stage through familiar patterns of behaviour and organisation.

## The Government of the UDP, October 1982 to August 1985

The popular euphoria that greeted the inauguration of Siles in mid-October 1982 at the head of the UDP coalition (MNRI, MIR, PCB) was not entirely misplaced. The armed forces were badly divided, demoralised, tarnished by association with *narcotrafico,* and now controlled by a determined group of generals who had taken up arms against the dictatorship in 1981, enjoyed US support and clearly favoured civilian rule (even if they were notably sympathetic to Paz's MNR). The anti-dictatorial mobilisations of September and October indicated a level of support for constitutionalism that cowed the civil police and effectively drove García Mesa's paramilitary apparatus underground (which, in local terms, meant that they stashed their weapons, kept their heads down and started looking for new jobs; whilst they had, occasionally, acted like the Romanian *Securitate,* they were never treated like them, for good or ill). Although the UDP contained communists, it was soberly welcomed by Reagan's White House, received much more resolute European support (particularly from France and Spain) and sent a clear signal from the conservative parties that they would respect the 1980 election results. On the international plane, the Malvinas defeat and economic recession had evidently reduced the spoiling capacity of the Argentine junta; Brazil continued to move cautiously towards civilian rule; Peru had already achieved it. Ecuador, Colombia and Venezuela all offered forthright support; the military's previous aggression towards the Andean Pact had bred abnormally warm sympathy for the civilian opposition, of which Siles was the clear figurehead.

Nevertheless, from its first day in office the new government faced considerable problems. Official figures for the third quarter of 1982 indicated a major economic crisis while estimates for capital flight in 1980 and 1981 stood at $370 million and $347 million respectively — more than a third of legal export earnings.[7] The UDP largely owed its restoration to power to the COB, whose rank and file had borne the brunt of the repression, had been unable to defend their wages against an inflation rate of nigh on 15 per cent per month, and were both well organised and in a boisterous mood. Although the PCB was in office (ministries of labour and mines), its capacity to influence the independent majority of the COB leadership and a traditionally suspicious membership was very limited. Equally, control of the executive was qualified by the fact that the UDP lacked control of congress, where the informal MNR–ADN bloc possessed an effective majority in the senate and was very close to one in the house of deputies. Fully aware of the pitfalls this threatened, Siles had resisted acceptance of the 1980 poll result and insisted upon new elections that would reflect the state of public opinion after two years of military rule (including the collaboration of senior *adenistas*). In this he was supported by the PCB, which called for fresh elections in December 1982. However, the MIR, whose Jaime Paz Zamora held the vice-presidency, joined the right in demanding an immediate ratification of the 1980 result under the slogan 'el hambre no espera'. This, together with manifest differences of opinion within the MNRI, signalled important tensions within the alliance even before it had entered office. At the same time, *institucionalista* control of the military did not extend to a purge of the officer corps beyond those very few figures publicly associated with *narcotráfico*. If the armed forces were, as a whole, compliant, there were still at large, and in important commands, officers appalled at the sight of the PCB taking cabinet portfolios. Moreover, the cocaine trade had not diminished at all, and the administration faced major — if not insuperable — difficulties in subduing it, with or without US support (which it clearly sought to avoid).

Finally, although Siles's frail appearance and gentle comportment contrasted favourably with the brusque demeanour of the soldiers who had preceded him, providing an avuncular image suited to a new era of consensus, it soon became clear that he lacked resolution and control over his cabinet, party and coalition allies. Despite enjoying broad sympathy, he was scarcely even *primus inter pares* within the government — a position of critical weakness with respect to managing the inevitable rush for the spoils of office (never enjoyed by the MIR and PCB, and not for over a decade by the MNRI) and still more so with regard to upholding executive authority against a congress that was able to mask its ideological enmity with demands for a full division of powers.

Siles saw his political role as one of averting conflict at all costs and maintaining public order without resort to violence. His past clashes with the COB, strong commitment to pacifism, and dedication to consensus politics betokened an outlook that was supremely suited to the tone of civilism and no less ill-suited to giving it substance. However, if the president's disposition aggravated the fissures and confusions within the UDP, these were equally the result of objective circumstances over which even the most determined government would have had little control. It should be noted here that comparisons between the UDP and MNR administrations are invidious insofar as Víctor Paz took office after Siles had endured a swathe of political problems that were intrinsic to any first post-dictatorial administration — a fact that could not have been ignored by the right when it supported the UDP's entry into government. (In this respect, the MIR rapidly learnt an invaluable lesson, for which it paid a high price as a party but a rather low one in terms of its most ambitious leaders.) Siles's preferred option was not only at variance with popular sentiment, it also appeared to be sectarian and ran the risk of prolonging the stalemates of 1978–1980. The right, by contrast, could maximise the advantages of opposition and what in technical parlance could be described as a 'depressed learning curve'. Although it had good reason to fear a flurry of radical policies, it could also perceive that the UDP was in a poor position to meet the very high expectations of the populace.

In sum, the UDP was faced with an unprecedented economic crisis when it lacked internal cohesion, decisive leadership, full military support and control over both congress and the economy's leading commodity, cocaine. It was not, then, surprising that within a year its popular support was greatly diminished and that in less than three it was comprehensively defeated at the polls. However, the scale of that defeat was by no means a foregone conclusion and reflects multiple errors, the opposition of the COB and the resurgence of the right.

## The Economy

The UDP's economic policies have been characterised — most frequently after Paz's 1985 deflation — as both technically inept and irresponsibly redistributionist. In fact, they were profoundly inconsistent, sometimes attempting stabilisation at the expense of capital and in defence of wages (November 1982; May 1985), sometimes seeking an orthodox deflation that clearly prejudiced labour, even if it did not appreciably assist productive capital (April 1984; November 1984; February 1985). Table 3.2 gives a summary depiction of the principal measures. Whilst the abject failure of all these initiatives is indisputable and borne out by the statistics, several less obvious points deserve brief comment.

The first is the least publicised by critics on the right: many entrepreneurs/ speculators made fabulous fortunes out of hyperinflation by either acquiring cheap dollars from the Banco Central and selling them on the parallel market (which existed throughout, regardless of periodic proscription) or simply 'informally repatriating' dollar savings to the same end. Equally, the consistently — and massively — over-valued exchange rate encouraged enormous profits through contraband, which was a far more 'socialised' activity but still the means for remarkable concentrations of wealth. (In contrast to the crisis of 1954–1957, goods remained available throughout, but only a miniscule percentage could be bought at subsidised rates, and there was no real effort, unlike in the 1950s, to exercise physical control over the black market except occasionally that in dollars.) The restrictions on the formal banking sector were also offset by the fact that it took loans at zero interest and extended them at nominal rates, thereby sharing in the government's short-term 'seignourage gains' made by printing money.

## Table 3.2: Major UDP Economic 'Packages'

| | |
|---|---|
| Nov. 1982 | Devaluation: Bs44.5–200 per US$ (parallel rate: 250); min. wage: Bs5,990–8,490 (US$42); indexation of wages; private banks excluded from exchange market ('de-dollarisation') |
| Nov. 1983 | Devaluation: Bs200 –500 per US$ (parallel rate: 1,200); reduced subsidies on foodstuffs; disputed indexation maintained; min. wage = Bs30,100 (US$33) |
| April 1984 | Devaluation: Bs500–2,000 per US$ (parallel rate: 3,000); formal indexation halted (average productive sector wage rise is 13 per cent; 40,000 public sector employees get food bonus at 50 per cent of wage). |
| July 1984 | Basic prices officially controlled; av. 30 per cent wage rise; official limit on debt service repayments at 25 per cent export revenues. |
| August 1984 | Devaluation: Bs2,000–5,000 per US$ (parallel rate: 6,500); dual exchange rate, treasury subsidising rate of Bs2,000 for 'essential imports'; reduced wage rises. |
| Nov. 1984 | Devaluation: Bs9,000 (single rate) per US$ (parallel rate: 17,000); reduced wage rises; min. wage raised to Bs 407,855 (US$20); general wage rise is by factor of 13.55 relative to Nov. 1983. |
| Feb. 1985 | Devaluation: Bs9,000–45,000 per US$ (parallel rate: 160,000); reduced wage rise (bonus of Bs 3.1 million) |
| May 1985 | Devaluation: Bs45,000–67,000 per US$ (parallel rate: 275,000); formal wage indexation restored; min. wage at Bs6.2 million (US$21). |

Secondly, whilst within months the UDP's management of the economy was badly 'in drift' by seeking simultaneously (and equally fruitlessly) to assuage the IMF and popular pressure, the administration started with a clear strategy that was partly misconceived and partly misapplied. This was the November 1982 'de-dollarisation', which converted all internal dollar obligations at a rate of Bs 145 and lifted state responsiblity for private dollar debts as well as the exchange risk of dollar deposits — realised two days later with a devaluation to Bs196. The aim here was to secure governmental control of all dollar transactions and fortify the peso; this failed almost at once as foreign banks closed, local institutions shifted their operations to the 'grey market' and private savers conducted their business on the parallel market. Confidence in the peso plummeted and the economy was rapidly 'redollarised' but now on informal terms with the state entirely lacking control.[8] The legality of this excessively aggressive measure was rejected by the courts in 1984, by which time its failure was apparent to all — the government began issuing gold and dollar bonds in August of that year — even those members of the COB for whom the *escala móvil* (indexation) was the economic defence equivalent to that of holding dollars for savers (of whom there were a great many with modest deposits who also earned wages and initially supported the UDP).

Thirdly, the UDP's much publicised resort to increasing emission of notes — characteristic of hyperinflation — should not obscure an equally critical factor: the collapse of public revenues, which fell from 9 per cent of GDP in 1980 to 1.3 per cent in the first nine months of 1985.[9] Collection time-lags under conditions of acute inflation, together with the fact that some three-fifths of central government revenues were related to the official exchange rate, meant that income fell faster than expenditure. It has been correctly noted that:

> The hyperinflation under Siles was not so much a result of new spending as the inability to restrain spending in the face of falling foreign loans, falling tax revenues, and higher debt service payments abroad.[10]

The notion that the UDP was 'spendthrift' is not, then, at all true in the popular sense of the term — the COB persistently made this point — but it may be applied insofar as the government was unprepared or unable — the degree varied — fully to pass on the structural and conjunctural costs of the crisis to the popular sector either through its own initiatives or by accepting those demanded by the banks in return for reducing the external pressure. Once the government's effort to control dollar deposits collapsed it simply trod water, trying to mediate internal and external pressures only when they became absolutely intolerable. (By 1984 the internal limits of tolerance corresponded to a general strike of more than a fortnight; the external ones extended to the impounding of Lloyd Aereo Boliviano's aged Boeing 707 at Miami airport.) Reductions in public investment were thus preferred to those of real wages although the effects were barely slower to emerge and would be fully exploited by the MNR after 1985.

The character of the UDP's 'packages' roughly reflects the administration's political fortunes. Between November 1982 and April 1984 it sought to protect real wages although the COB as well as private enterprise (CEPB) criticised all the measures of this period, fiercely disputed official assessments of the retail price index, and staged a number of effective strikes at the slightest hint of back-sliding by the ministry. From April 1984 to May 1985 the administration openly rejected indexation but was obliged at the end of May 1984 to acquiesce to the COB's demand for a formal limit on debt service repayments (although inflation was now so great that this was of little real consequence other than to harden the attitude of the banks, already determined in their opposition as a result of 'dedollarisation'). This period also witnessed a series of major strikes — particularly the general stoppages of November 1984 and March 1985 — the exceptional duration of which may be partially attributed to the relatively low real cost of lost wages. These destroyed first the UDP's capacity to serve out its term (the agreement of 21 November 1984 to advance elections) and then its hopes for a respectable election result. The May 1985 restoration of indexation (agreed, but renegued upon, in March) was the most palpable indication by the rump of the UDP (now effectively a section of the MNRI and some independent technocrats) that it had lost both the economic and political battles and would 'retreat in glory', complicating life for its successor.

The inconsistency of these policies — both in themselves and as a whole — should not simply be put down to ineptitude or the mesmerism induced by the scale of the crisis. It also reflected political divisions within the UDP, 'dedollarisation' being essentially a MIR initiative, the 'heterodoxy' of November 1983 to May 1985 being largely the product of independent technicians who tried to move towards the IMF but were forestalled tactically by the left, and the 'final fling', a traditional populist gesture in which the small clique around Siles, exasperated by rightist criticisms that it had pampered the workers, decided to do just that. Equally, while the IMF consistently refused to issue its imprimatur for any of the measures, it is noteworthy that the November 1982 package — arguably the most coherent and radical of all; certainly the most broadly unpopular — was attacked by Banzer for reducing real wages and exacting an unacceptable sacrifice from the poor.[11] The MNR also criticised it — a direct quote is permissible in view of later developments — because,

> it does not respond to popular interests but, rather, to the requirements of the IMF. It seeks to reduce the level of internal demand, and in order to do this uses as an instrument a pitiless reduction in the purchasing power of wages.[12]

In the same vein, following the November 1983 measures, the MNR tabled a bill in the lower house to increase wages by 100 per cent, and this was passed in the senate with ADN support (although the CEPB, now aware of the costs of political spoiling, reacted with disdain).

Thus, although an orthodox deflation would certainly have represented a surrender of the UDP's programme, the opposition was also fearful of this option and was careful not to pronounce it 'the only alternative' until the government's back had been broken in late 1984. This is understandable in political terms, but it should be borne in mind that the right, no less than the UDP, was apprehensive of the high social costs and threat of disorder; it also lacked familiarity with the techniques of managing high inflation (absent from Bolivia for the better part of three decades). Moreover, a significant entrepreneurial sector stood to lose heavily in terms of both reduced speculative opportunities and the inevitable reduction of a public sector upon which it was parasitic. To aver, as has one supposed expert, that Bolivians were stupid, forgetful or selfish in failing to embrace orthodoxy earlier is to display an unforgivable arrogance.[13] There were plenty of people — inside the UDP and out — who, by mid-1983, were making technically and morally informed judgements as to the relative social and performance-related costs of inflation and deflation. By the end of that year circumstances beyond the UDP's control determined that either could only prevail in acute and sustained form. Profoundly inequitable though the former was, its relative merit — in political terms — was that it was, at least until late 1984, corrosive rather than explosive. Pathetic and acquiescent though the government's position may appear, it was not simply bred of cowardice, and it upheld a shard of its original mandate not to provoke violence, the potential for which would be far greater through a decisive 'u-turn' than through an entirely new mandate. In this respect, then, electoralism was not simply formally desirable but also — from a managerial perspective — entirely necessary.

In the end, of course, Siles did deploy troops, and this initiative (March 1985) undoubtedly prepared the ground for the MNR, which during the ensuing election campaign kept its policy options very vague indeed, simply repeating the now familiar catechism that an agreement with the IMF was essential and more favourable conditions for private capital were the only means by which to resolve the crisis.[14] Mention should also be made of the fact that, despite the effective boycott of the UDP by the international banks and the IMF, the US government was apparently unwilling to force the Siles administration into a corner as resolutely as it had in 1956. This was certainly informed by the prospect of a conservative regime and the need to retain anti-cocaine operations, but increases in economic and military aid — from $19.7 million in 1982 to $78.1 million in 1984 — also reflect the perception that if the Siles government presided over a completely chaotic economy, at least it did so through constitutional means and on terms that were in reality barely less distinct from those demanded by the COB than they were from those espoused by Banzer (whom the State Department, at least, did not greatly trust) and eventually implemented by Paz and Sánchez de Lozada. Demonstration of the costs of irresponsibility were best left to the strictly economic domain; any manifestly political retribution carried an unnecessarily high price.

Whether purposefully or perforce heterodox, the UDP's economic policies did not enjoy even a brief flourish of success, as for instance did those of APRA in Peru. Even the diminished rate of contraction in 1984 may be ascribed to the recovery of agriculture after the climatic ravages of the previous year — a critical if conjunctural setback. In effect, by October 1982 the crisis was already too deep-seated and externally-determined to allow for remedies that fell short of absolute radicalism. Following the failure of 'de-dollarisation' — that, in terms of both inflation and exchange rates, took nine months to become fully evident — the UDP was doomed to manage rather than resolve the crisis although it could be argued that it was not until the second half of 1984 that a 'progressive remedy' was completely beyond hope. Certainly, it was between September and November 1984 that both the COB and the right moved into decisive confrontation with the government and each other, provoking a momentary revival of real wages but also the precipitate calling of elections that deprived the regime of any incentive to engage in structural remedies. At most, therefore, the UDP's political authority to deal with the economy lasted barely 24 months, and it was evident well before November 1984 that such authority would not resist a major challenge.

## Politics

The UDP years are widely viewed as a failure of the left both in government and outside it. However, as with the economy, the UDP's social policies were scarcely radical. Indeed, within three months of coming to power it could be said that only the presence of the PCB in the regime upheld any pretence of radicalism, sustained more by rhetoric and opposition attacks than by substantive policy. Nevertheless, when, in November 1984, the communist leader Marcos Domic defended the alliance in a final, futile effort to avert its collapse, he could legitimately point to a number of identifiably 'progressive' measures.

In foreign affairs relations were established with Sandinista Nicaragua and re-established with Cuba — a matter of anxiety for the high command, which was quick to inspect medical equipment donated by Havana to La Paz's Hospital del Niño on the grounds that it might be used for spying on the Estado Mayor General next door. Relations with the Soviet Union also improved (although, to the PCB's chagrin, the government condemned the occupation of Afghanistan), yet Siles took a very low profile on Central America as a whole. By contrast, an early and unique success was scored with the detention and extradition to France of Klaus Barbie by an interior ministry that promised to be just as competent at such operations as it had been under the military. Although at home the government was soon and justifiably seen to be weak and inactive in dealing with the extreme right, its image abroad was, at least for a while, far more impressive.

Perhaps the most notable and enduring success of the UDP was its health policy, and particularly the establishment of the Comités Populares de Salud, which effectively combined a progressive approach to preventative medicine with popular mobilisation in a campaign that eliminated polio and dramatically reduced the incidence of measles within two years through the inoculation of three-quarters of all infants. Indeed, despite the strongly collectivist thrust of this initiative, the right was obliged to recognise its popularity, and promised in the 1985 election campaign to retain the programme (a promise that was technically honoured although in practice the committees soon became a conduit for clientism and corruption).

If it was only in the field of health that the UDP even approximated to what was from its inception (in 1978) an exceptionally vague programme, it should be noted that the alliance itself effectively collapsed within weeks of coming to office. In formal terms the UDP was finally dissolved in December 1984, but it was the departure of the MIR from government in January 1983 that damaged the coalition beyond repair. Although the MIR, and especially Jaime Paz Zamora, staged this exceptionally early rupture primarily for sectarian ends, the plausible ostensible cause was in-fighting within the MNRI and the consequent failure to formulate coherent policy and eradicate the vestiges of the dictatorship's paramilitary apparatus.

The MNRI was indeed badly divided and would remain so to the end, the desertion of one faction led by Samuel Gallardo giving the opposition control of both houses of congress by 11 votes in

August 1984. By that stage dissidence was determined principally by the desire to protect political careers, readily achieved by 'rejoining' the MNR, which was ever open to erstwhile renegades and sufficiently lax in its interpretation of 'revolutionary nationalism' not to cause ideological inconvenience for those who had previously cavorted with communists and lambasted Víctor Paz — a man who harboured grudges with exceptional rancour but dissembled with the affability of a political genius. Opportunist though such moves were, they did not in reality break anything but the organisational boundaries of the MNRI's conduct since the party owed its existence less to a clear programmatic distinction from its forebear than a different set of allies at home and, to a lesser extent, abroad. It revindicated the more progressive features of the 'revolutionary era' and took a more principled stance on dictatorship, but its *modus operandi* remained very similar to that of the MNR.[15] Indeed, this shared clientelist inheritance was at the heart of the MNRI's early fissures (December 1982 to July 1983) when, shortly after coming to office, there was a very public and debilitating controversy over ministerial *feudos* and access to the placid Siles, with further personalist subfractions rapidly proliferating around them (Roncal, Velarde, Gallardo). These divisions were not entirely concerned with the spoils of office; they also related to treatment of the left, the COB and *narcotráfico*. However, the issues at stake never merited the degree of conflict and air of crisis that attended them, and the MNRI singularly failed to provide the discipline and sobriety necessary to contain the contagion of *politiquería*. Siles's personal involvement tarnished his reputation, and it is telling that although the MNR later suffered from comparable conflicts in government, Víctor Paz scrupulously kept himself above them, limiting public pronouncements to the absolute minimum required by the protocols of office (quite the reverse of his proclivity for personal attacks in previous decades).

Insofar as such disorganisation within the coalition's senior partner affected both the internal temper and external image of the government, it damaged the MIR and PCB. Yet the difficulties displayed by these parties were by no means reducible to this issue. The MIR came under pressure across the board, from initial disputes with the MNRI over appointments in the customs service, to limiting the damage caused by 'de-dollarisation' and assuaging a rank and file that had suffered sharply under the dictatorship and now saw very little effort being made to settle accounts with the paramilitaries. Although very loose, the MIR's rhetoric was notably more buoyant than that of the MNRI and PCB, and the expectations harboured by its generally youthful following, which had waited four years for power, were correspondingly higher. Moreover, as vice-president, Jaime Paz Zamora was closely associated with the administration whilst true to the traditions of his office — lacking even minimal influence over it. For some 15 months it appeared as if the MIR was reacting as one to its anomalous position of being in the government via Paz Zamora's position and its continuing membership of the UDP yet rejecting places in cabinet and acting — at the very best — as a fairweather friend in congress and the COB. Its attacks on the 'incoherence' of economic policy enabled the MIR to diminish its association with 'de-dollarisation' but also obscured a growing split between the party's right wing (Paz Zamora, Eid, Capobianco) and the more radical current that was itself divided between 'socialists' leaning towards the PCB (Aranibar, Ferrufino) and 'syndicalists' identified with the anti-PCB factions within the COB (Delgadillo). This process remained unclear for over a year in part simply because of the very bluntness with which Paz Zamora attacked Siles and the cabinet — even when he himself was acting as president during Siles's trips abroad — and in part because until mid-1984 the vice president found it easier to support anti-government initiatives from the left, notably the FSTMB's unilateral imposition of *cogestión mayoritaria in* Comibol in April 1983, which he had the temerity to welcome as a revival of the true traditions of 1952.[16] (It should be noted that this stance had the added advantage for Paz Zamora of embarrassing the PCB as well as Siles.)

Both the MNRI and the PCB justifiably distrusted the MIR's motives from the moment it quit the cabinet, not least because this seemed to presage a challenge for dominant influence, if not outright power. However, the MNRI was in no position to launch a complete assault on the *miristas,* and the communists disliked their replacement by Christian Democrats and independent technocrats as well as maintaining a greater commitment to unity than was recognised outside the party at the time. This, together with the fact that the MIR continued to enjoy appreciable popular support, delayed a complete schism within the UDP and permitted the party's return to government in April 1984. Yet the terms of re-entry into the fold rapidly revealed the tensions that had been gestating within the party itself. From Paz Zamora's perspective there was by this stage nothing mere to be gained — and indeed quite a bit to be lost — from continuing to act as a 'Trojan horse'. From the viewpoint of the MIR's radical wing there still remained the possibility of rapprochement between the UDP and the COB based on the initial redistributionist policies of the alliance. *Cogestión* had been obtained in Comibol; *cogobierno* was no longer a viable option; the PCB favoured their re-inclusion, and the right's growing challenge might still be resisted.

Nevertheless, the economic policy agreed by the majority of the cabinet following the MIR's return precisely ended indexation and sought to shift back to orthodoxy in controlling inflation — a telling fact in the light of developments in 1989. As a result, Delgadillo immediately quit both the cabinet and the party, establishing MIR–Masas, which would challenge the UDP within the COB as part of the Dirección Revolucionaria Unificada (DRU). The larger radical group led by Antonio Aranibar rejected this line as misguided in its aggression towards the PCB and its excessive economism. However, if the Aranibar faction appeared to be associated with official attacks on 'ultra-leftism', which escalated following the DRU's gaining of control of the COB at its sixth congress in September 1984, a second split was made inevitable by the polarisation of the final months of that year, the irreversible collapse of the UDP in December, and Paz Zamora's clear intention to stage an electoral campaign based on personalism and a concerted retreat from the party's radical heritage. This led, in January 1985, to the formation of the MIR–Bolivia Libre (MBL), which contained some of the party's most talented cadre and sought to restore the unity of the left under conditions of headlong retreat. The basis for such a recomposition was entirely absent prior to the election, the prolonged general strike of March 1985 exacerbating expectations of dual power through the COB and generating a fierce debate within the left over the viability of constitutionalism *per se*.

As befits its traditions, the internal response of the PCB to its participation in a chaotic and unpopular coalition was more modulated and less public. In terms of collective temperament and ideology the party was better adjusted to the vagaries of 'popular frontism'. However, it suffered the consequences to an unprecedentedly high degree despite the fact that Bolivian Communism had since its inception been obliged to contend with powerful forces to its left. Historically, these had been represented in the syndicalist sphere by Juan Lechín Oquendo, whose careering pragmatism easily embraced calls for armed struggle and workers' power, and in the political realm by Trotskyism; the two had often entered into short but effective 'anti-Stalinist' alliances. Under the UDP the Trotskyist threat was in itself of little consequence. Beyond the university, the Partido Obrero Revolucionario (POR) signally failed to capitalise on popular disenchantment; its clear-headedness with regard to the debilities of the local capitalist economy was accompanied by a remarkable misconception that the radical form of popular mobilisation reflected an equally strong commitment to political revolution. This cardinal error of failing to distinguish between appearances and reality was insufficiently mitigated by explaining several unrealised 'revolutionary situations' in terms of the 'absence of leadership' (either a truism or a damning self-indictment).[17] Nonetheless, if the POR had become petrified by sectarian propagation, the longstanding Trotskyist heritage had left its mark on a large number of activists for whom there appeared to be no alternative other than the COB to counteract the PCB's 'collaborationism' and consolidate a defence of the working class. Thus, the communists' problems in controlling the ministries of mines and labour throughout this period extended beyond a loss in rank and file support in the unions to confronting a radical critique of the contradictions of managing a capitalist slump under a proletarian banner.

In the first instance conflict took a familiar form through the FSTMB's occupation of Comibol (April 1983), which the party leadership first tried to avert, then mediate, and finally had shame-facedly to accept and join. After all, *cogestión* had been a leitmotif of the 1952 revolution, was part of the PCB's programme, and enjoyed broad support within its principal union constituency. Moreover, Simón

Reyes, one of the party's most prominent leaders, headed the new management structure, which did not in itself damage the popular front strategy and owed more to the *autogestionario* current in the COB than to the party's major political enemies rapidly grouping around Lechín. However, it was not long before what was a containable instance of 'workerism' was exacerbated by economic conditions into an irresistible militancy over wages. Here the PCB was comprehensively defeated by both policy and circumstances. It could not fail to be seen to be defending real wages and yet this entailed strike action against a government in which it was participating. Moreover, by mid-1984 such strikes were patently taking on a politically critical character, incorporating legitimate expectations as well as the 'demagogy' assailed by the party. It is, however, notable that it was only at the PCB's fifth congress in February 1985 — after the UDP had split and the party had left government — that dissidence took open form with a group led by Ramiro Barrenechea and based largely on the youth movement eventually breaking away in August.[18]

The role of the COB under the UDP naturally combined popular discontent over the economy with more politically motivated initiatives by factions of the left for which the organisation has traditionally been the premier site of competition. As noted above, one major axis of this conflict was between the PCB and Juan Lechín, who struck increasingly radical poses as the rank and file lost patience with the government. Although relations between the regime and a COB leadership dominated by forces unsympathetic to the UDP were fraught throughout and never escaped the cycle of devaluation and strike action, they deteriorated beyond repair in September 1984 when the sixth congress of the COB produced a clear polarisation between the PCB and the DRU, which went out of its way to distance formal support for constitutionalism from backing for the UDP (a 'bourgeois government') and continued to insist upon implementation of the COB's emergency plan — complete default on the external debt, full indexation, curbs on capital, and workers' control.[19] The ensuing strike in November produced Siles's effective abdication in the Church-sponsored agreement to advance elections.

It was, though, the strike of March 1985 that more profoundly determined subsequent developments, since the week-long occupation of La Paz by miners was unparalleled in its scale and appeared to promise a decisive settling of accounts amidst incessant discharges of dynamite that traumatised the middle class. For several days it appeared that a 'gentlemen's agreement' over elections would be swept away by proletarian activism, redolent of 1952 in its appeal to communitarianism. Whether by design or default, Siles let this wave roll unimpeded until it began to lose impetus. The COB leadership failed to present any new political proposal and, having already rejected the offer of *cogobierno* as a reheated trick of the 1950s, resolutely resisted any more radical option, for which it was even less prepared. Thus, although a state of virtual dual power prevailed for nigh on two weeks, this corresponded almost entirely to the stamina of the rank and file, prepared to face down the government for pay and denounce elections as useless but not to take state power. When the troops were deployed without major conflict the true limits of syndicalism were exposed. The end of the '*jornadas de marzo*' produced the single most emphatic deflation of the popular movement and the left. Mass mobilisation had not so much failed as demonstrated its essentially conservative character and thus a vulnerability which the right henceforth felt able to exploit by challenging the COB to 'showdowns' where the unions lacked an endgame.

In political terms the intransigence of the COB leadership stemmed from an acute anxiety to avert the compromises sprung on it by the MNR in the 1950s. This had instilled such a dedication to organisational independence that the syndicalist vanguard not only held to devices — *escala móvil* and *cogestión mayoritaria* — that optimised its distance from the regime but also preferred the risks of constant conflict to those of a social pact. These instincts were further deepened by prolonged experience of resistance to dictatorship that had enlivened skills of agitation but dulled those of negotiation needed to realise gains from it. Such proclivities had become ideologised less into a discourse of anarcho-syndicalism — although this lay close to the surface — than into a simultaneous celebration and denial of the limits of economism. The political forces seeking control of the COB fell prey to the slogans of its 'apolitical maximalism', either by stoking up expectations they could not meet (DRU) or by seeking to fulfil them at a 'capitulationist level'

(PCB/Escobar). This, of course, is a general pattern, but the political and economic circumstances prevailing in Bolivia between 1982 and 1985 gave it decisive importance within national political life.

The impasse reached in March 1985 was broken in the elections of July, and converted into defeat by Decree 21060, driving the left from the centre of politics and transforming what had hitherto been consequential debates over strategy into esoteric theoretical disputes. However, the objective dilemmas and difficulties encountered during the UDP period were clearly immense, and the failure to resolve them outside of slogans reflected the degree of popular pressure on the left no less than it did the political shortcomings of the principal parties. Indeed, in terms of incidence, popular mobilisation continued at an equal — and occasionally higher — rate under the MNR, suggesting that the left was responsible less for bringing people on to the streets than for orchestrating them once they were there, which was very often. Such matters are exceptionally hard to quantify, but it is telling that between October 1983 and June 1984 — 'quiet' at a national level by dint of the fact that there was only one 24-hour general strike — there was a total of 554 officially registered industrial or social 'conflicts'.[20]

Urban stoppages and conflicts dominated, but one key feature of this period was increased recourse by *campesinos* to road-blocks (*bloqueos*), which were highly effective, required a relatively slight physical presence, and could not readily be countered except through force, which the UDP only employed with the utmost reluctance. In 1983 and 1984 there were 18 major *bloqueos* which, following the example first set in opposition to the 1979 Natusch coup, both strengthened the confidence of the CSUTCB and its allied *katarista* currents and also suggested that the political imbalance between town/mine and countryside was being rectified.[21] In some sense this was true. Even after three decades of urbanisation the rural population remained substantial and could swing an election — a matter of unprecedented importance. Equally, the decline — soon to be collapse — of mining and the expansion of cocaine had already begun a process of migration to and within certain rural areas (notably from the altiplano to the Chapare) and greatly enhanced both the value of coca production and the resolution with which it had to be defended (see below).

Moreover, whilst it was to be some time before the experience of Sendero Luminoso in Peru was recognised to be a major phenomenon, fears of this example imbricating with a resurgent rural radicalism were harboured beyond the ranks of the military.

Yet these factors did not so much underlie a progressive polarisation in the *campo* as reflect a reduction in political control. As in the urban sector, mobilisation and direct action were aggressive but limited in their objectives; *caudillismo* and localism continued to prevail (one reason for the large number of incidents) and, if the parameters of the 'limited good' were palpably being eroded, they were still tighter than the right feared and the left hoped. Although the fact is often greatly exaggerated, inflation did prejudice rural labour less profoundly than urban workers; the drought of 1983 bred more survivalism than subversion; and the UDP's chaotic efforts at cooptation through *cogestión* (CORACA) increased bureaucratic in-fighting. The end result was sufficient discontent and activism to maintain political uncertainty in the countryside, but not enough for this to alter the balance of power at the national level. The MNR old guard, well aware that a similar situation had obtained prior to the coup of 1964, subsequently took the line of least resistance, excluding the countryside from its initial tax reforms and delaying introduction of modifications to the 1953 agrarian reform proposed by their technocrats. They still did not escape trouble, but it is probable that this would have been much more serious if the UDP experience had not clearly signalled a threat that had been obscured for several years by military government.

Conservative victories in the polls of 1985 and 1989 have led many commentators and the right itself to over-emphasise the degree to which it altered its *modus operandi* prior to the collapse of the UDP. Whilst it is certainly the case that both the COB and the parties of the radical left underestimated the degree and ramifications of conservative compliance with constitutionalism, their failure either to modulate a Manichaean vision bred of two decades of dictatorship or to move beyond a fundamentally cautious and defensive acceptance of liberal democracy was not solely the result of ingrained custom. Banzer's establishment of the ADN and acceptance of defeat in the polls of 1979 and 1980 signalled an important shift, but this had not forestalled the coups of Natusch and García

Mesa, and leading *adenistas* served these military regimes. Equally, although the US response to militarism after 1979 was more aggressive than in any other South American country, Washington's influence was far from decisive, and recidivist *golpistas* continued to agitate throughout the UDP period. The degree of their isolation is much more readily appreciated with hindsight than it was at the time. The kidnapping of Siles in June 1984 by elements of his bodyguard and the elite UMOPAR police unit; the 'passive mutiny' by the staff college in Cochabamba against General Sejas for four months in mid-1984; and the abortive rebellion by General Olvis at the end of the year all underscored the fragility of the constitutionalist entente at a time when military dissidence was breaking cover in Argentina and popular mobilisation against the Pinochet regime in Chile had been forced into retreat.

In each instance both the COB and the majority of the left rallied to the defence of the constitution, curbing their offensive against the government. Nonetheless, this desistance from escalating tension in the face of open rightist threats was paralleled by a deep suspicion of reactionary manoeuvres to subvert democratic institutions from within. Denunciations of '*golpes constitucionales*' often reflected reluctance to accept the new rules of governance, but they were not always baseless, especially once the relationship between Siles and Paz Zamora became antagonistic and opened the possibility (March and November 1983) of a 'formal succession', which had in the past been a mechanism for altering governments (1925, 1934, 1949). Eventually, of course, the UDP administration was terminated by an even more overt dispensation with the letter of the 1967 constitution, against which the left was poorly positioned to complain, partly because much of it had called for fresh elections in 1982, partly because the November 1984 accord was signed by all the major political forces and arbitrated by the Church, and in part because there now existed widespread support for any resolution of the stalemate. The right certainly helped to contrive such a situation by insisting on the impeachment of Siles's senior official Rafael Otazo over his discussions with the *narcotraficante* Roberto Suárez, by threatening to impeach Siles himself, and by effectively vetoing the president's amnesty for a handful of leftists captured by the army in the village of Luribay in unclear circumstances and given jail sentences, the harshness of which contrasted with the absence of any judicial action over scores of well publicised cases on the right. Indeed, if under the UDP attention remained focused on the relationship between a debilitated executive and an aggressive legislature, the interested immobility of the judiciary was a factor of consequence well before the disorganised efforts to replicate application of the rule of law in the neighbouring republics with the 'trial' of García Mesa from 1986. Siles's eventual recourse to his traditional tactic of hunger strike in October 1984 signalled an incapacity to secure even a minimum degree of cooperation between the powers of the state, where vested interests remained exceptionally strong even if they had been obliged to adhere to institutional protocols and the strategem of non-compliance.

The nature of Siles's response to his embattlement greatly facilitated the intervention of the ecclesiastical hierarchy, which constituted a peculiar amalgam of the first and fourth estates in that its appreciable authority was expressed through the country's leading daily *Presencia,* under the directorship of the conservative (and soon to be disgraced) Monseñor Genaro Prata, and its premier radio station Fides, dominated by the astute anti-communist Jesuit José Gramunt. Both stuck strenuously to the liberal voice that had been developed under the *banzerato* and lay at the core of their legitimacy, but the editorial impetus towards *concertación* was vital to sealing Siles's fate in that it provided a non-partisan imprimatur for the less high-minded horse-trading immediately dubbed as the '*golpe eclesiástico*' by the left.

The clergy remained politically divided, but the radical current was poorly represented in an aged hierarchy exhausted by its remonstrations over human rights under Banzer and García Mesa and preoccupied with administering aid and charity programmes amongst the poor, who continued to concentrate their political activity within the orbit of secular organisations. This general pattern — closer to that of Argentina and Peru than Chile and Brazil at that time — deserves a far fuller analysis than is possible here, but mention should be made of the historically weak position of Christian Democracy, which had suffered an early and decisive division in the 1960s and proved incapable of expanding a small confessional constituency. Although the 1988 papal visit witnessed some of the most robust language ever employed by John Paul II on the social question, this reflected the relatively low level of clerical radicalism, the exceptionally severe impact of the MNR's deflationary policies, and a justified perception that the Church no longer faced a challenge from Marxism. After November 1984 the good offices of the hierarchy were largely limited to the resolution of sectoral conflicts and almost exclusively directed towards obtaining a modicum of moderation from the government — a role to which it was accustomed and which bore little political risk.

The adroit use of congress by the right took the traditional form of obstructionism. Although there were very few precedents of a conservative legislature assailing a more progressive executive — certainly nothing of the order witnessed in Chile under Allende — conflict between these two arms of the state had arisen in the late 1950s through intra-MNR faction-fighting, re-emerging in 1979–1980. The MNR and ADN now stole a leaf from the left's book to stage a series of censures, impeachments and procedural obstacles that were sanctioned by law and required the UDP to govern by decree-law and ordinance within months of coming to office. No instance was in itself of critical consequence, but the accumulated effect was to cast the government in an unconciliatory light and strengthen the identification of the right with the strict letter of the law. It may be doubted that a great many electors took this to be more than self-serving *politiquería* of the old school. Still, the campaign increased from mid-1984 when the opposition won a majority in congress and immediately turned it to sharp effect with prosecution of the Otazo scandal, which significantly damaged the moral standing of Siles and the MNRI, if not the UDP as a whole.

The manipulation of this affair combined unremarkable hypocrisy — in 1988 senior members of the ADN were revealed to be in close and friendly contact with Suárez — with a more novel exploitation of the media, particularly television. Here it is worth noting that the parallel existence of widespread popular access to television and competitive politics had only previously existed in 1979–1980, when the state possessed an effective monopoly over broadcasting (the few disorganised university stations being closed to the right). By 1984 this position had changed sufficiently for the right to launch telling attacks on the regime across the board, from the press, where the UDP possessed no popular journal and was supported by none (even the weekly *Aquí* was critical from the left), to the radio, where the proliferation of independent stations diminished the impact of pro-regime broadcasting, to television, where the poor quality of the state channel and chaotic conditions of the university stations provided a commercial as well as political logic to the emergence of a private sector. Although this only came to flourish with complete — albeit semi-legal — deregulation under the MNR, when La Paz enjoyed the dubious benefits of six channels, during the last year of the UDP it expanded public access to the constitutional process. Moreover, it provided the right with the capacity to address a mass constituency that did not read the press or attend the relatively few rallies held by conservative parties. (The MNR remained a 'closed' and cell-based organisation whilst the ADN's more frequent public events were dominated by its youth and tended to be aggressive.) In the process, conservative politicians acquired new rhetorical skills, replacing the customary injunctions to sacrifice with a preparedness to field direct questions and engage in frank interviews. The results were not always impressive — Banzer remained a notably poor speaker — but television coverage undoubtedly assisted the 1985 election victory and laid the ground for much more concerted exploitation of the medium thereafter. The left, attached to the culture of mass meetings and pamphleteering, lagged badly even when it possessed access.

The importance of television as an effective 'journal of record' as well as the primary medium for political exchange was reflected by the attention given to the televised political forum of May 1985 organised by the CEPB. This event, which in the past would have taken place in the university (with the attendant disputes over access to the right), ratified the emergence of the entrepreneurs' corporate association as a major political actor, signalling a 'new right' that subsequently gained considerable influence — but not outright dominance — in the conservative governments of Paz Estenssoro and Paz Zamora.

Prior to 1982 the CEPB had operated principally as a lobby group and had a lower profile than that of the private mine owners' Asociación Nacional de Mineros Medianos (ANMM) which, along

with the *ganaderos* of the Beni and commercial farmers of Santa
Cruz, campaigned on a sectoral basis rather than through regional
chambers of commerce. The CEPB's rapid rise to prominence under
the leadership of Fernando Illanes may be attributed to a number of
factors. First, when the UDP entered office it was far from clear that
the MNR would consistently support the interests of private capital,
and while the ADN was far more reliable in this respect, its political
prospects did not look particularly good. Secondly, the inclusion of
the PCB in the government and the high profile taken by the COB
engendered a genuine fear of expanded state intervention. Thirdly,
the rapid deterioration of the economy damaged many productive
businesses. Fourthly, low expectations of military intervention
prompted local business to 'go public' where previously it would
have negotiated with officers behind the scenes. This had the added
advantage of demonstrating the CEPB's 'civic responsibility', and it
tended to give more prominence to the positive promulgation of
capitalist 'common sense' than to simple expressions of anti-
communism, although this was certainly not lacking.

Finally, it has been suggested that economic developments over
the previous decade had encouraged the emergence of a 'new entrepreneur' — a beneficiary of the expansion of agro-business and
cheap credit under Banzer, bolstered by the relative strengthening of
private mining (ANMM) and banking (ASOBAN), better educated
and less overtly 'political' than the generation that had arisen in the
1950s in the penumbra of the MNR's short-lived but extremely
powerful *Célula de Importadores*. It should be stressed that this interpretation is based on only impressionistic evidence and may easily be
qualified on a range of points, but it is far from implausible. Leading
figures such as Illanes, the Sánchez de Lozada brothers and Ronald
Maclean were by no means 'apolitical' — Gonzalo Sánchez de Lozada
(MNR) and Maclean (ADN) were highly active militants of their parties
— but they presented themselves first and foremost as entrepreneurs.[22]
Relatively young, bilingual and university educated (usually in the US),
they eschewed the customary reticence of local businessmen, and
possessed strong ties with both foreign capital and professional econo-
mists. Moreover, all shared a commitment to neo-liberalism, which by
no means enjoyed absolute hegemony within the CEPB but had

considerable external academic and political support, particularly from Chile, where these groups had long-standing links. Extreme caution should be exercised in viewing these attributes with relation to interpretative models for the restructuring of other South American political economies in the 1970s, not least because that of Bolivia was qualitatively smaller and more backward as well as being chronically dependent upon revenue from an illegal export. Indeed, it is indicative that the MNR's Nueva Política Económica (NPE) was devised by a Harvard professor (Jeffrey Sachs) and directed by a local businessman who had spent much of his life in the US (Sánchez de Lozada).

As has been noted, neo-liberalism was not rapidly embraced by either the ADN or the MNR, which initially preferred the short-term rewards of berating the UDP for failing to maintain real wages. However, by November 1984 it was clear that the economy would be the most important issue in an election that the right was almost certain to win. Heterodoxy had manifestly failed; true 'shock' had not been attempted since 1956; resumption of relations with the IMF and international creditors had become a priority after March 1984; and the internal opposition to deflation had already exhausted its political resources in combating a less than radical variant. The principal problem was the adoption and propagation of a mercantilist ideology capable of resisting the inevitable backlash under democratic conditions. Neither the (distant) memory of the 1956–1957 stabilisation nor the more recent experience of stability under Banzer provided sufficient conditions for this, although the former undoubtedly recommended the policy to significant sectors of both parties. In the event, the very scale of the crisis compelled the taking of an option that provoked widespread dissent, could only be realised through the use of force, and depended upon *narcodólares* for its success.

## The MNR–ADN Alliance, August 1985–1989

Within a fortnight of assuming office in August 1985 the government of Víctor Paz Estenssoro gave Bolivians a new phrase — 'veintiuno cero sesenta' — that was henceforth to occupy a central place in the lexicon of both daily life and politics. Decree 21060, introduced on 29 August, set a regional precedent for rapid and dramatic stabilisation measures adopted by incoming administrations. (The examples of Carlos Andrés Pérez in Venezuela and Menem in Argentina, both in 1989, most clearly follow the pattern.) Nowhere else in Latin America, however, were the results so emphatic and enduring — the very reason why this decree, alone of all republican ordinances (including those for the nationalisation of the mines and agrarian reform in October 1952 and August 1953 respectively), is known by its number of issue, which soon acquired a status akin to that of an alchemic formula to celebrants and detractors alike. For the government the decree was but the first — if the most vital — step of a 'New Economic Policy', but this term never achieved popular resonance, perhaps because it inferred a superior modernity for the many whom it prejudiced and who were less impressed by the stabilisation it brought to prices than by the acute contraction of jobs and welfare that accompanied it. The results of this were, as the authors of the policy readily admitted, conducive to existential instability and a substantial reduction in the standard of living — neither of which was properly measured or reflected in official statistics.

Although Decree 21060 will undoubtedly dominate both the formal history and popular memory of the 1985–1989 government, it was not, of course, the sole issue of consequence — even in the economic sphere, where the collapse of the international tin price in October 1985 and continued *narcotráfico* had a major impact. The axis of political life shifted substantially to the right but, despite the relative solidity of the MNR–ADN alliance until the final months of the Paz Estenssoro government, politics was by no means stagnant. The trial of García Mesa; increasing collaboration by the MIR with the administration; the emergence of a '*cholo populism*' headed by Carlos Palenque; and the holding in 1987 of the first municipal elections since 1949 all interacted closely with popular discontent over stabilisation and its attendant reductions of real wages and public expenditure to make public life both charged and unpredictable. Such conflict was no longer determined by the 'ultimatumist tests' of both policy and institutionalism witnessed under the UDP. Yet it signalled that, however widespread popular resignation and debilitated the mass organisations, activism remained vital and could not be ignored in either the formulation or implementation of official policy.

## The Economy

Sánchez de Lozada's prescription for economic recovery was one of orthodox neo-liberalism. Under Decree 21060 he sought to obtain a 'realistic' exchange rate, decrease the public sector wage bill, free almost all prices, and lift most restrictions on financial operations, including those on dollar transactions. Through Decree 21369 (July 1986) he effectively opened up the economy to full external competition by imposing a uniform import tariff of 20 per cent. In March 1986 the government introduced a major tax reform to enhance state revenue. In August of that year (Decree 21377) Comibol was 'decentralised' as a first step towards privatisation; in June 1987 the Caja Nacional de Seguro Social (CNSS) was deprived of many of its central welfare functions. In March 1988 the government declared the 'decentralisation' of the Corporación Boliviana de Fomento (CBF) to regional development corporations, and also attempted to devolve responsibility for education to local authorities.

Only some of these policies registered success in their own terms, but all were undertaken with the clear objective of maintaining tight control of the money supply and eradicating the fiscal deficit so as to restore finance flows from the IMF and foreign banks. Although these institutions had long urged both monetarist and free market policies, the Paz Estenssoro government adopted such policies of its own volition, and only later (March 1986) sought external support. The Sánchez de Lozada team was convinced of the merits of 'shock', determined to rectify the fiscal crisis in short order, and entertained few doubts as to the methods for 'restructuring'. Although the Fondo Social de Emergencia (FSE) was established in December 1985, and 'reactivation' of the economy formally begun under Decree 21660 of July 1987, the former was but a minor palliative and the latter remained moribund.[23] Despite protestations to the contrary in the period prior to the 1989 poll, the real thrust of economic management from August 1985 was towards deflationary stabilisation. This was affected in contradictory fashion by both the collapse of the tin price — which facilitated the break-up of Comibol but had a profoundly adverse effect on both export and fiscal revenue — and the continuation of *narcotráfico* — which provided an important source of dollars and 'informal' employment, alleviating some of the rigours of contraction, but also bolstering regional inflation and prejudicing US aid. In broad terms it is difficult to deny that the cocaine trade (see below) provided a critical support for stabilisation, and many account it a decisive factor, certainly offsetting the recession in mining. Nevertheless, proper weight should be given to the radicalism of government policy and the resolution with which its core elements were implemented.

The heart of Decree 21060 and its immediate impact lay in exchange rate policy. Here Sánchez de Lozada produced a *de facto* devaluation of the order of 93 per cent by unifying overnight the official and informal rates for the dollar. The official rate was subsequently allowed to float through the mechanism of daily dollar auctions by the Central Bank (BCB). Between December 1985 and February 1986 internal MNR disputes over the degree of contraction this was causing led to some relaxation in control of money supply with the result that the now legal informal rate began to rise faster. However, this was rapidly curbed, and thereafter the official rate shadowed that on the open market sufficiently closely for the general effect to be one of parity.[24]

The essential corollary to the unification of the exchange rates was a freeze on all public sector wages at pre-devaluation rates. Although the important and complex system of bonuses was consolidated into the basic wage, the impact of this measure was extremely severe. At the same time, indexation and the minimum wage were abolished in both public and private spheres, and legal curbs on redundancy were greatly relaxed. By the first half of 1986 total real wages had fallen to less than two-thirds of their level of the previous year, those in the public sector being significantly lower. Moreover, the state wage bill was further diminished by the 'voluntary retirement' of public sector workers as a result of the massive reduction in real pay. The number of state employees fell by at least 10 per cent within 12 months, the impact being sharpest in rural education, where perhaps 25,000 teachers left their posts.[25]

The liberalisation of prices that accompanied the fluctuation of the exchange rate produced an immediate increase in inflation as previously compressed prices rose to their 'real' levels. In September 1985 inflation was still at 57 per cent per month. But in October inflation became negative as demand all but disappeared and the collapse of the COB'S resistance made it plain that wage compensation would not be conceded. Notwithstanding the flurry of official nerves (bitterly opposed by Sánchez de Lozada) at the end of the year, the enforced contraction of the economy was secured. In 1986 GDP decreased by nearly 3 per cent, the per capita level by nearly 6 per cent. Overall growth thereafter oscillated between 2 per cent and 3 per cent — that is, barely retrieving the 1984 level — whereas per capita growth continued to be negative in 1987, and barely exceeded zero in 1988. In 1987 formal exports stood at 60 per cent of the 1980 level and were well below those registered under the UDP; reductions in imports proved extremely hard to achieve — narcodollars undoubtedly playing a part — but a trade balance was finally reached in 1988. This did not, however, produce a significant amelioration in the levels of un- and underemployment generated by stabilisation. The first rose almost instantaneously to 20 per cent whilst the second — in many respects more indicative of the health of an economy such as Bolivia's — touched 60 per cent.[26] By the end of the government, the official level of open unemployment stood at 11.5 per cent, but the real level was undoubtedly several points higher — probably 15 per cent — whilst underemployment had been reduced by a smaller margin.

The central objective of Decree 21060 to eliminate the fiscal deficit was pursued equally vigorously in terms of revenue and expenditure. Aside from the ordained and de facto reductions in the state payroll, a freeze was imposed on all public investment, tight controls placed on financial management, and ceilings on prices either lifted or removed altogether. Here the impact was most marked in the case of the state oil company, YPFB, the price of oil and its derivatives being raised from one day to the next by a factor of seven to slightly above international prices. Whilst this contributed to the immediate post-stabilisation inflation rate, it enabled YPFB to meet all its tax liabilities and thereby become the principal source of public revenue under the MNR, its contribution to the treasury rising from 12.7 per cent of the total in 1983 to 56.7 per cent in 1986.[27]

Exchange rate unification depended upon 're-dollarisation' — either directly or through indexation — of domestic accounts and the lifting of all but basic fiscal controls over the banking sector. A key factor in this regard was the maintenance of an open 'dollar window' permitting the circulation of narco-dollars. This legalisation of the 'grey market' undoubtedly bolstered the banks, which also benefited from processing tax payments and other state transactions. However, the new financial climate did little to suppress existing illegal or foolhardy customs with respect to loans, resulting in a number of collapses and closures as well as the withdrawal, in September 1987, of the banks' responsibility for administering 'reactivation funds'. On the other hand, the government proved more resolute and successful in removing a particularly powerful 'union mafia' from the BCB, restoring a semblance of sobriety to a nominally independent institution which had effectively been beyond the control of its directorate (and the government) for a number of years.

The introduction of the uniform import tariff at 20 per cent took place nearly a year after Decree 21060, and since to all intents and purposes it opened the borders to foreign commodities, it was predictably criticised by the Cámara de Industrias. However, the Cámara was a weak lobby and could not win support from the CEPB. Moreover, exporters were provided a modicum of help through a 10 per cent rebate on their inputs. In fact, in 1986 manu-facturing industry registered its first positive growth for nearly a decade, having experienced a much deeper and earlier contraction than any other sector. After being driven to the wall by inefficiency, contraband, extremely high interest rates and formidable foreign competition, a very small and backward industrial sector now began to exploit the suppression of wages, open labour market and the appreciable spare capacity left by the recession.

The dismantling of barriers to external trade was clearly signalled in August 1985, and by March 1986 the government had already secured the basis upon which to reopen relations with the IMF through the first stand-by loan agreement in the better part of a decade. In June the Club of Paris agreed to terms for renewed repay-ment of the external debt that, if not exactly as bountiful as the government claimed, was less onerous than some feared. This accord laid the basis for later and much-publicised purchases of debt on the discount market as well as a controversial 'debt for nature' swap.

What had initially seemed a strange — even ambitious — step by Sánchez de Lozada and Jeffrey Sachs (who harboured no amity for the banks) to administer the purge on their own first and then petition for help from the banks proved viable.

It is notable that agreement with the IMF was secured two days before congress approved the 1986–1987 budget — the first time in more than two decades that this process had been undertaken. Both the fund and the government were determined that there should be absolute compliance with budgetary limits, particularly by the state corporations, which had a very long history of exceeding their allocations from the treasury and were the principal source of official debt. In 1986 congress agreed to a fiscal deficit of $175 million, or 6 per cent of GDP. In fact, so efficient were the government's constraints that the year ended with a deficit of only 4 per cent of GDP, which must have been the cause of as much shock as gratification in Washington; the pupils were proving more zealous than their masters. Henceforth the government attempted, with partial success, to limit adjustments in public sector wages to the budget, but although this acquired unprecedented importance in terms of policy, it failed to become a dominant feature in broader political life, probably because it ceded very little in exceptionally straitened times.

In 1986 the budget certainly attracted far less popular attention than did the tax reform of May which had already been agreed with the IMF. This measure introduced a property tax and a value-added tax on consumption (initially set at 10 per cent). Although both the MNR and ADN had been quick to scupper the UDP's efforts at fiscal reform, it was evident that Decree 21060 needed substantial administrative and legislative supplementation if government revenue was to regain a measure of reliability. Between 1978 and 1983 the ratio of central government taxes to GDP had declined from 11.5 per cent to 2.8 per cent, not least because of collection time-lags in inflationary times. To oversee the new schemes the government established a separate fiscal ministry, but this was soon reintegrated with that of finance, and collection — but not assessment — was farmed out to the private banks. In 1986 all taxes rose to 13 per cent of GDP, and by 1988 they stood at 17.5 per cent; in the same period internal revenue taxes increased from 3.2 per cent to 6.3 per cent of GDP.[28] However, this

rather impressive scenario should be seen in the light of the fact that
between 1986 and 1988 the proportion of central government revenue
derived from these taxes rose from 24 per cent to 36 per cent whilst the
share provided by YPFB remained at over 50 per cent. Indeed, the Paz
government's policy of 'liberating' the corporation's prices and
enforcing its strict compliance with fiscal obligations meant that at the
end of the decade YPFB's share of treasury revenue was roughly four
times higher than at its start. (In the same period taxes on mining fell
from 16 per cent to 0.4 per cent.)

Fiscal recovery, then, relied more heavily upon the freeing of
prices in a single strategic sector than upon reform. In this regard it
should be noted that the majority of urban Bolivians use canister gas
for cooking and were thus directly hit by YPFB's price hikes — a fact
made abundantly clear by the frequent impromptu *bloqueos* of streets
by consumers whose empty containers provided most useful impedi-
menta. Equally, it is of no little consequence that the new property tax
was not applied in the countryside, where there were well-supported
demonstrations against the reform in June 1986 after the government
agreed only to delay implementation for one year. Renewed protests
in October 1987 forced a further delay, and in April 1988 (Decree
21923) small rural properties were formally excluded from the new
regime. However, the 1989 budget restored provision despite the fact
that no enforcement took place in an election year.

This official nervousness was not misplaced since in both the altiplano and the valleys there were tangible indications that the proposed
tax was suspected of heralding an attack on the agrarian reform of
1953. For many this was more of a concern than the direct financial
impact, although the contraction of agriculture throughout the MNR
government did not bode well in that respect either. Indeed, it may not
be fanciful to suggest that core sections of the *campesinado* viewed the
proposal as similar to the measures of the tyrant Mariano Melgarejo,
whose 'free market' legislation laid the basis for a concerted offensive
against communal lands in the last third of the nineteenth century.
Here one might also note that, immediately upon coming to office, the
MNR tried to levy a forced loan, which was the standard fiscal mechanism of the last century. This measure was opposed — for sound
political reasons — by the ADN, and was eventually rejected by
congress in January 1986, not to be heard of again.

The MNR was, in fact, planning to alter the structure of highland agriculture in particular, and in September 1988 it tabled before congress an agrarian development law that proposed, albeit in very vague terms, the reduction of the *minifundia* that had been propagated by the 1953 reform. These were correctly depicted as diminishing the overall efficiency of production. Yet if arguments based on economies of scale were irrefutable within the portals of the ministry and its think-tanks, they stood to cut very little ice indeed with those beneficiaries of the reform for whom title was sacrosanct and economic rationality only partly dependent upon input–output ratios. The legislation was withdrawn in January 1989, presumably because it threatened to jeopardise the MNR campaign for the May election. Whatever the reason, the government could scarcely afford to aggravate the problems it was already experiencing in the coca zones, and since Víctor Paz had relied heavily upon the peasantry in the 1950s and early 1960s as a counterweight to the miners and left, he would have been acutely aware of the importance of retaining at least a neutral constituency in the countryside. (In the event, on the basis of a calculation limited to the results of *provincias* — that is, all votes except those of departmental capitals — the MNR narrowly won the 1989 poll in the countryside from the MIR with 165,800 votes against 156,900, but it did not come first in any highland department and was forced into a poor third position in rural La Paz.) In 1985 the MNR had campaigned under the somewhat strange slogan of *agropoder,* which appeared to be equally addressed to the subsistence/local market and lowland agro-export sectors. However, little was heard of this catchphrase after 29 August and, following recovery from *El Niño* in 1984 and 1985, the recession in agriculture (most of coca and all of cocaine excepted) remained more consistent than in any other sector of the economy.

The crisis in mining was more acute and widely publicised because of the traditional importance of minerals to exports and central government revenue and the fact that progressive decline in the first part of the decade was rapidly brought to a head by the collapse of the tin price. Although this affected both public and private sectors, the immediate impact on Comibol was by a wide margin the most severe because of its size, relative inefficiency and simultaneous vulnerability to external pressure and direct state intervention. Between 1985 and 1987 both were applied without quarter, with the result that approximately 23,000 workers of a total labour force of 28,000 were made redundant, the core tin complex of Siglo XX-Catavi all but mothballed, total production scythed to a fifth of the levels of the 1970s, and public sector exports halted altogether for a year.[29] It is here that one encounters the single most important factor in the decline in legal exports that was, in fact, more pronounced than that witnessed under the UDP: from $827.7 million in 1982 to $759.6 million in 1984 against a fall from $665.4 million in 1985 to $580.6 million in 1988.

Although the government formally 'decentralised' Comibol into regional enterprises (Decree 21377, August 1986), the ministry retained direct control over *relocalización,* which was too large and conflictive an issue to be managed by small and effectively bankrupt holding companies dedicated to maintaining plant and administering the sale of easily realisable assets to the private sector. (This was also the case with YPFB, where central control was formally stronger and worker resistance to lay-offs more effective.)

Throughout the regime the FSTMB and individual plant unions battled over both closures and the terms of redundancy, proffering plans to maintain production and seeking to buy certain camps. However, with the partial exception of the Huanuni mine, the strike was now an impotent weapon and the rank and file divided over whether to defend jobs or fight for the best conditions in surrendering them. This became the central issue dividing the union, the first option generally being supported by the more political currents whilst the second was increasingly favoured by independents whose comrades were often voting with their feet out of resignation.[30] As pits were formally closed, *pulperías* left unsupplied, and funds for Comibol's schools and clinics cut off, the diaspora of miners and their families to the cities — principally El Alto and Cochabamba — and the Chapare marked a watershed in the country's industrial history. Even the gradual recovery of the tin price at the end of the decade did little to reverse this process, most of the upturn in production occurring within the private sector.

Whereas decentralisation in Comibol and YPFB amounted to little more than an ideologically convenient fiction, this policy had a sharp impact when applied (March 1988) to the management of the departmental development corporations, education and health. The corporations inherited the regional installations of the CBF with varying degrees of success depending upon existing infrastructure whilst the CNSS was effectively disestablished (June 1987) and sectoral health systems acquired increasing importance as the already impoverished public hospital network was subjected to withering cuts (administered directly through the central budget). As a consequence, the normally cautious medical profession made frequent recourse to strikes and found itself converging with the union movement to an unprecedented degree. (The Colegio Médico, which had been established under Banzer as a strictly professional association, now became the site of rising partisanship.)

This was far more the case with respect to education, where the efforts of the highly unpopular minister Ipiña (who had transferred his allegiance from the MNRI) first to reduce expenditure and then to make the departments responsible for administration and finance, were stalled by both union and regionalist mobilisation throughout the government's term. Indeed, it was perhaps this issue that most effectively concentrated popular antipathy to the consequences of Decree 21060 and damaged the regime's image. By 1989 Ipiña had not been able to realise his reforms and yet he had presided over four years of stoppages, demonstrations, growing truancy and radically reduced school rolls as the combination of absent teachers (notable transferees to contraband and the penumbra of *narcotráfico*) and the demands of maintaining family subsistence drove thousands of children into full-time 'informal' work.[31]

It appears that the government was rather taken aback by this development and failed to appreciate that grudging popular acquiescence in the imposition of mercantilist logic with respect to productive industry did not extend to basic services and welfare, where decentralisation was soon recognised to be cosubstantial with further budgetary decreases and an erosion of entitlement. The fact that education enjoyed a particularly high status and was still an inextricable feature of daily life gave this opposition a notably broad and non-partisan quality. This was channelled through the *comités cívicos*, which gained unprecedented authority and support in their battles with a government that was formally committed to devolution and yet strenuously resisted this in practice with regard to payments of the important departmental royalties from YPFB production (long an issue of contention between the capital and the departments). Facing an unexpectedly strong backlash from bodies it had assumed would be compliant, the government retreated and had to accept the political consequences of itself administering cuts from the centre. As was evident from the municipal elections of 1987, the MNR was unprepared for the revivalism of local politics that its economic policy generated.

## Coca and Cocaine

Table 3.3 presents the principal public developments in the political economy of coca and cocaine under both the UDP and MNR administrations. From this it can be seen that official efforts to suppress *narcotráfico* were hindered by a number of factors: lack of political will; the strength of the coca lobby; disagreements and inefficiency within the military; and confusion over policy. (It should be noted that the table does not include general, low-scale activity within the police and judiciary.) Such a picture is familiar and, indeed, conforms quite closely to the objections raised by Washington, which in 1986 and 1987 withheld some $17.5 million in economic aid as a result of failure to meet targets for the eradication of coca.[32] (A much smaller quantity of military aid was frozen due to problems with suppression of cocaine). However, the obstacles to this were truly formidable and encompassed much more substantial issues than the debility of the Bolivian state and questionable practices by elements of its servants. Important though these factors are, they remain symptomatic of a more profound crisis rooted in the collapse of the formal economy, popular desperation, and misconceived North American policy and actions. The debate over these issues is as complex as it is passionate, and it cannot be properly rehearsed here. Yet a few brief observations may serve to provide a broad context within which to approach this major phenomenon.

First, it should be noted that the illegal production of cocaine stems directly from the legal production and consumption of the coca leaf in the same country. As in Peru — but not Colombia — the market in coca has been an integral element of Aymara and

Quechua society for centuries, possessing important cultural and religious features that could only be criminalised at the cost of a major
breakdown in social order. As a consequence, the insistence of the
US that *narcotráfico* be attacked via an offensive on coca was from the
start riven with problems. Whilst the claim that the 'free sale in coca
is equivalent to legalising the production of cocaine'[33] may be
disputed, it is nevertheless the case that during the 1980s the connection became very strong. Moreover, coca bushes and leaves are more
readily detectable than is low-bulk, high-value cocaine paste. Yet, in
operational as well as political terms, concentration upon coca presents sharp difficulties that La Paz tried consistently to avoid and
Washington was late and reluctant to recognise.

## Table 3.3: Coca and Cocaine, 1983–1989

**1983**

| | |
|---|---|
| April | Visit of US Attorney General William French Smith; US–Bolivian agreement to reduce coca production to 'level of legitimate demand'; CSUTCB national *bloqueo* cuts off major cities, suspended upon government agreement to reconsider accord with US. |
| June | Rafael Otazo meets with Roberto Suárez. |
| Aug. | Confidential accord with US to reduce Chapare production by 4,000 hectares by end of 1985 breaks April agreement with growers. Government establishes permanent control of transport and sale of leaf, promises 'substantial police presence' in Chapare; US to channel development aid to region. |

**1984**

| | |
|---|---|
| Jan. | August 1983 agreement revealed. |
| Feb. | Cochabamba deputies attack agreement as unconstitutional. |
| March | 2,000 Chapare growers demonstrate in Cochabamba. |
| May | Congress of Chapare growers demands Supreme Court ruling on constitutionality of agreement with US. |
| Aug. | Military zone declared in Chapare; UMOPAR deployed. Coca growers' *bloqueo* of Cochabamba; action ends with official agreement not to intervene in coca market; UMOPAR withdrawn from area; military enters for six months. Otazo-Suárez meeting revealed. |

| | |
|---|---|
| Sept. | Sinahota cocaine market halted; trading shifts to Yapacani region. |
| Oct. | Government bans shipments of leaf from Chapare and controls movements within it; capture of Suarez ordered. |
| Nov. | *Bloqueo* of Cochabamba in demand of free sale of leaf and end to military occupation; transport ban and curfew lifted; military withdraw. |

**1985**

| | |
|---|---|
| Feb. | UMOPAR redeployed in Chapare. |
| June | Coca price at $800–850 per *carga* (100lb.); *bloqueos* of Cochabamba; three *campesinos* killed by police. |
| Nov. | Ministry of Interior agreement with representatives of Chimore and Chapare growers' federations to eradicate 1,000 hectares by mid-December at $350 compensation per hectare. Pact rejected by rank and file. |
| | US Foreign Assistance Act for FY 1986 stipulates that Bolivia eradicate 1,000 hectares by end 1985 to receive full aid. |
| Dec. | Coca price at $200–400 per *carga*. |

**1986**

| | |
|---|---|
| Jan. | UMOPAR camp at Ivirgarzama besieged by *campesinos* after rape of local woman. |
| April | 'Fuerzas Unidas' joint military operations with US forces. |
| May | Coca leaf price at $125–150 per *carga*. |
| June | Growers halt voluntary eradication due to government failure to release economic aid. |
| July | 'Operation Blast Furnace' with 170 US troops and six helicopters. Widespread protests; Chapare leaf price falls to $10–20 per *carga* (production costs at $30–40); resignation of Ñuflo Chávez from MNR in protest at US troop presence. |
| Aug. | Some 100 hectares eradicated under Nov. 1985 agreement; government petitions US for $500 million in aid to fight *narcotráfico*. |
| Sept. | Assassination of scientist Noel Kempff Mercado by traffickers at Huanchaca, Santa Cruz. |
| Oct. | UMOPAR attacked by populace of Santa Ana de Yacuma, Beni. Official closure of Huanchaca case; accusations of 'cover-up' of complicity/inefficiency of UMOPAR and DEA. |
| Nov. | US troops leave; leaf price rises to $40–50 per *carga*. Departamento Nacional de Sustancias Peligrosas (DNSP) |

|       | purged. Plan Trienal para la Lucha contra el Narcotráfico published; calls for eradication of 50,000 hectares of illicit coca by 1990, including half of Yungas production; $320 million 'reactivation funds' promised, 80 per cent to come from foreign donors; compensation for eradication set at $2,000 per hectare. |
| --- | --- |
| Dec. | Negotiations with Club of Paris include aid to fight cocaine trade. |
| **1987** | |
| Jan. | Plan Trienal introduced. |
| March | COB declares state of emergency in protest at Plan; draft drug law published. |
| May | Growers demand closure of UN agricultural project in Yungas. *Bloqueos in* La Paz and Cochabamba coca zones against Plan; four *campesinos* killed by police, many arrested. |
| June | Leaf price at $100 per *carga*. Official agreement with COB, CSUTCB and Yungas and Chapare federations for voluntary eradication; specifically excludes eradication by force and use of herbicides; guarantees legal status of cultivation; effectively nullifies Plan Trienal. |
| Aug. | Publication of US–Bolivian agreement to eradicate 1,800 hectares by August 1988. |
| Sept. | $8.7 million in US aid frozen for failure to meet 1986–1987 eradication target. |
| Nov. | *Campesino* leaders denounce government failure to pay credits and provide services under June 1987 agreement. |
| Dec. | Some 1,000 hectares eradicated since Sept. at compensation of $2,000 per hectare (mostly in Carrasco province). |
| **1988** | |
| Jan. | Leaf price at $25–40 per *carga*. National congress of growers (ANAPCOCA) in Cochabamba suspends voluntary eradication because of government's 'bad faith'. |
| Feb. | COB–ANAPCOCA–government agreement ratifies that of June 1987, provides for growers' participation in Plan Integral de Desarrollo y Sustitución (PIDYS) for coca zones. |
| March | Chapare growers halt eradication due to alleged UMOPAR abuses and lack of aid. |

| | |
|---|---|
| April | Visit of US Attorney General Edwin Meese; COB hunger strike over drugs law and budget. |
| | *Narcovideo'* scandal implicates leading members of ADN with Suarez. |
| May | *Campesino* demonstrations in La Paz and Cochabamba in opposition to proposed drug law defining coca as a 'controlled substance'; ANAPCOCA breaks negotiations with government. |
| June | Leaf price at $50–65 per *carga*. |
| | Growers' *bloqueo* of Cochabamba for two days; government offices occupied and 10 Bolivian and US officials held hostage. Suarez dubs Victor Paz 'the Viceroy of Cocaine'. |
| | Ten *campesinos* killed by UMOPAR in Villa Tunari, Chapare. ANAPCOCA–government talks collapse again. |
| July | Drugs law approved by congress; establishes maximum of 12,000 hectares for legal demand, the rest being subject to eradication (at annual target of 5–8,000 hectares); compensation retained at $2,000. Roberto Suarez arrested, in unclear circumstances, in the Beni. |
| Aug. | ANAPCOCA congress, Cochabamba, declares non-compliance with law. Leaf price at $120–130 per *carga*. |
| Sept. | 120 hectares eradicated since July. |
| Oct. | Removal of commander of army's VII Division for selling arms to traffickers; UMOPAR withdrawn from Guayamerín after clashes with populace. |
| Nov. | ANAPCOCA congress rejects eradiction under new law. |
| Dec. | Total of 200 hectares eradicated in last 12 months. |
| **1989** | |
| Jan. | Drugs law comes into operation. |
| | Jorge Alderete (as Subsecretario de Desarrollo Alternativo, in charge of coca/cocaine policy) accuses DEA of domination of operations and withholding information. |
| | Publication of extracts of 'narco-cassettes' in London and Madrid ties ADN leader Arce Carpio and others to Suárez; Arce later resigns. |
| March | Alderete resigns, accusing US of failure to reduce consumption. |
| April | ANAPCOCA resumes talks with government. |

| | |
|---|---|
| June | Ministry of Interior announces forcible eradication in Chapare from July but without presence of military. |
| | DEA criticises lack of local support in fighting *narcotráfico*. Six killed in Santa Ana de Yacuma in exchange of fire between UMOPAR and navy during operation to detain traffickers. ANAPCOCA–government agreement ratifies growers' participation in PIDYS. |
| | Cochabamba *campesino* leader Evo Morales arrested and tortured by police for 'protecting' trafficker 'El Cura'. |
| July | US Ambassador Gelbard declares 'the Bolivian government does not have control over its own territory' with reference to Santa Ana incident. |
| | Drugs law date for forced eradication in Chapare falls due; no action taken or forces deployed. |
| | Government postpones forced eradication *sine die* and calls for fresh talks with growers. |
| Sept. | PIDYS ratified by new government and given statutory basis in DS 22270; no move on forced eradication. |

The sheer scale of coca production presents a major challenge to control. By the mid-1980s Bolivia accounted for perhaps one-third of the world supply of leaf, and if estimates vary widely — in 1988 the Bolivian government put production at 155,000 tons from 60,000 hectares whereas the State Department figure was 56,500 tons from 40,300 hectares — they still reflect a significant economic activity that may properly be called an industry.[34] Although this tonnage was less than that produced in Peru (and Bolivia's production of finished cocaine lags well behind that of Colombia — in terms of direct imports into the US it probably stood at 15 per cent against 75 per cent), the industry has a far greater impact within the national economy than does coca/cocaine in the much larger and more diversified economies of the other two countries. In terms of revenue, coca production in 1986 was worth approximately $230 million — or 20 per cent of total receipts from agriculture — whilst income from cocaine was, in all likelihood, in excess of $600 million — barely less than formal export revenue.[35]

Sums of this scale do not simply reflect the high price of an illegal substance; in fact, the US wholesale price fell between 1980 and 1988 from $55,000 to $15,000 per kilo — the ratio between the prices of leaf and derived cocaine on US streets being of the order of 500:1.[36] They also indicate extensive participation in the industry. The estimate of the Bolivian senate of a total of 80,000 cultivators of leaf in the two core growing zones of Yungas (La Paz) and Chapare (Cochabamba) is not unreasonable.[37] However, to this figure must be added at least 25,000 *pisadores* (treaders of leaf), 20,000 other people employed in semi-skilled or skilled work, and at least 1,000 at the upper end of the trade. If the total of growers — identified as heads of family — is multiplied by three to allow for family and other labour, the resulting figure for those engaged directly in production of coca is 240,000 and those in cocaine at over 45,000.

Yet these figures still do not represent the full human reach of the industry, which not only depends upon protection and allied services (legal, financial, etc.) but has also generated a dynamic sub-economy of inputs — both at local retail level (e.g. kerosene and toilet paper in the city of Cochabamba) and at wholesale level (ether; sulphuric acid) — as well as local marketing (e.g. through established networks for trading in chicha beer in the Cochabamba valley, probably affecting 5 per cent of the population directly. The population of Chapare — the main cocaine-related coca zone — rose from 27,000 in 1967 to 120,000 in 1985, but even by 1981 over 400,000 people (29,000 vehicles) were entering this region.[38] This reflects the importance of seasonal migratory employment, initially undertaken largely through kinship ties but after the mid-1980s increasingly prompted by climatic disruption and economic slump in the altiplano (particularly Oruro and Potosí). These factors, together with the overwhelming concentration of coca production on small and modest plots, bestow a resolutely 'popular' character on all but the very highest echelons of the industry.

During the 1980s the price of both coca and cocaine was highly elastic, but even at its lowest level — in mid-1986 — coca yielded a revenue per hectare ($2,600) four times greater than that from citrus fruits or avocados, with which the US wished to replace it. (At the time of the highest prices — late 1984; $9,000 per hectare — the ratio was 19:1.)[39] Simple crop substitution was, therefore, contrary to all economic sense for the growers. Equally, government purchase of leaf — the main UDP strategy — could not match 'real' prices, and official compensation for eradication was, at $2,000 per hectare from early 1987, well below the growers' demands, which at $6,000 were realistic in terms of 'opportunity cost' if not in terms of the state's capacity to pay. The incentives to abandon an activity that provided a modicum of security against the process of pauperisation coursing through the rest of the economy were minimal. (This applied even more within processing, where a *pisador* could earn in a night more than a schoolteacher did in a month.)[40]

These major obstacles to both criminalising and suppressing production were accentuated by the fact that in those areas where the trade was largely in the form of semi-processed or (occasionally) finished paste — principally Santa Cruz and the Beni — the state was unusually weak and the control of wealthy *narcotraficantes* strengthened by long-standing traditions of contraband and landlord patronage. Here conspicuous consumption was complemented by significant expenditure on infrastructure and services, enhancing popular support for the trade and raising the threat of social conflict no less than was the case in the core cultivation areas (e.g. popular resistance in Santa Ana de Yacuma, San Borja and Guayamerín listed in Table 3.3).

More broadly, the close association of the military regimes of 1980–1982 with *narcotráfico* had not, principally for the reasons cited above, generated widespread repudiation of the industry as a whole. On the contrary, as the economic crisis deepened under the civilian administrations it acquired a measure of legitimacy, and the political scope for attacking it diminished significantly except in two respects. First, the pressure from Washington was considerable and required some form of response. (The real impact of moral pressure was negligible until mid-1989, when the scale of killing by the Colombian *narcos* engendered genuine revulsion and sympathy for the plight of that country; as a result North American sermons were treated with rather less disdain.) Secondly, outside of the *Oriente* the leading traffickers were popularly viewed as corrupt *arrivistes as* well as major beneficiaries of the dictatorship; outside their own regions they could not bank on much sympathy, still less stage a political campaign under their own colours. Yet, if suppression in general threatened to close off a critical economic safety-valve, compliance with US demands raised authentic problems with regard to sovereignty and claims on national pride. Equally, the failure to conduct all but the most token purge of the military and civil service after 1982 meant that many who were subsequently charged with directing suppression were simultaneously benefiting directly or, more often, indirectly from the trade. Thus, in addition to the overwhelming economic and logistical problems — never resolved despite appreciable US assistance — the governments were faced with an acute ideological challenge.

One notable feature of this was the convergence of interested parties on the right with the left in objecting to suppression on anti-imperialist grounds — which, it might be noted, were even employed by the García Mesa regime once it had been ostracised by the Reagan White House. The arguments for this opposition were simple. Reduction of the *cocales* directly prejudiced the means of subsistence of hundreds of thousands of poor *campesinos,* whatever its final objective with respect to cocaine. These small farmers produced a legal crop for which there was no substitute that yielded remotely comparable earnings. Destruction of the cocaine factories invariably involved the punishment of lowly workers, not major dealers, very few of whom were ever caught and fewer still brought to trial. These raids were staged selectively — often to settle scores — simply drove production centres deeper into the backlands, and had no lasting impact on prices or production; even the catharsis experienced by the gringos was ephemeral. Futhermore, 'interdiction operations' were frequently attended by violence on the part of the police and armed forces, and they depended increasingly upon US intervention. Perhaps most important of all, the entire strategy of attacking production and supply, rather than demand and consumption, stemmed from a North American determination to transfer the blame and cost from its own rich citizens and state to their impoverished counterparts in Bolivia. The opprobium attached to this was further sharpened by the fact that the US was viewed as directly responsible for generating the broader economic crisis that prompted the upsurge of popular involvement in *narcotráfico,* and by its strenuous resistance to provision of adequate recompense for the sacrifices incurred on its behalf for adhering to free market (outlaw) forces. Such a position was not only hypocritical; its immorality was decidedly imperialist.

Such an outlook is not, of course, unique to Bolivia; aspects of it are equally evident in both Peru and Colombia, where it had an even sharper impact on national political life. However, the Bolivian experience was distinctive in two important and related respects: the generally low level of social violence associated with *narcotráfico* itself (closer to Peru than Colombia) and the absence of any guerrilla movement or substantial paramilitary forces (different from both other countries). While not exactly peaceable, production was partly legal and exacted a relatively slight social cost, at least until the late 1980s, when growing use of the debased and dangerous cocaine derivative *bazuko* by youths, particularly in Cochabamba, began to sharpen anxieties.[41] Even then, the violence surrounding the trade was seen as stemming from suppression, the state and the US — not local *traficantes*, and still less the growers, whose principal means of resistance were passive (the *bloqueo* above all else), mass-based and in conformity with the traditions of the popular movement. Furthermore, since involvement in the upper reaches of the trade was less based on clearly defined clans outside the political system than linked to membership of all sections of its civilian and military elite, no amount of official blandishments could overcome popular cynicism.

The passage of events outlined in Table 3.3 shows that, despite its recourse to national and US troops and the introduction of major new legislation, the MNR fared little better than had the UDP. Its more decisive actions were met with greater resistance, obliging resort to negotiations in which the state made strictly limited progress towards eradication. The conduct of UMOPAR remained unreliable. The armed forces persisted in their reluctance to be involved in unpopular operations and dependence upon US support opened up conflict within the party (Alderete, Ñuflo Chávez) as well as outside it, and the threat of scandal was never far off. Judging solely (and thus very conservatively) on the basis of 'errors and omissions' in the national accounts, the formally registered infusion of *narcodólares* was at least $64 million in 1986 (much higher thereafter). It is unlikely, however, that the MNR actively contrived this situation, which might be best viewed as an embarrassing windfall resulting from forces that otherwise transpired to be more intractable than those it faced in stabilising the formal economy.[42]

Popular disdain for the North American position did not lack some justified foundation. The US was exceptionally reluctant to deal with its unwanted monopsony (the European market remained slight) other than in time-honoured fashion. It held to the policy of crop substitution long after it had been shown to be fruitless; the public pronouncements of its local representatives exhibited an arrogance — sometimes intended, sometimes depressingly ingénue — that infuriated senior Bolivian officials; and it could not break from a coercive and conditional approach to development aid for the coca zones where, according to Ambassador Corr (later 'promoted' to El Salvador), electrification would only 'allow narcos to work at night'.[43] (The fact that they already did casts an even more forlorn light on this remark.) The price to be paid for an alternative approach was deemed too high, even after cocaine became a major issue in domestic politics. Like the MNR's drug law, the Bennett report was conspicuous by its failure to introduce real change.

Aware of this, the MNR, which had already invested the great bulk of its ideological capital in stabilisation, adopted a distinctly opportunist course. Haunted (if not taunted) by its supposed policy of *agropoder,* if failed to match rhetoric with practice when it came to curbing the most *agropoderosos.* Realistically depending upon a reputation for managerial efficiency rather than outstanding moral probity, it shuffled past the option of launching a popular crusade. Exasperated by the exigencies of ministering to the protests of the victims of its economic policies, it forebore from tarnishing the growers as another group of 'anarchosyndicalists'. Last, but by no means least, it recognised that voluble inaction was the key to preserving the boon provided to stabilisation policy by cocaine revenue. This, quite naturally, was a hostage to fortune, but Víctor Paz had good cause to be unconcerned about it, and despite all the bravura complaint after the 1989 poll, many a *movimientista* had reluctantly accepted that the price of the fearlessness of stabilisation was a resounding *voto de castigo,* leaving others to deal with the consequences. In the event, this view was shown to be correct, but it is a reflection of the extraordinary vagaries of politics over the prior four years that it very nearly transpired to be false.

## Politics

After the tumult of the UDP, formal political life under the MNR became 'little' in the sense that it was primarily concerned with tactical manoeuvres and administrative issues. There were few 'grand events' to interrupt the institutional calendar, and those that did occur — the visits of the West German president, the King of Spain and the Pope — had a strictly marginal impact on policy. Víctor Paz's sombre comportment was a significant element in this picture, not least by containing the tensions within the MNR caused by the severity of stabilisation.

These rotated predictably about the person of Sánchez de Lozada, who some claimed — incorrectly — had never actually sworn loyalty to the party and others saw — justifiably — as little less than a heretic in his attitude to *movimientista* traditions. His leading critic was Guillermo Bedregal, foreign minister and recent returner to the ranks after splitting with Paz over support for the coup of Colonel Natusch (whose short-lived cabinet Bedregal had effectively led). Since Bedregal had headed the initial effort in the early 1960s to restructure Comibol in the face of bitter union resistance, it was somewhat ironic that he should baulk at the social cost of this two decades later; a more plausible cause for his ill-concealed rancour lay with ambitions to succeed Paz as *jefe* or at least to become presidential candidate in 1989. Although Bedregal failed on both counts, this was not before he had succeeded in summoning appreciable support from the party's 'old guard' headed by the eternally unpredictable Ñuflo Chávez, who could still command some authority beyond his stronghold of Santa Cruz. The traditionalists disliked 'Goni's' refusal to adhere to rhetorical customs, his independent outlook and mercurial disposition, and, perhaps most of all, his bourgeois background — none of which was typical of the party leadership (except Víctor Paz himself). The fact that his policies also threatened to damn the MNR to electoral defeat provided the unstated impetus to this campaign, which emerged in the first months of the government and then receded until the pre-electoral period once it was clear that their success had ensured that Paz would support Sánchez de Lozada's policies and endure his candour in presenting them.

The insistence upon making a virtue out of a necessity in defending stabilisation was distinctly novel and won the minister a surprising degree of respect that only began to erode when his abject inability to resist a good joke or telling insult came to be seen in the context of the presidency from late 1988. At that stage it became plain how complementary the characters of Paz and his *de facto* chief minister had been; the prospect of the troubleshooter operating on his own was far from reassuring. (In this sense the party would possibly have been better advised to by-pass both Sánchez de Lozada and Bedregal, who had a widespread and far from undeserved reputation for mendacity, and present a more 'statesmanlike' candidate, such as vice-president Julio Garret Ayllón, to preside over the squabbling factions.)

The MNR was historically a party of 'sectors' and internecine intrigue, originally based upon authentic ideological divisions and feudal competition (often localist as well as over the spoils of office and patronage). Subsequently this tendency was sharpened by the high incidence of expulsions, repudiations and prodigal homecomings in exile, opposition or at the service of military governments. By 1985 there were no significant survivors from the left of the party — the initial appointment of the old FSTMB activist Sinforoso Cabrera as minister of mines reflected nothing more than a personal conversion. Nevertheless, both long-standing animosities and the infusion of 'newcomers' to the cabinet — notably defence minister Fernando Valle, previously of the ADN and a senior adviser to García Mesa — provided ample potential for schism. That this did not occur may be attributed to a number of factors. First, Paz, as founder and historic leader of the MNR was personally *intachable* and possessed binding powers of arbitration. Secondly, there was minimal disagreement over the basic necessity of stabilisation, and since this — rather than 'reactivation' — preoccupied the government for most of its term, the authors of Decree 21060 held the initiative. Thirdly, the MNR was only able to govern with the support of the ADN, and the extremely sharp challenge made by Banzer immediately following the 1985 poll on the basis of his superior vote was not forgotten once he had been denied the presidency by congress (with the support of the left) and then became a party to the Pacto por la Democracia in October. Unity within the MNR was essential both to the preservation of the pact — and thus the maintenance of office — and to any successful emergence from its demise (which was more widely anticipated within the MNR than was publicly recognised). The support of both Washington and the armed forces, where there were many more or less closet militants, together with the absence of a concerted challenge from the left, provided further, unprecedented incentives to keep the party cohesive and disciplined.

The Pact of October 1985 was undoubtedly the linchpin of the administration although it should be noted that it did not formally provide for a coalition, merely collaboration at legislative level, thereby largely overcoming the conservative sectarianism so evident in the election campaign. It is significant that the agreement, which lasted until February 1989, was not sealed until after the government had survived the COB's general strike of September and the consequent declaration of a state of siege. Although the ADN fully supported Decreee 21060 — and indeed declared that it had been all but stolen from them and their adviser Juan Cariaga — it studiously awaited the outcome of the inevitable clash with the unions before pledging its strategic support. Moreover, it did not gain a foothold in the cabinet until Sánchez de Lozada had outfaced Bedregal over the necessity of keeping firmly to the government's initial economic policies. Thereafter differences were of a strictly secondary order within an alliance that permitted appreciable latitude in terms of local competition and appeared to rest on the understanding that, in a variant of the Colombian and Venezuelan 'models' after 1958, Banzer would be allowed to reap the benefits of the 1989 poll. (Here the MNR acted no less opportunistically in ending the Pact than had the ADN in entering it.) There was plenty of confident talk of the accord taking Bolivia into the twenty-first century.

As the 'junior partner', the ADN celebrated its 'responsibility' and 'selflessness' rather more quickly than the resulting Pact, especially in the initial stages of the administration when it appeared that the MNR would gain the lion's share of benefit from directing the economic policies the agreement was primarily designed to support. *Adenista* dissidence was relatively slight in extent, but it did lead to the loss of Banzer's running mate Eudoro Galindo, who left with a section of younger, more 'ideological' cadre and eventually entered the ranks of *movimientismo*. As a result, the party became a more firmly personalist organisation. Nonetheless, the high profile of the ex-mayor of La Paz, Ronald Maclean, provided a forceful and modern entrepreneurial image that contrasted markedly with that of his successor Raúl Salmón, an independent but traditional machine-politician who had previously served under sundry regimes with no apparent prejudice to his reputation — under-lining, perhaps, the dangers of ascribing to 'modernity' the qualities of unambiguous appeal. Security through familiarity was no less a requirement in troubled times.

It was the MIR, which most lacked authority gleaned from experience in office, and most assiduously promoted its 'newness', that attempted to court Salmon. Their short-lived liaison following the 1987 municipal elections was perhaps the most prominent — certainly the most erratic and contentious — feature of the party's strategy of expanding its activity through the development of a loose alliance of sympathisers under the name of *Nueva Mayoría,* which soon became a permanent suffix to the party's acronym.[44] This initiative yielded significant reward in the elections of 1987 and 1989 in that it offered some shelter for politicians and middle-class activists who wished to remain in mainstream politics and retain their progressive *bona fides.* They could no longer countenance support for the left, and neither could they succumb to the lure of *movimientismo,* which, for all its new-found dynamism, was tacking the most conservative course in its 40-year history. The loss of its left wing deprived the MIR of both organisational strength and ideological coherence. Jaime Paz had already begun to move further rightwards, but within congress the MIR stood as the only significant party of opposition after the Pact of October 1985; the logic of this position was that it attacked the MNR–ADN alliance from the left. Thus, under circumstances very different from those prevailing under the UDP, the MIR was confronted with a number of taxing challenges whereby it had, on the one hand, to divorce itself from a discredited left and yet maintain its progressive pretensions, and, on the other, take a critical position on the NEP that did not evoke a return to the *status quo ante* and enable the government to dismiss it as the shame-faced rump of the UDP.

The MIR's relative success in manoeuvring through these uncharted waters owed much to the MNR's moderation in assailing it. Amongst the reasons for this were the need to be assured of cooperation in both houses of congress, particularly the senate, where the balance of forces was more delicate; the (correct) perception that there was little to be lost by celebrating the constitutional opposition of a 'moderate and civilised' left; and, to some degree, the affinity felt by Sánchez de Lozada for the MIR leadership, whom he excoriated with characteristic panache but whom he also treated seriously. (This was a prescient attitude in view of the 1989 election results and could have laid the basis for the much vaunted 'second phase' of stabilisation in 'reactivation' under an MNR–MIR alliance were it not for 'Goni's' tardy shift from campaign invective, at which he excelled, to overture, for which his skills were indifferent.) The MIR's own trajectory may plausibly be viewed as a combination of Jaime Paz's single-minded presidential vocation (no doubt sharpened by his experience as vice-president yet extraordinary in that he so ardently coveted the office without any corresponding explanation as to why); the 'hegemonic' status of stabilisation; and a broader transition within international social democracy away from Keynesianism — and its modern corollary in equitable association with organised labour — towards managerialism, wherein neither pragmatism nor the discourse of moderate welfarism were greatly altered. In this latter respect, the increasingly desperate gyrations of Alan García's APRA government across the border in Peru certainly exercised a sobering influence.[45]

The combination of the pact, the MIR's dedication to compliant opposition, and the weakness of the parliamentary left accounts for the relatively subdued conduct of affairs within cabinet and congress. At government level more attention was paid to disorderly conduct — the unprovoked assault on a traffic policeman by the industry minister (December 1986) and defence minister Valle's drunken speech to congress (April 1987, when the high command protested that he had revealed 'matters of national security') — than to the residual animus displayed by Bedregal and Sánchez de Lozada. Within congress, matters such as the MIR's barter of support for tax reform in return for the new electoral law (April 1986) raised minimal public interest — the statute is inordinately complex,

possibly purposefully so — compared with the legislators' concern
to award themselves munificent pay rises (October 1986, July 1988).
This provoked sufficient ire within the public that an acutely embarrassed government was obliged to take rapid action in order to avoid
a critical loss in that institutional legitimacy which constituted a
major prop for its own programme.

This also came under challenge in a more novel fashion from the
referendum — *consulta popular* — organised by the COB in July 1986 on
the tax reform, payment of the external debt, and the deployment of
US troops. The threat posed by this poll lay less in its result — an overwhelming repudiation of government policies by a surprisingly large
'electorate' (1,428,000, of whom 898,000 voted against the policies) —
than in its restitution of the impulses of 'popular democracy'. The level
of participation indicates at the very least that these were not dormant
since the government waged a strong campaign against the referendum
and came close to banning it altogether. Held less than a year after the
introduction of Decree 21060, the *consulta popular* may simply be viewed
as a predictable expression of discontent in much the same light as the
result of the 1987 municipal elections. However, it also indicated a
significant shift on the part of the COB, which had perforce to move
beyond reliance on strikes and the diminishing membership of its
constituent unions. In this sense the referendum marked the first step
in a process whereby the COB acquired a more reactive role in relation
to popular discontent, coordinating rather than leading protest.
Increased resort to hunger strikes similarly indicated a defensive position in which appeal to popular sentiment replaced industrial strength
as a means of bargaining. This approach was most closely determined
by the position of the *relocalizados* from Comibol, whose wretched fate
was the subject of incessant disputes throughout the government and
reached its apogee in the mock 'crucifixion' of redundant miners in La
Paz in April 1989. Following the visit of the Pope, and after three years'
experience of penniless miners and their families camped in El Alto,
the populace of the capital responded to such acts of desperation with
a sympathy that stood in sharp contrast to its hostile reaction to the
March 1985 occupation. There was an increase in talk of the country's
historic debt to the miners, public recognition of their sacrifice, and
some qualification of earlier emphatic epitaphs for the industry.

Of course, such matters neither cost the government very much nor offered the miners more than ephemeral consolation in what was an indisputable defeat. Only at the Huanuni mine was the FSTMB able to retain any substantive resistance (tellingly, on health and safety grounds), and after the government's use of troops in September 1986 to halt the union's 'March for Peace and Life' from Oruro to La Paz — which accumulated great popular support and threatened a major political crisis — the FSTMB was thrown into confusion over how to react. Conflict over the form and degree of response produced three major shifts in its leadership in 1986 and ended in an uneasy compromise whereby the balance between the radicals of the DRU/Eje de Convergencia and the PCB was publicly sustained by Víctor López — associated with Lechín but also autonomous from him — and practically determined by Filemón Escobar — erstwhile *porista* and now the most ardent advocate of *autogestionismo*. This pattern was broadly reproduced within the COB itself at the seventh congress of July 1987, when Lechín's fiat was finally eliminated, first López and then Simón Reyes presiding over a tense truce between two weakened blocks, neither of which possessed the capacity to realise their antagonistic stratagems outside the debating hall.[46]

Such a scenario evoked the experience of the dictatorial era and reflected a loss of authority and direction more profound than that witnessed after the 1957 stabilisation, when the mines were not greatly affected by redundancies. It raised the pertinent question of whether the traditional leadership of the COB by the FSTMB could be maintained. However, the reiterated claims to this role by the CSUTCB were undermined by its own deep divisions, which the COB itself had to arbitrate and which emphasised the continued preponderance of *caudillismo* and dubious practices of patronage over ideology in a sector that was poorly suited to operate according to the norms of industrial syndicalism. Yet if this presented a major organisational challenge to the COB, it did not, as has been seen, marginalise the *campesinado* from wider political life, even if the succession of *bloqueos* and the emergent influence of the federations of the coca zones were — like the protests over health, education and local administration — only loosely associated with the orthodox political opposition.

In one sense, the fact that the left had strictly limited influence over these movements complicated life for the government, which found little relief in stock anti-communist and anti-syndicalist invective and had to contend with a variety of organisations that lacked firm control over their supporters. The price of victory in the realm of formal politics was an uncontainable fluidity in regional and sectoral disputes, none of which posed a threat to the government's national authority but which, in sum, severely constrained its writ. Whilst this corresponded in part to a 'natural' retreat by the effectively disenfranchised constituency of the left that redeployed its political energies in a more quotidien and tactical fashion, it also raised the spectre of a dangerous anomie conducive to the emergence of forces similar to Sendero Luminoso. Fears of this grew from mid-1988 as it became evident that some elements associated with *katarismo* were abandoning faith in either constitutionalist or quasi-syndicalist/collectivist methods of struggle and seeking more direct and violent means. At the same time, occasional scares about *senderista* intromissions gained some substance when, in December 1988, the Peruvian naval attaché was assassinated in the middle of La Paz. The subsequent killing of three Mormon missionaries by the hitherto unknown Fuerzas Armadas de Liberación Nacional–Zárate Willka (FAL–ZW) sharpened apprehension in this quarter although the little available evidence — far exceeded by rumour — suggested both that the group was tiny and isolated and that the government was determined at all cost to avoiding provoking Sendero, which probably did make use of Bolivian territory around Lake Titicaca but continued to experience greater problems with the Aymara communities of the border region than it had with the Quechua majority around Cuzco. Although the progression from participation in legal politics to those of subversion is rarely linear, and the two are seldom as mutually exclusive as theorists and proponents of counter-insurgency claim, this space had evidently been crossed by very few. Perhaps because of a flexibility endowed by the very weakness of the state, the system neither generated such despair nor unlocked enough residual millenarian convictions to promote a movement comparable to that in Peru.

As in Peru, the continued existence and very modest recovery of the orthodox left played little part in this. The reconstruction of electoral unity around the MBL and PCB as Alianza Patriótica (1987 municipal elections) and then Izquierda Unida (1989 poll) and the spirited but strictly limited activity of the PS-1 and MRTKL had minimal impact on the national balance of forces. But, in contrast to the Peruvian case, the retention of some systematic equilibrium may be attributed to the rise of a new form of populism that succeeded far better than the left in voicing the preoccupations of the poor. This movement may be characterised as reactionary in that its principal protagonist — Carlos Palenque — had good right-wing credentials (part *movimientista,* part *barrientista*), a considerable fortune, and manifest talent for constructing alliances with a status quo that he simultaneously berated for its callow indifference to the commonwealth. Moreover, whilst Palenque's exploitation of radio and television was overwhelmingly dedicated to the expression of individual complaints and tales of misfortune (the hourly 'Tribuna libre del pueblo'), its concentration on CONDEPA's distribution of free spectacles, food and other hand-outs was understandably more insistent than was the promulgation of indecipherable 'autochthonous' economic policies by which the fledgling party proposed to resolve the wider crisis that made this old-style clientelism so necessary and popular.

On the other hand, the synthesis of an unmediated *vox populi,* attacks on a 'dictatorial' and 'uncaring' government, effusions of sympathy for the miners and coca growers, and celebration of popular culture — from Cantinflas to El Gran Poder — unnerved the established parties and rapidly dislocated customary political allegiances in the capital and surrounding provinces. If *Compadre* Palenque himself was too 'white' and accomplished a media personality — he had previously played in a popular folk group — to pass himself off as an authentic member of the newly urbanised Aymara underclass, he was exceptionally adept at projecting its travails. Moreover, his co-presenter on television, *Comadre* Remedios Loza, operated as a perfect foil in that, as an articulate, bilingual and attractive *chola,* she generated considerable appeal amongst women — very poorly represented in other parties — across the class and ethnic divide whilst inviting but failing to provoke a macho backlash. Both Palenque and the instinctively more radical Loza concentrated their attention on the domestic sphere, which was either ignored or dismissed with pious platitudes by the orthodox politicians. They thereby largely circumvented the greatest potential obstacle to CONDEPA in the widening economic chasm between impoverished recent migrants and the enriched market traders and rentiers of similar social and ethnic background whose operations appeared petty but who had, for some, become a veritable bourgeoisie.[47]

It is telling that the emergence and rapid rise to prominence of CONDEPA in La Paz followed the 1987 municipal elections, which in the capital witnessed a quite extraordinary decomposition in both protocol and mores amongst the established forces. The real casualty of this was Salmón, who was supported for his first election for the post of mayor by the MIR and a loose grouping known as the 'Friends of Don Raúl' against the candidacy of Ronald Maclean, backed by the ADN and MNR. The poll resulted in the election of six *concejales* (aldermen) for each bloc, opening up a tortuous process of negotiation that soon collapsed into an *opera bouffe* when one of Salmón's supporters changed sides upon the alleged — and never fully denied — payment of $100,000 by the government parties. However, just as the partners of the pact were set to ratify and celebrate their 7–5 victory on television, the Machiavelian qualities of Don Raúl surpassed even their literary depiction by Mario Vargas Llosa in the offer by his camp to Walter Mur, a prominent *movimientista,* to back him as mayor. This utterly unexpected proposal so enticed Mur that he cast aside party loyalty and voted against Maclean, thus returning the contest to a stalemate from which neither side emerged with a modicum of credit although one was a great deal worse off financially and the other had inherited the services of a mathematical dunce.

This unedifying spectacle continued for a full three months after which the office was given to each of the original candidates for half the term, beginning a race for popularity through expenditure on grandiose projects, particularly by Salmón, whose remodelling of Laikacota hill for a new 'central park' was but a transient triumph of civic imagination over geological realities. Subsequently Salmón threw in his depleted lot with the MNR as the best means by which to exact revenge on the bourgeois upstart Maclean, but he was soundly defeated in the 1989 senatorial race. The MIR, for its part, perhaps reconciled to the loss of the city under the twin pressures of

Palenque's media appeal and Maclean's cash, set its sights on the rural vote through alliance — under the auspices of the Nueva Mayoría — with the dissident *movimientismo* of Carlos Serrate Reich, whose close supporter Zenón Barrientos Mamani could still command a sizeable proportion of the votes he had delivered to the MNR from the northern altiplano in the 1950s and early 1960s.

Such manoeuvres produced results, but it is clear that these were obtained at a rising cost in terms of legitimacy, the myriad paths for tactical *votos de castigo* amongst contestants of comparable ideological hue threatening to lead all into a cul-de-sac. Disenchantment was not lessened by the much-publicised failure to bring the García Mesa trial to a conclusion, even in the absence of the defendant, who absconded from military supervision with an ease that only fortified popular disdain for claims to resolute impartiality on the part of the authorities. This sentiment was further enhanced by the fact that when Suárez and Palenque attacked Víctor Paz they were either apprehended or punished with unusual celerity and efficiency. However questionable their past or motives, they had at least stood up to the system and therefore deserved sympathy. This distinguishes them from another aggressive *arriviste,* Max Fernández, who had bought La Paz's highly profitable brewery with funds of uncertain origin and now tried to contest the 1989 poll by distributing largesse, particularly in the Oriente. However, Fernández soon discovered that overnight purchase of a political party is a problematic undertaking when his bargain-basement apparatchiks — mostly from the moribund FSB — simply took the money and ran. His later response to the *triple empate* in calling for a military coup endeared him to very few, but the fact that he could make such a bold entrance into the political arena suggested that Palenque was not a singular phenomenon and that the rules of politics were undergoing a disturbing transformation.

The results and immediate consequences of the 1989 poll, however, indicated that these new political figures posed a more limited challenge to the status quo. CONDEPA won the vote in the capital by a very clear margin (121,024 against second-placed ADN with 82,524), but it lost to the MIR in the departmental provinces and trailed very poorly elsewhere in the country, amassing just 11 per cent of the total vote. This score was roughly equal to the combined vote of the left (IU — 7.2 per cent; PS-1 — 2.5 per cent; MRTKL — 1.5 per cent). Equally, it should be recalled that the MIR polled only 19.6 per cent of the vote — enough to give Jaime Paz the presidency, albeit under tight ADN control in cabinet. In these circumstances it can be appreciated that any percentage of the vote in double figures had to be treated seriously, and CONDEPA had concentrated its support most effectively for the purposes of winning congressional seats and thus negotiating terms. Its opposition to the MNR was immovable and based almost exclusively on the closure of Palenque's television station in 1988. However, the *compadre* was quick to join in talks with Jaime Paz and Banzer, and although no formal agreement was signed, CONDEPA's voting record in the new parliament proved consistently supportive of the governing alliance. The cost to the ADN and MIR would be loss of the city council and the departmental development corporation, taken over to much fanfare shortly after Jaime Paz's inauguration with immediate promises — conditional upon treasury support — to start construction of a road from La Paz to Pando. CONDEPA thus set down a marker for its ambitions and the direction of blame should they not be fulfilled. Nonetheless, the limits of cooptation had not been stretched very far to incorporate the party.

A similarly sober interpretation of the fragility of the political system may be derived from the process of negotiation between the country's three leading forces. Here the MNR's decision early in 1989 to abandon the Pact of October 1985 and make an independent 'dash for power' constituted a calculated risk that came close to success in simple electoral terms. However, it also helped to sharpen the incidence of malpractice before, during and after the poll, pushing the party extremely close to repudiating an election held under its government but effectively controlled by the ADN and MIR, which dominated the electoral courts and now felt little need to curb manipulation by their supporters. Yet despite extensive partisan intervention in the results, these stood and a new government was elected according to the constitutional timetable. The fact that it began as a coalition suggested that the division of the dominant political bloc into three was not as debilitating or dangerous as many feared. Indeed, some held that the *triple empate* provided the best electoral foundation for *concertación*. Moreover, following Jaime Paz's inauguration, all parties accepted the need for electoral reform, and Sánchez de Lozada adopted the role of leader of a responsible opposition without undue difficulty.

Amongst the chief features identified as underpinning this outcome were the flexibility and skill of Banzer and the erosion of *movimientismo*. The former may be accepted only with the caveat that Banzer was no longer in any position to pose an authoritarian alternative and had, alone of the three leading candidates, already served as president; his ambitions for office were not as sharp and had been further reduced by physical frailty and the death of his sons. Under the circumstances his actions were unremarkable, providing the ADN with a dominant voice in policy-making whilst Jaime Paz attended football matches and signed agrarian reform titles. Equally, notice of the death of the MNR was somewhat exaggerated, even if the generation and many of the traditions of 1952 were in advanced decline. Between 1985 and 1989 the party's exploitation of the revolutionary legacy was slight and indirect, revolving principally around the figure of Víctor Paz. It will not, of course, be entirely jettisoned since it lends some gravitas and resolution to the image of the MNR. Yet a further diminution of 'historical' *movimientismo* would little affect the substance of the party's conduct.

Certainties with respect to the weakness of the left were no less well founded in mid-1989 than in mid-1985, at least in terms of established party organisations. However, a degree of caution is in order here in terms of the wider potential for a renewal of a radical movement. In the first place, the electorate will by 1994 have experienced government by all components of what might be termed the 'triple conservative alliance'. From a purely electoral viewpoint this may simply enhance the degree of tactical voting on the basis of a more informed logic of the *mal menor*. (It should be noted that the MNR–MIR option remains untested.) On the other hand, the prospect of 'more of the same' is likely to be upheld by all these parties and, after prolonged period of recession in the poorest country in mainland America, this may well exasperate the evidently large number of uncommitted voters as well as supporters of

CONDEPA. In order to evade this scenario, the right will have to achieve not only the economic growth that has persistently eluded it but also a qualitative expansion of welfare and an authentic resolution to the dilemmas posed by *narcotráfico*.

The prospects on all three fronts are less than bright, as is that of a thorough reform of state institutions, where the customs of malpractice and partisanship persist to growing popular discontent. If these issues have long been the left's stock-in-trade and offer fertile ground for recovery, a less familiar challenge lies in adjusting to the decline of the COB and the emergence of forces such as CONDEPA. Failure to address these critical developments could well result in more than the left being reduced from the status of a minority to that of an entirely peripheral entity; it might also encourage the incidence of social violence, drawing Bolivia much closer to the Peruvian experience. The *disiderata* in this regard are peculiarly taxing since they include a simultaneous move away from surpassed traditions and defence of those that take a similar form but remain vital — as demonstrated by Palenque for La Paz — in affirming ethnic and social identity. As yet the full gamut of distinctions is unclear, even within the discourse of 'western' ideologies and practice. Yet failure to address both the 'American' and 'European' features of this dilemma is likely to produce a far nastier future than that of Bolivia quietly queuing up to take its modest place in 'the end of history'.

## Notes

1    The most contemporary English language study of Bolivia is James Malloy and Eduardo Gamarra, *Revolution and Reaction: Bolivia 1964–1984* (New Brunswick, 1988). Although Malloy and Gamarra employ the terms 'populism' and 'authoritarianism' quite extensively, their study seeks to discover inflections within these very broad categories, and I would not wish to attribute to them a single-minded commitment to model-building, just as I reject their characterisation of my narrative survey, *Rebellion in the Veins: Political Struggle in Bolivia, 1952–82* (London, 1984), as reductionist and class determinist. Salvador Romero reviews both texts in *Estado y Sociedad*, vol. 4, no. 2 (1988). Perhaps the widest disseminated caricature of Bolivian personality is the scriptwriter in Mario Vargas Llosa's novel, *Aunt Julia and the Scriptwriter*

(London, 1983), an individual based closely on Raúl Salmón, mayor of La Paz in the 1980s and a personalist political figure of some consequence although distinctly vulnerable to his own grandiose ideas. If Bolivians felt ambivalent about Vargas Llosa's lampooning of Salmón, there was a far wider and deeper sense of outrage at the publication in the *Atlantic* of an article, 'A Cowboy High in the Altiplano', by the former press attaché to the US embassy, Mark Jacobs, who referred to Bolivians as primitive 'gnomes'. The piece — in fact, a very mediocre ramble — was reproduced in two Sunday papers and generated sufficient indignation to prompt the embassy to issue a disclaimer.

2   See Dunkerley, *Rebellion in the Veins*; Malloy and Gamarra, *Revolution and Reaction*; Laurence Whitehead, 'Bolivia's Failed Democratization, 1977–80,, in G. O'Donnell, R. Schmitter and L. Whitehead (eds.), *Transitions from Authoritarian Rule. Latin America* (Baltimore, 1986).

3   See, in particular, Juan Antonio Morales, 'Inflation Stabilization in Bolivia', in M. Bruno, G. Di Tella, R. Dornbusch and S. Fischer (eds.), *Inflation Stabilization. The Experience of Argentina, Brazil, Bolivia, Israel and Mexico* (Cambridge, Mass., 1988), for an assessment of the 1985 stabilisation plan by one of its principal overseers (but not one of its architects). A less detailed survey may be found in J. Morales and J. Sachs, 'Bolivia's Economic Crisis', Working Paper no. 2620, National Bureau of Economic Research, Boston (1988). The original document behind the plan is República de Bolivia, Decreto Supremo 21060 (29 August 1985), whilst the principal agreements and documents supporting it are collected in Muller and Machicado (eds.), *Acuerdos y documentos de la nueva política económica 1986* (La Paz, 1987). Excellent assessments of the economy are given in Coyuntura Económica Andina (La Paz, anual 1985), and a radical critique is provided in Pablo Ramos, *¿Hacia dónde va el neoliberalismo?* (La Paz, 1987). Full statistics are provided in Muller y Machicado Asociados, *Estadísticas Económicas*, La Paz, anual 1985–. A full background to the tin industry is given in Mahmood Ali Ayub and Hideo Hashimoto, *The Economics of Tin Mining in Bolivia* (Washington, 1985), and its collapse is surveyed in Latin America Bureau, *The Great Tin Crash: Bolivia and the World Tin Market* (London, 1987). The important 'informal' economy is outlined in Samuel Doria Medina, *La economía informal en Bolivia* (La Paz, 1987).

4   See, in particular, Kevin Healy, 'The Boom within the Crisis. Some Recent Effects of Foreign Cocaine Markets on Bolivian Rural Society and Economy', in Deborah Pacini and Christine Franquemont (eds.), *Coca and Cocaine. Effects on People and Policy in Latin America* (Cambridge,

Mass., 1987); Kevin Healy, 'Coca, the State and the Peasantry in Bolivia, 1982–1988', in the special issue of *Journal of Interamerican Studies,* vol. 30, nos. 2 and 3 (1989). For background material, see G. Flores and J. Blanes, *¿Dónde va el Chapare?* (Cochabamba, 1984); R. Bascopé, *La veta blanca. Coca y cocaína en Bolivia* (La Paz, 1987); and J. Canelas, *Bolivia. Coca y cocaína* (La Paz, 1983); IEPALA, *Narcotrafico y política* (Madrid, 1982). Rensselaer W. Lee III, *The White Labyrinth. Cocaine and Political Power* (New Brunswick, 1989), provides a very useful synthesis of the main policy issues but some of its considerable factual information should be treated with caution.

5   There is, as yet, little consolidated literature on this important issue, which relates closely both to the political failures of the UDP regime and the collapse of the mining proletariat. See, *inter alia,* FLACSO, *El sector minero. Crisis y perspectivas* (La Paz, 1986); Jorge Lazarte, 'Movimiento sindical y transformaciones del sistema socio-político boliviano', *Estado y Sociedad,* vol. 4, no. 2 (1988); MIR–Bolivia Libre, *Repensando el país* (La Paz, 1987). *Autodeterminación,* nos. 6 and 7 (1988), reproduces an interesting debate between leaders of various radical currents.

6   My comments here are, of course, highly contentious and are developed later in the chapter. For an alternative view that proclaims the unambiguous victory of conservatism, see Javier Hurtado in *Presencia,* 2 August 1989.

7   Kenneth P. Jameson, 'Dollarization and Dedollarization in Bolivia', mimeo, University of Notre Dame 1985; Ramiro Carrasco, in Facultad de Ciencias Económicas, Universidad Mayor de San Andrés, *Dinámica Económica,* no. 8 (1982), p. 97.

8   For details see Jameson 'Dollarization and Dedollarization'. The MIR disowned the policy as fast as possible, but for an appreciation of its intended aims and the context in which it was understood to operate, see Rolando Morales, 'La crisis económica', *Informe R, May* 1985.

9   Morales and Sachs, 'Bolivia's Economic Crises', p. 25; Arthur J. Mann, 'The Political Economy of Tax Reform in Bolivia', mimeo 1986, p. 6.

10  Morales and Sachs, 'Bolivia's Economic Crises', p. 21.

11  *El Mundo ,* Santa Cruz, 9 November 1982.

12  *Presencia,* La Paz, 10 November 1982.

13  See the comments of Gail E. Makinen in Bruno *et al., Inflation Stabilization* (Cambridge, 1988), pp. 347–51.

14  At the *Foro Político* of 25 May 1985 Víctor Paz indicated that an agreement with the IMF would be necessary and that he would grant favourable conditions to private capital. Significantly, it was at this meeting that Hugo Banzer declared, 'No me voy a sentir incómodo si el Doctor Paz gana las elecciones', despite the fact that the MNR

presented itself to the voters as 'inserta en la izquierda nacional, anti-imperialista y democrática'.

15 It should be recalled that the coup of Colonel Natusch in November 1979 received support from leading figures in the MNRI as well as the MNR.

16 Whilst Siles declared the FSTMB occupation of Comibol illegal and ultra-leftist, Paz Zamora welcomed the move fulsomely. *Presencia,* 21 April 1983.

17 For example, 'Durante el gobierno del general Vildoso se dió una clara situación revolucionaria y el POR fue el único partido político que asi lo dijo', G. Lora, *La insurección* (La Paz, 1983), p. 7. For a rather more sober analysis, still couched in boisterous rhetoric, see the opening two pages to G. Lora, *Lo que será y hará la dictadura del proletariado* (La Paz, 1985), drafted in the immediate aftermath of the March general strike.

18 For the internal polemic over strategy, see *Unidad,* no. 639, 19 July 1985 (for the official line) and *Unidad,* no. 641, 20–26 July 1985 (for the dissident line). Both factions issued their own versions of this paper until September.

19 For an outline of this and other congresses, see Jorge Lazarte, *Movimiento obrero y procesos políticos en Bolivia* (La Paz, 1989). A fuller picture is given in Hisbol, *VI congreso de la COB. Protocolos y tesis de la discusión política* (La Paz, 1985). It is noteworthy that at this congress a leading *cobista,* Filemón Escobar, effectively sided with the PCB against the DRU although he argued for the development of the COB itself as a focus of political struggle. The DRU's position was that 'there are only two alternatives: either to advance the objective of social and national liberation through transforming the process into a revolutionary one, or to perish under imperialism and fascism'.

20 Renzo Abruzzese, 'Formas democráticas en los procesos de transición: el caso de Bolivia', *Estudios Sociológicos,* Mexico, vol. 4, no. ii (1986).

21 Kevin Healy, 'The Rural Development Role of the Bolivian Peasant *Sindicatos* in the New Democratic Order', Paper to the XII congress of LASA, Albuquerque, April 1985.

22 For a full and suggestive discussion of the emergence of the 'new right', see Carlos F. Toranzo Roca and Mario Arrieta Abdalla, *Nueva derecha y desproletarización en Bolivia* (La Paz, 1989).

23 *Coyuntura Económica Andina,* June 1989; Pablo Ramos, *¿Hacia dónde?*

24 Juan Antonio Morales in Bruno *et al., Inflation Stabilization,* pp. 337–41.

25 *Ibid.,* p. 319.

26 *Ibid.,* p. 329.

27   Mann, 'Political Economy of Tax Reform'.
28   *Ibid.*
29   *Ibid.*
30   Ricardo Calla, *La derrota de Lechín. Luchas políticas en el XXI congreso minero, mayo 1986* (La Paz, 1986); Lazarte, *Movimiento obrero.*
31   Rolando Morales and Fernando Rocabado, *Los grupos vulnerables en las economías de desarrollo. El caso boliviano* (La Paz, 1988).
32   Lee, *White Labyrinth,* p. 1.
33   *Ibid.,* p. 60.
34   *Ibid.* p. 23.
35   República de Bolivia, *Plan trienal para la lucha contra el narcotráfico* (La Paz, Nov. 1986), p. 6.
36   Lee, *White Labyrinth,* pp. 8 and 30.
37   Hon. Senado Nacional, 'Informe preliminar sobre el narcotráfico' (La Paz, 1986), pp. 23–4.
38   J. Blanes, *De los valles al Chapare* (La Paz, 1983); Healy, 'Boom within Crisis', pp. 102; 115; Temas de política social, *Efectos del narcotráfico* (La Paz, 1988), pp. 53–73.
39   Lee, *White Labyrinth,* p. 27.
40   *Ibid.,* p. 46.
41   *Efectos del narcotráfico,* pp. 13–51.
42   *Coyuntura Económica Andina,* 1986, p. 19. This is the IMF figure and thus conservative.
43   *Narcotráfico y política,* p. 152.
44   A full account of the 1987 local elections is given in José Baldivia, *Balance y perspectivas: elecciones municipales* (La Paz, 1989).
45   The platform of the MIR and other parties for the 1989 elections is reproduced in Asociación de Periodistas de La Paz, *Foro debate. Elecciones nacionales 1989* (La Paz, 1989). For a humorous but telling view of the campaign, see Paulovich, *Elecciones a la boliviana* (La Paz, 1989).
46   Lazarte, *Movimiento obrero.*
47`  Toranzo and Arrieta, *Nueva derecha.*

# 4

## Barrientos and Debray: All Gone or More to Come?

The prominence and popularity of biography in explaining politics have been surprisingly little affected by the advent of social science. Moreover, we have in recent years seen the re-emergence of a rather distinct genre — that of 'parallel lives' — which was most notably developed by Plutarch in the first century AD, with more than two dozen sketches of Greek and Roman figures.[1] Plutarch's influence has, of course, proved enduring, not only through Shakespeare's use of North's translation but also via Dryden, Racine and Emerson amongst others. It is, then, somewhat surprising to discover no mention of him in three modern studies: J.H. Elliot's *Richelieu and Olivares,* Michael Beschloss's *Kennedy and Khrushchev,* and *Hitler and Stalin. Parallel Lives* by Alan Bullock.[2]

Perhaps this silence on the part of such eminent scholars, at least one of whom received a 'classical education', simply reflects modern acceptance of an approach that Plutarch himself never fully explained or defended. Yet even if this is the case, it is worth quoting the observation of D.A. Russell:

> either character or circumstance may be the basis of a *sunkrisis* (comparison); similar events affecting dissimilar persons and similar persons reacting to contrasting events alike provide a suitable field for the exercise. It is basically a rhetorical proce-dure; but it is rescued from purely rhetorical ingenuity by its value as a way of concentrating and directing the moral reflec-tions which are the primary purpose of biography.[3]

Of course, I don't have the time to provide even a proper biograph-ical sketch of René Barrientos and Régis Debray. Furthermore, one doubts the contemporary usefulness of an approach as didactic as that of Plutarch with respect to virtue and vice, even when reflecting on the politics of Latin America through the experiences of a conservative general and a radical intellectual.

Nevertheless, Russell's argument is far from wholly redundant for these two individuals, who in fact never met each other and yet were the principal surviving protagonists on either side of the guerrilla war staged by Ernesto Che Guevara in Bolivia in 1967. They may, then, plausibly be taken as representative not only of polarised political traditions and outlooks but also of a binding antagonism. Although these phenomena are by no means ancient, memory is frequently tyrannised by fashion, especially when this operates as mercilessly as it does within academic life. At the same time, for most of us Bolivia is a place as obscure as it appears to be exotic. Let me, therefore, look at each man before reflecting very briefly on the proposition that the qualities with which they are most closely associated now belong to a surpassed age and have been rendered redundant and ridiculous by the consolidation of a liberal democratic culture based upon modern capitalism and the hegemony of consensus.

General Barrientos's reputation has not stood the test of time or resisted the invective and denigration of his many enemies. But in the last decade of his life — including four years as president of Bolivia — he possessed an impressive image at home and abroad as a charismatic military strongman or *caudillo*. In his recent biography of De Gaulle — himself scarcely a besuited wimp — Jean Lacouture says that Barrientos's reputation 'made people tremble'.[4] This is exaggerated but unsurprising since the picture abroad was very much that painted by *The Times* in its obituary of … a handsome … airforce general (who) was the target of many assassination attempts, (a) dark-haired president (who) carried three bullets in his body'.[5] This, too, was not strictly true, but it pales in comparison with some of the home-grown descriptions heaped upon Barrientos when he was at his zenith: Condor of the Andean Skies; Creator of the Second Republic; Paladin of Social Democracy; Restorer of Faith in the National Revolution; and General of the People.[6] This last title is also that of a hagiography written for wages by Fernando Diez de Medina, who includes in his 350 pages the phrase, 'Barrientos was Bolivia, Bolivia was Barrientos'.[7]

Such an assertion strikes one as innocently foolish until we recall the declaration made by Rudolf Hess at a Nazi rally in 1934 that, 'Adolf Hitler is Germany, and Germany is Adolf Hitler'.[8] Even if — as is quite likely — Diez de Medina was simply borrowing from the not inconsiderable corpus of National Socialist literature that had made its way into Bolivia in the 1930s and 1940s, this resonance between euphoric nationalist sentiment and personalist political leadership is not uncommon in modern Latin America.[9] Barrientos, for all his authoritarianism, was no Nazi, and he never succeeded in organising a proper political party to replace the Movimiento Nacionalista Revolucionario (MNR), the movement which had led the revolution of 1952, to which he himself had belonged even before that revolution, and which he overthrew in a coup in November 1964 when he was serving as constitutional vice-president.

René Barrientos Ortuño was born in 1919 in the small provincial town of Tarata in the department of Cochabamba. Not untypically for this region, he was of mixed Quechua and Spanish blood, and his fluency in the Quechua language was later to play a key part in developing both regionalist backing and something of an indigenous identity in one of the two Latin American countries — the other is Guatemala — which still had a majority Amerindian population.

Barrientos's parents were of humble, rather than poor, background, but he was orphaned young and, losing his brother César in the Chaco War against Paraguay, his upbringing was overseen by sisters Corina and Elena, upon whom he later depended heavily. His passage from local seminary to military college was not unusual for somebody of his background. Nor, in fact, was Barrientos particularly distinctive in his admiration for the radical nationalist officers Germán Busch and Gualberto Villarroel, who from the late 1930s attempted to curb the power of the large tin companies and reduce Bolivia's political dependency on Britain and the US. Too junior to belong to the nationalist military lodges that supported these leaders, Barrientos nonetheless opposed the conservatives who came to power in 1946, and he penned a very short and rather uninspiring pamphlet calling for 'the glorious and valiant army to free itself from vulgar obeisance to the tin companies'.[10] Cashiered, but having already qualified as a pilot, he flew missions for the insurgent MNR in the civil war of 1949, and in April 1952, following the party's eventual capture of power in a three-day insurrection, it was Barrientos who volunteered to bring the MNR leader Víctor Paz Estenssoro back from exile in Buenos Aires.

The MNR nationalised the major tin mines, decreed an extensive agrarian reform, and introduced universal suffrage for the poorest country in mainland America. Under strong pressure from the left-wing miners' union, the party had little choice but to acquiesce in the formation of popular militias, which for a while threatened the very existence of the regular armed forces. Perhaps wisely, Barrientos spent a fair part of the 1950s on postings and courses abroad, including, according to his enemies, a spell in a US psychiatric hospital. In all events, it is only in the early 1960s, following the Cuban revolution and the accelerating division and right-wing drift of the MNR that he came firmly into the public eye. As the party's authority decomposed and its rule became more violent, Barrientos exploited his dual role as commander of the air force and leader of the MNR's military lodge to promote the restoration of the armed forces, staging a thinly disguised Bonapartist campaign that attracted increasing support from Washington and the very private companies against which he had railed in the 1940s. Indeed, once he came to office, the general reversed a great many of the political positions that he had championed a decade earlier.

If Barrientos was widely denounced as an opportunist and traitor, at least he staked out his ground emphatically, using language that manifested little or no modulation:

> The *Patria* is in danger. A vast Communist conspiracy, planned and funded by international extremism, has exploited the good faith of some sectors of labour in trying to pit the people against the armed forces ... It doesn't matter than the snipers, the masters of blackmail, demagogy and lies heap up mountains of calumny against the armed forces. They are frustrated; their epilepsy and maladies do not impress our glorious institution, effectively at the service of the people and against the traffickers who feast on the credulity and goodwill of the workers.[11]

The same man who expressed these sentiments ensured that he was made a freemason days before coming to office, and having done so promptly appointed eight close relatives to ministries, ambassadorships or directorships of state corporations.[12] He was, perhaps, not overly prejudiced in such a macho culture by the fact that, rather like John Kennedy, he had a high sex drive over which he exercised poor control, although to describe him as Priapic is probably to give his activities an undeserved classical gloss.[13] Only recognising eight children as his own but promising to adopt more than 50, Barrientos was thrice married, once bigamously, to his 'first lady' Rosemarie Galindo — a union that he failed to regularise, he said, 'because of pressure of work', instead contracting nuptials with Cati Rivas a month before he died.[14]

Such antics greatly exasperated the prelates, but the populace as a whole seemed more perplexed by Barrientos's efforts to justify the outlawing of trade unions, manipulations of the constitution, erratic suppression of opposition parties, and attacks on the student movement:

> 'I am,' said the President, 'a man of the Christian left — nationalist in economics, democratic in doctrine. But this democracy is just, active, belligerent, dynamic and profoundly revolutionary because I am seeking only social justice and the happiness of the peasant, worker and middle class majority; in sum, the happiness of the people.'[15]

Of course, one should never underestimate the power of even the most incomprehensible and leaden rhetoric when it is delivered with energy and conviction. And it is to this, I feel, that Barrientos owed his significant popularity. He was, above all else, a man of action for whom heroic feats were essential and sheer movement an adequate substitute for rationality.

Barrientos was by far the most peripatetic of Bolivia's presidents. Often he would conduct essential business in La Paz early into the morning so that he could spend the daylight hours moving around the republic, dropping into the smallest and most isolated communities to shake hands, share a drink or meal, distribute footballs and bicycles, speechify and, above all, ratify the existence of the president. Such paternalism was, of course, an integral feature of traditional patterns of authority, the exchange of hospitality and fealty for gifts and recognition reaffirming identities in a manner that is only partially understood in terms of patron and client. It was all made possible in an exceptionally mountainous country courtesy of the helicopter, first used over the Bolivian altiplano in mid-1962 and rapidly adopted by Barrientos, who enjoyed the permanent loan of a Bell craft from Gulf Oil, one of the companies favoured by his 'open-door' economic policies.

One civic-minded citizen concerned at the expense of such activity wrote to the press to observe that in two years these trips must have cost at least $700,000, the president having travelled the equivalent of two-thirds of the distance between the earth and the moon.[16] This comparison is telling because, of course, Barrientos ruled Bolivia, and ruled it from the air, at a time when space travel had captured the global imagination. Sometimes this occurred rather too vividly, as when a puma was reported to have landed from outer space near the town of Ayo Ayo, just a fortnight before Telstar was launched and while John Glenn's capsule was on display in Mexico City.[17] In such a context, though, even an aviator of most illiberal outlook and attachment to 'order' might appear not only glamorous but also dazzlingly modern.

It seems unlikely that René Barrientos would have compre-hended Aristotle's bracketing of the virtue of courage with the vice of audacity as well as cowardice.[18] Yet if he vacillated over major political decisions in a manner that belied his impulsive personal style, he could never be accused of bodily cowardice.[19] Indeed, it might even be said that his career hinged on three instances of phys-ical fortitude or suffering.

Barrientos first won widespread popular acclaim in October 1961 when some 20,000 people gathered at the El Alto aerodrome above La Paz to watch a demonstration of parachuting, which had been attempted only twice before in the country — in 1939 and 1947. This event — central to a much-publicised aeronautical week organised by the general — went horribly wrong when the parachutes of three of the 15 soldiers who made the drop failed to open and they fell to their deaths in front of the crowd. Faced with accusations of allowing his men to use inferior equipment, Barrientos simply invited the press back to El Alto, put on one of the dead men's parachutes and executed a faultless jump himself.[20]

In February 1964 the general staged an energetic but futile effort at the MNR's Ninth National Convention to have himself nomi-nated as vice-presidential candidate for the general elections to be held in August of that year. Upon hearing of his defeat, he got heartily drunk and indulged in a number of emotional outbursts that did not augur well for president Victor Paz and the apparatchiks who had manipulated the convention. A month later, at two in the morning, Barrientos was shot as he left the home of his sister Corina following a meeting with supporters. The attack, which was very probably staged by the MNR's political police, the Control Político, seemed finally to have removed a threatening loser as Barrientos, hit in the chest, collapsed to the ground. However, the bullet had struck the metal United States Airforce insignia habitually worn by the general, shattering on impact with the result that no organs were damaged and he suffered only slight flesh wounds, caused by splinters.

Perhaps the most sober lesson which can be drawn from this incident is that the important thing about uniforms is that they are different. But Barrientos and his US friends were taking no chances. At 8.45 am, following a brief operation, he was taken to El Alto, and by 6.15 pm he was in the Panama Canal Zone, recovering in a US military hospital. Víctor Paz, fully able to read the writing on the wall, moved quickly to have the elected vice-presidential candidate resign and, after an enterprising re-interpretation of party statutes, he was able to send a cable to Panama offering Barrientos the position as his running-mate.[21] This was readily accepted, the office being exploited within six months to depose Paz and end a dozen years of MNR rule.

A year later, having taken dictatorial power, the general was again shot, but because he was driving a jeep and wearing protective clothing, of the three bullets that struck him only one caused a major wound — in the buttocks. This shooting took place on the road between Tarata and Cochabamba, and Barrientos was immediately ferried to the house of his sister Elena, where he remained for several days in what appears to have been a deliberately contrived atmosphere of crisis — almost melodrama — as delegations of officers visited him to express their backing and urge a return to the capital. The tenuous gravity of the moment was not assisted by the fact that the detectives sent to investigate the crime had to exclude the general's underpants as evidence because they had, quite fittingly, already been laundered in 'Ace' washing powder by Leonor Lezama, Elena's maid.[22] The tension cultivated during this incident was again exploited by Barrientos, who, having tested his support within the high command, and probably his own self-confidence as well, called a precipitate halt to the truce with his opponents and launched a major offensive against the left.

It is tempting — especially within the academy — to ignore all but the folkloric qualities of such matters. This, though, would be a mistake — one, I sense, made by Che Guevara and Régis Debray in 1967. It is certainly true that René Barrientos had by then become a figure loathed by many in the working class for his violent record of repression, and he was despised by much of a middle-class youth negotiating the rapids between the elitism of adolescent Christian Democracy and that of a socially deracinated Leninism. It is also the case that Barrientos himself played a minimal role in the military operations against Guevara. Moreover, his propaganda war against the guerrilla was seen abroad as complete buffoonery. And yet one has to ask oneself why his regime was so little threatened by this insurgency when, despite a multitude of errors made by the radical left, so many of its charges were entirely accurate and widely accepted. Undoubtedly, the calculating young rationalists were spectacularly wrong-footed by an expressive, instinctive politician whose populist edge lay precisely in his unpredictability, and whose vulnerability was masked — not revealed — by his capacity for mouthing gibberish.

Barrientos survived Che Guevara by some 18 months. He died — as might have been expected — in a helicopter crash on one of his dashes around the country. For a while foul play was suspected — not least on the part of Cati Rivas's ex-husband, the ebullient Captain Faustino Rico Toro — but the laborious autopsies practised on the defunct president could not shake the most sober explanation. Unable to accept this, some, including police Colonel Oscar Vargas Valenzuela, resorted to the astral plane of investigation and consulted the general's spirit — an inadvisable course of action since the Bolivian Church lacks a qualified exorcist, and there stands in the city of Oruro a house, once occupied by German dabblers in the occult, that remains empty and haunted even after the ministrations of officials sent from Rome. As it happens, Colonel Vargas was informed by the general's shade that his death was 'due to a simple accident'.[23]

When he was in the realm of the quick Barrientos had declared, 'to die is part of life. Those who fear death cannot command'.[24] This is one of the few sentiments that he assuredly shared with Guevara. It is also, perhaps, not surprising, in view of his experience in Bolivia 25 years ago, to find in Debray's *Critique of Political Reason* the declaration that, 'Death is the lyrical core of the individual, the site where he discovers that he is irreplaceable'.[25]

In turning to Régis Debray one might legitimately expect some relief from the kind of excitements that have just been described. This, however, can only be partial for although Debray may properly be described as an intellectual, he was very young when he resolved to harness his analytical skills directly to the struggle for revolutionary socialism. To the best of my knowledge, the only time that he has been fully employed in an academic post was in 1966, in Cuba. It is, then, not entirely surprising that when, on 20 April 1967, Debray was detained by elements of the Bolivian army's Fourth Division near the village of Muyupampa in the middle of the guerrilla zone of operations his protestations that he was only covering the campaign as a journalist were not readily accepted. Several days later a rather elated General Barrientos told the international press that Debray was a guerrilla and agent of Fidel Castro whose adventures would end in Bolivia.[26] In fact, neither claim was proved to be true, but the first was more than plausible and, for a while, the second seemed highly likely.

Jules Régis Debray was born in Paris in September 1940, the son of relatively affluent lawyers who were soon to become members of the Resistance. When he was arrested in Bolivia his mother, Janine, active in conservative politics, was vice-president of the municipal council of Paris, on which she had served for 20 years; his father, Georges, a distinguished attorney, was a member of the Council of Lawyers and a Chevalier of the Legion of Honour. Such a respectable bourgeois background later proved vital in promoting a high-profile campaign in Debray's defence, but it did not apparently provoke an exceptionally talented youth to acts of social rebellion or idle iconoclasm. Indeed, Régis appears to have fulfilled the exacting expectations of his parents, receiving the 1957 national philosophy prize for secondary students from his mother's hands and graduating first from the Lycée Louis-le-Grand in 1959. That year his parents rewarded him with a holiday in the US, but when in Miami he diverted to Havana for several weeks in order to witness the recently triumphant Cuban Revolution. On his return Debray entered the École Normale Supérieure to study for a master's in philosophy with Louis Althusser. In 1961 he visited South America for several months; and he returned

there in 1963 for a stay of 18 months, visiting every country except
Paraguay. Subsequently he began to study for a doctorate in social
anthropology under the supervision of Maurice Godelier.

Debray was, therefore, scarcely wet behind the ears when he was
arrested in Bolivia. However, local opinion seems to have been that the
combination of his intelligence and self-esteem — even some sympathetic commentators talked of arrogance — had transformed the
Frenchman into what is known in that part of the world as a *s'unchu
luminaria* — the sense of which might be translated as 'somebody
whose fine words mesmerise only momentarily'. Another reaction was
that Debray was a *q'incha qhara,* which literally means 'unlucky
European' but which can also signify 'European who brings bad luck'.
Certainly, as he awaited a court martial on the eve of his twenty-seventh
birthday, charged with murder, robbery, grievous bodily harm and
rebellion, Régis Debray appeared to be paying a very high price for a
*folie de grandeur* that compounded the assurance of a comfortable metropolitan upbringing, the pretensions of Althusser's Marxist theoreticism,
and the presumptions of Cuban revolutionary internationalism. It is a
heady mix and — combined with his significant literary talent — it
should remind us that Debray, like Barrientos, can only be taken as
'representative' by virtue of his being outstanding.

A week after he had been arrested, beaten into a coma and threatened with death, Debray, understandably pessimistic about his
prospects, started to write down some reflections on his short life.
Initial declarations, such as 'Memories don't interest me', reverberate
with the petulance with which he responded to his interrogators. But
this brief memoir settles down as soon as its author casts his mind
back to the regime at the rue d'Ulm and the outlook of the young
philosophers at the École Normale Supérieure:

> '... we thought', he tells us, 'we could analyse our world and
> our hearts at arm's length ... a fine philosopher who was
> guiding our steps as students, and had introduced us to Karl
> Marx, gave us the entrée to the kingdom that he was himself
> exploring, that of theoretical rigour and dialectical materialism,
> as a theory of general praxis ... All very fine: theory draws its
> effectiveness from its rigorousness, and its rigorousness is effec-
> tive because it separates "development in reality" from

"development in thought", the "operation of society" from the "operation of knowledge". In other words, all we had to do to become good theoreticians was to be lazy bastards.'[27]

Under the circumstances this is a pardonable exaggeration, but it is also quite a justified response to Althusser's progressive elimination of the core philosophical problem of the guarantees of knowledge and truth as well as his relentless invective against the ideological illusions of immediate experience.

This passage is from Althusser's book *Reading Capital,* published in 1965 when Debray was back in Paris:

> We must take seriously the fact that the theory of history, in the strong sense, does not exist, or hardly exists as far as historians are concerned; that the concepts of existing history are therefore nearly always 'empirical' concepts ... that is, cross-bred with a powerful strain of ideology concealed behind its 'obviousness'.[28]

As Perry Anderson has observed, such a position is an almost exact replica of Spinoza's logical progression from the monist dictum that 'Truth is the criterion both of itself and of falsehood' to the assertion that the primary delusion of humanity is the conviction that individuals are free in their volition, or, as Spinoza puts it, 'Their idea of freedom is simply their ignorance of any cause of their actions.'[29]

It is not too difficult to see how such an approach complicates the issue of political commitment and daily practice for the radical philosopher. Certainly, it places a large question mark over Che Guevara's slogan that it is 'the duty of the revolutionary to make the revolution' — a call to which Debray was exposed even before he was to grapple with Althusser's rejection of, 'the empiricist model of a chance "hypothesis" whose verification must be provided by the political practice of history *before* we can affirm its "truth"'.[30]

Combine these two positions and you can readily attempt to make the revolution free of any prior 'historical' verification of your ideas, or, alternatively, you might stoically restrict yourself to contemplation and criticism. Althusser tended to the latter option, albeit at some cost to his real-world relations with the leadership of the French Communist Party. It is perhaps telling that, on 1 March 1967, just as Debray was making his way from La Paz to the guerrilla zone,

Althusser wrote his student a letter, commenting on Debray's recently published book *Revolution in the Revolution?* Althusser says:

> The struggle poses urgent demands. But it is sometimes *politically urgent* to withdraw for a while, and to take stock; everything depends on the theoretical work done at that time ... Time thus taken away from the struggle may ultimately be a saving of time ... I see this as being the duty of all working class and revolutionary intellectuals. They are entrusted by the people in arms with the guardianship and extension of scientific knowledge.[31]

It was, of course, too late. Debray, like many students, had drawn rather different conclusions to those of his professor. 'The intellectual,' he wrote in *Revolution in the Revolution?*:

> will try to grasp the present through preconceived ideological constructs and live it through books. He will be less able than others to invent, improvise, make do with available resources, decide instantly on bold moves when he is in a tight spot. Thinking that he already knows, he will learn more slowly, display less flexibility.[32]

Some might think this observation good for most occasions, but Debray was applying it to guerrilla warfare, with which strategy for the Latin American revolution he had already become closely identified through the publication in 1965 of an extended essay, 'Castroism: the Long March in Latin America'.[33] Perhaps, despite the pious disclaimers just mentioned, he saw in guerrilla warfare more than just a repudiation of the *mores* and experience of the École Normale Supérieure. Maybe he discerned in the conjunction of intellect and force that praxis about which Althusser had lectured and around which no small part of classical literature revolves.

Whatever the case, Debray's writing on this subject is not essentially original. Despite a distinctive polemical flair and analytical insight, its central thrust is clearly derived from the interpretation of the Cuban revolution made by Che Guevara, who within months of the overthrow of Batista's dictatorship produced an admirably cogent defence of what became known as *foquismo*. Guevara tells us,

> We consider that the Cuban Revolution contributed three fundamental lessons to the conduct of revolutionary movements in America. They are:

Popular forces can win a war against the army.

It is not necessary to wait until all conditions for making revolution exist; the insurrection can create them.

In underdeveloped America the countryside is the basic area for armed conflict.

Of these three propositions, the first two contradict the defeatist attitude of revolutionaries or pseudo-revolutionaries who remain inactive and take refuge on the pretext that against a professional army nothing can be done, who sit down to wait until in some mechanical way all necessary objective and subjective conditions are given without working to accelerate them.[34]

Of course, the disastrous defeat of Guevara's own guerrilla was but the most poignant example of the insufficiencies of this compelling voluntarism, against which the political objections and historical evidence mounted up with tragic velocity. For our purposes there is no need to detail this process, which is the subject of a rich literature.[35] However, it is certainly worth noting that the appeal of a political philosophy rooted so positively in *making* a revolution and overcoming objective constraints through *action* is not limited to periods of radical optimism and advance; it may also — if not equally — acquire a constituency in times — such as our own — of embattlement and despair.

Debray's practical experience of conducting this struggle was short and sobering. Arriving at Che's camp in the first week of March 1967 together with two other foreign visitors, he was initially anxious to become a combatant although he had entered Bolivia officially and as a journalist for a Mexican magazine. Guevara, however, immediately asked him to organise a solidarity campaign in France, and noted pithily in his diary that the suggestion that Debray return to Europe via Cuba was 'an idea which coincides with his desires to marry and have a child with his woman'. A week later Guevara, who gave Debray three interviews, noted that, 'the Frenchman stated too vehemently how useful he could be on the outside' — an account that Debray, to his considerable credit, himself volunteered before Che's diary was published.[36] Indeed, at his trial the Frenchman — whom the guerrillas nicknamed 'Danton' — made an eloquent defence speech around his declaration, 'I regret that I am innocent'.[37] In this he stresses that Guevara even gave his increasingly burdensome visitors a choice of how and when to leave the force — an offer which, given the progressively vulnerable position of the guerrilla, clearly indicated that they were not subject to military discipline.[38]

The fact that Debray was able to make an unashamedly heroic defence speech owes not a little to his lawyer, Raúl Novillo Villarroel, whose enterprising but careful demolition of the loose case made against his client revealed the determination of the three military judges to pass a verdict of guilty and impose the maximum sentence of 30 years. This should not surprise us — a score of young conscripts had been killed during the seven weeks of Debray's presence with the rebels, and yet now not only De Gaulle and Sartre but also Malraux, Robert Kennedy and Bertrand Russell were requesting a pardon and scrutinising the legal procedures and moral rectitude of their country. Moreover, the guerrilla had clearly been set up and led by Cubans, and here was this Frenchman who supported the whole enterprise and yet expected with Olympian condescension to get off because he had not himself squeezed a trigger. Recognising the odds — but not, I think, quite why they were so poor — Debray cast aside caution. In a closed session, following an officially contrived outburst by spectators, he informed the colonels,

> Each one has to decide which side he is on — on the side of military violence or guerrilla violence, on the side of violence that represses or violence that liberates. Crimes in the face of crimes ... You choose certain ones, I choose others, that's all.[39]

But it is not quite all, for while a colonel might indeed *commit* a crime, an intellectual would only *be on its side*. Debray, then, standing on firm legal ground, makes a moral virtue out of a necessity. 'Guilty of what?' he asks his judges. 'And on what grounds? Political? Granted. Criminal? Inadmissable'.

> .... tell me: 'We are condemning you because you are a Marxist-Leninist, because you wrote *Revolution in the Revolution?*, a book that was read by some guerrillas in your absence. We are condemning you because you are a confessed admirer of Fidel Castro and came here to speak with Che

without first requesting permission from the authorities ...'
That's fine. I have nothing to say.[40]

Debray's wish was not granted. Apart from anything else, the international furore caused by his trial had persuaded Barrientos to execute Guevara summarily in order to avoid an even worse outcry. Now that this had been done and still held the world's attention a month later, there was nothing whatsoever to be gained from indulging the Frenchman.[41]

Debray spent over three years in prison before being released by a military president. In February 1968 he was allowed to marry his sweetheart, Elizabeth Burgos, who was given visiting rights for ten days every three months. He had, of course, nothing to do with the events in Paris of that year — a fact that might explain his subsequent interpretation that their 'real meaning' was the establishment of a new bourgeois republic on a 'modern or American individualist agenda'.[42] Upon his release he interviewed the Chilean president Salvador Allende, the leading regional exponent of 'the peaceful road to socialism', but whilst there are clear signs of Debray being chastened, he showed no major shift in his line. Indeed, after Allende's death in 1973, the Frenchman wrote in his account of Guevara's last campaign that 'it is right to fight'.[43]

The shift, I think, comes after Debray has settled his analytical accounts with the guerrilla experience in the two-volume work *La critique des armes,* the publication of which in 1974 coincided with the onset of dictatorial regimes in South America. Aside from several novels, apparently written for personal catharsis and not without some quite nasty things to say about readily identifiable individuals, Debray leaves Latin America and concentrates upon France itself.[44] It is unremarkable, even from what little has already been described, that he should write a study of modern intellectuals — a survey that was predictably controversial and unusually 'empirical' in its approach.[45] Indeed, it is refreshing to find — even if only in a footnote in the *Critique of Political Reason* — this author declaring, 'No concrete analysis of a given historical period can proceed by deduction (the use of categories). At most it can infer certain localised results and contrast them with a global conception of social history.'[46]

At times the sheer eclecticism and lack of focus of this work put one in mind of Ortega y Gasset's comment of Stendhal — that he 'possessed a head full of theories; but ... lacked the gifts of a theoretician'.[47] This may sound harsh, but to a non-theorist it looks like pretty good company to be keeping, and the view, I think, is justified by Debray's reluctance to develop theories beyond his immediate polemical needs. This is the case in his latest work, *Que vive la república,* a quite emotional text that places its author in the tradition of Michelet and Durkheim as he revindicates the state and the collective — even when known or felt through myth — against the particularities of civil society. One does not baulk when Debray effectively fingers post-modernism as landscaped ethnomethodology, but when he protests that the media today pays inordinate attention to the death of a celebrity from AIDS, wondering why it cannot take corresponding interest in the grandeur of a speech by Saint-Just, one feels that this — rather than 'Danton' — would have been a more fitting *nom de guerre* for his earlier incarnation.[48]

Debray, of course, has been a servant of the state for over a decade, first advising president Mitterand on third world affairs and subsequently joining the Conseil d'État as well as serving as secretary of the South Pacific Council. It is, perhaps, a fitting irony that in this latter capacity he not only promoted a new regional university to 'combat Anglo-Presbyterian morality' but also defended the testing of nuclear devices on the Mururoa atoll by approving the detention of protesting squatters, including one Mr Charlie Chang and 17 members of his Taata Tahiti Tiana party who were found guilty under a 1935 statute relating to economic crimes. One does not, of course, imagine that Mr Chang and his followers played any part in Mitterand's recent call for other states to follow his 'unilateral' halting of nuclear tests, but one is grateful that the choice of violence on offer was so clear-cut.

Since we have have moved on rather precipitately 25 years from 1967 let me turn briefly to the question raised in the title — 'All gone or more to come?' — which, apart from a not entirely misplaced evocation of infantile loss and deferred gratification, signals the lurking presence of some very grand theory in the shape of Francis Fukuyama's *The End of History and the Last Man.* This text, published in 1992, declares quite unambiguously that the ideal-types represented for us by Barrientos and Debray have no significant role to play in future world events although they may possibly linger on the margins of the stage until market economics and liberal democracy have finally seeped into every last cranny.

This is assuredly not the place to get to grips with Dr Fukuyama's expansive thesis, but we should at least take note of the extraordinary confidence with which it is propounded.

> 'Technology,' Fukuyama informs us, 'makes possible the limitless accumulation of wealth, and thus the satisfaction of an ever-expanding set of human desires. This process guarantees an increasing homogenization of all human societies, regardless of their historical origins or cultural inheritances. All countries undergoing economic modernization must increasingly resemble one another; they must unify nationally on the basis of a centralized state, urbanize, replace traditional forms of social organization like tribe, sect, and family with economically rational ones based on function and efficiency.[49]

For Fukuyama this is clear because we have already crossed the threshold of 'the end of history'. He is in no doubt that there will be, as he puts it, 'no further progress in the development of underlying principles and institutions because all of the really big questions (have) been settled'.[50] Moreover, he gives Latin America a quite significant role in a transition that nobody could sensibly deny has started to take place but that few would deign to insist — even with such a glorious mélange of borrowed philosophy, poor history and wholesale wishful thinking — is going to end where he says it will, still less that it is the final transition of all. Nonetheless, one has to accept that this is a theory that — rather like post-modernism — has proved quite resistant to the collapse of many of its particular features, reflecting more than a purely philosophical mood. Indeed, it might even bear out some of Debray's laconic ruminations on 'developments in thought' and 'developments in reality'.

There is no need to embark upon a detailed survey to comprehend why the present conjuncture in Latin America might contribute to the conviction that 'liberal democracy remains the only coherent political aspiration' and free markets, or liberal economics, an inevitable destiny.[51] As Victor Bulmer Thomas showed us so clearly some weeks

ago, the last five years in particular have seen an emphatic shift in
regional economic policy away from corporatist capitalism towards free
market principles, producing in several countries a notable reduction in
inflation as well as state intervention; overall economic performance
has registered a significant improvement.[52] Moreover, the imposition of
invariably harsh and initially inequitable and unpopular deflationary
policies has almost everywhere been undertaken by elected civilian
administrations — the result of an impressive if still unfinished transfer
from dictatorship to constitutional rule over the last decade. Since 1988
every country has held an election, and some — including Bolivia —
have been governed by three or four successive civilian administrations
resulting from the popular vote. Even in those cases, such as El
Salvador and Guatemala, where the electoral process began very much
as a US imposition and unashamedly excluded the left, there has been
some — occasionally much — progress towards a negotiated truce.

It is surely telling that the region's one communist state — Cuba
— has not made this transition, but it is also a widely held view that
spiteful US policy has played a major role in fortifying the nationalist
resolve of the leadership in Havana. It may even be that poor Cuba
is having to represent her sister republics in defying the arrogant
Gringo with a kind of dusk chorus of denunciation. If Fidel Castro
retains a remarkable popularity throughout the region, this now rests
heavily on nostalgia, and in many ways he would serve as quite a
passable amalgam of Barrientos and Debray.

Today the internationalist is not a European left-wing philosopher
but a conservative North American economist — Professor Jeffry
Sachs of Harvard, who, having presided over the Bolivian stabilisation plan of 1985 proceeded to Warsaw and Moscow, and, although
he may perforce have to dally there awhile, one can readily imagine
him pushing on to Beijing via Hanoi.

In the political realm the fact that the Latin American dictatorships were generally able to determine the nature of their departure
sets them apart from the experience of the east in 1989 and the west in
1945. It has also left a distinctly disturbing set of dilemmas between
revenge and reconciliation that are largely being handled at an official
level by a retreat from prosecution to amnesty to outright 'forgetful-
ness', as well as through a clear shift from the naming of those alleged

to have committed crimes to those known to have been their victims. This may be successful in terms of statecraft, but it is much less so at the level of civil society, especially for the direct victims of repression and their families. Anybody who knows Ariel Dorfman's recent play *Death and the Maiden* cannot fail to appreciate this.[53]

The question of human rights has not, in fact, provoked open conflict to the same degree as have economic policy and corruption. Moreover, if a refusal to forget or forgive remains at the core of both survival and deterrence, it is worth noting José Woldenberg's observation that, as the victims and their repressors die, the objective effects of this sentiment necessarily decline. In the case of Latin America, where the savagery of dictatorship has occurred very recently, the more likely scenario for *de facto* acquiescence is the coming maturity of a generation too young to have remembered — half the present population of Chile, for example, was born after Pinochet's coup in 1973.[54]

This picture may not fully accord with Fukuyama's bouncy predictions, but it would appear to herald the disappearance of the likes of Barrientos and Debray. On the one hand there is the warrior who grasps office with scant regard for policy and holds it by a combination of dashing deeds, demonisation and unabashed political dependency, and on the other, the radical thinker for whom foreignness and the terrible risks of failure on the insurrectionary road to civilisation are strictly secondary considerations in a decisive culture of commitment. Whether or not we deem these attributes even partly worthy, they are widely seen to be anachronisms. One is reminded of that passage in Gabriel García Márquez's *The General in his Labyrinth* where Bolivar admonishes a Frenchman: 'stop doing us the favour of telling us what we should do ... Damn it, please let us have our Middle Ages in peace!'[55] Except, of course, that after 160 years the Middle Ages are over, and, Fukuyama assures us, there is now on earth no apparent problem that is not soluble on the basis of liberal principles.[56]

Some caution is evidently called for. In the first place, not even Fukuyama's sources concur on whether the linear ascent of human history to this felicitous apogee will greatly reduce the incidence of warfare. As a result, we might expect the ancient disparities between the warrior and the scribe to continue for a while yet.

Secondly, it is typical of intellectuals to assign transcendent importance to underlying principles when ordinary folk are far more
concerned with the tactile reality pressing in on them every day. One
should not, then, underestimate the indisputably harsh price being
paid by Latin America's poor for economic stabilisation or the cholera
that is presently afflicting them or the sense of injustice over past
violations of human rights and present corruption. It would be even
more unwise to assume that these are consciously traded for acquiescence in liberalism on the belief that this is the true 'development in
reality'. Unlike in Eastern Europe, a great deal of what is currently
occurring has been seen before and illusions are more modest in a
region that has been far more and much longer market-oriented than
some theorists — right- and left-wing alike — recognise.

Against the impressive quietude of Argentina and Chile over the last
two years one must pitch the eruption of popular fury in Venezuela and
the suspension of constitutional guarantees and government in Peru.
Furthermore, one might note that in this latter country a particularly
violent and remarkably resourceful insurrectionary movement —
Sendero Luminoso — is headed by a man — Abimael Guzmán —
who has not been seen in public for over ten years, suffers acutely from
diabetes, and is the author of a thesis on Kant's theory of space. These
are not obvious components of a charismatic leader although among
several Bolivian figures who exercise an influence well beyond the
customary parameters of public respect I would single out Eduardo
Nava Morales, for many years Dean of Economics at San Andrés
University in La Paz, a man whose work on Keynes in the early 1950s
had an influence on the MNR, and who now, with the loss of his
middle ear aggravating a famously bad temper, poor eyesight and a
tendency to obesity, may be seen each day being assisted down the
street to his classes by students whom he will shortly berate.

It is, though, much more often a combination of healthy physique
and oratorial energy that one associates with charismatic authority, as
illustrated by the description given in the Mexican daily *La Jornada* of
Comandante Hugo Chávez, the officer who led a violent coup attempt
in Venezuela this last February against the deeply disliked regime of
Carlos Andrés Pérez. Given Chávez's subsequent popularity, it would
seem clear that many people shared *La Jornada' s* view of him as,

young and slim. His trim and clean *mestizo* features highlighted
a smooth sensuality. The contrast with the palid and flaccid
masks of the parliamentary bureaucracy was striking ... the
sense of self-control and military discipline, honour and serene
conviction in the face of uncertain destiny distinguished the
soldier as a classic hero ... his words invoked with tenderness
the name in which independence is rooted: Bolívar ... the
soldier accepted full and absolute responsibility for the events of
the night — something which surprised public opinion, tired of
a political system that, in the name of anonymity, permits social
crimes to be committed with impunity.[57]

This contrast, which is not too exaggerated, evokes that between
Barrientos and the MNR. More importantly, however, the inclusion
of Bolivar's name in the title of the rebel movement underlines the
dangers of adopting Fukuyama's unproblematic division between
ancient and modern, or the post-historical. For the fact is that in
Latin America the two are not separate — not even parallel — but
passionately entwined. It is not, then, simply a question of arguing
that Latin American 'modernity' began in 1922 with the publication
of César Vallejo's poem *Trilce*, or in 1946 with the opening of the
Volta Redonda steelworks, or in 1973 with the coup in Chile. Rather,
it is a matter of unburdening ourselves of the unilinear perspective
that confuses the 'development' of political economy with the
'nature' of a society in its entirety.

Last month I attended a clandestine meeting in an industrial
suburb of Mexico City where a man known as *el hermanito* and reckoned to be inhabited by the spirit of the great lord Cuauhtémoc
conducted major surgical operations with a regular household knife
and without anaesthetic on patients who included qualified doctors
and computer programmers as well as peasants and street-sellers. As
a result, I am probably too impressed by and indulgent of the
regional propensity for metaphysics in general and rebirth in particular, but one ignores such phenomena at the cost of gravely
misunderstanding the people for whom they possess great meaning.
There is undoubtedly a quality of innocence about the persons and
activities of Barrientos and Debray; they belong to a bygone age.
Yet innocence is defiantly relative.

I want to finish by upholding the claims of 'the third man'. By this I mean a representative of those who died in defeat, as opposed to Barrientos, a victor felled in his prime, or Debray, one of the vanquished who was spared to ruminate. 'All gone' means 'disappeared', which in Latin America is immediately understood to signify physically executed with the body destroyed or hidden. As a result, there are very many names that one could pin on this third figure, but today I choose Jorge Ríos Dalenz — a man whom I never met and who does not appear in the report of the Rettig Commission set up by the new Chilean government. This is because investigation of those killed under Pinochet depended upon a submission by family or close friends, and Ríos was a Bolivian without relatives in Chile.

Chichi Ríos Dalenz, a member of the Movement of the Revolutionary Left exiled from Bolivia two years earlier, was executed at the same time as the singer Víctor Jara — on 15 or 16 September 1973 — in the Estadio Chile, where they had been held for three days.[58] Once described as 'the flower of the Bolivian left' for his restless creativity and organisational energy, he is now little more than a sentimental footnote in the past of Jaime Paz Zamora, who was his friend, admirer and party comrade, and who today subscribes to many of the views held by Fukuyama and is president of the Republic of Bolivia.

It is testimony to the generosity of the people of Chile that last year Jorge Ríos and the other foreigners who died in the Estadio Chile were each remembered in song alongside their compatriots as that place was subjected to a secular and remarkably optimistic 'purification', or exorcism. Perhaps a response more fitting to the present occasion would be to reserve a quota of doubt with respect to both the inevitability of history and the full identity of its authors.

## Notes

1    There is no contemporary English edition that reproduces Plutarch's 'coupling', but for a sampling see Ian Scott-Kilvert's translations for Penguin: *The Rise and Fall of Athens: Nine Greek Lives* (London, 1960), and *Makers of Rome* (London, 1965).

2    J.H. Elliott, *Richelieu and Olivares* (Cambridge, 1984); Michael R.

Beschloss, *Kennedy v. Khrushchev: The Crisis Years, 1960–63* (London, 1991); Alan Bullock, *Hitler and Stalin: Parallel Lives* (London, 1991). Elliott understandably organises his text around the Mantuan crisis whereas Beschloss is concerned only with a three-year period, within which the October 1962 'Cuban missile crisis' clearly provides a focal point. Bullock adheres to a much more precise (and extended) chronological parallelism, pausing for comparison in the year 1934, with Hitler newly established in power over a one-party state and Stalin about to embark on the purges.

3 D.A. Russell, *Plutarch* (London, 1973), p. 114.

4 Jean Lacouture, *De Gaulle: The Ruler, 1945–70* (London, 1991), p. 411.

5 *The Times,* London, 28 April 1969.

6 José Antonio Llosa, *René Barrientos Ortuño: Paladín de la bolivianidad* (La Paz, 1966).

7 Fernando Diez de Medina, *El general del pueblo* (La Paz, 1972), p. 15.

8 J. Fest, *Hitler* (London, 1974), p. 445.

9 Such a conjunction frequently produces a relationship described as 'charismatic'. For Charles Lindholm this is a 'concept of a compulsive, inexplicable emotional tie linking a group of followers together in adulation of their leader', in *Charisma* (Oxford, 1990), p. 6.

10 Teniente René Barrientos, *Mensaje al ejército: Gestación histórica de la revolución boliviana* (La Paz, 1948, reprinted 1965).

11 *El Diario,* La Paz, 18 April 1965.

12 Raul Peña Bravo, *Hechos y dichos del general Barrientos* (La Paz, 1982), pp. 73–74.

13 However, the close contemporary association of 'sex appeal' with charisma is not one that would be readily recognised by Max Weber and would be difficult to square with the political standing of, say, Winston Churchill. Even the more frequently postulated linkage with sexual abstinence and religious order provides only a partial explanation. Max Weber, 'The Nature of Charismatic Domination', in W.G. Runciman (ed.), *Weber: Selections in Translation* (Cambridge, 1978), pp. 226–50.

14 Peña, *Hechos y dichos,* pp. 120–23.

15 'Meditación para los bolivianos', in Diez de Medina, *El general,* p. 289.

16 *Presencia,* La Paz, 30 November 1968.

17 *El Diario,* 11 July 1962. The animal, rarely found in this region, had been killed by local *campesinos,* whose reports excited such attention that the Chief of the US Military Mission, Colonel Paul Wiemert, went to investigate and acquired the hide — apparently without exchange of cash — in his words, 'as a reward for travelling to test sensationalist reports', *El Diario,* 12 July 1962.

18    Aristotle, *Nicomachean Ethics,* 4.1.
19    Between January and May 1965 Barrientos publicly changed his posi-
      tion at least six times on whether he would stand in the planned
      presidential elections. Of course, this was partly a ritual to promote
      expressions of support, but close colleagues report a similar indeci-
      siveness before the 1964 coup. Interview with Colonel Julio Sanjines
      Goitia, La Paz, August 1989. Peña Bravo, a distinctly unsympathetic
      author, does not hesitate to charge cowardice, asserting that Barrientos
      was nicknamed 'huallpa Melgarejo', or a palid, insufficient version of
      the nineteenth century tyrant Mariano Melgarejo, who was also from
      Tarata. Peña, *Hechos y dichos,* p. 29.
20    *El Diario,* 15, 18, 19 October 1961.
21    *El Diario,* 25 January, 26, 28 February, 1–7 March 1964.
22    *El Diario,* 23–28 March 1965. Far less publicity was given to a not dissim-
      ilar occurrence in 1976 when, according to immovable popular
      conviction, General Hugo Banzer was shot in the posterior by his formi-
      dable wife Yolanda because of his liaison with a young lady from Tarija.
23    Tcnl. Oscar Vargas Valenzuela, *La Verdad sobre la Muerte del General
      Barrientos a la Luz de Investigaciones Policiales, Técnicas y Esotéricas* (La Paz,
      1984), p. 179. Peña also attended a seance but did not himself
      commune with any spirit, *Hechos y dichos,* pp. 132–6.
24    Diez de Medina, p. 15.
25    Régis Debray, *Critique of Political Reason* (London, 1983), p. 15.
26    An excellent condensed account of Debray's trial and its background is
      provided in *Keesing's Contemporary Archive,* vol. XV1I1, 1969/70,
      pp. 234–93f. The present account of Che's *guerrilla* and Debray's links
      with it draws primarily on the following sources: Daniel James (ed.), *The
      Complete Bolivian Diaries of Che Guevara and Other Captured Documents*
      (London, 1968); Luis J. González and Gustavo Sánchez Salazar, *The Great
      Rebel: Che Guevara in Bolivia* (New York, 1969); José Luis Alcázar, *Ñanc-
      ahuazú: la guerrilla del Che en Bolivia* (Mexico, 1969); Gary Prado Salmon,
      *The Defeat of Che Guevara* (London, 1990); Régis Debray, *Che's Guerrilla
      War* (London, 1975) and *Prison Writings* (London, 1973), together with the
      reports of *The Times* and *The Guardian* of London and *Le Monde,* Paris.
27    Régis Debray, 'Some Literary Reflections', in *Prison Writings,* pp. 171;
      1867.
28    Louis Althusser, *Reading Capital* (London, 1972), p. 210.
29    Benedict Spinoza, *Ethica,* II, Propositions XLIII and XXXV, quoted in
      Perry Anderson, *Considerations on Western Marxism* (London, 1976),
      pp. 64–5.

30  Althusser, *Reading Capital,* p. 59.
31  Reprinted in Régis Debray, *A Critique of Arms* (London, 1977), p. 267, and also partially cited in Gregory Elliott, *Althusser: The Detour of Theory* (London 1987), pp. 68–69. In the Spring of 1968 Althusser repeats the same advice to Maria Antonieta Macciocchi, a militant of the Italian Communist Party: 'Politics is a protracted war. Do not be in a hurry. Try to see things in advance, and know how to wait today. Don't live in terms of subjective urgency. Know, too, how to put your defeats to use.' But in the same letter he appears to capitulate to 'empiricism' by declaring, 'Impressions are important, but above all it is the *facts* that count'. Maria Antonieta Macciocchi, *Letters from Inside the Italian Communist Party to Louis Althusser* (London, 1973), pp. 21 and 23.
32  Régis Debray, *Revolution in the Revolution?* (London, 1968), p. 21.
33  Reprinted in Régis Debray, *Strategy for Revolution* (London, 1970).
34  Ernesto Che Guevara, *Guerrilla Warfare* (New York, 1961), p. 1.
35  See, *inter alia*, Leo Huberman and Paul Sweezy (eds.), *Régis Debray and the Latin American Revolution* (London, 1969); Richard Gott, *Rural Guerrillas in Latin America* (London, 1973); Geoffrey Fairbairn, *Revolutionary Guerrilla Warfare* (London, 1974).
36  Guevara, *Bolivian Diaries,* pp. 127, 132.
37  The full speech, which was taped and released to the press the following day, is reproduced in Debray, *Strategy for Revolution,* pp. 227–73.
38  *Ibid.,* p. 242.
39  *Ibid.,* p. 244.
40  *Ibid.,* p. 238.
41  A long-standing view recently restated by both General Gary Prado and CIA agent Félix Rodríguez in interviews with Amalia Barrón of *Tiempo,* Madrid, reproduced in *La Razón,* La Paz, 3 November 1991.
42  Régis Debray, *Modeste contribution aux discours et cérémonies du dixième anniversaire* (Paris, 1978), p. 15.
43  Debray, *Che's Guerrilla,* p. 11. It is perhaps telling that in this text Debray continues to use an analogy employed seven years earlier in *Revolution in the Revolution?* — that of the *guerrilla* as a 'small motor' (and external cause) starting up the 'large motor' of the Bolivian mass movement. *Ibid.,* p. 143. This image is borrowed from Althusser, who states that Marx and Engels' declaration in *The Communist Manifesto* that, 'class struggle is the motor of history' is a 'basic Marxist proposition', *For Marx* (London, 1965), p. 215. Although he pushes the point too far, E.P. Thompson is surely right to insist that it is, rather, an

analogy that has been misinterpreted in a dangerously functionalist fashion. *The Poverty of Theory* (London, 1978), pp. 295–96. In all events, its appearance in a text written by Debray after his return to France clearly indicates a continued Althusserian influence, even as the philosopher entered decline and, eventually, tragic illness.

44  Régis Debray, *Les Masques* (Paris, 1987), which suggests that the differences between left-wing and right-wing are due to distinct 'sensibilities' but demonstrates little sensitivity towards Carmen Castillo, Debray's long-time companion who had previously been the lover of the Chilean revolutionary leader Miguel Enríquez.

45  Régis Debray, *Teachers, Writers, Celebrities: The Intellectuals of Modern France* (London, 1981).

46  Debray, *Critique of Political Reason*, p. 346.

47  José Ortega y Gasset, *On Love: Aspects of a Single Theme* (London, 1967), p. 19.

48  *Que vive la république* (Paris, 1989). It is notable that John Berger, writing about the photographs of Guevara's corpse in December 1967, meditates upon the role of Saint-Just in introducing a 'modern heroism': 'I despise the dust of which I am composed, the dust which is speaking to you; anyone can pursue and put an end to this dust. But I defy anybody to snatch from me what I have given myself, an independent life in the sky of the centuries'. *Discours et rapports* (Paris, 1957), p. 90, quoted in John Berger, *Selected Essays* (London, 1972), p. 49. It is perhaps telling that the last recorded words of Saint-Just were, 'I am the one who wrote that', with reference to the constitution of 1793, whereas Danton is widely reported to have addressed his executioner, 'Above all, don't forget to show my head to the people; it's worth seeing'. Norman Hampson, *Saint-Just* (London, 1991), p. 227; *Danton* (Oxford, 1978), p. 174. This latter incident is also compellingly captured in Andrzej Wajda's film *Danton,* which properly depicts this revolutionary figure as possessing more than a touch of Barrientos's populist flair, indecision and opportunist instincts.

49  Francis Fukuyama, *The End of History and the Last Man* (London, 1992), pp. xiv–xv.

50  *Ibid.,* p. xii.

51  *Ibid.,* p. xiii.

52  Victor Bulmer-Thomas, 'Life after Debt: the New Economic Trajectory in Latin America', Inaugural Lecture, Queen Mary and Westfield College, University of London, 5 March 1992, Institute of Latin American Studies Occasional Paper, no. 1, 1992.

53  Ariel Dorfman, *Death and the Maiden* (London, 1992). See also the impor-
    tant essay, 'Political Code and Literary Code: the Testimonial Genre in
    Chile Today', in Dorfman, *Some Write to the Future* (London, 1991).
54  Interview with José Woldenberg in *La Jornada,* Mexico City, 1 April 1992.
    Woldenberg's first novel tackles some similar themes in its attention to
    the Jewish experience in Mexico: *Las ausencias presentes* (Mexico, 1992).
55  Gabriel García Márquez, *The General in his Labyrinth* (London, 1990),
    p. 124.
56  Fukuyama, *The End of History,* p. xxi.
57  Eduardo Subirats, 'Venezuela: crónica de un golpe inacabado', *La
    Jornada, 5* April 1992. The brief radical manifesto of the Movimiento
    Militar Bolivariano is reprinted in *Latin American Chasqui,* London,
    March/April 1992.
58  Details of the fate of those held in the Estadio Chile are recounted in
    *Informe de la Comisión Nacional de Verdad y Reconciliación* (Santiago, 1991),
    vol. I, pp. 143ff.

# 5

# The Origins of the Bolivian Revolution of 1952:
## Some Reflections

Mr Mann then referred to the fact that Bolivia is a one-economy country with the Government dependent upon the mining industry and particularly the tin industry, for a very large part of its tax revenues and virtually all of its foreign exchange. He recalled the income of the average Bolivian is about one-fortieth of the income of the average US citizen and there abounds in Bolivia not only economic misery but social strife which makes Bolivia one of the most unstable countries in the hemisphere ... [Mr Symington] stated that while he recognised that the cost of producing a portion of the Bolivian tin from the marginal-type mines was higher than it was in other countries, he thought that question of preventing a collapse of the Bolivian economy should be met by grants from congress if they were needed rather than by subsidizing the economy through artificially high tin prices.

State Department Memorandum, 15 June 1951[1]

It is sheer incomprehension to assume that Bolivians will cause an upheaval against themselves. The United States and the American people have a substantial venture in Bolivia and I was sent here by the president of the United States, Harry S. Truman, to protect that venture. I therefore implore the Department of State to look for the roots of Bolivia's evils in countries other than Bolivia, for La Paz is as safe a city now as Norfolk, Virginia.

Ambassador Irving Florman, 2 August 1951[2]

Hay que reconocer que el capitán Sanjinés, a la cabeza de la Escuela Militar de Ingeniería, subió por la Avenida Arce, decididamente. Cuando pasaba por la Belisario Salinas y Arce, desde un edificio en construcción donde estaban Álvaro Pérez del Castillo y otros, armados, hubiera sido matado como pajarito, pero Pérez del Castillo reconoció a Sanjinés y dijo a sus compañeros que no dispararan: era su amigo.

Mario Sanjinés Ugarte[3]

## Points of Departure

L et's start at the end. Within the country there was very little public celebration of the fiftieth anniversary of the Bolivian revolution. The MNR held a formal act of commemoration in the Plaza Murillo of the capital, and its *subjefe*, Guillermo Justiniano, produced a dutiful essay for *La Razón* that identified the insurrection of 9–11 April 1952 as opening 'la era moderna, de la integración nacional, de la inclusión social, de la recuperación de los excedentes mineros para reconstruir el país, de un proyecto de desarrollo'.[4] But there was rather more attention paid to the promise by the party's presidential candidates, Gonzalo Sánchez de Lozada and Carlos Mesa, to distribute hundreds of thousands of hectares of state land to 12,000 families in Santa Cruz: 'Carlos Mesa afirmó que en 1952 se avizoró a este departamento como el futuro, y ahora es el presente de Bolivia.'[5]

It is understandable that even in an election campaign as uninspiring as that of 2002 the concerns of the present and aspirations for the future should prevail over recall of the past. (It could also be that these lines, written in London immediately after the funeral of the Queen Mother, reflect a local approach to ritual and ceremonial commemoration that is poorly calibrated to international sensibilities.) However, I have the sense that what might be termed the 'low commemorative profile' of 1952 in 2002 has less to do with the pressures of actuality than with a misfit between its formal historical calendar and the life-cycles of its principal leaders and figureheads. Subsequent improvements in life expectancy mean that there are still tens of thousands who recall the uprising of three days and two moonlit nights in Holy Week half a century ago. Indeed, at the end of the millennium there were still drawing a pension some 7,500 veterans of the Chaco War, which began twenty years before the revolution and which is often deemed to be its principal cause.[6] This particular anniversary is not 'historical' in the sense that there is nobody alive who can remember its origin, as was the case with the centenary of the foundation of the republic in 1925. Nor does it possess exclusive claim upon a set of martyrs. The deaths of Germán Busch (23 August 1939) and Gualberto Villarroel (21 July 1946) are sensibly remembered as sacrifices on behalf of a process that *would become* the revolution, but even if both men drew on the services of Víctor Paz Estenssoro, neither of these soldiers could fully incarnate a memory that possesses only in part a military character. Juan José Torres, the third officer to be interred in the Museo de la Revolución, was arguably a better representative of the populist military tradition rooted in the Chaco and post-revolutionary armed forces than René Barrientos, who flew Paz in from Buenos Aires to take power in April 1952. However, Torres' own death (Buenos Aires, 2 June 1976) is much more associated with the ideological battles of the late Cold War.[7]

Now these three have been joined by the civilian remains of Juan Lechín Oquendo (27 August 2001, aet. 89), founder of the FSTMB and the COB, eternal champion of syndicalism whose blend of rousing rhetoric and glycerine opportunism infuriated and mollified by turn:

> Soy exáctamente un boliviano y la vida me ha honrado con lo más profundo de nuestras pasiones del siglo XX: futbolista, soldado y minero. He vivido de acuerdo con los valores humanos en que creo. Creo en la bondad, en el coraje y en la honradez. He vivido peinando a la muerte como todo minero de nuestra tierra y quizá este coqueteo me previno de buscar regazo en el poder y hogar en el dinero. Para muchos, estos fueron errores, para otros fueron aciertos. No lo sé. No soy juez. Quiero y querré una Bolivia no sólo mejor, sino buena para todos.[8]

Lechín was an essential foil to the enigmatic Paz Estenssoro, whose more provincial demise (Tarija, 7 June 2001, aet. 93) masked a longer and more decisive historical role. The passing of 'Doctor Paz' was of a person who had mutated in true family fashion into a genteel rural patriarch. Moreover, the politician who died was one who not only built and led the revolution of 1952 but also played a big part in bringing it down in 1964 as well as reversing some of its core public policies when he returned to the presidency, for the fourth time, in 1985. Paz was the core figure of the revolution but never constrained by or fully symbolic of it.[9]

Had he lived another year, Víctor Paz might have provided the focus for a fuller, more energetic remembrance of 1952, but he was, of course, outside of the country, thousands of miles away, during the capture of power. The acknowledged leader of the uprising itself was Hernán Siles Zuazo, a less complex but equally controversial character whose final years were marked by public disappointment. Siles' death abroad (Montevideo, 6 August 1996, aet. 83) may have matched those of Jefferson and Adams by coinciding with national Independence Day. Yet he had generated much less historical respect than personal sympathy — as a man who reacted valiantly to circumstances rather than crafting events. Siles' was the 'human face' of 1952, but his own return to the presidency in 1982 was marked by economic and social chaos so profound that they have all but drowned out his Herculean efforts of the late 1950s to reconcile US pressure with popular expectations unleashed by the April uprising.

In keeping with republican and Bolivarian custom, we should mention the other recently departed presidents and vice-presidents around whom the memory of 1952 moved: Walter Guevara Arze (1996, aet. 84), who split from the MNR even before it fell and whose markedly *cochabambino* contribution remains under-valued, together with Ñuflo Chávez Ortiz (1996, aet. 73), the 'Lion of Inkahausi' in the civil war of 1949, *cruceño* proponent of an agrarian reform that barely touched the population of his own department, and a man more prepared even than Lechín to resign high office. Most particularly, we ought to note the passing of the oldest of the old guard, the writer Augusto Céspedes (11 May 1997, aet. 94), one of the first MNR militants to hold government office, only to lose it almost immediately (on 5 April 1944, just after Carlos Montenegro, who was removed on 11 February by the same US pressure). Céspedes' fierce, fluid prose acquired major book form once a decade — *Sangre de Mestizos* (1936), *Metal del Diablo* (1946), *El Dictador Suicida* (1956); and *El Presidente Colgado* (1966) — in a compelling combination of fiction, reportage, polemic and historical narrative.[10] These four titles — more than the writings and speeches of all those mentioned above — popularised and consolidated the MNR's vision of modern Bolivia and the role of the revolution for several generations at home and abroad.[11] Indeed, as we shall see, so successful has been this *óptica movimientista* that it is still a major target for academics, who are almost obliged to treat the *oeuvre* like the Bastille — a fortress that has to be stormed because it possesses such symbolic importance.

This does not apply to the only text which, in my view, competes with Céspedes' output — *Nacionalismo y Coloniaje* by Carlos

Montenegro. The reason is simple enough — this inspired interpretative essay was written in the immediate wake of the Catavi massacre of December 1942 and published in May 1944, within six months of the Villarroel government coming to power — the book forms part of the *ideológico*-intellectual origins of the revolution, not a subsequent defence or justificatory recasting thereof. Although its effective rejection of a distinctive colonial identity, dismissal of class conflict in the independence struggle, narrowly dichotomous presentation of political life thereafter, and celebration of the emancipatory power of the journalistic word are all legitimately open to critique, Montenegro's work is so palpably in and of its time that it has to be taken as an historical rather than critical subject. Few of those (many) who have a view on Montenegro argue that he is any less important because incorrect.

This might have been different had he continued to publish and polemicise what José Antonio Arze bluntly called his 'fundamentally Nazi ideas'.[12] But Montenegro died within a year of the MNR reaching power, killed by a cancer of the bladder that limited his government service to a few weeks as ambassador in Santiago (New York; 11 March 1953, aet. 49). His was the first state funeral of the revolutionary era but Montenegro could not be considered a martyr in the same way as, say, Vicente Alvarez Plata, who also died (15 November 1959, aet. 35) in the service of the MNR, but at the violent hands of others.[13]

Montenegro's intellectual legacy was most effectively carried forward by René Zavaleta Mercado, who never shook off this influence, nor that of Céspedes' pungent historical characterisations, nor the sobering experiences of official life (deputy 1962; minister of mines 1964) and exile (1971–1984), even as he dug deep into new reserves of Marxist theory. Zavaleta belongs to the next generation — the mestizo who will consult the *yatiri* when the enlightenment runs out of puff; the nationalist who is sufficiently socialist to be published by Casa de las Américas; and the Marxist sensible enough to leave political parties before they became doctrinal, let alone sclerotic. His early death (Mexico; 23 December 1984, aet. 47) deprived us of a fully developed vision of that original historical sensibility already so distinct from that of his contemporaries, such as Fernando Baptista and Guillermo Bedregal.

Of course, historiography is never the exclusive property of the victors, and it is definitely not so when those victors spent a scant dozen years in power, and retook it only 20 years later with many of their original policies reversed. Yet the MNR's effective 'move to the right' after 1964 — and certainly after 1985 — had the effect of limiting and softening a conservative criticism that had been so vitriolic in the 1940s and 1950s.[14] It may have been a higher democratic vocation that led Hugo Banzer to decorate the dying Lechín in May 2001, but such a public act would have been inconceivable in 1951 and 1961, let alone 1971 and 1981 (and Lechín had plenty of upper-class and right-wing mates). The MNR's exchanges with the orthodox right were almost always interesting, and they confused most US observers, whose own ideological outlook meant that when Paz returned to power in 1952, they could depict him as 'Communist of the Right' leading a 'blood-drenched comeback of the totalitarian MNR' whereas he had left office in 1946 directing a 'Nazi-type tyranny'.[15]

The left, by contrast, was comprehensively split by the MNR, which after 1946 quickly recruited a good portion of those who preferred direct action to earnest reading groups.[16] The pro-Moscow current lost such ground in the late 1940s that the PIR dissolved itself in 1952 and the Young Communist Party (1950) ventured little beyond the provision of 'popular front criticism' and a stern invigilation of Lechín's FSTMB leadership. For these militants the MNR may well have been 'insufficiently radical', but the PCB was completely unprepared for the subsequent arrival of Che Guevara and the imposition of a Cuban 'praxis'. Proletarians with a narrow syndicalist history, they did not need the likes of Debray to instil confusion and humiliation, but they got him and a good deal else besides. Bolivian Communism never acquired an authoritative historiographical voice, not even in Sergio Almaraz, whose critique of the tin oligarchy in *El poder y la caída* (1967) postdated his departure from the party, and whose critique of the MNR in *Réquiem para una república* (1969) showed an even more marked shift from dialectical materialism to social psychology.

On the other hand, that sector of Trotskyism which had enjoyed a quite healthy existence in the 1940s preying on the 'Stalinist treason' of the PIR and the 'petty bourgeois opportunism' of the MNR did manage to elbow itself a distinctive interpretative niche. According to Zavaleta, Bolivian Trotskyism was akin to the Salvation Army, but the righteous distribution of paper and ink in pursuit of an heroically

unattainable ideal was rarely accompanied by a charitable instrumen-
talism (operational or musical).[17] It was certainly predictable that
Guillermo Lora (born Uncía, 1922 and still vocally very much in the
quick) should remark, upon being informed of Lechín's death, that he
had never represented the workers' movement — 'yo le dijé a él que
cabalgaba en dos potros, en la derecha e izquierda, y le advertí que
desde ese momento sería mi enemigo y que lo combatirá . . .'[18]

Once exceptionally rich for its almost ethnographic attention to
detail in the industrial relations of the mines, Trotskyism in general,
and Lora's variety in particular, lost most of its interpretative
authority with the collapse of the 1971 Asamblea Popular, which
had fleetingly proffered a practical escape from the deadening hand
of abstract formalism and the repudiation of all and any political
creativity. Lora has reposed on his omniscient invective, and enough
young people have followed this for it to have subsisted in sterility
for at least two decades. It is, though, not so hard to see a productive Trotskyism tincture in the work of those who quietly slipped
the corral — to feminism, *indigenismo*, critical theory, anthropology
— in the mid-1980s, once 'resistance' palpably demanded intellectual risk and originality. It is not in the Trotskyism style and method
of denunciation that the younger, archive-based generation of
Bolivian historians is taking up the still daunting challenge of
writing on 1952. Yet Trotskyism example has provided them with a
species of critical precedent and a sturdy set of hypotheses.

**Issues at Stake**

At this point I should clarify that I am pragmatically treating the 'origins'
in my title as inclusive of 'causes', the possibility of which even historians
sometimes recognise when processes mutate into events, and when
synoptic presentation takes precedence over full narrative account.[19]
Equally, I am sure that the 'twentieth century' endowed by world time
has meaning for Bolivia, and in terms that are chronologically about
equidistant between the original and the Hobsbawmian 'shorter version'
of 1914–1989. This 'Bolivian twentieth century' would begin with the
federal revolution of 1899, which established liberalism in office and La

Paz as the seat of national power on the basis of a burgeoning tin industry, and it would end in 1985, with the collapse of the world tin price, the end of mining as a significant factor in national economic and cultural life and, under Paz's final presidency, an enfolding of the nationalist tradition associated with 1952 back into liberalism.

On such a schematic basis the narrow causes of a revolution-as-event and the broader origins of a revolution-as-process must include the politics of the tin industry, which, as we can see from Table 5.1, was in continuous productive growth up to 1930, contracted fiercely in 1930–1933, but continued to dominate the export economy thereafter, averaging 73.4 per cent of total exports in 1929–1949.

## Table 5.1: Tin Exports, 1900–1930

| Year | Metric tons (average p.a.) | Index | Value (£) | Unit price (£) | % total exports |
|---|---|---|---|---|---|
| 1900 | 9,139 | 100 | 1,331,466 | 145.7 | 41.0 |
| 1901–1905 | 13,163 | 144 | 1,483,941 | 112.7 | 58.7 |
| 1906–1910 | 19,333 | 211 | 2,620,547 | 135.8 | 56.3 |
| 1911–1915 | 23,282 | 254 | 4,013,239 | 172.4 | 51.3 |
| 1916–1920 | 27,158 | 297 | 7,769,616 | 286.1 | 63.3 |
| 1921–1925 | 29,129 | 318 | 4,984,102 | 170.6 | 70.5 |
| 1926–1930 | 39,981 | 437 | 6,600,753 | 165.1 | 73.6 |

**Source:** CEPAL, *El desarrollo económico de Bolivia* (Mexico, 1958), p. 7.

Table 5.2: World Production of Tin, by Country,
1900–1952 (000 tons)*

|  | 1900 | 1929 | 1935 | 1940 | 1948 | 1952 |
|---|---|---|---|---|---|---|
| Germany/ Austria | 0.1 | 0.1 | 0.0 | 0.6 | – | 0.4 |
| Portugal/ Spain | 0.0 | 0.1 | 0.1 | 2.0 | 1.0 | 2.4 |
| UK | 3.9 | 3.3 | 2.0 | 1.6 | 1.3 | 0.9 |
| Nigeria | – | 10.7 | 7.0 | 12.0 | 9.2 | 8.5 |
| South Africa | – | 1.2 | 0.6 | 0.6 | 0.5 | 1.0 |
| Congo | – | 0.1 | 6.5 | 12.3 | 12.9 | 12.3 |
| US | – | 0.0 | 0.0 | 0.4 | – | – |
| Bolivia | 9.1 | 47.1 | 27.1 | 42.1 | 37.3 | 33.0 |
| Burma | 0.1 | 2.6 | 4.5 | 4.5 | 1.1 | 1.1 |
| China | 2.9 | 6.8 | 9.4 | 6.3 | 4.9 | 5.6 |
| Indo-China | – | 0.8 | 1.4 | 1.5 | 0.0 | 0.2 |
| Japan | 0.0 | 0.9 | 2.2 | 1.8 | 0.1 | 0.7 |
| Malaya | 43.1 | 69.4 | 46.0 | 83.0 | 44.8 | 58.9 |
| Thailand | 3.9 | 9.9 | 9.8 | 17.1 | 4.2 | 9.7 |
| Indonesia | 17.6 | 35.7 | 24.7 | 41.3 | 30.6 | 36.2 |
| Australia | 4.3 | 2.2 | 3.1 | 3.9 | 1.9 | 1.6 |
| World | 85.0 | 192.2 | 146.8 | 235.0 | 152.0 | 176.6 |
| Bolivia % | 11.2 | 24.5 | 19.7 | 16.1 | 24.6 | 18.7 |

*Columns do not tally exactly because of rounding.
**Sources:** all but last row: John Thoburn, *Tin in the World Economy*
(Edinburgh, 1994), Tables 2.1, 3.1, 4.1, pp. 48, 68, 88. Last row: Mahmood
Ali Ayub and Hideo Hashimoto, *The Economics of Tin Mining in Bolivia*
(Washington, 1985), Table SA.13, pp. 87–88.

Moreover, as can be seen from Table 5.2, Bolivia's place in the international tin market was such that it was often subject to direct global pressures as well as possessing a quite commanding position. The importance of mining, then, requires us to return to it specifically, but even on the most generous estimates of the labour force involved — the figure of 43,000 at the end of the Second World War is generally accepted — it was less than 3 per cent of the population, dwarfed in human terms by the agricultural sector and rural society (in which perhaps one-third of all mineworkers in 1930 had begun their lives).[20]

On the eve of the revolution, agriculture accounted for a third of national GDP, against less than 15 per cent for mining. Thus although the rural/ *campesino* aspects of modern Bolivia are fully and expertly considered in other papers, their sheer and simple importance should be signalled here, not least because most comparative accounts depict the revolutionary role of the Bolivian *campesino* movement as subsequent to — and consolidatory of — that of the working class and urban middle class:

> Although *campesinos* did not officially take part in the Bolivian revolution as they did in Mexico, they in fact 'made' both revolutions. Those *campesinos* in Bolivia who seized land, facilitated by the breakdown of army and police authority in the provinces after 1952, helped undermine the political and economic power of the *hacendados* as a class. Had land not been redistributed, Bolivia at that time would have experienced little more than another coup. Labor already formally gained access to power in the 1930s and 1940s through its ability to name — directly or indirectly through political parties closely associated with labor — government ministries. However, the labor alliances with a segment of the petite bourgeoisie were not sufficiently forceful to displace 'la Rosca'.[21]

And just as we need to register the problems with neat sectoral frontiers, so is it necessary to recognise that international circumstances could rapidly and radically reverse approaches to the civilization versus barbarism dichotomy. The very same British diplomat who apologised to Foreign Secretary Eden for 'being wearisome' over the length to which he expatiated in May 1945, at the end of the Second World War, on the Congreso Indigenal — 'an event fraught with great

importance for the future history of Bolivia' — was two years later, in
the depths of the Cold War, ready to declare,

> when the low mental state of the average Indian, his innate
> bestiality and his hatred of the white, or near-white, are borne
> in mind, it will be realised what dangerous consequences such
> propaganda is likely to engender, particularly with the help of
> alcoholic stimulants.[22]

This is just the sentiment that, had he known of it, Augusto Céspedes
might well have quoted in *El president colgado*, where the congress is
depicted as a 'superficial reform', even though its 'decretos aboli-
cionistas sobresaltaron a los terratenientes feudales que engrosaron las
filas de la contrarrevolución'.[23] For Céspedes only the victory of April
1952 would settle the essential social score. His later texts, like the less
ebullient *movimientista* accounts, tend teleologically to depict a periodisation of 'immediate origins' in which the deeper challenge of nation
against colonialism etched by Montenegro is accelerated by the Chaco
War (1932–1935) and initial *post bellum* labour militancy (Tejada Sorzano,
1935–1936); erratically expressed by the 'military socialist' regimes of
Toro and Busch (1936–1937 and 1937–1939); repressed and rolled
back under the *Concordancia* (Quintanilla and Peñaranda, 1949–1943);
revived in 1943–1946 by the MNR in sub-optimal circumstances
because of the Second World War, its own lack of experience, and the
need for an unreliable military alliance (RADEPA/Villarroel); and
repressed anew (1946–1952) but with enhanced ferocity because of the
betrayal of the PIR and the Cold War.

Writing pretty much at the same time as Céspedes drafted his study
of Villarroel, Herbert Klein argued persuasively for the strength of we
might term the 'nationalist interpretation' because the numbers for
sustaining any explanation of the 1952 revolution through economic
immiseration and social mobilisation did not, to put it bluntly, add up;
or at least they did not do so until the late 1940s:

> To almost all Bolivians, the key to the understanding of the
> revolutionary process lies in the disastrous results of the
> Chaco War of 1932–15 ... (Yet) while most commentators
> have assumed that the Chaco War created social discontent
> and economic dislocation, a careful examination of the post-
> war period reveals neither of these effects. The Indian peasant

masses were easily reabsorbed into the feudal land system after the conflict, and the urban proletariat felt no unusual adverse effects or bitter hostility toward the system. As for the popularly accepted thesis of economic dislocation, that too is a myth. The national economy during and immediately after the war showed surprising resilience, and the immediate post-war years brought full employment, constantly rising imports and exports in a favourable balance of trade, and at first only moderate inflation ... The impact of the war must rather be seen in terms of political dislocations and basic changes in the political structure of national leadership and ideology.[24]

There can be little dispute over the impact of the Chaco War itself. The numbers, necessarily inexact, 'add up' simply by order of magnitude. The campaign of some 36 months — between April 1932 and June 1935 — was mostly fought hundreds of miles from established Bolivian settlements, in an environment thoroughly alien to the 250,000 men sent to the front — a very high percentage of all males aged between 17 and 50 in a population of some 2 million. Those sent to the front line in May 1934 had originally undertaken military service in 1915; the average age of the cohort demobilised that October was nearly 40, but their replacements included 17-year olds who would be under 40 in April 1952. (Lechín, who served in the Regimiento Abaroa and was wounded in action at Kilómetro Siete, was twice rejected for service because of his youth.)

Only from January 1935, when the Paraguayan offensive on Villamontes was repulsed, were Bolivian forces operating on remotely favourable logistical terms and in familiar terrain. Effective counter-attacks over the next four months led Asunción to seek a ceasefire. The fact, though, is that hitherto Bolivia had raised three entire armies and lost thousands of square kilometres of territory, 52,400 men dead (overwhelmingly through natural causes), 21,000 captured, 10,000 deserters, arms worth at least $4 million, and any lingering claim to efficiency and legitimacy on the part of its high command and the old political order which had done much to provoke the conflict in the first place.[25]

In one sense it is remarkable that a state could fund a major international war conducted with the most modern weaponry when it had

just declared inconvertibility and defaulted on its international debts
in the wake of the Wall Street crash. On the other hand, the fact that
between 1931 and 1935 the Bolivian government received some £2.5
million, or a quarter of the national budget, in direct loans from
three companies — and some 78 per cent of that sum from Patiño
Mines and Enterprises Consolidated (PMEC) — shows how starkly
dependent it was upon a powerful industrial elite. In a way, the 5,000
new lorries, the tanks, flame-throwers, fighter and bomber aircraft,
machine guns, howitzers and mortars bought from Europe and the US
may be viewed as offensive equivalents of the new extractive and
concentration equipment installed by Patiño in his Llallagua operation,
but all this weaponry proved to be entirely unproductive. It was not the
capacity of the new cannon effectively used by Sergeant Víctor Paz's
artillery unit in the defence of Villamontes that he recalled, so much as
the shared experience of adversity (often fraternity) between men of
distinct rank, class and race as well as between all those of *sangre mestiza*.

If the Paraguayans happened to be the enemy in the opposing
trench — and, remarkably, the Chaco Boreal was contested as if it
were a Flanders field — there had never been enduring animus
between the two peoples, and the nationalism that emerged from the
war was not narrowly xenophobic. For René Zavaleta,

> el país tiene razón cuando se siente frustrado porque, en la
> movilización, en la conducción de la Guerra, en la lucha de
> los días descubre que no es verdaderamente una nación. Los
> bolivianos van a conquistar o a defender el país territorial,
> descubren que hay que conquistar el país histórico cuyo
> enemigo no es, desde luego, el Paraguay.[26]

The likes of Paz, Siles, Céspedes and Montenegro — all of whom
saw front-line action — were quick to declare this baldly and boldly
— Céspedes' spell as ambassador in Asunción in the 1940s was
famously successful. And it may well be, as once suggested by René
Arze and increasingly supported by new scholarship, that the rural
population was not quite so readily reincorporated into the established structures of power. Dissonant, if not yet dissident, energy
was building up, less precipitately, volubly or directly — the timing is
more distended than in what Zavaleta terms 'seigneurial space' —
but the spark is shared.[27]

Reading Walter Guevara's *Manifiesto a los campesinos de Ayopaya* of May 1946, one is today struck by the incongruous addressing of a Marxist elite rhetoric to a rural audience. But one staccato passage tellingly combines nationalist zeal with the 'horse sense' of common folk:

> ¿Cómo pueden los americanos del norte, que no conocieron jamás la servidumbre feudal, entender nuestro problema del indio? ¿Quién tuvo mayor vocación democrática, Busch o Peñaranda? La respuesta es simple para los bolivianos, no lo es para los extranjeros. ¿No ensayó Busch la dictadura? ¿Cómo pudo entonces ser un demócrata más sincero que el General Peñaranda? La apariencia superficial, la única que se ve desde el extranjero, engaña fácilmente. Lo que no se sabe en los Estados Unidos o en el Uruguay es que no hay hogar pobre en Bolivia en donde no hay un retrato de Busch mientras que el general Peñaranda ha sido piadosamente olvidado, incluso por los que se aprovecharon de él.[28]

It was Busch who personally beat up the 70-year old Alcides Arguedas for writing a critical newspaper article, and he was only persuaded with difficulty not to shoot the tin magnate Mauricio Hochschild for failing immediately to comply with a decree requiring the tin companies to lodge all their foreign exchange with the Banco Central.[29] Yet Zavaleta has a point as strong as Guevara's when he tells that Busch, 'representa la concepción heroica de la nación. Insuficientes resultan esquemáticas, menguadas, pálidas las explicaciones racionales de la derrota y de la frustración.'[30]

However whimsical one deems such a poetics of frustrated collectivity, it was rejected at great cost by the Marxist left, which, having largely gone into exile during the Chaco conflict, sought in the late 1930s and early 1940s to lay the bases for a new and radical syndicalist movement. The Second World War immensely complicated the challenge facing the militants of the PIR, but they were, after all, Bolivians, and so presumably had the choice between responding to local opinion and borrowing foreign categories, tactics and alliances. The twisting tale of their dilemma is too complex to bear even the briefest paraphrase here. I would, though, argue that it is precisely a failure to comprehend the sentimental and imaginative legacy of the Chaco — rather than their militant pacifism during the war itself — which lay behind the inability of the party leadership to hold on to a significant popular constituency built upon a radical social programme and then lost to the MNR.

In Zavaleta's telling depiction, Busch — together with Villarroel and RADEPA five years later — sought to impose a military solution on an historical problem.[31] It was hardly in the nature of orthodox Marxists to sign up to such a proposal.[32] They could not grasp that although Busch, no less than Hochschild, possessed a bank account, his ultimate means for handling economic matters had to be the methods and kit in which he had been schooled and with which he had won fame as a patriot. Busch, however, is a hero because he eventually decided to kill himself and Villarroel because he effectively allowed himself to be killed.

The members of RADEPA responsible for the November 1944 executions at Chuspipata and Caracollo stand no higher than Luis Arce Gómez, responsible for the 1980 assassination of the MIR militants in the calle Harrington, and their murderous actions are, to my mind, direct precursors of the lynching of their comrade Villarroel and his aides in July 1946. By the time of the completely unnecessary elimination of Lieutenant Oblitas in September, a macabre kind of moral equivalence had been reached, and the customary rules of moral economy was restored. Thus, the repression of the protesting but unarmed *Potosino* miners in February 1947 — at the hands of forces directed by the baleful PIR — created great outrage, whilst the rebel casualties of the September 1949 Civil War, when both sides were armed and the question of power openly recognised to be at stake, were valiant casualties, not mere victims.

This, then, is not an entirely capricious ethical arena, but it is one that has to be respected for the purposes of making an appraisal of the fuzzy field of legitimation. That is the aspect that worries me about John Hillman's comments on Busch's decree of 7 June 1939 requiring all the large mining companies to lodge their foreign exchange with the Banco Central: 'The indispensable technical problem of just how the mining industry was to function under these new conditions was swept aside with a vacuous moral argument about the need to make amends for the past sins of capital flight.'[33]

This is a very good point — we shall have to return to it in a moment — but it is not the most important one. Even as late as June 1939 moral argument prevailed over technical policy. Capital flows were essential, but the Chaco was still the driver of the system. I reckon that Patiño and Aramayo — arriviste and aristocrat respectively, but savvy alike — intuited this and back-peddled on protestations over profit margins and lesser desidcrata of capitalist accountancy. The ever-calculating Hochschild, however, missed the indispensable point that there are markets in sentiment as well as commodities.

The crisis over the decree of June 1939 was certainly exceptional but still part of a pattern that is no longer presentable — whether from *nacionalista* or Marxist perspective — as a seamless, unproblematic and unchallenged class rule. This, I feel, is at the heart of Klein's original focus on the Chaco as historical driver, but it can be seen in other features too. Laurence Whitehead's careful analysis of the electoral record in the mining zones over the period 1923–1951 reminds us of the importance of studying local conditions when testing headline hypotheses:

> What emerges is that the pre-1952 system of political representation shaped the process of social mobilisation to a considerable extent. The image of unmediated political control exerted by the propertied classes over the disenfranchised masses requires substantial modification. Certainly the electoral system was narrowly based, and had been traditionally subject to manipulation by local elites. However, in the mining zone, such 'oligarchic' patterns of electoral control had started crumbling as early as 1920 ... Each brief interval of electoral freedom in the mining camps witnessed an upsurge of political and trade union activity, in which intransigent opposition to the mining management became the touchstone of electoral success.[34]

For our present purposes the key issue here is that of pacing. If, at least until 1946, it is the Chaco that dominates the 'strategic sphere' of political culture, this is hardly an evolutionary impulse; it cannot grow in its own terms alone. Indeed, in some senses, even when revivified by the Second World War, the Chaco is destined only to fade — to form part of historical memory, a moral marker and evocative index of agency and identity. Its momentum is expediently halted in the name of democracy upon the deaths of first Busch and then Villarroel; each time its revival is more diffuse and discursive. Yet underneath it, moving fitfully backwards and forwards, is a set of socio-political conflicts rooted in the mines. After 1946 those came to dominate the political dynamic, the dislocations caused by the Chaco now a familiar feature of the ideological landscape. Nevertheless these class conflicts certainly began before the war and deserve consideration in their own terms, even if we do not expect to find in them a determining explanation of 1952.

## Political Economies, Public Policies

It is much easier to assert the general existence of a tin oligarchy/*rosca minera*/*superestado minero* than it is to demonstrate in detail how such an elite secured its interests and enforced its rule. It is correspondingly tempting entirely to follow or comprehensively to reject the MNR account of the large tin enterprises as omnipotent, the principal bulwark against the attainment of national economic independence, and the main conduit for imperialist interests in the country. In practice, as we have seen, there were plenty of ideological challenges at the top, and from the early 1920s progressive organisation of the labour force in the mines meant that industrial relations became increasingly demanding. Labour costs could no longer be treated as entirely secondary to technical and financial issues, still less as unproblematic items on the balance sheet.

The sparkling exchange between Laurence Whitehead and Herbert Klein of some 30 years ago over the nature of inter- and intra-class power at the time of the Depression yields an interpretative balance in which the big companies (Aramayo, Hoschschild, Patiño), whilst relatively well protected by their international ties and facing an uneven challenge from labour, still had to contend with significant local pressures with respect to rail rates, the demands of small and medium miners for devaluation, and the financing of a state without other significant sources of internal revenue or, after 1931, the ability to borrow abroad. If, as Klein suggests, the companies were not unhappy with president Salamanca's belligerence towards Paraguay, then, as Whitehead indicates, the price of their own domestic belligerence was widespread resentment and sectoral opposition even before war broke out.[35]

More recently, Carmenza Gallo has provided a lucid review of the Bolivian state's dependence on the companies. Equally, Manuel Contreras has highlighted the previously under-valued role of the small and medium mining enterprises as well as revealing the extent to which, from the mid-1930s, the large companies were taxed through state control of their foreign exchange as much as by standard levies on exports and profits (Table 5.3).[36]

### Table 5.3: Tax Burden of Patiño Mines, 1924–1949

| | Export tax | | Profit tax | | Exchange tax | | Others* | |
|---|---|---|---|---|---|---|---|---|
| | £000 | % | £000 | % | £000 | % | £000 | % |
| 1924–1929 | 205.1 | 50 | 119.8 | 30 | – | – | 90.3 | 20 |
| 1930–1934 | 69.8 | 42 | 7.5 | 4 | – | – | 95.5 | 55 |
| 1935–1939 | 74.6 | 19 | 19.3 | 5 | 216.4 | 54 | 84.5 | 22 |
| 1940–1944 | 134.0 | 12 | 290.4 | 24 | 682.8 | 59 | 60.2 | 6 |
| 1945–1949 | 137.6 | 11 | 120.8 | 9 | 808.1 | 66 | 164.8 | 13 |

*Import and municipal; universities; Potosí centenary; Cochabamba–Santa Cruz road.

**Source:** Derived from Manuel Contreras, *Bolivian Tin Industry,* p. 43.

### Table 5.4: Mining Taxes and State Revenue, 1928–1952
### (Bs m, current)

|      | State revenue | Mining taxes | % Revenue from mines | Export value | Taxes % exports | Tin % exports |
|------|------|------|------|------|------|------|
| 1928 | 44.89 | 10.56 | 23.5 | 108.04 | 9.8 | 75.1 |
| 1930 | 34.83 | 4.18 | 12.0 | 87.67 | 4.8 | 76.2 |
| 1932 | 20.50 | 3.65 | 17.8 | 45.56 | 8.0 | 72.3 |
| 1934 | 32.40 | 13.55 | 41.8 | 165.44 | 8.2 | 79.5 |
| 1936 | 102.06 | 32.81 | 32.1 | 144.01 | 22.8 | 61.5 |
| 1938 | 274.27 | 142.84 | 52.1 | 647.30 | 22.1 | 63.3 |
| 1940 | 606.02 | 299.64 | 49.4 | 1,678.51 | 17.9 | 71.3 |
| 1942 | 976.35 | 606.83 | 62.2 | 3,082.63 | 19.7 | 66.8 |
| 1944 | 1,094.99 | 647.26 | 59.1 | 3,094.39 | 20.9 | 68.4 |
| 1946 | 1,037.64 | 491.17 | 47.3 | 2,772.05 | 17.7 | 70.6 |
| 1948 | 1,393.94 | 764.20 | 54.8 | 7,360.60 | 10.4 | 71.1 |
| 1950 | 1,755.44 | 853.97 | 48.6 | 8,253.19 | 10.3 | 70.8 |
| 1952 | 3,050.89 | 1,392.55 | 45.6 | 22,070.69 | 6.3 | |

**Source:** Walter Gómez D'Angelo, *La minería en el desarrollo económico de Bolivia* (La Paz, 1978), Table 12, p. 191.

Table 5.4 relies on the statistics of Walter Gómez, whose numbers are at the core of Gallo's study and also used by Contreras. Here they show the official levels of tin company contributions to the national budget over the two decades before 1952. It can be seen that, even before Busch's decree of June 1939, open mining taxes were increasing both absolutely and relative to revenue as a whole. It is, then, not so surprising that after the decree Patiño, who was safely ensconced in Paris, should feel obliged to give Busch his unalloyed views of the matter:

in a moderately organised country the burdens of a war and post-war period would have been equitably distributed, but in Bolivia this could not happen; all these burdens have weighed exclusively on mining ... with a tin price of about £160 per ton the mining industry has paid to the state practically 100% of its profits.[37]

In a series of detailed and energetic articles over the last 15 years John Hillman has drawn attention to this position and gone beyond Patiño himself to challenge the *nacionalista* account of the social forces in the pre-revolutionary era. For Hillman,

it is no longer feasible to see that weakness [of the state] as a function of the *superestado*, a power above the state, but rather as a result of the distinctive pattern of class and fiscal relations which makes it impossible for any group, including the large miners, to secure stable alliances.[38]

In what is perhaps the most revisionist facet of his ongoing reappraisal of the large tin corporations, Hillman shows that it was not only ideologically unsympathetic regimes, such as those of Busch and Villarroel, that retained the 'exchange tax' on the companies (indeed, under Villarroel, Víctor Paz's management of the economy ministry was one of the more friendly): 'all governments, regardless of ideological persuasion, would ... be compelled to continue to rely on exchange control', because of overbearing socio-economic realities.[39] Moreover, this dependence constituted a paradoxical form of power on the part of an inefficient state over the technically efficient but politically and fiscally vulnerable enterprises:

The companies were never able to reverse the fiscal policy of the state whereby they provided the major source of revenue, and they always had to recognise its power to allocate quotas ... While the state claimed authority over the mining industry, it lacked the administrative capacity with which to sustain it. Conceptualising the weakness of the state as though it were a function of the large companies misses its internal source.[40]

Here the polemical qualities of the argument may be stretching somewhat too far ahead of its evidence, but Table 5.5 does at least suggest a consistency of behaviour by the administration of

1932–1952 with respect to controls over the companies' foreign exchange holdings.

### Table 5.5: Foreign Exchange Policies, 1932–1952

| Government | Foreign exchange control (%) | Concessions | Other factors |
|---|---|---|---|
| Salamanca | 65 | Dividends excepted | Exchange rates of Bs 20 (necessities) and 80 per £ |
| Tejada Sorzano | consolidated | | |
| Toro | consolidated | | 13 exchange rates |
| Busch | 100 (7 June 1939) | None | *impuesto adicional* of 41% for consolidation of exchange rates; 30% profits tax |
| Quintanilla | 50 (1 Octobler 1939) | None | *impuesto adicional* set at 30% |
| Peñaranda | 42 (15 May 1940) | None | *impuesto adicional* cancelled |
| Villarroel | 100 (13 April 1945) | 40% retained for costs; 15% profit remittance | |
| Hertzog | | | |
| Urriolagoitia | 100 (11 August 1950) 52 (21 October 1950) | None | |
| Ballivián | | | Tin exports halted (October 1951) |

Let us follow Hillman through to the logical conclusion of his argument:

> The *superestado* thesis was a very convenient way of simplifying a very complex pattern of politics, but it came at considerable expense. In exaggerating the power of the large mines, it overlooked not only the significance of the struggle between Patiño and Hochschild but also the importance of the underlying features of the tin industry, and the need to build the administrative capacity of the state with which to address them.[41]

## Endgame

One senses here the next — unknown but much anticipated — step in Professor Hillman's project whereby the mines nationalised by the MNR will be shown to be much less effectively managed than under the private companies. This, of course, would hardly be an original position, but it has never been so fully analysed with respect to the experience of the 1930s and 1940s, and it has rarely been discussed in non-partisan terms. At the same time, Hillman's emphasis upon competition between capitalist firms is a most welcome qualification to past insistence upon the unity of the corporate bloc. His distinction between Patiño's high-grade Llallagua ores and Hochschild's operation based on lower quality primary material at Unificada might carry less weight by the mid-1940s — as shown in Table 5.6 — but it is still germane to policy differences that extended well beyond national frontiers and, eventually, into international relations.[42]

Hillman also picks up on Klein's early emphasis on the international nature of the large firms (although in the case of Aramayo this, to the best of my knowledge, extends little beyond company registration in Switzerland from 1915). Here the argument might be expected to play more directly towards the MNR's theses on 'imperialism'. Hillman, however, provides a plausible rebuttal of the notion that the enterprises — and indeed the governments alongside which they had to negotiate in an essentially regulated international market — 'sold out' to the US for lower prices than they could have secured during the Second World War. Given that, in a way, he is up against Céspedes and Almaraz, Professor Hillman's prose is suitably pithy: 'the notion that the war created a special opportunity for the Bolivian government to secure a substantially greater transfer of real economic resources from the wealthy to the poor is . . . . sheer fantasy.'[43]

### Table 5.6: Tin Production by Firm (Annual Average, Metric Tonnes)

|  | Patiño | | Hochschild | Aramayo | National |
|---|---|---|---|---|---|
|  | Total | Llallagua |  |  |  |
| 1940–1944 | 19,601 | 14,616 | 10,192 | 2,678 | 48,921 |
| 1945–1949 | 16,022 | 12,118 | 9,666 | 2,607 | 36,571 |
| (1945) |  |  |  |  |  |
| grade % |  | 1.9 | 2.6* |  |  |
| Recovery % |  | 74.5 | 71.4* |  |  |
| Shifts/tonne |  | 208 | 303* |  |  |
| $/tonne$^3$ |  |  |  |  |  |
| Labour |  | 444 | 405* |  |  |
| Other |  | 556 | 874* |  |  |
| Depreciation |  | 39 | 55 |  |  |
| Total |  | 1,039 | 1,334 |  |  |

*Colquiri
**Source:** derived from Hillman, *The Mining Industry and the State*, Tables 3 and 4, pp. 60–61.

This is an unusually complicated issue, but the layperson can make some progress through recognition that no 'free market' for world tin existed between 1931 and 1945, there first being a cartel set up as the International Tin Council, which administered three production quota agreements (1931–1933; 1934–1936; 1937–41, all of which treated the Bolivian firms quite favourably), and then a US government price, which, as Hillman convincingly shows, the

British were effectively obliged to match. Secondly, Bolivia had never possessed a smelter, and so could not achieve full vertical integration within her own borders, giving relatively technical issues of production a strong international projection. Thirdly, the US neither produced tin itself nor smelted it until 1942.[44]

Until the World War, all the Bolivian companies sent their ore to be smelted in Europe, where Patiño owned a major stake in the large Williams Harvey smelter at Bootle (Liverpool). After the outbreak of hostilities in Europe, Washington built its first industrial facility at Texas City, and from early 1942 began to supplement its imports from the Belgian Congo by buying ore from Aramayo and Hochschild, who eagerly sought to exploit this unprecedented opportunity. Washington had earlier accepted the request from the Peñaranda government not to allow Patiño to build a second smelter of his own in the US, even though this would have allowed optimal application of the expertise built up at Bootle, because it would also have strengthened the effective monopoly of the company. Equally, after the Catavi massacre, Judge Magruder's report to the US government on labour conditions in the Patiño mines gave PMEC a particularly poor reputation within the Roosevelt administration. Nonetheless, in 1944 the US did buy small quantities of Patiño ore, the high quality of which made a perfect 'sweetener' or catalyst for the smelter of lower-grade mineral.[45] However, there was no substantial shift of the Patiño trade from the UK, not least because London needed to replace the loss of its Malayan imports and also required a high-quality mix to fully exploit the processing of Nigerian ores. Accordingly (and after the requisite bluff-calling and hand-wringing), the British were prepared to match the higher prices offered by Washington. Indeed, they conceded relatively generous allocations of hard currency to both Patiño and Aramayo.

In sum, then, there did exist some margin for the Bolivian companies to negotiate, and Hillman suggests that the Allies only coordinated their tin pool with any real effectiveness in 1942, the first year of its full operation. As measured by import capacity, the companies, which palpably sought to improve their position on both sides of the North Atlantic, increased their real income to 50 per cent above that prevailing before the Crash.[46] Quite whether this chimes with the claim made above by Hillman that any major transfer would be limited to the realm

of fantasy is a matter for discussion. It does, though, have an important link to the post-war position since, whatever the reasonableness of
the price and efforts to secure it, increased production permitted the
accumulation by the consumer states of buffer stocks, which were
subsequently depicted — and not only by *nacionalistas* — as being vital
to the capacity of the US to 'fix' a notionally free world market price,
and to do so at a time when demand was falling. It is this issue, and how
it played through into the labour policies of the firms after the fall of
Villarroel, when the ousted MNR needed desperately to secure a
stronger working class alliance, that strikes me as more salient than
charges over missed opportunities from 1941 to 1945.

We cannot know the precise extent of the US buffer stock after the
war because this was a state secret. However, Table 5.7 provides a broad
indication of the wartime position from which some sensible extrapo-
lation can be undertaken. One should bear in mind that although tin is
not a metal extensively used in the construction of armaments, demand
would naturally have fallen after the end of the war. On the other hand,
the return of supplies in South East Asia was rapidly followed by the
threat of their loss under a communist takeover, most directly, of
course, in Malaya in the early 1950s. Under such circumstances,
including the communist capture of power in North Vietnam (1946)
and China (1949), these 'buffers' could have appeared to strategic plan-
ners as less generous than they might seem today.

### Table 5.7: US and UK Tin Stocks, 1942–1945 (Long Tons, Metal Content)

|      | Ore and metal | | Weeks' supply | |
|------|---------|--------|------|------|
|      | US      | UK     | US   | UK   |
| 1942 | 132,369 | 28,072 | 112  | 40   |
| 1943 | 135,043 | 23,335 | 121  | 42   |
| 1944 | 118,338 | 29,943 | 96   | 75   |
| 1945 | 100,808 | 32,600 | 88   | 87   |

**Source:** Derived from Hillman, *Bolivia and British Tin Policy*, p. 305.

In the event, of course, it was in Korea that war broke out, driving the open price of tin, which had fallen to around 80 cents per pound, back up to $1.03. But that was in June 1950. The depressed market of the immediate post-war years meant that the Bolivian companies' production in 1947–1952 was a fifth lower than in 1940–1946, and they were now earning less in real terms than in the mid-1920s. Furthermore, the prospects looked worse: ore content was falling, and whilst workers as a whole were not as militant as some suggest from the experience of Patiño mines in 1947 and 1949, the labour force was more pugnacious than 20 years earlier. Those laid off for commercial reasons or sacked as political agitators, particularly in 1947 and 1949, not only constituted the first substantial redundancies for a decade but also took their ill-will back into a new inflationary environment — the level of 33 per cent in 1951 was the highest since 1939. Could the rise in tin prices prompted by the war in Korea perhaps salvage the industry and stave off a wider economic crisis?

The irony is that the price rise brought the US government straight back into the market. When the level touched $2 per pound in February 1951 Washington halted all purchases of metal for the buffer stock, reimposing a state monopoly on imports of the metal (through the RFC). Indeed, the North Americans now effectively drove the price down. Just as John Hillman doubts that the Bolivian companies could have secured a better deal in 1940–1942, so I wonder whether by the first months of 1951 even the kind of price rise being sought by La Paz ($1.50) could have held the crisis at bay. But the fact that the State Department was having problems pushing the RFC into an offer of even $1.15 suggests that the numbers were very far from adding up. The issue had now taken on a directly political character and, although the traditional account properly stresses the cancellation of the MNR's victory in the presidential poll of May 1951 and the imposition of military rule, we should not lose sight of the enduring contradictions at the level of political economy.

So parlous was the state of the Bolivian economy at the outbreak of the Korean War that in August 1950 even the reactionary regime of Mamerto Urriolagoitia had felt obliged to emulate Busch and reimpose total state control over tin company foreign exchange earnings. A fierce debate with the firms ensued — Patiño had died in

April 1947, and Aramayo took the lead protest role — and in
October concessions were duly made on that front (Table 5.5), but
within weeks the tin price was again being forced back down. The
junta which replaced Urriolagoitia in May 1951 had no hope of
resorting to full control of foreign exchange and was unable to
persuade the US to improve the terms of even three-month
contracts to purchase. It therefore resolved to cease export of tin
altogether in a frankly desperate effort to force Washington's hand.

Aramayo, possibly recalling Víctor Paz's management of the
economy in 1944–1945, had already considered backing the MNR,
whose victory at the polls he knew reflected much more than a
protest vote.[47] At the same time, ex-president Hertzog, who had led
the anti-MNR campaign of 1947–1949, advised the junta itself to
nationalise the mines so as to steal the thunder from the party, which
had at its fifth congress in February 1951 settled on that policy,
agrarian reform and universal suffrage as its platform.[48]

In Washington the full consequences of this impasse were, by
November 1951, beginning to be recognised:

> We understand that the RFC in its negotiations with the
> Bolivians has argued that the price should be based on the
> average cost of production in Bolivia. In order to keep the
> mines operating on this basis it would be necessary for the
> Bolivian government to control all tin revenues and to
> distribute them to individual producers so that the cost of each
> would be met. This is a very dangerous proposal to make to a
> foreign government. The United States is engaged in trying to
> protect the interests of American investors in underdeveloped
> countries against the strong desire of those countries to expro-
> priate and nationalise. If other countries were to learn that the
> United States Government were proposing such action in the
> case of Bolivia it would be very difficult for us to protect the
> American owners of low cost mining properties in other coun-
> tries. It would be an open invitation to the Chilean
> Government, for example, to redistribute to locally owned
> copper mines the profits of Anaconda and Kennecott.[49]

The prophetic qualities of this reflection need no extra emphasis
here, but it is worth reiterating the fact that, six months before the

revolution, the US government had contemplated a price arrange-
ment which was a surrogate for nationalisation, and that the Bolivian
government — an anti-communist military dictatorship installed to
keep the MNR out of power — felt it had no choice but to confront
Washington by withholding supplies of a strategic commodity at a
time of war. Moreover, a leading tin capitalist was considering collaboration with the party that depicted him as anathema to the economic
interests of the nation. That same party, observing the deadlock from
exile or conditions of domestic repression, was itself jettisoning the
strategy of management through exchange control for one of outright
expropriation, which at the very least could be conducted in openly
nationalist language and draw directly on the legacy of the Chaco War
rather than being mired in obscure financial formulae. In that sense,
then, the MNR, rather than trimming its ideological sails, was actually
reversing its prior economic conservatism. This obviously owed much
to the FSTMB and pressure from the left, but it also had its own logic
(just as would reversion to a deeper history in 1985).

The economic stalemate at the end of 1951 may well not be
deemed a 'cause' of the Bolivian revolution, but it was a decided
mess within which the status quo was unravelling as fast as its opponents were consolidating. Few, then or now, had much sense of the
finer strategic issues at stake, but one could apply to the years
1946–1952 the comment made by Laurence Whitehead with respect
to the period 1930–1935: 'los bolivianos políticamente activos
estaban escasamente interesados en un debate académico sobre si las
compañías de estaño actuaron peor en la guerra o en la depresión.'[50]

The better known stories of the *sexenio* that we have not told here
— of the strikes, repression, the thwarting of a democratic
campaign, and of the distillation of a partisan programme into a
common civic cause — all served to marginalise such academic
debate. Yet, between the depression that followed a war (1946–1952)
and the war that followed a depression (1932–1935) one finds rather
more in common than the univocal account of either *nacionalismo* or
political economy can comfortably handle.

Historians, of course, draw a salary for being wise after the event,
but in recent years this relatively simple task has been made much
more exciting by enthusiasm for counter-factual speculation (some-

thing to do with the micro-climates of the Isis and Cam?). In that spirit I should place all the above discussion under a final shadow of doubt. In December 1951 the Ballivián junta set about a task in which it possessed experience and about which it felt confident — the annual process of conscription of some 15,000 young men into military service. By mid-January 1952 these soldiers were in their barracks with the customary crew-cuts and rough uniforms. But their regime was rather different from those of previous cohorts because the regime, in an effort to improve its dire political position, had managed to secure from Chile agreement to repatriate the remains of Eduardo Abaroa, hero of the War of the Pacific. Accordingly, all the way through to the service of reinterment at the end of March the conscripts exclusively drilled for the march past. None of the six regiments stationed in and around La Paz had begun to provide their new troops with training in the shooting of a weapon when the uprising took place on 9 April. Perhaps, if they had, Álvaro Pérez del Castillo could have shot Julio Sanjinés and there would still have been no Bolivian revolution?

## Externally Oriented Conclusion

Even with our inter-disciplinary vocation and sense of collegiality at a peak — and even working within a regional context — it is always a challenge to undertake international comparisons. Alan Knight has argued that it is particularly so with respect to the origins or causes of political phenomena:

> the complexity of the 'great revolutions' is such that common features or patterns are hard to find, *especially* at the level of cause or process ... theories which posit patterned causes or processes ... offer little by way of genuine insights into the Latin American experience, or, indeed, any such experience ... In this sense revolutions are probably no more amenable to general theories than holes in the ground.[51]

One should not despair: here, I feel, we have a sensible comment on practicalities rather than a severe stricture on epistemology. If we can understand revolutions as both processes and events, then it should be possible to speak with at least some usefulness of the (probably more diverse) processes that led to similar events, even if it is surely easier to address the (probably more unified) processes that emanated from those events. But here one is 'speaking', not building theories.[52]

We need also to note the simple fact that similar processes often do not produce similar events. Within Latin America, Bolivia's experience between 1946 and 1952 was not so much at variance with the regional pattern as to make the National revolution thoroughly extraordinary, and yet it was not only unique but also alone. I don't believe that Guatemala between 1944–1954 amounted to a revolution comparable to the cases of Mexico, Bolivia, Cuba and Nicaragua although, as Jorge Domínguez has shown, Washington's treatment of the two processes was not objectively adjusted to the local radical impetus. Nor, following on from our counter-factual foray above, does it seem likely that, had the radical forces in Guatemala been overthrown by Arana in 1949 without outward and material US support — that is, in a manner comparable to 21 July 1946 in Bolivia — they would later have been able to retake power and defend an agrarian reform of the type they introduced before the 1954 counter-revolution. Still less, in my view, could the PGT (Communist Party) have emulated the leading role of the MNR. In short, the vital specificity of the Guatemalan experience is the endurance of the immediate post-war political conjuncture whilst that in Bolivia is the experience of rupture, which both steeled and changed the MNR.[53]

Something similar happened in Venezuela, where Acción Democrática ruled between 1945 and 1948 on terms comparable to the Villarroel regime in both programme, balance of civil–military relations, and ambiguity about political alliances, particularly with communism. Yet, whilst they were of almost exactly the same chronological generation as the Bolivian parties, AD and COPEI were struggling in the wake of a *cesarismo democrático* very different from that of Toro and Busch, with much less political experience and significantly less proletarian influence upon them. Moreover, Pérez Jimenez's regime proved more resilient than any of the governments of the *sexenio*. Understood in its broadest, systematic sense, Venezuelan social democracy was honed through the experience of a decade-long opposition that took it into the same time-frame as the Cuba revolution, endogenous and exogenous factors alike conspiring to squeeze out precisely those radical features — bar universal suffrage — upon which the Bolivian revolution was founded.

Something similar equally happens in the case of Costa Rica, but with different timing since Figueres's capture of power in 1948 is provided with external protection by the fact that it is undertaken against communist forces (not to mention Somoza next door). Figueres, of course, had strong personal ties with the US, but in the early 1940s his trajectory was not so different from that of Víctor Paz, and by the early 1960s these two figures were widely treated as belonging to the same political family. Yet in 1948–1949 Figueres was able to take the extraordinary step of abolishing the country's armed forces, whilst by 1956 Washington was adamant that this should not occur in Bolivia, where it was not seriously expected that the economic plan devised by George Eder for the IMF could be implemented without the restoration of the military. As in Guatemala, the issue of logistical projection of US military power must be factored into the equation, but so also must North American direct investment as well as the distinctiveness of local social forces. If Guatemala at least had a 'land question' comparable to that in Bolivia, there was no problem of a comparable order in Costa Rica, either in the germination of the PCN in the early 1940s or in the constitutional era that followed the civil war of 1948.

Of course, the Bolivian revolutionaries themselves resisted both analogies with other experiences and charges of foreign influence in their own. Theirs was always a 'national revolution' and as much disposed to repudiate models in 1946 as in 1952:

> The Bolivian revolution [of 20 December 1943] was wrought in a purely Bolivian atmosphere. We recognise and have severely criticised the mistakes of the revolution, but we cannot admit — it disgusts us even to think of it — that the Bolivian revolution, which embodies the hopes of the majority of Bolivians, should have been inspired and helped even by the Argentines, still less by the Nazis.[54]

This retort was in response to the State Department's 'Blue Book' of January 1946 which boldly alleged the direct and undemocratic intervention of the Argentine government in Bolivian affairs after December 1943. The charges which did little good for US policy towards Argentina under the Perón government, were firmly rebutted by the governments in both La Paz and Buenos Aires, and received a fairly cool response from the British, who broadly sympathised with the aims of the exercise but were underwhelmed by its tone and technique. Nonetheless, the sense has remained that at least until 1952 the MNR's strongest external relations were with Peronism, which may well have provided it with a vital lifeline (or a shorter spell out in the cold) lacked by, say, AD in the 1940s or Arbenz/the PGT, in 1951–1954 (when one might have expected stonger state-to-state support from Mexico).

This question has not yet received full scholarly attention, but the existing circumstantial evidence suggests that, whilst in 1943–1945 they may have been some direct and consequential backing from Buenos Aires, between 1946 and 1952 the Peronist government took a distinctly cautious approach. Víctor Paz himself remarked, 'como la situación política no se tomaba favorable al MNR, Perón, que era un político pragmático, hizo una apertura hacia el nuevo gobierno, realizando una entrevista con Hertzog en Yacuiba'.[55] Moreover, in May 1949 the Argentine frontier police physically halted a *movimientista* column invading in support of the miners' strike, and in July of that year Paz himself was expelled to Uruguay (where members of the Argentine UCR initially spurned him as a *peronista*). It was only in January 1951 that Perón permitted Paz to return to Buenos Aires — according to Paz because the Bolivian ambassador Gabriel Gosálvez had joked too freely about Evita — and even then the Argentine government tried to dissuade him from standing against Gosálvez in the presidential poll of May.[56]

Official bilateral relations between 1952 and 1955 were warm enough, but Perón was himself now on the back foot and could offer little beyond food supplies — critical enough in themselves, as it soon transpired. The MNR–Peronist link may, upon deeper investigation, prove to be more substantial, but my present sense is that between 1946 and 1952 it amounted to a neutrality somewhat less benign and practical than that offered to the Sandinistas by the Carazo administration in Costa Rica in 1978–1979. Without it life would have been significantly harder, but the outcome probably not so different.

What of the revolutions that did occur? Only the Mexican, of course, predated the Bolivian uprising which, at the level of broad social forces and ideological currents, looked, as Skocpol has noted, not dissimilar. And yet, for all the strikes, invasions and provincial *revueltas*, the armed phase of the Bolivian revolution is not at all comparable: 72 hours maximum, in two towns (General Blacutt did put up resistance in Oruro, and we should not forget that scores died there). Precious little infrastructure was destroyed, no regional armies *strictu sensu* were amassed, and the party thwarted in the 1951 poll did, upon the capture of state power, immediately take office. The comparison here properly belongs to other papers, but I should signal the likelihood that different patterns after the assault on power relate to the very distinct political origins of the two movements, with the long *porfiriato* possessing no match in Bolivia (even, to my mind, if we take the Liberal-Republican regimes as one 'regime' from 1899 to 1930). Finally in this regard, there is only modest evidence of the MNR promoting Mexico as a 'model' before 1952 although it was palpably a source of inspiration and influence. Perhaps the MNR, steeled from its earliest days by resistance to communism, discovered a subordinate aversion to the external promotion of even nationally based models?

Certainly, there was little either in the mid-1940s, when the party was in office (and well represented at the Chapultepec conference) or later in the decade, when it was experiencing its first period of consolidated repression, that could draw it into very close ties with APRA which, besides being a poor model for taking power and notably personalist in character, possessed altogether too much of a 'greater Peru' aura about it to settle into any comfortable alliance with a major Bolivian party. All these ties would in time, of course, be amiably routed through the Second International, belatedly compensating for the fact that the Andes lacked an equivalent of the Caribbean Legion in the 1940s.)

The case of political pacing in Cuba likewise lends itself to a number of comparisons with Bolivia. The 1933 overthrow of Machado could in some senses at least be seen as a parallel to the Chaco, and the 1940s worked through quite rapidly the local contradictions of the international alliance imposed by the World War. However, after 1945 the pattern starts to diverge, Batista seizing dictatorial power on 11 March 1952 — precisely a month before the uprising in La Paz — and holding on to it for more than half of the period that the MNR was in office. The Cuban revolution did not take place in qualitatively different 'historical time' from that in Bolivia, its origins likewise developed over a phase of erratic political experimentation (1933–1952) followed by one of outright repression (1952–1959), and one may indeed discern some influence of the Bolivian experience in the State Department's response to the Cuban rebels immediately before and after Batista's fall. The points of similarity, though, do not form part of a compelling pattern, even if one ignores (as few can) Guevara's comprehensive misreading of Bolivia in the late 1960s — a 'mistake', perhaps, that owed much to a projection of pre-revolutionary Cuba onto post-revolutionary Bolivia.

The Nicaraguan revolution was a full generation younger, but its origins are unusually prolonged and may sensibly be traced back to Sandino's campaign of 1927–1934. (I would, in fact, be prepared to accept a 'long nineteenth century' for Nicaragua that began with William Walker's invasion in 1854 and ended in July 1979, but this is to be too chronologically clever by half. The point is that the wider isthmian and Caribbean features of the country are so vital that the nation-state 'level of analysis' can never be sufficient in itself.) The experience of original *sandinista* resistance to the Marines and the new National Guard under Somoza senior surely lends itself to comparison with the role of the Chaco in seeding a nationalist legacy and giving it a belligerent, tragic timbre. We might also find analogies between the failure in 1944–1947 of the two communist parties (PSN in Nicaragua and PIR in Bolivia) to break out of a narrow, class-based politics and promote alliances with a breadth and energy of the popular-frontism of the 1930s.

Nevertheless, the differences of political epoch between the revolution-as-event are as great as between Mexico and Bolivia, and the points of correspondence are rather too constrained by historical context to be remarkable. On the other hand, the origins of all four revolutionary cases do share a vital element of nationalist sentiment, which, whilst it is by definition distinctive in character, does also possess a common focus on the US. There is a real sense in which all begin as 'American revolutions against America'.

## Notes

1   National Archives (hereinafter NA) 824.2544/6-1551, reprinted in
    *Foreign Relations of the United States, American Republics, 1951,* II
    (Washington, 1972), pp. 1152, 1154. Mann was Deputy Assistant
    Secretary of State for Inter-American Affairs. Symington had served
    six weeks as administrator of the Reconstruction Finance
    Corporation.

2   'Bolivian Political Psychosis', NA 724.00/8-251.

3   Quoted in Alfonso Crespo, *Hernán Siles. El hombre de abril* (La Paz,
    1996), pp. 134–35. Those who later identified Sanjinés as the 'intellec-
    tual author' of the coup of 4 Nov. 1964 which overthrew the MNR
    might have preferred Pérez del Castillo to have shut up in 1952, but I
    am inclined to believe Julio Sanjinés' account that he was 'set up' by
    US air attaché Colonel Edward Fox, who certainly was the guiding
    hand behind Barrientos' revolt. Interview, La Paz, 24 Aug. 1989.

4   *La Razón,* 10 April 2002.

5   *Ibid.*

6   8,603 *beneméritos* and 13,571 widows in 1997. *Hoy,* 9 March 1997.

7   I am here repeating a commonplace that needs refinement. Paz trav-
    elled from Ezeiza to El Alto in a meat cargo plane owned and piloted
    by Walter Lehm, who was suspicious of the military craft put on offer.
    Barrientos was the co-pilot.

8   *Memorias* (La Paz, 2000), p. 9.

9   'He was no populist rabble-rouser, but a pragmatic technocrat,
    committed to modernising Bolivia. It is given to few individuals to
    change the course of their country's history, let alone to do so twice. Yet
    that is what Víctor Paz Estenssoro achieved in Bolivia'. *The Economist,*
    23 June 2001.

10  His robust approach to criticism and historiography is nowhere better
    exemplified than in this *riposte* to,

>   un tal Roca, escritorcillo en vía de desarrollo ... me refiero
>   únicamente a sus dos premisas iniciales: *El Presidente_Colgado* es
>   un típico libro cespediano: historia indocumentada, escrita en
>   primera persona ... Si yo no hubiese sido iniciador de un
>   movimiento obrero en las minas; acusado en el putsch nazi;
>   preso y confinado; luego ministro de Villarroel; más tarde
>   diputado (como lo fuí también con Busch); si no hubiese sido
>   uno de los fundadores del partido más grande de la historia de
>   Bolivia; subdirector de *La Calle* y acusado en el juicio de respon-

sibilidades contra el gobierno Villarroel — y fuera sólo un arribista silvestre venido a la capital — realmente no podría escribir en primera persona.
*El presidente colgado*, 2nd ed. (Buenos Aires, 1975), p. 187.

11  Although they have acquired great fame, I confess to finding Paz's congressional speeches pretty pedestrian in their reliance upon statistics, quotation and rather laboured irony. The competition, though, is rarely sharp, and, in the wake of the Catavi massacre it was surely only necessary to ask why, if the miners had attacked the army first, there were no injuries among the troops: 'Es la clásica fábula, sorprendentemente confirmada en nuestra política, de las palomas contra las escopetas.' *Discursos Parlamentarios* (La Paz, 1955), pp. 149–50.

12  Valentín Abecia López, *Montenegro* (La Paz, 1997), p. 187.

13  Alvarez Plata is generally accepted to have been killed on the orders of the 'cacique' of Achacachi, Toribio Salas ('Huila Saco'), denounced as a 'red' as assiduously as is his contemporary equivalent Felipe Quispe ('El Mallku'). For an interesting discussion of the background of the MNR leadership, see Christopher Mitchell, *The Legacy of Populism in Bolivia. From the MNR to Military Rule* (New York, 1977), pp. 18–26.

14  Compare, for example, Alfonso Crespo's *Hernán Siles* with the same author's *Enrique Hertzog: el hidalgo presidente*, Lima 1997. In 1979 the *falangista* Gonzalo Romero wrote a prologue to the 5th edition of *Nacionalismo y Coloniaje*.

15  *Time*, 21 April 1952, quoted in Kenneth D. Lehmann, *Bolivia and the United States. A Limited Partnership* (Athens, Ga., 1999), p. 99; Joseph Flack to Washington, 'Diary of a Successful revolution', 25 July 1946, NA 824.00/7-2546.

16  'Las diferencias básicas en el funcionamiento político del POR y el MNR, es decir, entre los marxistas ortodoxos y los nacionalistas revolucionarios, fundamentalmente, se resumían en lo siguiente: entre los primeros primaba la capacidad y la audacia doctrinal y teórica, y entre los segundos, la agresividad y la intrepidez práctica en la vida militante.' Edwin Moller Pacieri *El dios desnudo de mi conciencia revolucionaria* (La Paz, 2001), p. 32.

17  *La formación de la conciencia nacional*, (1967) (La Paz, 1990), p. 89. Having a passing acquaintanceship with both Trotskyism and the Salvation Army, I can see the point of the analogy, but the latter certainly provides a much more congenial environment for those who are in a stable heterosexual union and enjoy brass band music.

18   *La Razón*, 11 Aug. 2001. The diary of Juan Carlos Ríos relates a telling
      exchange from 1954:

> El otro día en una reunión del partido le pregunté al fiero: 'El
> día que triunfe la revolución obera-campesina, camarada Lora,
> qué cargo ocupará usted, Comisario del Pueblo, Presidente de
> la República o qué se llamara?' Me contestó: 'No, yo no ambi-
> ciono nada; lucho por mis ideas. Con tal de abrir una librería yo
> estaré contento y seguiré trabajando.' Esto me ha decepcionado
> — les dijé a los dirigentes de la COB — yo luchaba para que mi
> Jefe por lo menos que sea Presidente; como no es así, algo anda
> mal. Quiero luchar junto a ustedes, aunque sea sin entrar el
> MNR. Usemos el poder para las masas.

*Hoy*, 6 Sept. 1992

19   If there were space for such a narrative account, I would probably
      follow the style of Donald Cameron Watt, *How War Came. The
      Immediate Origins of the Second World War 1938–1939* (London, 1989).

20   Manuel E. Contreras, *The Bolivian Tin Industry in the First Half of the
      Twentieth Century* (London, 1993), pp. 4; 42. Ricardo Anaya cites the
      Banco Minero for a total figure of 57,000 in 1948, *Nacionalización de las
      Minas de Bolivia* (La Paz, 1952), p. 85

21   Susan Eckstein, 'The Impact of Revolution: A Comparative Analysis
      of Mexico and Bolivia', *Contemporary Political Sociology* series, 06-016
      (London, 1976), pp. 42–43. Ian Roxborough and Alan Knight intro-
      duce similar depictions in wider comparisons designed to test the
      theories of Theda Skocpol, Barrington Moore and Eric Wolf: 'It is
      unlikely that [major transformations] would have happened if, in the
      months following the revolution, much of Bolivia's peasantry had not
      acted spontaneously to take over many of the country's landed estates.'
      Ian Roxborough, 'Theories of Revolution: the Evidence from Latin
      America', *LSE Quarterly*, vol. 3, no. 2 (1989), pp. 105–6. 'As the victo-
      rious MNR began to sponsor a (somewhat calculating and
      instrumental) agrarian reform, Indian peasants organised, rebelled and
      mobilised, breaking the traditional political and economic controls of
      the landlord class', Alan Knight, 'Social Revolution: a Latin American
      Perspective', *Bulletin of Latin American Research* (hereinafter *BLAR*),
      vol. 9, no. 2 (1990), p. 189.

22   T. Ifor Rees to Eden, 16 May 1945, no. 38; Rees to Bevin, 11 June 1947,
      no. 68, in *British Documents on Foreign Affairs*, Part III, Section D, Latin
      America, Vol. 11 (Bethesda, 2000), p. 106; *ibid.*, Part IV, vol. 4, p. 183.

23   *El Presidente Colgado*, pp. 196–97.

24 *Parties and Political Change in Bolivia,* 1880–1952 (Cambridge, 1969), p. xii. The Bolivian edition of this book, which rapidly became the standard account, is entitled *Los orígenes de la revolución,* (1968), which could, I feel, also have been employed for the original as it devotes 250 pages to the years 1880–1943 and only 40 to the period 1943–1952, when the economic and social factors were arguably as sharp as those in the realm of ideas and ideology.

25 The loss of traditional values was, of course, an uneven process. In the aftermath of the Battle of Campo Via, Paraguayan Captain Oscar Corrales reported, 'Una patrulla halló a 200 metros de nuestras posiciones, bajo un arbusto, en su catre de campaña, el cadaver del Tnt. Urriolagoitia, junto a él su fiel ordenanza, quien no quizo dejarlo abandonado. "Acaba de morir", nos dijo," "pertenece a una familia distinguida de Bolivia".' Quoted in James Dunkerley, *Orígenes del poder militar en Bolivia* (La Paz, 1988), p. 173.

26 *Formación,* p. 49.

27 René Danilo Arze Aguirre, *Guerra y conflictos sociales. El caso boliviano durante la campaña del Chaco* (La Paz, 1987). Antonio Álvarez Mamani reminds us of the more obvious reasons why the immediate impact of the war was not uniform: 'la guerra fue un fracaso porque no se podía comunicar. Los campesinos no sabían manejar ninguna clase de armamentos, el clima no les favorecía y nadie era amigo de nadie. Todavía había mucho regionalismo, los aymaras se juntaban en un lado y los quechuas en otro, y se insultaban en sus dialectos … Pienso que el único aspecto de la guerra fue la toma de contacto entre campesinos de todo el país que nunca se habían encontrado.' *El camino perdido* (La Paz, 1987), pp. 65–66.

28 In Walter Guevara Arze, *Bases para replantear la revolución nacional* (La Paz, 1988), p. 230.

29 Entonces llegó a mí y con un gesto rápido me cogió por la solapa, me atrajo hacia sí y me dió un golpe violento sobre la ceja derecha con la mano cerrada y armada de un enorme anillo de oro … Repitió el golpe sobre el otro lado de la cara … Brotó la sangre a chorros por la ceja abierta, la nariz y la boca. Y el dolor, la sorpresa, la indignación, el estupor, el asco, la cólera me dejaron clavado en el suelo, suspenso, inmóvil. Aquello, era tan insólito, tan ordinario, tan bestial y tan salvaje, tan primitivo que hasta la noción de la defensa sentí anularse en mí. No acostumbro llevar armas ni nunca practiqué deporte alguno. Pertenezco, ¡ay! a la casta, la pobre casta de estudiosos que viven en el aire confinado de las bibliotecas y descuidan cultivar el músculo de los brazos para únicamente la sustancia del cerebro.

Alcides Arguedas, *Cartas a los Presidentes de Bolivia* (La Paz, 1979), p. 203 Hochschild was a naturalised citizen of Argentina and probably owed his life to the petition for mercy from president Ortíz.

30   *Formación,* p. 60.

31   *Ibid.,* p. 111.

32   ... un exceso de identificación con la mentalidad militarista le haría correr el riesgo de ver los hechos de la Vida Social muy 'en militar'; sabido es que la psicología del militar es muy inclinada a admitir la violencia como la ley suprema de la conducta colectiva, a despreciar a los hombres de pensamiento, a los predicadores de ideas pacifistas, etc., por considerarlos unos 'ilusos', a juzgar con cinismo y frialdad los dolores físicos y morales de las masas sacrificadas en los planes belicistas. José Antonio Arze, *Sociología Marxista* (Oruro, 1963), p. 119.

33   'The Mining Industry and the State: The Politics of Tin Restriction in Bolivia, 1936–1939', *BLAR*, vol. 21, no. 1 (2002), p. 64. At the time the decree was seen as enshrining rather more than 'vacuous moral argument': 'it fits in neatly with a general plan of coordination with Axis principles, and in particular with those of Nazi Germany. There has been a disposition, in many quarters to take the most favourable view of the decree, and to see in it only a measure of the financial extremities of the Bolivian Government resulting in a more drastic control and further appropriation of the profits of the mining industry ... there seems little justification for this optimism,' *Mining Journal,* vol. 29 (1939).

34   'Miners as Voters: The Electoral Process in Bolivia's Mining Camps', *JLAS*, vol. 13, no. 2 (1981), pp. 344–45.

35   Klein, *Parties and Political Change,* pp. 153–4; 'The Crisis of Legitimacy and the Origins of Social Revolution — the Bolivian Experience', *The Journal of Inter-American Studies,* vol. X, no. 1 (1968), pp. 103–8. Laurence Whitehead, 'El impacto de la gran depresión en Bolivia,' *Trimestre Económico,* no. 45 (1972), pp. 72–80.

36   Carmenza Gallo, *Taxes and State Power. Political Instability in Bolivia, 1900–1950* (Philadelphia, 1991); Manuel E. Contreras, *Bolivian Tin Industry;* 'Debts, Taxes and War. The Political Economy of Bolivia, c. 1920–1935', *JLAS*, vol. 22, no. 2 (1990); (with Marco Napoleón Pacheco), *Medio Siglo de Minería Mediana en Bolivia, 1939–1989* (La Paz, 1989).

37   Quoted in Charles Geddes, *Patiño. The Tin King* (London, 1972), p. 281.

38   'The Mining Industry and the State', p. 42.

39   *Ibid.,* p. 67. The corrective features of this work should properly be recognised by those, such as myself, who argued that after Busch's

death his decree of June 1939 was 'left to collect dust on the statute books'. James Dunkerley, *Political Suicide in Latin America* (London, 1992), p. 34.

40 'The Mining Industry and the State', p. 68.

41 *Ibid.*, p. 69.

42 Patiño worked established mines with high grade ores while Hochschild looked to the development of entirely new kinds of mines with low grade deposits that could only be worked profitably through extensive mechanisation ... Patiño's response [to the Depression] was defensive and he cooperated with the British and Dutch in forming the ITC to preserve the value of existing mines. Hochschild took the decline in prices as an incentive for cost reduction through mechanisation, and had no interest in production restriction ... Patiño's position was ultimately based on the assumption that the past successes of Llallagua provided a reliable guide to its future. Hochschild's was based on the assumption that he could reinvigorate a declining mining complex at Unificada. Both were profoundly wrong, and the criticism that each made of the other's position was therefore correct.
*Ibid.*, pp. 41, 1. 'Sic transit gloria mundi'.

43 'Bolivia and British Tin Policy, 1939–1945', *JLAS*, vol. 22, no. 2 (1990), p. 313.

44 In 1903 the British had imposed a 40 per cent tariff that saw off the burgeoning challenge to its world monopoly staged by the works at Bayonne, New Jersey.

45 Patiño tin was exported to the US for the first time in March 1944, *The Times*, 19 April 1944. The British ambassador in La Paz reported of Hochschild, 'He is very pro-United States and not sufficiently grateful for help which he has received in the past from the UK ... He is in continuous strife with the Patiño group of mines but the latter with their greater resources generally get the better of him.' Rees to Bevin, 16 Aug. 1945, no. 71, in *British Documents on Foreign Affairs*, Part III, Series D, vol. 10, p. 43.

46 'Bolivia and British Tin Policy', pp. 307, 313.

47 'Si el MNR hace, por su parte, honor a la legalidad y se somete a las normas de respeto a la dignidad humana, será *La Razón* la primera en reconocerlo.' *La Razón*, 11 May 1951. 'Víctor Paz Estenssoro the new Finance Minister, said the Government would not burden the mining industry, Bolivia's main source of wealth, with taxes beyond its capacity. He added, however, that the Finance Ministry would not be "a lawyer for the mining companies".' *The Times*, 27 Dec. 1943.

48  Crespo, Enrique Hertzog, p. 181; Eduardo Trigo O'Connor d'Arlach, *Conversaciones con Víctor Paz Estenssoro* (La Paz, 1999), p. 104.

49  'Position Paper Prepared by the Acting Deputy Director of the Office of International Materials Policy (Evans)', 2 Nov. 1951. NA 824,2544/11–251, reprinted in *Foreign Relations of the United States. American Republics 1951*, vol. II, p. 1162.

50  'El impacto de la depresión', p. 80.

51  'Social Revolution: A Latin American Perspective', pp. 178–79.

52  I believe that Theda Skocpol is effectively 'speaking' rather than theorising when she notes that the three 'great revolutions' she studies — in France, Russia and China — were not the only ones, and that, after the Second World War,

> Yugoslavia, Vietnam, Algeria, Cuba, Bolivia, Angola, Mozambique, Guinea-Bissau and Ethiopia ... all share certain broad resemblances to the French, Russian and Chinese revolutions. They occurred in predominantly agrarian countries, and they became possible only through the administrative-military breakdown of pre-existing states. Peasant revolts or mobilisation for guerrilla warfare played a pivotal role in each revolutionary process. Furthermore, in every one of these cases, organised revolutionary leaderships (recruited from the ranks of previously marginal, educated elites) emerged or came to the fore during the revolutionary crisis ... Industrial proletariats have played key roles in many instances (such as the Bolivian and Mexican Revolutions).

*States and Social Revolutions* (Cambridge, 1979), pp. 287, 291.
Barrington Moore mentions Bolivia not once, and John Dunn, *Modern Revolutions,* Cambridge 1989, twice — in relation to Che Guevara's guerrilla movement in the 1960s.

53  Bolivia is analysed by Laurence Whitehead and Guatemala by myself in Leslie Bethell and Ian Roxborough (eds.), *Latin America between the Second World War and the Cold War, 1944–1948* (Cambridge, 1992).

54  *La Noche,* editorial (probably by Gustavo Chacón), quoted in Rees to Bevin, 8 March 1946, in *British Documents on Foreign Affairs*, Part IV, Series D, Latin America, vol. I, p. 135.

55  Trigo, *Conversaciones con Víctor Paz Estenssoro*, p. 97.

56  *Ibid..*, p. 105.

# 6

## Reassessing *Caudillismo* in Bolivia, 1825–1879

... successive revolutions; revolutions in the south, revolutions in the north; revolutions prepared by my enemies, led by my friends, hatched in my home, breaking out all around me. ... Good God — they condemn me to a state of perpetual warfare ... Bolivia has become totally incapable of sustaining any government.

President Manuel Isidoro Belzu, 1855[1]

The turmoil of Bolivian politics in the nineteenth century is notorious. In 1918 Nicanor Aranzaes, one of that rather insubstantial group of literati who thrived on the hegemony of the Liberal party, translated the events of the period 1826 to 1903 into figures, and discovered 185 'revolutions'.[2] Often these were no more than passing infringements of public order in the provinces but they were, nevertheless, decidedly frequent, and there were few years up to the War of the Pacific that were free of disorder. In the red year of 1848 there were 15 rebellions, eight of them led by General Belzu himself who, despite claims that he was an avid reader of Proudhon and Saint Simon, was as yet concerned with little more than the stentorian productions of the barracks.[3] The rules of war appeared to be the stuff of politics.

Writing from Chuquisaca in 1843, the perceptive Frederick Masterton, first British Chargé d'Affaires to Bolivia, offered a synopsis of developments since independence which essentially complements Aranzaes' positivist tabulations:

nothing has been attended to but a series of perfidious revolutions and usurpations of power, shameless robberies of the publick treasury, exortations of tribute from the indigenous Indians, and constant wars with Peru without a national

object. Military force has ruled everything by caprice; and
right, though ever pompously and theoretically spoken of, has
never been practically acted on by any government.[4]

Six years later Masterton's North American colleague spent over
three months finding a government to which he could present himself, there being two armies in the field, both issuing decrees and
levying taxes.[5] Of the 20 regimes that had more than a completely
spurious claim on authority, only three were led by civilians (two belligerent gentlemen, more than disposed to cast aside from coat and
take up the sword), only four surrendered power voluntarily, while six
presidents were assassinated (two whilst holding office), and four
died in exile (see Table 6.1).[6]

## Table 6.1: Principal Administrations, 1825–1884

| | | | |
|---|---|---|---|
| Simon Bolívar | 11/8/25–1/1/26 | | |
| Antonio José Sucre | 1/1/26–1/1/28 | | |
| José Miguel Velasco | 12/8/28–14/12/28 | Sucre/Potosí | |
| Pedro Blanco* | 25/12/28–1/1/29 | Pro–Peru | Peruvian invasion |
| J. M. Velasco* | 2/1/29–24/5/29 | Sucre/Potosí | |
| Andrés Santa Cruz | 24/5/29–20/2/39 | La Paz | Debasement of coinage (*peso feble*); Peru–Boliva Confederation (1835–38) |
| J. M. Velasco* | 22/2/39–27/9/41 | Sucre/Potosí | |
| Jose Ballivián* | 27/9/41–23/12/47 | La Paz | Peruvian army defeated at Ingavi (1841) |
| J. M. Velasco* | 18/1/48–6/12/48 | Sucre/Potosí | |

| | | | |
|---|---|---|---|
| Manuel Isidoro Belzu* | 17/12648–15/8/55 | La Paz | Protectionist high–point; artisanal mobilization |
| Jorge Córdova | 15/8/55–21/10/57 | La Paz | |
| José María Linares*+ | 19/12/57–14/1/61 | Sucre/Potosí | *Peso feble* issue halted; tariffs reduced |
| José María Achá(1)* | 6/5/61–29/12/64 | Cochabamba | |
| Mariano Melgarejo* | 29/12/64–15/1/71 | Cochabamba | Renewed debasement; assault on indigenous communities |
| Agustín Morales* | 15/1/71–27/11/72 | La Paz/Sucre | |
| Tomas Frías(2)o+ | 27 !11 /72–6/5/73 | Sucre/Potosí | Free trade established |
| Adolfo Ballivián | 6/5/73–31/4/74 | Sucre/Potosí (4) | |
| Tomás Frías (3)t+ | 14/2/75–4/5/76 | Sucre/Potosí | |
| Hilarión Daza* | 4/5/76–27/12/79 | Sucre/Potosí | War of the Pacific (1879) |

t = 'elected'
* = came to power through revolt
o = vice-president/president of congress/provisional administration
+ = civilian

**Notes**

1   Junta of ministers removes Linares, followed by four-month crisis from which Achá emerges the victor.
2   Following the assassination of Morales.

3    Following the death of Ballivián from natural causes.
4    Daza in effective control of the army 1872–1879, 'strong man' for
     Frías and Ballivián,
5    Campero proclaimed president after two separate revolts remove Daza
     in midst of the War of the Pacific. The main force behind the throne
     is Colonel Eliodoro Camacho, a Liberal northener with whom
     Campero shared an attachment to continue the war.


It is evident that the politics of insubordination were contagious, and
arguable that within the army they were structurally so: 'Those officers who have reached the rank of Colonel do not simply consider
the possibility of becoming president or dictator, but believe that
they have a right to these positions.'[7] President José Ballivián gave
this sentiment his official imprimatur when he stated, probably to his
own detriment, 'The soldiers amongst us, in much the same way as
in ancient times, are not simply called to serve in the army but also
in the highest office.'[8] There was a wealth of vehement condemna-
tions of this state of affairs, much of it unfortunately couched in the
resigned tone adopted by Manuel José Cortés who, writing in 1861,
pointed out that while the 'laws of progress' were fulfilled by the
actions of men, they were enacted by God alone.[9] The more secular
and far from disinterested mine owner Avelino Aramayo, who was to
play a major part in securing the conditions that would provide for
the eradication of *caudillismo,* denigrated the 'pitiable farce', but was
content to explain it away in terms of personal ambition.[10] The
Manichaean vision of the epoch was nurtured by a species of amateur
psychoanalysis, and various protagonists defended on the most tenuous terms according to a writer's ideological affinities, the most
celebrated exponent of this art being Alcides Arguedas.[11] Melgarejo,
damned as the epitome of *caudillismo,* is alone denied such exoneration.
According to that prolific jacobin Tristán Marof, 'Melgarejo is the history of Bolivia.'[12] On the other hand, Masterton's successor, Bruce,
ascribed the lack of order and progress to the absence of a 'middle
class', a view unsurprisingly not too distant from that of the MNR
ideologues Carlos Montenegro and José Fellmann Velarde, the only
difference being that they found that class in the urban artisanate, its
champion in Belzu, and its unworkable salvation in protectionism.[13]

There is an undoubted danger of regression to a sanitised version of Whig history in concentrating on the manifestation rather than the framework of this chronic instability. This is not to deny the importance of personalist elements of power, which clearly corresponded closely to social and political conditions. While purely coercive activity does not enjoy explanatory primacy, it is apparent that what might be seen as an exotic sub-culture needs to be given an anthropology in much the same way as it is today necessary to decode the pernicious gobbledegook emanating from the Casa Rosada, the Moneda or the Palacio Quemado. However, we are not yet in a position to explain the predominance of the *condottieri* of the *altiplano* in terms of a comprehensive political economy, for the historiography of nineteenth century Bolivia remains very weak despite the impressive achievements made by the young intellectuals grouped around the journal *Avances.*[14] The purpose of this chapter is simply to outline in discursive and suggestive fashion some of the principal features of the process.

For Bolivia, as for most countries in nineteenth century Latin America (perhaps the only exception would be Francia's Paraguay), one can only talk of 'militarism' in a very specific sense for, as vividly depicted by Belzu, military dominance operated not through monolithic unity but by successive schism. Indeed, it is somewhat misconceived to refer to 'the army' rather than 'armies' plural. It was more a case of the judiciary and legislature lending ephemeral, but by no means entirely worthless, legitimacy to the passage of victors than a case of the institution underwriting the redundancy of the formal division of powers.

In very broad terms, explanations of this pattern of political power tend to revolve around the following factors: the struggle for land; *empleomanía* (pressure for employment) expressive of a more general tendency for the state to constitute little more than an arena for plunder; the renewed need for social control of the lower classes in the wake of their not insubstantial incorporation in the struggle to overthrow colonial control, which itself had to a high degree integrated its repressive apparatus within the production process and its immediate administrative superstructure (*mita, encomienda, corregimiento,* etc.);[15] the sectoral division of the economically dominant bloc which rapidly became structured around the conflict between free trade and protection as local economies were drawn into the world market directly rather than through the mediation of the colonial power; and regional antagonisms, resulting from a combination of factors but most immediately influenced by the inheritance of colonial boundaries. These, apart from being negotiable in juridical and spatial terms, effected a substantial dislocation of the unifying features of the imperial economic network. All these features inform and interpenetrate each other but in different cases we can identify priorities; for Bolivia, the system had its axis around the bounty offered by control of the state and the pressure for employment.

## 'Empleomanía' and Its Costs

Fifteen years of intermittent but increasingly extensive and bitterly contested warfare bequeathed to the new republic a glut of soldiers and an empty exchequer. Wars with Chile and Peru during the first decade of independence consolidated this legacy and established the defence of pay and station as a residual feature of military activity. If *empleomanía* was the bane of society, it was only in the military sphere that it had a real impact on state funds since it was provided with the optimum means of self-perpetuation. Yet this is not immediately apparent from the size of regular forces which, in line with the exigencies of petty skirmishing campaigns, were generally small. In 1828 Sucre maintained a force of 2,700 men, which was considered large by the standards of the day. If Santa Cruz and Ballivián raised armies of 4,500 and 3,700 for the confederation and Peruvian wars, these were demobbed as rapidly as possible. Belzu, under constant pressure, rarely kept a force larger than 2,300 while Melgarejo's armies fluctuated wildly from 500 in 1865 to a highly unreliable 3,300 on the eve of his overthrow in 1870. Daza, who more than anyone cultivated 'institutionalism' within the orbit of personalist rule, limited the army to 1,500 men right up to the outbreak of the War of the Pacific.[16] Nevertheless, all these armies were top-heavy with officers. In 1843 Ballivián, attempting to reduce the excess stock accumulated over a decade of almost continuous war, removed 100 officers but three years later 650 officers and 36 generals remained on the lists.[17] In 1869 Melgarejo retained seven generals, 119 *jefes* and 345 officers to command 1,996 men, a state of affairs that Daza did nothing to ameliorate, paying 384 officers and 637 NCOs but only 825 troopers in 1876.[18]

Although these figures are not extraordinary for the Latin America of the day, they only reveal part of the story, for constant revolts bred equally persistent transfers of allegiance, and made uninterrupted incorporation in the *escalafón* the exception rather than the rule. Perhaps the most 'institutional' figure of the era was Colonel Juan Sarabia y Espinoza, who was promoted to general in 1886 having managed to serve every government since 1842, loyal service which must have entailed support for seven 'revolutions' at the very least. Of the 21 generals who at some time supported Melgarejo, 14 had previously backed his arch-rival Belzu and six had been out of the army for up to 20 years. Many officers certainly had either more at stake or less skill in such manoeuvres to sustain a regular career, and there rapidly accumulated a reserve labour army of warriors who under the rules of the game were hardly dispensable and had to be paid off. Ballivián's 1843 purge cost 50,000 pesos when pensions already stood at 112,145 pesos against serving officers' pay of 100,346.[19] Aramayo claimed that Melgarejo paid out twice as much in pensions than he did in regular pay — a claim that may well hold weight since, in 1869, 20 generals, 358 *jefes* and 204 officers drew a pension.[20] Even after the 1871 revolt that removed Melgarejo, and occasioned extensive attrition inside the officer corps, pensions were 50 per cent above regular pay.

Although Ballivián survived the endeavour of pruning the establishment, neither Velasco (1848) nor Linares (1861) was able to repeat the experiment, even when they had a clear mandate from the civilian elite. Consistent with his policies of relieving the fiscal burden on the slowly expanding mining sector, Linares attempted to cut military spending to below 40 per cent of the national budget. He was summarily removed by his military backers, who announced that their new regime, 'will, for its part, fulfil the duty of promoting, paying and increasing the pensions of various veterans as far as possible, making good the injustices inflicted on many soldiers by the previous administration'.[21] Throughout a period when national revenue remained stuck at between two and three million pesos, the formal costs of sustaining the military were consistently high: never less than 40 per cent and under Melgarejo as high as 70 per cent. The real economic cost was, of course, much greater, as evidenced by constant extraction of forced loans, the formidable looting of insurgent towns, and the *ad hoc* requisitions of produce to sustain levies that lacked the slightest vestige of quartermanship and were often only retained by the lure of bounty. Melgarejo's methods of raising revenue were so predictable that news of his impending arrival resulted in the almost complete depopulation of Cochabamba in 1865 and, when a five peso levy was decreed to 'reconfirm citizenship' this rich and populous region yielded only 7,000 pesos, necessitating the immediate withdrawal of the army.[22] In similar fashion, the rebels who finally overthrew him in the name of fiscal sobriety as well as freedom unleashed a welter of forced loans, seizing 50,000 pesos from the mint at Potosí and an equal amount from the mine owner Alfredo Durells, bestowing upon him the rank of colonel in lieu not only of interest but also of principal.[23] Morales, who had lost considerable property in Cochabamba under Belzu and presided over a very uneasy and temporary popular free trade alliance in 1871–1872, did not break from the practice, attempting to wrest a number of important mines in Aullagas from Luis Arteche for alleged non-payment of taxes, a demand that precipitated an immediate political rupture and may well have been the direct cause of the new president's assassination.[24]

Nevertheless, contingent and directly coercive extraction was neither the mainstay of the *caudillos* nor the principal issue of complaint for the civilian oligarchy. The deadweight of sinecure and the endlessly peripatetic business of maintaining authority were primarily maintained by the tribute paid by the indigenous population (on both private estates and communities) and — a matter of far greater contention — revenues acquired through state control of the silver market, closely combined with debasement of the currency.

## The Politics of Silver

The state monopoly of the purchase of silver through the Bancos de Rescate, a central legacy of the colony, and the typical absolutist recourse to reduction of the intrinsic value of specie were the two most important issues of the day for the civilian elite not only because they fortified protection, fuelled inflation and constituted an undeclared but real tax burden on the mining elite but also because they enabled the military to play a major role in controlling production and circulation as well as to appropriate a major portion of the surplus through the national mint.[25] Thus, until 1873 a tacit alliance may be said to have existed between the employees of the Casa de Moneda in Potosí and a succession of bankrupt generals and their followers, acting as a brake on the liberation of market forces, and inserting a critical space — 'relative autonomy' — between the dominant class and the direct control of policy. We cannot consider the precise co-ordinates and full implications of this here, but a few brief remarks are necessary.

First, the economic impact and political crises engendered by protection were not consistent. Between the heady and transient boom of commercial activity in the first years of independence and the gradual recovery of silver mining in the mid-1850s (effected by a combination of more favourable external conditions and the concentration of ownership in the hands of a comprador faction of the commercial-landowning class) the issue remained contentious but not acutely critical.[26] Secondly, while we still need to know much more about the textile interests that provided the main impetus for protection, it is evident that they were on the wane, if not in deep recession, and desperate for resuscitation through colonial safeguards.[27] These they obtained with only minor interruption and without substantial contest until the 1850s when the entire system came under concerted challenge. This stemmed from the deep social conflict during the Belzu and Cordova regimes, which were forced to adopt an unprecedented Jacobin stance in order to defend the interests of both the urban artisans and the state employees, civilian and military. Henceforth, the free trade bloc was consistent in its pressure and its consolidation as a coherent political force was only gradual, with the realisation of its policies only partial until 1873. While Linares was able to halt the issue of the debased coinage known as *peso feble* and reduce tariffs on cloth and bark in 1859, he was still unable to free silver, the key commodity. This uneven development of social and political weight on the part of the mining interests also goes some way to explaining why Melgarejo, who came to power with the backing of the heirs of Linares' *rojo* group, was able to break loose for a while, imposing debasement in 1866.[28]

Although monopoly and debasement operated in unison, they underwent different developments. The price paid by the Bancos de Rescate for silver increasingly moved towards the world market price, being 26 per cent below it in 1829 and only 2 per cent in 1865. This was a gradual increase, not directly determined by the nature of the regime in power, and may well have corresponded more closely with levels of contraband than shifts in the world price which remained very stable until the early 1870s.[29] On the other hand, the *peso feble*, first issued by Santa Cruz in 1830, increasingly dominated the currency, representing 14 per cent of issue in 1830–1834 and a staggering 85 per cent in 1850–1859.[30] Antonio Mitre has calculated the combined revenue from these two sources at an average of just under 23 per cent of total government income in the 1860s (it is likely to be much higher for the previous decade), compared with approximately 30 per cent from the indigenous tribute. It is worth bearing in mind that, since an increasing proportion of the price paid for silver ore by the *Bancos de Rescate* was in *febles*, the entire system imposed a tax of perhaps 25 per cent on production until well into the 1860s.[31] Finally, there is the important and provocative point that whereas the mine owners considered silver a commodity, and needed to realise the surplus value from its production on the world market in order to prompt accumulation, the governments of the day almost uniformly saw it as 'money', which may have been a happy elision for the purposes of monopoly but was a disastrous manifestation of backwardness for Bolivia's nascent capitalist class.

### The Impact on Labour and Land

The impact of military activity upon the markets in labour and land was of secondary importance compared with this intervention in the silver industry. While we do not yet possess a full picture of conscription, it is clear that it did not amass large numbers of men under the colours at any one time, that it was highly random and, in common with many other Latin American countries, bred an extremely high level of desertion; even in the 1880s, regimental turnover of 75 per cent was common in an army that numbered less than 3,000 men.[32] Moreover, it seems that the towns were hardest hit by conscription and the countryside by the direct appropriation of goods.[33] Military service continued to be as much socialised as institutionalised with more or less homogenous levies being raised by governments and rebels from a hard core of veterans, the shoddy national guard (urban militia) and the not insubstantial vagrant population. Clearly this caused periodic disruption of production, but it does not appear to have led to a major drain on the labour force as, for example, in Guatemala.[34] From 1838 conscription of *comunarios* (covering the entire population of the communities, not just the *originarios*) was expressly forbidden, and if it took place it was never on such a scale as to excite major complaint. The sole major mobilisation of the indigenous communities in this period was during Melgarejo's rule (principally 1866–1871). This was compelled by the attack on the communities and organised independently of the 'constitutionalist' rebels, and so was not actively inspired by them. The eventual success in co-opting and subduing this movement did not, however, erase the memory; in the 1890s when there was renewed and extensive *campesino* mobilisation, the oligarchy resisted demands from the army to extend recruitment to the communities, and was outraged when Pando organised a number under the federal flag in the civil war of 1898–1899.[35]

There were complaints from landlords about lack of labour, principally due to flight in order to evade recruiting sergeants, and particularly common in the 1830s, when production in Cochabamba and the Yungas was said to have suffered for this reason.[36] However, it was the mine owners who were most outspoken on this score, and there does appear to have been a proclivity to recruit in Potosí, where a relatively large and concentrated population was collected around the mines. Occasionally this burden was recognised and regions given dispensation from providing conscripts.[37] But, as Mitre points out, at least until the 1870s the mine owners were incapable of guaranteeing employment for any length of time and, therefore, unable to attract large numbers of workers from the fields. One by-product, no doubt, was a residual pool of un- or under-employed men in the mining regions.[38] It is possible that similar situation existed in the northern mines; in 1859 we find working at Corocoro 300 men who had served in Belzu's army and were ready to take up arms against Linares.[39] By the 1870s mine owners, able to pay better wages and offer secure employment, were actively assisting their workers to avoid the draft — a practice that was to endure well into the twentieth century.

The question of land is more complex but cannot be separated from that of labour for exploitation of one depended on control over the other. The central issue in this respect is whether land was obtained *manu militarii* with generalship effectively co-substantial with proprietorial status as in the platine states. In general it was not. Of course, some political and military leaders — Santa Cruz, Velasco, Ballivián, Achá — were landlords of more than modest standing, and Ballivián, like Campero at the end of the period, had mining interests. But others, Belzu, Córdova, Melgarejo, Morales, Daza — made their way up the ranks to supreme power without acquiring important lands. They certainly obtained property, and often at the expense of their adversaries, but they never transformed themselves into leading *hacendados,* and *caudillismo* as a system was not structured around the battle for land. For this to be the case there would have to have been a far greater shift in the pattern of owner-ship than actually took place within both the private domain and in terms of expropriation of community lands. In the latter case there was indeed constant pressure but it does not appear to have been markedly more acute than that under the colony until the War of the Pacific.[40] This issue has traditionally been centred on Melgarejo's untempered offensive of 1866–1870 which carried most weight in the provinces of the *altiplano,* especially La Paz, and may be seen as the endeavour of a coalition of a faction of the landed oligarchy, state employees, and the incumbent military apparatus to generate funds rapidly and secure a basis as rentiers on the richest community holdings.[41] Erwin Grieshaber has produced evidence from tax returns to refute the standard thesis that this offensive was both successful and symptomatic, showing that it was convincingly resisted with a quite impressive degree of repossession taking place, at least in the short term.[42] We still need to know a lot more about this process but it should be stressed that the land-owning class was deeply divided over the issue of community lands with an important sector, which included mine owners such as Aramayo, arguing that communal pro-duction was high, its produce cheap, and agriculture as a whole of marginal interest to capital.[43] Moreover, the standard liberal-positivist thesis was greatly debilitated insofar as its optimistic proposals were seen as certain to generate rural unrest on a massive scale, prejudicing the collection of the tribute, which was still the largest single item of national revenue. Thus, in 1838, Santa Cruz reversed his earlier measures designed to implement Bolívar's Cuzco and Trujillo decrees. Ballivián also failed to take to its logical conclusion his 1842 declaration that communal lands were held in enfiteusis, and when Achá tried so to do in 1863 he was promptly stalled by a high vocal congress. One subsidiary point that may be drawn from this picture is that it further qualifies the image of the military as existing principally to repress, or indeed being consistently capable or repressing, the 'lower orders' in the interests of the oligarchy, a function that was generally secondary to that of mediating relations within the dominant bloc.

The other major factor in this connection, that of spatial expansion and the institution of an economic sub-system that is often rather unhelpfully denominated 'the frontier', was noticeably lacking throughout this period. The various isolated military colonisation schemes were never transformed into a dynamo for the conquest of the interior and the operation at a structural level of differential rent. This was, no doubt, largely because of physical conditions but it may also be explained in part by the fact that Bolivia's frontier, in the expanded sense of the term, was internal and rapidly becoming centred on the mining regions of Potosí and southern Oruro.[44]

## Regionalism

The final question that ought to be considered at least in outline is whether regional antagonisms were the main propellant for political conflict, a case made forcefully in a recent study by José Luis Roca.[45] It would seem more accurate to describe the process of the transformation of the Audencia de Charcas into Bolivia as one fraught with internal imbalances, which at determinate moments prejudiced the coherence of the territorial unit, rather than as one embodying persistent centrifugal tendencies. Some regions — present-day Beni and Pando — remained cloistered in virtual autarky, and even Santa Cruz was marginalised for much of this period.[46] The principal focus of tension was between the northern entrepôt of La Paz, closely integrated in an economic sub-system with Tacna and Arequipa, and the southern axis of Sucre–Potosí, the interests of which lay in maintaining its trade links to the north as well as to the Plate.[47] The most acute manifestation of this rivalry was the threat of annexation of La Paz by Peru, a threat that was not subdued until after the battle of Ingavi in the wake of the failure of that grandiose variant of lower Peruvian hegemony, the confederation. In the first decades this question undoubtedly had a deep and direct impact upon military activity, and organisation for the caucus of the Bolivian soldiery was drawn not only from Sucre's Liberation Army (which contained a large number of Peruvians) but also the expeditionary forces from Buenos Aires, the armies of the crown (which had split in the final year of the war along lines that were by no means wholly foreign to localist sentiment), and the indigenous guerrilla groups of Padilla, Lanza, Warnes and others, pledged to an often radical localism.[48]

This led to a series of highly fluid alliances in the early years, reaching a peak of confusion in 1828–1829 but, largely as a result of Santa Cruz's achievement of internal order at the same time as he attempted a quasi-Bolivarian enterprise in the confederation, they came to be more firmly structured from the 1830s onwards. The clearest signpost can be found in the persistent but usually short-lived incursions of the eastern *caudillo* Velasco, whose challenges for power generally coincided with an escalation of Peruvian ambitions. This proved to be an adequate rectifying balance until the 1850s when the question of regionalist sentiment increasingly became bound up with that of free trade, a point unwittingly signalled by Julio Méndez when he remarked that the practice of horsemanship must be inherently conducive to liberal thought since liberal armies were largely composed of calvary — almost exclusively raised in the southern pastures of Tarija and Chuquisaca.[49] Yet even Linares, a *potosino*, civilian and ardent free-trader, was neither able nor apparently willing to preside over a wholesale shift of political power to the south once he had removed Belzu's acolyte Córdova. The undeniable importance of La Paz as the nation's largest city and trading centre meant that once the Linares regime fell, something of a stalemate was reached, necessitating the temporary arbitration of two regimes that had their base in Cochabamba while the two main epicentres undertook negotiation and internal realignment of their forces. Significantly, it is only at this point that the advocates of federalism really make themselves heard. We do not hear of federalism again until the end of the century with the breaking of the dominance of silver and the hegemony of Sucre, and then too it was quickly and efficiently suppressed by the unitarians inside the Liberal party. The 1876 rcbcllion in Santa Cruz led by Ibañez, while certainly no mere aberration, conformed more closely to the lack of centralised control and the wave of populist and egalitarian mobilisation sweeping the country in the 1870s than to a major secessionist drift.[50]

## Conclusions

The epoch of *caudillismo* has almost without exception been held to end in 1879 when the ostensible axis of conflict moved from north–south to east–west. The war of the Pacific was the cause of the final collapse of the system, if indeed it merits such a term. Although there were survivals in terms of military organisation and political style, there can be no doubt that the war acted as a major watershed. Yet a more incisive periodisation must give weight to the partial but qualitative advance of liberalism under Linares. From 1857 onwards, no military regime was able fully to turn the clock back. This is true even for Melgarejo who, although he transgressed even the very generous contemporary norms for malfeasance, posed fewer problems for the dominant bloc than Belzu would have done; it is telling in this regard that Belzu's final attempt to regain power by overthrowing Melgarejo in 1865 was defeated with the assistance of the new southern military strong man, Narciso Campero. The post-Linares military regimes proved costly and unpleasant but they provided necessary barriers against a restless artisanate, and neither Morales nor Daza attempted to redress the balance in favour of protection. In the decade before the war, the political challenge to the power of the *chuquisaqueño* elite was identified as emanating less from the army than from a reformulated, fundamentally confused, yet far from impotent *belcista* populism. Its leaders, such men as Méndez and Casimiro Corral, were still obliged to cling to the coat tails of such dispossessed generals as the veteran *melgarejista* Quintín Quevedo but they also provided the germs of *post bellum* liberalism, and in their challenge to the *rojo/consti-tucionalista* current heralded the arrival of a form of party politics.

While the conflict between free trade and protection is now granted importance in the structuring of political power in nine-teenth century Bolivia, this has largely been as a result of the interpretative work of Guillermo Lora (who has been a Trotskyist militant for 35 years and a university professor for only nine months). Lora's work has certainly had the effect of stalling the momentum of epic studies — a veritable discipline in its own right — but it remains to be consolidated and expanded in terms of pri-mary research. What we have suggested here is that the mechanism of the state monopoly over the purchase of silver, the keystone of protection, is critical to the understanding of the rapid, internal schisms of the military as well as of the broad development of social classes; that control over bullion goes a long way to explain the more precise character of political conflict in addition to determining the longer-term formation of regional armies and power blocs.

This is not to dismiss the importance of land at all but, rather, to qualify the centrality it is generally supposed to have had in determin-ing the phenomenon of *caudillismo*, and to revise the notion that, in Bolivia at least, the early republican period was characterised principally by spatial dispersal of power with the system as a whole representative of an amalgam of essentially regional authorities, for which there was no organising principle of consistent importance beyond the mainte-nance of competition between landed capitals and their internal relations of production. By recognising that this system interacted, albeit in an uneven and intermittent manner, with one in which control of bullion, and thereby both local accumulation and access to the world market was contested, we can appreciate that while the modern state may have progressively come into being from 1880 onwards, the state itself was not previously absent, or some kind of secondhand sham, but a real power base, weak in that it was constantly 'invaded' but strong inasmuch as it was in many respects the commanding citadel. This is less a paradox than the starting point for a model.

# Notes

1   *Mensaje del presidente constitucional* ...*1855* (unpaginated).
2   Nicanor Aranzaes, *Las revoluciones de Bolivia* (La Paz, 1918).
3   M. Rigoberto Paredes, *Melgarejo y su tiempo* (La Paz, 1962), p. 45.
4   FO 11/1, 30 Jan. 1843.
5   John Appleton to Washington, no. 3, 13 Dec. 1848.
6   N. Andrew N. Cleven , *The Political Organization of Bolivia* (Washington, 1940), p. 120.
7   Tomas Caivano, *Historia de la guerra de América entre Chile, Peru y Bolivia* (Iquique, 1904), no. I, p. 321.
8   *Gaceta del Gobierno,* vol. I, no. 7, 18 Jan. 1843.
9   Manuel José Cortés, *Ensayo sobre la historia de Bolivia* (Sucre, 1861), p. 94.
10  Avelino Aramayo, *Apuntes sobre el congreso de 1870* (Sucre, 1871), p. 4. See also his *Apuntes sobre el estado industrial, económico y político de Bolivia* (Sucre, 1871). A more perceptive viewpoint, but doomed for the purposes of political programme, is to be found in Julio Méndez, *Bolivia antes del 30 de Noviembre de 1874* (Tacna, 1875).
11  A. Arguedas, 'Los caudillos bárbaros; la plebe en acción; la dictadura y la anarquía; los caudillos letrados', in *Obras completas* (Mexico, 1959).
12  *Ensayos y Crítica* (La Paz, 1961), p. 73.
13  FO 11/8, No. 4,16 July 1850; Carlos Montenegro , *Nacionalismo y coloniaje* (La, Paz 1953); José Fellmann Velarde, *Historia de Bolivia,* II (La Paz, 1970).
14  Only two issues of *Avances* were published before the coup of 1980 which resulted in the exile of many of its leading contributors. The second number, November 1978, is entirely given over to the question of *latifundismo* and the oligarchy. Much. of the best work may also be found in *Estudios bolivianos en homenaje a Gunnar Mendoza L.*(La Paz, 1978) and the *cuadernos* of the Centro de Investigación y Promoción del Campesinado (CIPCA). See also, Brooke Larson, 'Economic and Social Change in an Agrarian Hinterland: Cochabamba (Bolivia) in the late Colonial Period' (Ph.D., Columbia University, 1978); Antonio Mitre, 'Silver Mining in XIX Century Bolivia' (Ph.D., Columbia University, 1977); Fernando Cajías, *La provincia de Atacama 1825–42* (La Paz, 1976).
15  Gunter Kahle , 'Die Encomienda als militarische Institution im kolonialen Hispanoamerika', *Jahrbuch für Geschichte von Staat, Wirtschaft and Gesellschaft Lateinamerikas,* vol. 2 (1965); Alfonso García Gallo, 'El servicio militar en Indias', *Anuario de Historia del Derecho Español,* vol. XXVI (1965); Leon G. Campbell, *The Military and Society in Colonial Peru*

(Philadelphia, 1978); Enrique Tandeter, 'La rente comme rapport de production et comme rapport de distribution. Le cas de l'industrie Minière de Potosí, 1750–1826', Thèse de 3e Cycle, École des Hautes Études en Sciences Sociales (Paris, 1980).

16   Cortés, p. 115; Julio Díaz A. (1945), *El gran mariscal de Montenegro. Otto Felipe Braun* (La Paz, 1945), p. 71; José Manuel Aponte, *La batalla de Ingavi* (La Paz, 1911), p. 124; *Memoria del ministro de guerra* (MemMG) ... 1843; FO 11/10, no. 12, 7 Sept. 1852; Hall to Washington, no. 49, 24 Sept. 1865; MemMG ... 1870; *ibid.*, ... 1877.

17   *Gaceta del Gobierno*, II, no. 58, 23 Dec. 1843; José María Dalence, *Bosquejo estadístico de Bolivia* (Chuquisaca, 1851), p. 351.

18   MemMG ... 1870; *ibid.*, ... 1877. According to the army's organic law, there should have been one Major General for every 3,000 men and one Brigadier for every 1,000. In 1846, an average year, there was a general for every 106 soldiers and an officer for every six.

19   *Gaceta del Gobierno*, II, no. 11, 22 Aug. 1843; *ibid.*, I, no. 80, 3 May 1843.

20   MemMG ... 1870.

21   Ramón Sotomayor Valdés, *Estudio histórico de Bolivia bajo la administración del general Don José María de Achá* (Santiago, 1874), p. 139.

22   Hall to Washington, no. 46, 17 July 1865.

23   Rand to Washington, no. 15, 9 Nov. 1870.

24   Markbreit to Washington, no. 226, 28 Nov. 1872; Federico Lafaye, *Apuntes para la historia de Bolivia* (Tacna, 1873).

25   Aramayo, *Congreso*, pp. 28–43; *Informe sobre los asuntos de Bolivia en Europa* (Paris, 1877), p. 57; Mitre (1977), pp. 55–76.

26   Gustavo Rodríguez, 'Libre cambio y el carácter del capitalismo; el caso Boliviano' in *Estudios en homenaje a Gunnar Mendoza*, pp. 231–48; Mitre, pp. 46–50.

27   Rodríguez, pp. 236–7; Guillermo Lora, *Historia del movimiento obrero boliviano* I (La Paz 1967), pp. 73–100. See Larson, pp. 247–71, for *tocuyo* production in Cochabamba at the turn of the century. She contends that 'by 1850, all Bolivians except the highland Indian population clothed themselves in cloth manufactured in England or one of its colonies ...', (p. 269). This is a position commonly held for Peru at this time, but in the case of Bolivia it might be questioned whether imports were so great, not solely on the basis of Dalence's probably inflated figures for 1846 of 3,572 wool workshops (production valued at 36,681 pesos) and 359 cotton workshops (66,584 pesos) but also on the basis of bad communications and the continued high tariffs until 1859.

28   Julio Benavides, *Historia de la moneda en Bolivia* (La Paz, 1972), pp. 58–62. On debasement see Luis Peñaloza, *Historia económica de Bolivia*, II (La Paz, 1947), pp. 7–42; Watt Stewart, *Henry Meiggs; Yankee Pizarro* (Durham, NC, 1946), pp. 232ff. and, especially detailed, the reports of US Consul Rand in La Paz, 1870.

29   Mitre (1977), p. 61.

30   *Ibid.,* p. 282.

31   *Ibid.,* p. 65.

32   In 1896 the Batallón Sucre lost 197 deserters out of an establishment of 254 men, a not unrepresentative example. Archivo Nacional de Bolivia, Ministerio de Guerra, 1896,

33   For details see James Dunkerley, 'The Politics of the Bolivian Army; Institutional Development 1879–1935' (D.Phil., University of Oxford 1979), Chapter 2.

34   Manuel Rubio Sánchez, 'Breve historia del cultivo del añil o xiquilite y de la grana o cochinilla' in *Economía de Guatemala en los siglos XVIII y XIX* (San Salvador, 1976).

35   The rebels of 1871 were keen to disown all responsibility for mobilising the indigenous population. *Memoria del secretario general del estado, Dr Casimiro Corral* (Sucre, 1871), p. 2. On the opposition to conscription in the 1890s, *Interpelación del sr ministro de guerra, Dr Luis Paz 1895* (Sucre, 1897), and on 1898 Ramiro Condarco Morales, *Zarate. El temible willka* (La Paz, 1965); Andrew Pearse, *The Latin American Peasant* (London, 1975).

36   José Agustín Morales, *Monografía de las provincias del Norte y Sur Yungas* (La Paz, 1929), pp. 191–92; Aramayo, *Estado*, p. 79.

37   For example, Chichas, Omasuyos, Oruro, Tarija, Tarapacá and Poopó for two years in 1842, and Tarija and Chichas for ten years in 1861. There were often political motives behind such measures. *Gaceta del Gobierno, II, 10* Oct. 1843; José Agustín Morales, *Los primeros cien años de la república de Bolivia, II* (La Paz, 1926), p. 32.

38   Mitre (1977), pp. 202–5.

39   John Cotton Smith to Washington, no. 6, 13 March 1859.

40   Erwin P. Grieshaber, 'Survival of Peasant Communities in Nineteenth Century Bolivia' (Ph.D., University of North Carolina at Chapel Hill, 1977), pp. 132ff., 242; Silvia Rivera Cusicanqui, 'La expansión del latifundio en el altiplano boliviano. Elementos para la caracterización de una oligarquía regional', *Avances*, vol. 2, pp. 95–118.

41   According to the Chilean ambassador, 'a multitude of vagrant soldiers, public employees owed back-pay, relations and retainers of govern-

ment ministers' were the main beneficiaries, Ramon Sotomayor *Valdés, La legación de Chile en Bolivia* (Santiago, 1912), p. 93. For details of the 1866 and 1868 measures combined with orthodox interpretation, liberal and 'anti-imperialist' alike, see Luis Antezana, *El feudalismo de Melgarejo y la reforma agraria* (La Paz, 1970), pp. 19–73; Arturo Urquidi, *Las comunidades indígenas en Bolivia* (Cochabamba, 1970), pp. 62–64; Peñaloza, I, pp. 252–9; Fellmann Velarde (1970), pp. 179–214, passim; Alfredo Sanjinés, *La reforma agraria en Bolivia* (La Paz, 1930).

42 Grieshaber, p. 200.

43 Aramayo, *Congreso*, pp. 21–4; José María Santivañez, *Reivindicación de los terrenos de comunidad* (Cochabamba, 1871). For support for alienation see José Vicente Dorado, *Proyecto de repartición de tierras y venta de ellas entre los indígenas* (Sucre, 1864); Juan de Diós Zambrana, *Dos palabras sobre la venta de tierras realengas* (Cochabamba, 1871).

44 See, inter alia., José Cardus, *Las misiones franciscanas entre los infieles de Bolivia* (Barcelona, 1886); J. Lavadenz, *La colonización de Bolivia durante la primera centuria de independencia* (La Paz, 1925); Julio Díaz A., *Expediciones y exploradores del suelo boliviano* (La Paz, 1971); Cristián Suárez, *Exploraciones en el oriente boliviano* (La Paz, 1919).

45 'The history of Bolivia is not a history of class struggle. It is rather the history of its regional struggles,' J.L. Roca, *Fisonomía del regionalismo boliviano* (La Paz, 1980), p. 9.

46 Matías Carrasco, *Descripción sinóptica de Mojos* (Chuquisaca, 1830); Antonio Carvalho Urey, *Bosquejo socioeconómico del Beni* (Sucre, 1976); Chelio Luna Pizarro, *Ensayo monográfico del departamento de Pando* (Sucre, 1976).

47 J. Valerie Fifer, *Bolivia: Land, Location and Politics since 1825* (Cambridge, 1972).

48 Charles W. Arnade, *La dramática insurgencia de Bolivia* (La Paz, 1972); William Lofstrom, 'The Promise and Problems of Reform: Attempted Economic and Social Change in the First Years of Bolivian Independence' (Ph.D., Cornell University 1972); Tambor mayor Vargas. Diario de un soldado de la independencia altoperuana en los valles de Sicasica y Hayopaya , ed. Gunnar Mendoza (Sucre, 1954); Julio Díaz, A., *Los Generales de Bolivia* (La Paz, 1929).

49 Méndez, p. 19.

50 Lora, pp. 417ff.; Roca, p. 378; Hernando Sanabria Fernández, *Bosquejo de la contribución de Santa Cruz la formación de nacionalidad* (Santa Cruz, 1942), which challenges the separatist theses of Plácido Molina, *Observaciones y rectificaciones a la historia de Santa Cruz de la Sierra* (La Paz, 1936).

# 7

## The Third Man:
## Francisco Burdett O'Connor and the
## Emancipation of the Americas

## What's in a Name?

For the last 500 years most people in Europe have been given at least two names. In a few countries, such as Spain, they hold three, retaining the surname of the mother after the patronym, and some married women add that of their husband to their maiden name. With the exception of native North Americans, this pattern has generally been followed in the colonies established by the European powers, so that a name normally indicates a family as well as a personal history.

Parents face a constrained choice in bestowing one or more forenames on their expected or recently-born child insofar as subsequent usage will bear only partly on the aesthetic or allusive routes to nomination. In childhood the rhyming and rhythmical potential of a name can be positively tyrannical, and even for adults the degree of formality used in address does not fit any common threshold of familiarity. It is a banal fact of life that we address many people with whom we have but the slightest acquaintance by their forenames in the same way as do those who know them with the greatest intimacy. A name is only a starting-point, and it can obscure as much as it reveals. Besides, names can be changed.

This is what happened in the case of my subject this afternoon. After September 1819, when he arrived in Venezuela from Dublin to join the independence campaign for Spain's colonies in the Americas, Francis — or, as his family and friends called him, Frank — O'Connor became Francisco Burdett O'Connor. This might seem to be an unremarkable hispanisation of a forename. However, I think it telling that this process would restore to O'Connor the qualities precisely of a Christian name, and it may well be that such an early translation helped to ensure that over the rest of his life — some 52 years — he would never return to the British Isles.

At the same time, O'Connor proudly provided himself with a new surname, placing 'Burdett' in the position of the patronym — that is, where hispanic custom locates paternity — and so causing open and subliminal confusion as to his inheritance or, in the demotic of our own day, his identity.

Those inclined to the Viennese school of analysis will discern a rich and deep motivational field here, but none of us can quiz

O'Connor on that now, and the fact is that until his death he continued to be known by his original surname. Burdett loitered as a quasi-forename. It was, though, no mere embellishment. When he signed his will, O'Connor simply included the initial 'B', but the first article of that document of 1866 studiously indicates that his father was Roger O'Connor, his mother Wilhelmina Charlotte Caroline Bowen, and his godfather Sir Francis Burdett. Moreover, when Frank had been a teenager Burdett had acted *in loco parentis* in a serious and practical fashion. His godchild might well have had political or psychological reason to promote him and adopt his name, but he had been a genuine *padrino,* as it is put in Spanish.

Today one of the provinces of the Bolivian department of Tarija carries the name of O'Connor — it includes the farm Francisco built up near the town of San Luis — and in the 1830s the division he commanded as a general of the Bolivian army was also named after him. O'Connor was personally associated with the establishment of a third of the units that comprised the armed forces in the first century of the republic, and he is the only man to have served three times as their chief of staff.[1] In 1826 the congress of the new state awarded him 5,000 pesos as a 'liberator', but he himself never used that title despite the rare honour it bestowed, and all these institutional vestiges have now been lost outside the mustiest of books.

Only one of O'Connor's children survived — a daughter, Hercilia.[2] So, if tradition had been followed his name should also have disappeared from the family within a generation. However, his grandsons adopted his own voluntarist attitude to nomenclature: they not only retained their matronym but also converted it into a patronym.

Hercilia had married one Adhemar d'Arlach, which in the valleys of Tarija had no less exotic an echo to it than did O'Connor — which may explain why, even though they traded places, these two possessive surnames have stuck together over the generations as a composite, O'Connor d'Arlach today being a single surname in southern Bolivia. Indeed, the origins of this lecture lie partly in a request from the deputy foreign minister of the country, Eduardo Trigo O'Connor d'Arlach, for an explanation of the appearance of Burdett in the name of his forebear.

The name Burdett appears in most textbooks on modern British history as an opponent of the Pitt and Liverpool governments, a

forceful advocate of civil liberties — particularly *habeas corpus* — and
an architect of parliamentary reform. The name of O'Connor is
usually associated with the Chartist leader Feargus, also an MP but
more widely known for his ability to mobilise the masses and his
frequent arrests in the campaigns of the 1830s and 1840s for political change. This O'Connor was born three years after Frank and
was, indeed, his younger brother.

In the simple sense of localised public knowledge Francisco
Burdett O'Connor is a 'third man' in that the owner of a forename
stands behind two famous surnames that in historical memory
belong to other people before they do to him. In some respects,
then, the earliest parts of the present story are the most important.

This is particularly so because we have the interesting challenge of
the relationship between siblings — not just between Frank and
Feargus but also between their ebullient father Roger, a sportsman and
spectacular spendthrift who exercised his charm equally upon the
greatest of Whig grandees and the most humble of countrymen, and
Roger's brother Arthur, renegade MP, hardline leader of the *United
Irishmen* and convicted traitor to the British Crown, who was idolised
by his nephews as a persecuted and heroic patriot.

The imbalance between their father and uncle in terms of public
profile and achievement possibly helps to explain why both Frank and
Feargus maintained throughout their lives that the family descended
from the kings of Connaught, thereby providing some dynastic
compensation — perhaps even excuse — for the fact that Roger was,
in the words of Graham Wallas, 'a semi-lunatic'.[3]

Of course, a romance like ours begins bereft of both innocence
and rigour. It is bad form even in Whig and Freudian terms to put
the *craich* in place of the deconstruction. Blood-ties provide struc-
turalists with the most numerous and least stimulating linkages. Karl
Marx himself thought Feargus 'patriarchal and petty-bourgeois' —
the ultimate put-down, even coming from the accused in the second-
biggest ideological paternity suit in two millenia.

I'm not myself sure whether any publicly practising post-
modernists really exist east of Gander and north of Calais, but if so
the chances are that they see biography less as fragmented irony than
the metanarrative of solipsism. And for many sophisticated people

in receipt of funds from the public purse for purveying to the young ideas ancient and modern, the notion of an improving tale is utterly primitive — a veritable Chernobyl of the mind.

Nevertheless, as that great historian Johan Huizinga reminds us, 'sophistry, technically regarded as a form of expression, has all the associations with primitive play ... The sophism proper is closely related to the riddle. It is a fencer's trick'.[4] Jules Michelet, a contemporary of the O'Connor boys, is no less persuasive of the pleasures and profit in managing the affairs of the dead in our day — when he is celebrated for his treatment of sex and magic — than he was in his own — when he was famous for democratic demands and dates.

*

The central date for our purposes is some 208 years ago — 12 June 1791 — when Francis or Frank was born in the city of Cork to Whilamena Bowen, second wife of Roger O'Connor, who had previously been married to Louisa Strachan. The son of that earlier union, Roderick, was the elder brother to whom Frank and Feargus both looked for a lead and who later established the Commonwealth branch of the family by settling in Tasmania in 1824. Today his descendent Roderic has preserved a family tradition by occupying in Cressy a house called 'Connorville' after the original family estate in County Cork. Feargus would establish a settlement with the same name in the 1840s, when he sought to establish a yeoman-based land company in England as part of a political vision of self-sufficiency and the citizen-as-producer which he shared with Frank, which they both inherited from Arthur, and which Arthur in turn derived from a close reading of Adam Smith.

That notion of the farm and the home as the basis of a republican civilisation has strong roots in the family experience, and the first six years of Frank's life were comfortably set within it. His grandfather had bequeathed a considerable income of £10,000 a year to his four sons, and the eldest of these, Daniel, had already sold his inheritance to Roger in order to fund his elopement to Bristol with a Mrs Gibbons. For a child, life on the Connerville estate at Bandon must have been exciting enough in a family so devoted to the chase that when the season for foxes closed they took to hunting hares. After 1795, when Frank's uncle Arthur made an arresting speech in the House of Commons in favour of Catholic emancipation the comings and goings increased further still.

One central reason for Arthur's unexpected initiative was the suicide by drowning of his sister Anne, who had been prohibited from marrying her Catholic love. A family that for three generations had combined political conservatism, commercial success and social stability was plunged into such a fierce conflict that the second son, Robert, who was the local sheriff, tried to have Roger executed as editor of the nationalist *Harp of Erin* well before both Roger and Arthur were accused of treason for their part in the French invasion plans of 1796 and 1798 and their role in the failed uprising of the latter year.

When, on the eve of his own detention, Arthur published an article in the radical Dublin paper the *Press* praising the Gracchi brothers — the reformers of late republican Rome murdered by conservatives — he was surely displaying more than knowledge of the classical tradition, offering an autobiographical reflection, if not a hostage to fortune.

Arthur took the lead in this shift to what we would now call the left. Roger organised clandestine meetings in Cork and occasionally visited London to frequent those Whig salons where it was fashionable to cherrypick policies and attitudes from revolutionary France, but it was Arthur who actually went to France to negotiate an alliance with the Directory, who did deals with the real radicals of the London Corresponding Society, and who was followed by Pitt's spies in both London and Ulster. According to Marianne Elliott, Arthur's 'confidence, his informed loqaciousness and oratorical abilities won more support for the movement than it might otherwise have attracted', but 'his obvious desire to run the show' also split a fractious and underprepared organisation.[5]

Today names such as Horne Tooke, Wolf Tone and Napper Tandy sound quaint and antique — almost as if they were penned by Tolkien — but 200 years ago their ideas about freedom of the press and association and the claims of popular and national sovereignty made them dangerous enemies of the state which — especially in times of war — sought to have them hanged, drawn and quartered. In none of these cases did Pitt succeed — Theobold Wolfe Tone came closest but killed himself on the eve of execution. Nonetheless, in the 1790s Britain had a regime which so combined the rule of law with the apparatus of dictatorship that opponents were generally given enough rope with which to hang themselves. Ireland was still a different polity and jurisdiction, but it was ruled by the same monarch and cabinet; and there the frontier between privileged security and outlaw status was much more readily crossed.

Frank O'Connor's innocence ended before his seventh birthday, in February 1798, when his uncle trespassed across that fateful line. Roger followed Arthur into prison almost immediately, and the boys were left with their younger sisters in the care of their mother and their godfather Burdett.

Arthur had been arrested at the King's Head, Margate the day before he was due to flee to France in the company of the radical priest the Reverend James Coigley. O'Connor's life was saved by some good luck — the state was reluctant to produce as evidence papers its agents had intercepted in the mail, and his servant succeeded in flushing other incriminating material down the privy in the hotel before the Bow Street Runners broke down the door. However, Arthur also owed much to the fact that before Roger was arrested he had persuaded Arthur's Whig friends to testify to his good character and innocence at the trial held in May — the subject of one of Gilray's most laconic and telling cartoons.[6]

Father Coigley benefited from neither such oligarchic solidarity nor Arthur's emphatically selfish defence strategy, which even moved the judge to remark, 'Mr O'Connor, do you not see how much this is to the prejudice of the other prisoner?' However, Mr Justice Buller did not hesitate to pass the death sentence on the priest, whose guilt seemed to be sought at any cost by all other parties and was sealed by the papers found on his person.

Arthur was acquitted in what Thomas Packenham describes as,

> one of the strangest scenes in a British court of justice. O'Connor could be re-tried under Irish law on exactly the same charge of which he had been acquitted under British law. Accordingly, two Bow Street Runners were waiting by the dock ready to re-arrest him. But no sooner had the death sentence

been passed on the unfortunate Coigley than O'Connor rushed
from the dock to the bar, and from the bar into the body of the
court, with the police in hot pursuit. The court was plunged
into confusion. Outraged Whigs, including O'Connor's council
and Lord Thanet, tried to snatch him to safety. Swords were
drawn — the swords that were lying as evidence on the table.
Furniture was smahed and heads broken. O'Connor might
have got clean away, but for the quick-wittedness of the judge's
coachman, who bought him crashing to the floor.[7]

Although Arthur was duly dispatched to Kilmainham jail with some
80 other United Irishmen facing charges of high treason, the state
was almost as tarnished by the trial as was the embattled republican
movement. Pitt eventually won the day although he had to execute
four more people before the rest of the convicts agreed to a trade of
their confessions for life. In the process Roger joined Arthur in the
Scottish prison of Fort George, and it was only in 1803 that he was
permitted to return to Ireland on condition that he settle within 30
miles of Dublin. Arthur took the logical step of exile in France,
where, at the age of 44, he married Condorcet's daughter Eliza, who
was just 17, buying Mirabeau's estate at Le Bignon and being
gazetted by Napoleon as a divisional general.[8]

Arthur O'Connor rather misjudged the balance of forces in
1814–1815, but he never came close to a real battle and was able to
draw a military pension from the French taxpayer for a full 47 years.
This was probably just as well since Roger soon either squandered or
stole his brother's share of the family inheritance, and Eliza, who
until the Whigs came to power was alone permitted to enter Ireland,
proved to be no match for her brother-in-law.

In 1848, at the age of 85, Arthur published a sprawling three-
volume work — *Monopoly — the Cause of All Evil* — the ill-discipline of
which he compounded by styling himself Arthur Condorcet
O'Connor. That work added little or nothing to his 110-page pamphlet,
*The State of Ireland,* published in February 1798, where one finds a fluid
and compelling mix of Smithian logic, the scepticism of Hume, and a
Kantian appetite for freedom, equality and independence. The piece,
although over-stretched, still constitutes a major document of a republican movement striving to escape the stain of Jacobin excess.[9]

Perhaps Arthur's most practical legacy to his nephews was an insistence upon the power and importance of the press to a democratic politics.[10] Feargus took the injunction seriously enough to found a new *Northern Star* in the 1830s as a mouthpiece for Chartism, and although there would be no newspaper in Tarija until the early 1850s, Frank wrote in *El Cóndor* of Chuquisaca within six months of its establishment in 1825, and his grandson Tomás, to whom we owe the publication of the general's memoirs, was editor of *La Estrella de Tarija* for 27 years.

The O'Connors shared a healthy appetite for expression: Francisco alone published no book in his lifetime and positively shied away from speechifying — on Bolivian social outings he would often accompany the ladies so as to avoid the elaborate and inebriated toasting that was the masculine order of the day. Yet, in addition to the published memoirs, which had been written up until 1839 when he died, we have five volumes of diaries dating from 1849, in a varied state of repair but their sparse Spanish — never English, not even Spanglish — is generally readable even for those untrained in palaeography. The two inalterable features of each day's entry are the weather and O'Connor's location. We are usually also given the state of his health and transactions. Sometimes we get a reflection on the wider world, very much less often an inner thought. There is very little mention of Francisca Ruyloba, the 17-year-old daughter of a family of clerks and priests whom he — twice her age — married in 1827. O'Connor unfailingly refers to Francisca, of whom we have a firm and attractive photographic portrait, as *La Señora*, and he sometimes has the good grace to allude to advice she has given and he accepted.[11]

As he grew old in Tarija, O'Connor imbibed more of the ethos of the Franciscan brothers whose monastery dominated the centre of the small Andean town and, with 5,000 books, possessed the best library of the region. In his will he ordained that every school in the department should be donated a copy of his favourite book, Marmontel's *Belisaire,* but also that — following the example of the censors of pre-revolutionary France — its mildly deist Chapter 15 should first be excised. Perhaps predictably, his legacy came to nought, saving *Tarijeño* youth from some rather tiresome ruminations on Byzantine affairs as well as the risk of passing on to Procopius's

*Secret History*, a text which, by virtue of its references to the more intimate forms of animal husbandry, was unlikely to appear even in an O'Connor syllabus for the history of the book.

Francisco's sympathy for the Catholic Church was not so evident early on — as military governor of Tarija in 1826 he closed all the monasteries except that of the Franciscans (who numbered then, as they do today, just three friars) — although it may well have been a reaction against his father, who habitually declared that Voltaire was his only God.

Frank and Feargus had spent much of their youth and early adulthood coming to grips with Roger's behaviour, which, following his release from jail in 1802, became increasingly extravagant. On one occasion the boys fled his house, stole two horses belonging to their brother Roderick, sold them in Dublin to fund the trip to London, doorstepped Burdett at his home in Stratton Street off Piccadilly, and asked to move in.[12]

At the time Burdett, whose marriage to Sophia Coutts, daughter of the banker, had provided him with more than enough cash to fund his political campaigns, was serving as an MP and publishing incendiary material — much of it on the sale of parliamentary seats — in Cobbett's *Register*. Whilst he was happy to subsidize the boys, and to show them the town and the radical demi-monde, he was not prepared to test further domestic arrangements made very fragile by his affair with Lady Oxford and his frequent clashes over parliamentary privilege with the Speaker and the magistrates. Frank and Feargus returned to Dangan Castle, County Westmeath, which Roger had bought in 1803 for £40,000 from the Wellesley family, declaring the mansion to be of a grandeur sufficient for receiving Napoleon when Ireland was finally liberated. And, indeed, a few months later the emperor sent Arthur an undertaking that he would not conclude a peace with England until Ireland was free.[13]

When, five years after its purchase, part of the Dangan building burnt down with only a portion of the price paid in cash, it was widely believed that Roger had planned an insurance fiddle. However, writing his memoirs 60 years later General O'Connor records that he had started the fire, by accidentally spilling molten lead on the floorboards when casting bullets for his target pistols.[14]

Whether he thought so at the time is unclear, but in his old age O'Connor ruefully presents the blaze as the main reason for his mother's early death, which left the children even more exposed to Roger's antics even as he ran off with a Mrs Smith, took up with her maid Dora Reynolds, and then, in 1817, settled down with a woman uniformly described by the distinctly secondary sources as 'a young peasant girl' at Ballincollig.

By that stage Frank was 26, physically and fiscally independent, having completed his military training; Burdett had already been obliged to talk him out of joining Napoleon's comeback campaign. It is unlikely that he was still lodged at Dangan, but the evidence suggests that he had been around in October 1812, at the time of the infamous robbery of the Galway mail, which was carrying a large sum of cash for the purchase of cattle at the annual fair of Ballinasloe.

Roger was immediately suspected of organising the ten high-waymen who staged the assault, in which the coach's guard was killed. The day after the robbery it was he who informed the police that much — but by no means all — of the loot had been found in the grounds of his home. It is just possible, but unlikely, that Frank and Feargus were aware of the plot, which understandably appears nowhere in their memoirs even though five years later Roger was formally charged with the crime as the result of a plea-bargain struck by a criminal in another trial.

The case was heard before Mr Justice St George Daly at Trim Assizes in August 1817. Burdett, recently re-elected MP for Middlesex, rushed across to give evidence on behalf of the father of his godchildren. On the day of the trial the heat was so intense that Roger fainted into Burdett's arms, but his friend provided an even more critical form of support in convincing the jury that he had no need to rob the mail in order to secure funds. Under examination, Burdett was as studiously reliable in an uncertain cause as had been Sheridan some 20 years before in order to save Arthur's neck:

> If Mr O'Connor had occasion for a particular sum in 1812, would you have advanced it for his accommodation?

> Undoubtedly, and I can hardly mention the sum to which I would not go to accommodate him.

You were surprised at such a charge as this being made
against him?

I felt ready to sink to the ground.[15]

Roger, who was now 55, proved unable to accept his acquittal as a
salutary warning. Later that year he enraged his saviour by preferring
charges of perjury against the main prosecution witness in the case,
putting it about that the aim of the heist had been to recover
Burdett's letters to Lady Oxford now that she had transferred her
affections to Lord Byron. Henceforth Burdett stayed with Roderick
on his visits to Ireland despite the fact that Roger dedicated to him a
book published in 1822 under the title *The Chronicles of Erin* with the
purport of being the only true account of Ireland 'translated from
the original manuscripts in the Phoenician dialect of the Scythian
language'. Described in the *Dictionary of National Biography as* 'mainly,
if not entirely, the fruit of O'Connor's imagination', this text
contains a great many grammatical errors, as did Feargus's later writings, opening him to the lampoons of enemies who in their youth
had been obliged to undertake classical studies.

*

In tracing this trajectory, I am deliberately tripping around a caricature — the etching of the pantomime Irishman that is the engine of
English condescension — for the purpose of asking a second question: why does a person cross the Atlantic? I should also reassure the
reader that I do not propose to survey the rest of Frank O'Connor's
life at a pace proportional to that struck hitherto; this has been
undertaken with a view to establishing a distinct perspective on our
subject's private emancipation in the Americas even as he partici-
pated in their public liberation.

Today, of course, people cross the Atlantic to and fro the whole
time, but until at least 1945 — and maybe until the days of Freddy
Laker — most made the trip from east to west with much greater
thought of arriving and staying than of returning. It was, historically, a journey of escape, and there were usually strong push- as
well as pull-factors.

Roger O'Connor had provided his children with a superabundance of the exotic which is so frequently hung on Latin America and popularly associated with the 'magical realist' school represented by Gabriel García Márquez's *One Hundred Years of Solitude*.[16] Yet, at close quarter and within familiar distance, such 'otherness', as it is now dubbed by dowdy Anglo-Saxon scholars, could be distinctly disturbing, far from alluring, and conducive less to associational admiration than to the living grief of embarrassment at a life conducted on the very margins of its own ambition.

Terry Eagleton has commented that, 'if Ireland is raw, turbulent, destructive, it is also a locus of play, pleasure, fantasy, a blessed release from the tyranny of the English reality principle'.[17] Elsewhere I have argued that Ireland is usefully looked upon as an American country unaccountably located in the wrong continent, but here I certainly do not want to postulate some kind of ectopian utopia.

Rather, I should like to suggest that whilst the English bayonets were forever the avowed cause of Francisco Burdett O'Connor's voluntary exile from his homeland, the 'collateral damage' wreaked by an eccentricity raised in response to them is an additional factor. We are here, in a sense, dealing with an inversion of the picaresque.

O'Connor was not escaping metropolitan drudgery simply for adventure although this he would experience to intense and dangerous measure — over the rest of his life I estimate that he spent some 24 hours in direct combat, three weeks within an hour's ride of enemy forces, seven years in military campaigning, and 45 years farming. His life was transformed by no luxuriant apparitions of butterflies, no wondrous ice-making machines, and no dusky seductions — well, just the one — but, instead, by a land of regularity and modesty, naturalism and the rigours of the real. It was a life dedicated more to construction than creativity, and, of course, such a path can be transcendental in a wider philosophical sense as well as within subjective fulfilment.

What is of particular interest to us here is how this trajectory passed through and beyond the paraphenalia of heroism. Francisco Burdett O'Connor was no representative man in the Emersonian sense, and just as Carlyle could write the 70 pages of *Chartism* without once mentioning Feargus, so would he have encountered problems, had he known of Frank's existence, slotting him into

*Heroes and Hero-Worship.* In saying this I do not mean to infer that O'Connor was resistant to fame and adulation; he certainly bridled at lack of recognition. But he treated the heroic with an affectation so light as to suggest that it was almost wholly attributable to an inescapable genetic endowment.

We need less to promote O'Connor or rehabilitate him to some overdue iconic status than to go back behind the superficial surrealism that still infects the image of Latin America and interrogate a deep culture of heroism which remains so resiliently attached to the origins of its independence. That sanitised vision has already been subjected to distinguished critical inquiry at a variety of levels and for different regions by all four of my predecessors as Director of the Institute.

Here I simply note that the heroic version derives from the needs as well as the condescension of posterity. It is not easy to resist the crisp, sub-Bonapartist iconography populated with handsome, focused and beautifully attired young generals. Of those who led the struggles few survived long enough to have their photo taken, and such portraits generally reflect the weight of exhaustion and pain visible in the picture we have of O'Connor (although I persist in the conviction that there is gentleness in those fair eyes).

The telescope given to him by Bolívar has disappeared, as have the many artefacts that most families lose through carelessness and pilfering and that we know from his will were still held in his final years. In that final testament O'Connor claims,

> I entered marriage with capital of 26,000 pesos, without counting the value of my silver service, shotguns, firearms, horses, mules, books etcetera etcetera, about which I say nothing more here because my wife denies it, saying that she has never seen any of it, but in the distribution of my possessions she will receive one half of everything.

Even if we believe Francisca here, we can be sure that Frank did not leave for the Americas in order to make a fortune. When, in July 1819, he boarded the *Hannah* with 200 other members of the Irish Legion he carried Burdett's letter of credit for £500 drawn on the Bank of England. Two years later when stationed in Panama he would issue a bill for £1,000 to be drawn on Coutts, and just as during the campaign he often kitted out his men from his own purse, so as a landlord he was accustomed to pay small fines and forgive the debts of his tenants and workers, even if in every case he kept a detailed record and in most instances registered a careworn complaint.

Most of all, O'Connor went to America for political reasons. There is no sign that he wished to practise politics himself — and he never did so in Bolivia — but we should not underestimate the extent to which people left Europe, including Great Britain, in the early nineteenth century because it was an unfree and counter-revolutionary place. In 1801 Ireland lost those vestiges of self-government that were still in place when Arthur had tried to drive through to full independence. This, of course, would only be obtained 120 years later, under the aegis of Eamonn de Valera, born in the US of a Spanish father.

A fortnight after the Irish Legion set sail for Venezuela in 1819, a total of 11 people were killed and more wounded when the militia charged with sabres upon a political reform meeting held not in Caracas but in Manchester. It was not until ten years after that 'Peterloo Massacre' that any Catholic was allowed to vote or hold public office, and it was three more years before there took place a British parliamentary election in which a large number of seats were not effectively bought and sold; even then the franchise was restricted to propertied men. There was no World Bank, IMF or other multilateral agency to tutor the Westminster and Whitehall of the day in the manners of good governance.

Of course, a popular vote for the presidency of the US was not held until 1824, but it is today easy to forget how, compared to a reactionary post-Waterloo Europe, the Americas offered the only real prospect for a democratic, republican politics. Nowadays that is accepted almost by default in the celebration of Anglo-American 'exceptionalism' and in the lamentations over the collapsed promises in the south of the continent — a disappointment which is explained with depressing frequency in terms of some cultural blindness or mimetic clumsiness, without any sense of the wider world which posed such a political challenge.

O'Connor could not but recognise that dual feature of independence. Soon after it was achieved — probably in 1827 — he began drafting an essay on the political economy of Bolivia that is strikingly

similar to his uncle's *State of Ireland.*[18] In June of that year he
published a proclamation encouraging 'Men of Ireland' to settle in
the 'New Erin' of Tarija, 'where the poor of my flesh and blood will
be received with open arms and provided with a good cow, a horse,
a pig and some farmyard fowl … They will be absolute masters of
their own destiny'.[19] This now familiar motif of liberty residing in
an industrious rural community averse to luxury and extravagance
also lies behind O'Connor's consistent advocacy of protectionism
against British textiles — an anti-imperialism which was kept alight
by the daily sight of even the most humble of Bolivians wearing
clothes of foreign-made fabric.[20] The image we have of him as a
patriarch decked out in Palmerstonian check and English cashmere
was one most reluctantly assumed.

Feargus would likewise inveigh against free trade as just 'a substitute for landed monopoly at home'.[21] He, however, did not take the
critique as far as his Spartan elder brother, who on 28 January 1850
noted in his diary,

> Upon my arrival [at Tarija] I paid to Don Antonio Cortés 43
> pesos and one *real,* which I owed him from last week for the
> clothes … I bought in his shop, and this is the first expendi-
> ture of this size that I have made for the purpose of
> clothing my person in 13 years, but I had nothing left to
> wear … It would have pleased me much to have spent this
> money on a product of national manufacture, but all the
> money leaves the country for Europe, where it maintains
> the industries of those countries, and I am caused great
> discomfort by the idea of contributing to the ruin of my
> *patria,* where I eat my daily bread …

Naturally, neither that *patria* nor any other aside from Spain existed
when Frank O'Connor set out from Dublin, and it is, above all, as a
soldier who fought to make their existence a possibility that history
recalls him. In 1999, with the outbreak of the first major armed
conflict in Europe for over 50 years, more than one generation is
acquiring for the first time a sharp sensibility as to the physical and
mental consequences of warfare. Even those predisposed to accept
claims made for modern weaponry on the basis of scream-free and
bloodless videos know that the exercise is not and cannot be free of

butchery, cruelty, privation and that volunteered madness which is required to kill and court death.

In a campaign fought with the ordnance of Waterloo the scale of damage inflicted was certainly different. Not a single shot was fired at the Battle of Junín in August 1824, when O'Connor was chief of staff of a Patriot army of 1,500 ranged against the Viceroy's 7,000 troops and nine artillery pieces,; an engagement confined to cavalry charges ended within an hour. Four months later at the Battle of Ayacucho, the last set-piece of a 15-year conflict, the Patriots fielded just one cannon, and the Royalists only managed to fire ranging shots with theirs.

On the other hand, the Patriot cavalry won at Junín largely because the Royalists had cut down their lances to six feet in order to lessen the stress on the backs of horse and rider ('lumbago' was a complaint common to all soldiers but experienced especially by lancers, and O'Connor suffered it all his adult life). The fact that the Patriots had not done the same meant that they had a three-foot advantage with which to impale their enemy or his horse. The wounds suffered were not neat bullet-holes but dismemberment and evisceration. When treatment could be administered it was undertaken with anaesthetic comprising the same liquor served up in slightly more modest quantities before the start of the battle. At Ayacucho over 1,500 men were killed and more than 1,000 wounded in a couple of hours.[22]

Moreover, at Junín and Ayacucho prisoners were taken. When O'Connor first arrived in Venezuela in 1819 this was not the case, the war being formally and practically 'to the death'. Even for a professional soldier whose father had twice escaped capital punishment this was a nasty shock. O'Connor reports that after the Battle of Ciénaga de Santa Marta in November 1820,

> there were two badly wounded Spaniards, unable to move, lying on the field. An adjutant to the commander approached him when I was sat beside him, and asked permission to slit the throats of the Spaniards. It was in vain that I opposed such barbarism ... and the next day the officer told me that he had hung the prisoners upside down over the river before decapitating them with his sword.[23]

It is not surprising that almost the entire Irish Legion had deserted or died within six months of its arrival in Isla Margarita. No amount of promotions and promises could compensate for such experiences, although it was disease that was the main fear and the principal cause of death. Yellow fever and cholera were the two greatest killers in the lowlands, into which the commanders tried to hem their enemy. Tuberculosis, of course, kept mortality rates generally high, but although he frequently coughed up black blood O'Connor seems to have been resistant to it. He also escaped the attacks of diarrhoea that ravaged troops and officers alike. However, as the army moved south through the territories that would become Colombia, Ecuador and Peru he became increasingly concerned about his 'terciana' — a less virulent strain of malaria — and 'Peruvian wart', also caused by insect bites and with the unpleasant symptom of discoloured tumours on the face.

These ailments meant that he was constantly compelled to experiment with remedies, from the familiar 'Dover salts' based on magnesium sulphate and opium to local potions of chocolate, celery and chicha, often prepared by his orderly, to whom he attributed the saving of his life on two occasions. Years after the campaign the general — who was often in pain, usually on the farm and seldom mentions a doctor or dentist — would administer himself formidably powerful purges, usually with an opiate-base of 'English salts' drenched in Jalapa pepper, honey and calomel or mercurious chloride.[24]

*

There is a second sense in which I see Francisco Burdett O'Connor as a third man.

Some seven years ago I gave my first inaugural lecture in this university, at Queen Mary and Westfield College. I confess that for some time thereafter I looked upon that experience as agreeably accomplished and rather like the loss of one's virginity in that it was by definition resistant to repetition. Now that I discover the fun to have become habit-forming, I shall obviously have to seek advice from colleagues in the philosophy programme of the School of Advanced Study as to where I committed epistemological error.

In that earlier lecture I placed between two historical stereotypes — a warrior felled in his prime and a scribe spared to ruminate —

the figure of a third man representing those who died in defeat, the disappeared forgotten as individuals by all bar family and friends.

This evening I seek a much less tragic shadow, but I cannot fail first to notice that in 1992 my exemplar for it was a man — Jorge Ríos Dalenz — who had been executed in Santiago de Chile on 15 September 1973, following the coup led by General, now Senator, Augusto Pinochet. I do recognise that there are in this hall today distinguished persons convinced that Pinochet's detention last October in this city at the behest of the kingdom of Spain was a denial precisely of the kind of republican sovereignty fought for at such cost by O'Connor and the other founding fathers.

England and Spain have, indeed, been the villains of my piece this evening. Nonetheless, I am of the firm if inexpert view that the arrest of the former dictator on such charges, whilst it undeniably further alters the ever-mutable condition of national sovereignty, provides welcome support precisely for those rights of man — what we today call human rights — and that individual sovereignty without which no civil society — let alone a nation — may flourish in freedom. Many of the claims for an increasing internationalisation of society in the post-Cold War world are both exaggerated and misconceived, but the evolution of law in this field clearly does promise progress beyond both property-based ideologies and Westphalian frontiers.

As I have already intimated, the third man I discern today is both warrior and scribe, and he is a victor who survives, but he is a technician, planner and strategist, not the heroic leader. This is the O'Connor who stands behind Bolívar and Sucre in the campaign of 1824 in Peru, and this is the same man who stands behind Sucre and Santa Cruz in the construction of Bolivia until the late 1830s.

In his own account O'Connor was told by Bolívar that after the campaign for independence he would lend a regiment of hussars to help the Irish cause. The offer was, of course, even less serious than that made 20 years earlier by Bonaparte to Arthur.[25] However, Bolívar had quickly gained a high regard for the young Irish colonel, whom he appointed chief of staff of the united army of liberation within six months of his joining it from Panama early in 1824. It was O'Connor who kept the Patriot forces coordinated and supplied as they manoeuvred under Sucre's command in distinctly hostile territory to bring the last Spanish viceroy in mainland America to battle and defeat.[26]

This was a far more demanding task than it might appear today.
Even the modest rebel army required a cattle train of some 6,000 head,
which had to be kept close enough to afford regular supply but sufficiently distant to avoid enemy raids. A horse is more primitive than an
armoured car, but it still needs considerable upkeep — not only in
terms of forage but also shoes, and nails for those shoes, and farriers
to fix them, and forges to melt down the requisitioned iron, which was
so precious that even carbines were converted in order that the chargers
might be shod on all four hooves, uncommon at that time.[27]

Moreover, for every horse the army needed several mules, not
just to carry the stores across the Andean fastnesses — 300 mules
were required for the reserve depot alone — but also to provide
fresh mounts for marches and counter-marches at altitudes which
sickened beasts as well as men. O'Connor's equestrian youth underpinned his aptitude for logistics of this type, but his assiduous
quartermastership reflected a far less naturalistic factor, and sometimes his liking for dispatch and detail drove other members of the
command to distraction.[28]

In his will O'Connor scrupulously notes that he was not chief of
staff on the day of the Battle of Ayacucho but chosen by Sucre to
determine where the Royalists should be engaged. The disgrace of
being replaced by a Peruvian — General Agustín Gamarra — for
political reasons when the engagement was imminent was felt most
deeply, even bitterly. O'Connor sourly notes that no unit of the
Patriots' Peruvian Division was actually commanded by a Peruvian,
and all the officers who had been born outside the Americas must
have taken some umbrage at the fact that only one of their number
— the Irishman Colonel Arthur Sandes — was mentioned in Sucre's
official despatch after the battle.

Otto Braun, the commander of the grenadiers already denied
proper recognition for his action at Junín, adopted a Germanic
brown study. William Miller, who led the hussars in the charge that
swung the battle, remarked that the last cannonade of the day had
signalled the moment for all foreigners to get out. By contrast,
O'Connor, who showed no sign of leaving, protested to Sucre, who
then withdrew his promotion to general — he would have to wait six
years to receive the rank.[29]

However, it is telling that following this very public difference of opinion Sucre put O'Connor in command of the operation to hunt down the remaining Royalist forces under General Pedro Olañeta, whose escape into Alto Peru would lead the angry but disciplined colonel into his new *patria,* shortly to be renamed Bolivia.

This was a command entailing considerable confidence, and indeed, it would seem to revindicate O'Connor's achievement at Ayacucho, where the Royalist army of over 9,000 troops had been nearly twice as large as that commanded by Sucre. O'Connor knew that a battle could only be won by choosing terrain which permitted an attack to be pressed home before the enemy could collect all his forces, and that this would most likely happen as a result of surprise, when La Serna's troops were descending rather than climbing the steep gorges of the zone.

After an initial encounter in which the Patriots lost most of their baggage train and so many of their rearguard that the veteran Sandes wept as he reported their deaths, the two armies manoeuvred for nearly a week. In the eyes of his former chief of staff, Sucre began to lose his nerve, and O'Connor, who now formally held only a regimental position, had difficulty in persuading him not to make a defiant stand but to continue marching the exhausted and demoralised force to Hauicho and then engage the Royalists as they confidently approached from the heights of Condorcunca. Despite his many years of attachment to the turf, Francisco Burdett O'Connor was not a betting man, but on 9 December he wagered his pay on the result.[30]

Something similar is discernable almost 15 years later when O'Connor, then in his late 40s and much more familiar with the terrain, rejoined forces with Otto Braun to inflict a defeat on the invading Argentine army at the Battle of Montenegro. That victory was also obtained by a series of flanking manoeuvres and feigned retreats through hill country in a manner that might be expected of a fox-hunting man. It came too late to save the Peru–Bolivia Confederation that Santa Cruz had laboriously assembled as a counter-weight to conservative Chile and the pugnacious power of Governor Rosas in Buenos Aires. However, Montenegro consolidated the present south-west border of Bolivia as well as allowing the Hibernian commander to retire from military service for the

third time — he always refused to serve in times of peace — and
recover his farms, which the invaders had occupied, slaughtering and
selling off cattle that in those same times of peace were rustled only
by the Chiriguano Indians.

At one point Santa Cruz had placed his hopes for the
Confederation's future in the purchase of a new European warship
for a million pesos, which he asked O'Connor to take to Britain.[31]
The reply received by the president indicates that Francisco was
never going to revert to Frank:

> If any friend asked me to accept this proposition I would not
> accept it ... when I left my homeland I did so with the inten-
> tion of never returning to it because my family suffered the
> persecutions of the English government, but I owe [you] the
> obedience due to my commander, and [you have] the right to
> order me to undertake this task.[32]

Perhaps it was just as well that the money was never raised. Indeed,
a few years later there arrived in Tarija a letter from Feargus which
would have surely confirmed his brother's fears about political
repression in Britain and probably revived others about personal
eccentricity in the family.

These were no longer focused on Roger because, as Feargus
reported,

> Our Father died in 1834 of apoplexy, having got up in the
> morning in perfect health and being dressed, he stooped to
> put on his boot, seized the bed post and never spoke more,
> although he lingered some days in perfect consciousness. He
> also died a Catholic and was buried according to the cere-
> monies of that religion.

Roger's death does, however, appear to have unleashed something in
Feargus, who was described by Sir Robert Peel as a man who
'appeared to take fire very easily and boil at a very low tempera-
ture'.[33] Feargus himself told his brother in Bolivia,

> Since [1837] I have had to sustain seven government prosecu-
> tions, for two of which ... I was sentenced to 18 months
> confinement in York Castle, which I spent in one of the
> condemned cells in solitary confinement, and upon the day of

my liberation I was received by delegates from all parts of England, Scotland and Wales and honoured with a triumphal procession in a splendid triumphant car covered with velvet and drawn through the City of York with six horses ... While I was in York Castle I read 200 volumes of the best works and wrote a number myself. I have published several works, some of which have been stereotyped and all of which sell well ... I should tell you that on every occasion I have been prosecuted I have defended myself, and upon my last trial at York I spoke for 5 hours and 37 minutes, when the Judge directed an acquittal but the Special Jury found me guilty ... More I need not tell you of myself other than that after all, and having travelled more than any other man living during the last ten years and having been knocked down, and awfully and brutally mangled by hired mobs with stones, sticks and iron bolts, yet I am as well in health and constitution as when you and I used to jump over the six feet poles ... [at] a hopping match at the Pigeon Ground at Battersea ... I did 306 feet in thirty consecutive hops, never putting the second foot to the ground.[34]

Feargus gave as good as he got to almost everybody — from the chancellor of the exchequer, whom he ridiculed at one remove,[35] to hissing audiences of northern aristocrats, whom he abused directly and with relish.[36] Perhaps his greatest defeat in debate was in 1844 at the hands of Cobden over free trade. He has certainly gone down in history as a turbulent, unreliable braggart hated by his companions in the Chartist leadership but loved by the masses. Even Marx's description captures a critical contrary strain: 'He is essentially conservative, and feels a highly determined hatred not only for industrial progress but also for the revolution ... He unites in his person an inexhaustible number of contradictions which find their fulfilment and harmony in a certain blunt *common sense*.'[37]

Such common sense — allied with the convictions of this most physical of men about the superiority of moral force — led Feargus to persuade the thousands gathered on Kennington Common on 10 April 1848 not to march on Westminster and so avoid an almost certain massacre at the hands of troops assembled by Wellington.[38]

Here, though, there is also tragedy because Feargus, stressed by the pressures of 1848 beyond even his Promethean limits, did even-

tually go mad. The sad arena for the final collapse was the House of
Commons, where he sat for Nottingham and where his prior antics
had so exasperated the Speaker that he was held in custody by the
Serjeant-at-Arms for a full week until, after petitions from his sister
Harriet, the true nature of his ill-health was recognised.[39] Feargus
died three years later, believing, not without a certain logic, that he
was still being detained by the state.

Francisco Burdett O'Connor would have recognised his brother's
common sense beneath the hype, but he must also have had reason
to contrast his own life with that lived publicly and privately on the
edge and so insistently within the idiom of heroism.

O'Connor's diary gives the lie to the image of a nineteenth-
century Bolivia wracked by constant anarchy and utterly unhinged
from the residual concerns of civilisation. The reality was by no
means shining, just more prosaic. The entry for 17 December 1849
is quite representative:

> I went to the Fort after lunch and spent a long time with the
> Reverend Father and the magistrate. I made a visit to the
> governor with some complaints about the abuses of
> authority caused by reserve officers posted to this frontier —
> he promises me satisfaction and we leave it at that. During
> my visit he gave me to understand that the Reverend Father
> had offered him six pesos and that he, for his part, would
> match them towards the building of a small school-house for
> the village. I greatly approved of his plans, and I promised
> six pesos of my own ...

In view of what had gone on in his life before and what he learnt of
events in the British Isles it is perhaps unsurprising that on 6 August
1849 — Bolivia's national day and the 25th anniversary of the Battle
of Junín — the general noted,

> Now I'm a man forgotten by all ... reduced to seeking my
> own subsistence at an age — 58 years — when there is little
> strength left in the body, and even less energy, but obliged to
> undertake manual work by necessity. Thanks to God, who
> endowed me with a disposition for this. If it had been other-
> wise, I'd be delivered up to sadness and revisiting my past life,
> and who knows what would happen to me.[40]

\*

I have told this tale — now nearly done — very much for its own sake, so that O'Connor might not be forgotten by all. However, when one is generously furnished with a platform before a distinguished audience it would be idle not to make at least one wider point.

These days one discerns a certain slack-jawed hubris in the world's metropoli with respect to the phenomenon of 'globalisation'. Now, of course, we cross the Atlantic every day and night, courtesy of our televisions, our telephones and our computers linked up to the internet. This transportation is not physical, but it is real. We are told that it is producing a qualitative transformation of the human condition even if the energy required and the effect produced sometimes seem to match those of a gerbil at leisure.

It is possible that — from the perspective not of technology but of the human mind and experience — we have been here, or very near here, before.

Certainly, there is a narrow sense in which I need to signal an institutional precedent. The first monograph published for the Institute of Latin American Studies 30 years ago by the Athlone Press was *The 'Detached Recollections' of General D.F. O'Leary,* edited by the founding director, Professor Robin Humphreys. Daniel O'Leary was Bolívar's principal aide de camp, a decade younger than his friend O'Connor but also a Cork man and capable of turning a fine phrase. It was O'Leary, not García Márquez, who described Bolívar's death in 1830 as 'the last embers of an expiring volcano, the dust of the Andes still on his garments'.[41]

Professor Humphreys himself died last month, in his ninety-second year. He was not only the first Director of the Institute but also, from 1948, the first holder of the established chair in Latin American history based at University College. That chair was subsequently occupied with great distinction by John Lynch and Leslie Bethell, both with us this evening, but in the early 1990s it was frozen. This is a great shame because it was the only established chair related to Latin America in the University, and it helped to ensure that the existence of the Institute was not used as an excuse to reduce or remove the study of the region elsewhere.

Indeed, that chair was one of only a couple in the country as a whole, so I am here concerned not just with the opportunities for our field within the new, more autonomous and less coordinated University of London but also throughout the United Kingdom. The Institute plays a critical role promoting Latin American studies at national level in collaboration with other institutes and centres with which it sometimes has to compete for scarce resources. The balance is fine and the challenge is sometimes considerable but it is also entirely consonant with our place and mission within the School of Advanced Study.

My predecessor, Victor Bulmer-Thomas, was the man who so enthusiastically and energetically oversaw our entry into the School, simultaneously expanding the Institute's activities on all fronts. The extent to which he has has really 'retired' may be judged from the fact that he is this evening giving a lecture in Salamanca, prior to attending a committee in New York. Last Autumn I caught sight of him briefly on Institute business in Boston and Chicago on either side of a trip to China.

I won't even attempt to match such activity, but it gives me great pleasure to announce today that the Institute will, in memory of its founding director, appoint each year to a Robin Humphreys Visiting Research Fellowship a past or present British public servant with experience of the Americas. The first holder of the Fellowship is to be Philip McLean, formerly British Consul in Boston and latterly Ambassador to Cuba — or, to borrow another title from Graham Greene, 'Our Man in Havana'.

Mr McLean's prior posting in Hibernian Massachusetts reminds us that O'Connor and O'Leary were a military vanguard of a major diaspora; and that diaspora was, in turn, simply one of the more recent movements of peoples — very seldom of a voluntary nature — throughout the globe.

It is a common observation that there are in America more people of Irish ancestry than in the island itself. It is less well known that there are now in US schools more pupils of a Hispanic background than there are young African-Americans. The Irish Famine began just months before the US invasion of Mexico and the annexation of that territory now being peacefully repopulated by the descendents of those defeated in 1847. It would take the better part of two more decades before slavery was abolished in the US, and 20 more years would lapse before the system which had over several centuries transported millions of people in chains from one continent to another would be entirely eradicated in that second place.

When we ask what's in the name 'America', then, we find a plethora of responses even within the two Institutes of the School directly concerned with that continent. Moreover, each of the other Institutes — to which I think I have now alluded directly or indirectly — in its own scholarly expertise gives the lie to any notion that the globe came into a complete spatial and self-knowing integrity with the advent of the micro-chip or the collapse of a wall built in Berlin after Fidel Castro came to power in Havana.

I don't mean to cast aspersions. We need fashion; it keeps us on our toes, sometimes literally. I would simply register some scepticism as to any unprecedented, seamless and centrifugal process of homogenisation. In that vein I have today employed the nearly anachronistic terms 'the Americas'. Pluralism is not just normative niceness — if, in fact, it is that at all. It is also a better class of scholarship — one which seeks excellence but without elitism. General O'Connor is, to my mind, best understood as a Jeffersonian, and there are many others and much more south of the Rio Grande profitably to be studied from that perspective of similarity as well as difference.

Indeed, a little more concern with comparison as a dual process — and a little less timidity in exploring and explaining it — would rectify the unwarranted exoticism of 'otherness' and test vacuous notions of hogomenisation-through-hybridity. It would enrich the understanding of Latin America and fortify area studies as a whole.

We cannot, after all, complain at the undoubtedly miserable funding of UK research and teaching in area studies if we do not confront the belief that they constitute little more than parochialism craftily practised abroad and protected by factors of space and language from the glare of scholarship heroically based on pure discipline. We need, in short, to enhance our disciplinary expertise (usually with a couple of others besides) and energetically to demonstrate how area studies has been made more, not less, valid in the contemporary world, where phenomena that we have studied for decades are now in the mainstream of daily life.

*

Francisco Burdett O'Connor died in Tarija on 5 October 1871. At this stage of proceedings one baulks at further tale of audacity, but it is a matter of record that at 8 o'clock in the evening he refused to receive the last rites at home and was assisted to the monastery, four blocks away, where they were administered. Eighty-one years of age, he died at 10 pm. Francisca and Hercilia survived him. Burdett had died a dozen years before Feargus. Now, of course, Frank dies too.

The name, we know, has been kept alive. Perhaps its most celebrated owner in recent years has been Cecilia O'Connor, who was the red-haired and post-globalist representative of Bolivian pulchritude at the Miss Universe contest of 1994 staged at Manila.

The family that's in the name of O'Connor has flourished since the patriarch died in the midst of his memoirs. This evening I choose as its representative Octavio, from the third generation, because he carried his forebear's educational concerns into the twentieth century that we are so noisily about to leave:

> The ceremony to mark the opening of the school year was exceptionally well attended, the teachers and populace of Tarija overflowing the stalls of the '15 April Hall'. In the wait before ascending the platform the Director of Education, Dr Octavio O'Connor d'Arlach, slowly lit his pipe and took a few contented puffs as he listened to the talk about him. Then somebody came up to him to say that people were getting impatient of waiting. O'Connor snapped to, put the pipe in his back-pocket, as you would a handkerchief, and requested the committee to take their seats.

> Following the solemn act of inauguration, Dr O'Connor, who was standing to the right of Don Víctor Navajas Trigo, prefect of the department, began to read his annual report. Immersed in his speech, he was unaware of the mounting consternation around him. But just as he was describing with some passion the infrastructural needs of the district, he sensed both the odour of burning and the gentle elbow of the prefect in his ribs. The smell came from his trousers, which the increasingly concerned audience could not see to

be on fire. The boss was unharmed, the trousers were a write-off, and the pedagogic community most gratified.[42]

We have happily evaded the combustion which terminated that inauguration. It is not the prefect but the clock that is now nudging me. The reality principle beckons, and I must thank you all for both indulgence and attention.

## Notes

1 Julio Díaz, A., *Historia del ejército boliviano, 1825–1932* (La Paz, 1971), p. 65.
2 In 1850 he wrote to his old friend Marshal Otto Philip Braun that his wife had lost 'six or seven' girls, 'todas muertas de resfrío', and was then nursing a son of ten months with great apprehension. O'Connor, Tarija, to Braun, 12 Dec. 1850, in J. Barnadas (ed.), *El mariscal Braun a través de su epistolario* (Cochabamba, 1998), p. 204.
3 *The Life of Francis Place* (London, 1898), p. 51.
4 *Homo Ludens* (London, 1949), p. 148.
5 *Partners in Revolution. The United Irishmen and France* (New Haven, 1982), pp. 100, 173.
6 My Heart's Beloved, knowing how anxious you will be, I send [this], though the Trials will be over some time tonight. Matters, we think, look good for O'Connor, but I am resolved not to be sanguine. I got to speak to him this morning. His mind is composed, but his nerves badly shaken. He was greatly affected when his poor brother was brought into court yesterday, and when the other took his hand, he burst into tears. The usage of Roger O'Connor, who is one of the finest fellows I ever saw, has been merciless beyond example. We are all very anxious and very busy, for the counsel want assistance. Here is Fox, Grey, Erskine, Grattan, Moira, Norfolk, etc.
Quoted in Walter Sichel, *Sheridan* (London, 1909), II, p. 284. See also Fintan O'Toole, *A Traitor's Kiss. The Life of Richard Brinsley Sheridan* (London, 1997), pp. 325–37.
7 *The Year of Liberty. The History of the Great Irish Rebellion of 1798* (London, 1972), pp. 129–30. In his maiden speech of March 1797 Burdett declared to the Commons, 'Good God, that treason to Ireland and the name of O'Connor should be preposterously linked together, as he is capable of everything that is great, generous and noble for his

country's good.' Quoted in M.W. Patterson, *Sir Francis Burdett and his Times (1770–1844),* II (London, 1931), p. 58.

8     Having met Arthur in January 1805, Benjamin Constant noted in his diary, 'O'Connor is a sophisticated man. When joking he has a lighter touch than foreigners usually do, and so has something of the French defect of joking about one's own opinions. He is more ambitious than he is a friend of liberty, and yet a friend of liberty nevertheless, because to be so is the refuge of ambitious men who have missed success ...' *Journaux intimes* (Paris, 1952), p. 189.

9     *The State of Ireland,* (1798) ed. James Livesey (Dublin, 1998). Frank MacDermott calls *Monopoly,* 'a boring mixture of economics, politics and anti-clerical rant'. 'Arthur O'Connor', *Irish Historical Studies,* vol. XV (1966–1967), p. 67. In his introduction to the pamphlet Livesey quotes Lady Wycombe, writing in March 1798 to Lady Holland, in similar vein: 'when he is in company, by the aid of a good memory he talks a few pages out of Adam Smith in lieu of conversation'. *The State of Ireland,* p. 9. MacDermott makes no mention of the pamphlet and is much more interested in matters of espionage than those of ideology.

10     The press is the palladium of Liberty. What has heretofore made England celebrated over the nations of Europe? — the press. What overturned the Catholic despotism of France? — the press, by the writings of Montesquieu, Voltaire, Rousseau, Diderot, Seyes, Raynal and Condorcet. What has electrified England and called down its curses on a Pitt? that press he in vain attempted to silence. What illumined Belfast, the Athens of Ireland? the *Press* and the *Northern Star.* Why did America triumph over tyranny? — a journeyman printer fulminated the decree of nature against the giants of England — and the pen of a Franklin routed the armies of the King.'

Quoted in D. Dickson, D. Keogh and K. Whelan (eds.), *The United Irishmen. Republicanism, Radicalism and Rebellion* (Dublin, 1993), pp. 275–6. In 1843 Feargus wrote to Frank, 'The press of this country is much more shackled than ever the French press was — the difference is just this — that of France had to undergo governmental censorship; while the aristocracy and middle classes hold the press of England in close and close and much more destructive bonds'. Feargus, London, 28 Sept. 1843, to Francisco Burdett O'Connor, original in possession of Eduardo Trigo O'Connor d'Arlach, to whom I am most grateful for access to this and other papers belonging to General O'Connor.

11   In a letter to Braun some three years after his marriage, O'Connor
     wrote that, having lost most of his men in a small-scale operation to
     capture some rebels, he himself was about to be lanced down and tried
     to kill himself but his pistol failed. He was spared and managed to
     escape but later suffered a collapse:

> En fin, mi amigo, los trabajos que padecí ese día me reventaron
> el corazón. Desde entonces no me conozco a mí mismo, ni
> Usted me conociera: estoy lastimado interiormente y expuesto
> a continuos ataques de enfermedad. Regresé a Tarija, en donde
> pasé tres meses en cama, merecí mil atenciones de la familia, en
> la cual me casé por gratitud, pensando morirme y dejar lo que
> poseía en esa familia. Tal no fué mi suerte. Aún existo ... Mi
> mujercita es apreciable, porque — pobre! — no me trajo un
> real, y es por eso que la elegí.

     O'Connor, Retiro-Frontera de Tarija, to Braun, 13 March 1830, in *El
     mariscal Braun,* pp. 50–51.
12   G.D.H. Cole, *Chartist Portraits* (London, 1941), p. 308.
13   Elliott, *Partners in Revolution,* p. 329.
14   Patterson, *Burdett,* II, p. 433; D. Read and E. Glasgow, *Feargus O'Connor.
     Irishman and Chartist* (London, 1961), p. 13; Francisco Burdett
     O'Connor, *Recuerdos* (1895) (La Paz, 1972), p. 5.
15   Quoted in Patterson, p. 441.
16   The space between reality and invention is shown to be magically
     minimal in this letter from Roger to Lady Burdett:

> Dear Lady Burdett,
> Your good opinion is most gratifying to me. The greatest
> misfortune of my life would be the loss of it. I did not think to
> write now, but a note I wrote in my wild mountains (which I
> pray Heaven that you will look upon next Summer) in answer
> to one Burdett wrote to me calls for a little history. Of these
> mountains I can give you no idea — the messenger handed me
> the letter, which demanded an answer, a written one from me
> for fear of mistake. How was this to be done was the point;
> people there were to hand, but they were all on the chance trip
> to meet Sir Francis. What am I to do, lads, say I; is it possible to
> get pen, ink and paper anywhere near? What, says one, is there
> no pen among you? No. Is there no goose here, says another?
> Yes. Off with the speaker from his horse, catches a goose —
> plucks a quill — no knife — may be the smith (there chanced
> to be a smith's forge not far off) has a razor. The pen was made.

> There was no ink. Run down one of you boys to the forge and
> make up some forge water pretty strong. Up came ink; there
> happened to be a pedlar who had a little book — out goes a leaf
> of a little bit of paper — a fellow takes off his hat for a table
> — and *thus* was I enabled to make out my note. Never let it be
> said that the Irish are not people of rare invention.
> Your faithful servant.

Quoted in Patterson, pp. 451–52.

17  *Heathcliff and the Great Hunger* (London, 1995), p. 9. In 1848 Aubrey de
Vere wrote that, 'charges made against Ireland, it is true, derive a
certain verisimilitude from the stories in circulation amongst you; but
you cannot be ignorant that for such tales the supply, according to the
ordinary laws of trade, will always be proportionate to the demand'.
*English Misrule and Irish Misdeeds* (London, 1970), p. 44.

18  Neither uncle nor nephew confused the rights of man with the qualities of men. Francisco opens his untitled essay in distinctly sober
voice:

> A true desire to render a service to the Republic of Bolivia and
> to all the new States of America obliges me to exercise strict
> control over my nature, violating it to the extreme of writing for
> the multitude, ungrateful though I know it to be, always to have
> been and always to be ... My conscience tells me that [in this] I
> provide a service of greater value than those ... in nine years of
> work in the fields of destruction of tyranny and victories for
> the rights of man ...'

19  Parts are reprinted in Edmund Temple, *Travels in Various Parts of Peru,
Including a Year's Residence in Potosí,* II (London, 1830), pp. 354ff.

20  In the mid-1830s, arguing that the sale of public lands on the US model
would not work in Latin America, O'Connor proposed to president
Santa Cruz that all Bolivians who wore foreign clothes should be taxed
twice as much as those with locally produced garments. Although there
was evidently a huge problem with the practicality of such a scheme,
O'Connor reports that Santa Cruz reacted in a positive manner:

> Do you know General, he said, that my little Simon's nurse is an
> Indian from the Puna, to Whom my wife gives presents of yarn,
> shawls and scarves of foreign fabric. Her relatives see this when
> they come to the house in La Paz and are themselves wearing
> such garments when they visit the following Sunday. I expect to
> see all our Indians dressed in foreign clothes instead of the rude
> garments they now wear. And, General, it will then be necessary

to find new sources of tributary tax because when the Indians who now pay it are clothed in foreign materials they will not have a *real* left to pay for their *fiestas* or ecclesiastical obligations. *Recuerdos,* p. 217

21 *Northern Star,* 3 Nov. 1838.

22 John Miller (ed.), *Memoirs of General Miller in the Service of Peru,* II (London, 1828), p. 170. According to Miller there was not a single qualified doctor in the Peruvian department of Puno, and when, after the war, San Martín's surgeon-general, the Irishman Michael Crawley, set himself up at Lampa it was not as a medical practitioner but as an owner of mines. An English dentist by the name of Dudley did open a clinic in Arequipa, where he had a child with the great Argentine writer Juana Manuela Gorriti, at whose earlier wedding General O'Connor had been *padrino.*

23 *Recuerdos,* p. 28.

24 *Recuerdos,* pp. 62, 78–79; Diary entries for 22 Nov. 1849; 27 March 1850.

25 *Recuerdos,* p. 56. Morgan O'Connell, the son of Daniel, 'the Liberator', also joined the Patriot forces in 1820, encouraging his father to stage a fervent defence of John Devereux, the Waterford man charged with illegally recruiting members of the Irish Legion. In April 1820 O'Connell wrote to Bolívar to register 'my respect for your high character and ... my attachment to that sacred cause which your talents, valour and virtue have gloriously sustained — I mean the cause of liberty and national independence'. By the end of the year, though, he was writing to his wife with more parental concern and candour:

> You have seen our darling Morgan's letter to Ricarda Connor. Would to God we knew where he is at present. Admiral Brion's letter which appeared in the *Freeman's [Journal]* of yesterday distinctly says there will not be any more troops recruited from Ireland. He calls them a banditta. In my opinion that gentleman has not behaved by the Irish troops as he should have done. I hope he will be made to suffer for his conduct.

O'Connell, Dublin, to Bolívar, 17 April 1820; O'Connell, Tralee, to his wife Mary, 5 Oct. 1820. *The Correspondence of Daniel O'Connell,* II (Shannon, 1972), pp. 277–78, 284.

26 In January 1824, a month after he first met him, Bolívar wrote to Sucre, 'Major O'Connor should be detached from his batallion to oversee the carrying out of your instructions to the Grenadiers as I think he is the best officer to use at the advanced posts'. Bolívar,

Pativilca, to Sucre, 24 Jan. 1824, in V. Lecuña (ed.), *Selected Writings of Bolívar*, II (New York, 1952), p. 247. In April the Liberator had enough confidence in him to think of using him as an emissary to negotiate with Viceroy LaSerna. Bolívar, Otuzco, to Sucre, 14 April 1824, in V. Lecuña (ed.), *Cartas del Libertador*, IV (Caracas, 1929), p. 127.

27   'Such was the scarcity of iron that most of the fire-arms had been converted into nails and horse-shoes', *Memoirs of General Miller*, II, p. 124.

28   'The Liberator instructs me to inform you that there are here 700 loads of wheat which should betaken to the hill, and that he does not know how this is to be checked because O'Connor does not belong to this world and knows nothing; and the intendent is worse than O'Connor because he is useless.' Tomás de Heres, Huánuco, to Sucre, 12 July 1824, in *Correspondencia del Libertador* (Caracas, 1974), p. 240.

29   *Recuerdos*, pp. 99–104. In fact, O'Connor had previously used his powers of persuasion to stop Sucre executing the Kassel-born Braun for disobedience when he was conducting himself in a rather teutonic and not ingratiating fashion. Aside from Miller and Braun, both of whom would serve the young Bolivian republic, O'Connor mentioned Wright, Ferguson, Harris, Gregg, Duxbury and Hallowes as foreign-born soldiers who fought at Ayacucho with distinction. Foreigners served on the other side too. O'Connor failed to extract a single intelligible word from Paul Eccles, a native of Switzerland whom he and Sandes had interrogated in French, Spanish, English and Celtic when Eccles was detained near Oruro carrying a flask of poison and instructions from General Olañeta for the murder of Sucre and the rebel guerrilla commander Miguel Lanza. *Ibid.*, pp. 109–10; C. Arnade, *La dramática insurgencia de Bolivia* (La Paz, 1972), pp. 196–97.

30   *Recuerdos*, p. 97. Miller's account stresses the superior numbers, weapons and resources of the Royalists but also their political divisions and low morale. *Memoirs of General Miller*, II, pp. 163ff.

31   'Señor O'Connor, because of his birth, his honour and his knowledge seems to me to be the most obvious choice to obtain a boat for us in Europe'. Vice-President Enrique Calvo, Tapacarí, to Santa Cruz, 10 June 1836, in R. Querejazu (ed.), *Oposición en Bolivia a la confederación Peru-boliviana* (Sucre, 1996), pp. 149–50.

32   *Recuerdos*, p. 248.

33   Quoted in Norman Gash, *Sir Robert Peel* (London, 1986), p. 661.

34   Feargus O'Connor, London, to 'My dear Frank', 28 Sept. 1843. Typed copy in the possession of Eduardo Trigo O'Connor d'Arlach. Feargus shared the family love of equestrianism, but 'in 1834 all my horses

were thoroughly licked at the races of Fermoy. I lost £750 upon them, sold them all, and gave up the Turf. Since then I have never bet a farthing on horseflesh'.

35     'Harry Brougham said they wanted no poor law as every young man ought to lay up a provision for old age, yet while he said this with one side of his mouth, he was screwing the other side to get his retiring pension raised from £4,000 to £5,000 a year. But if the people had their rights they would not long pay his salary. Harry would go to the treasury, he would knock at the door, but Ceberus would not open the door, he would ask, 'Who is there?' And then luckless Harry would answer, 'It's an ex-chancellor coming for his £1,250 a quarter's salary', but Ceberus would say, 'There have been a dozen of ye here already, and there is nothing for ye'. And then Harry would cry,        'Oh!    what    will become of me? What shall I do?' And Ceberus would say, 'Go into the Bastille that you have provided for the people.' Then, when Lord Harry and Lady Harry went into the Bastille, the keeper would say, 'This is your ward to the right, and this, my lady, is your ward to the left; we are Malthusians here, and are afraid you would breed, therefore you must be kept asunder.'

Quoted in R.G. Gammage, *History of the Chartist Movement, 1837–1854* (London, 1894), p. 26.

36     Yes — you — I was just coming to you, when I was describing the materials of which our spurious aristocracy is composed. You gentlemen belong to the big-bellied, little-brained, numskull aristocracy. How dare you hiss me, you contemptible set of platter-faced, amphibious politicians? ... Now was it not indecent of you? Was it not foolish of you? Was it not ignorant of you to hiss me? If you interrupt me again, I'll bundle you out of the room.

Quoted in Mark Hovell, *The Chartist Movement* (London, 1918), p. 94. The threat would have been taken seriously, according to Gammage, who was writing when Feargus was still alive: 'No member of the prize ring could fight his way with more desperate energy through a crowd than could this electioneering pugilist; and it was not alone with his fists that he was useful to his friends.' Gammage, *History*, p. 14. In 1843 Feargus told Frank, 'I am six feet and one inch high, and weigh 14 stone ... I have had four duels in which I received three apologies on the ground, and was once fired at in the neighbourhood of Cork when the bullet whizzed by my nose.'

37   Review of May–October 1850, *Neue Rheinische Zeitung Revue*, in D.
     Fernbach (ed.), *Marx. The Revolutions of 1848* (Harmondsworth, 1973),
     pp. 308–9.
38   I take my lead in this unfashionable interpretation from John Belchem,
     '1848: Feargus O'Connor and the Collapse of the Mass Platform', in
     J. Epstein and D. Thompson (eds.), *The Chartist Experience: Studies in
     Working-Class Radicalism and Culture, 1830–60* (London, 1982). In his
     1843 letter to Frank — who as Francisco was a republican and warrior
     — Feargus wrote,
          You must know that I am not a Republican nor would I seek for
          any change by violence, while you have learned enough of
          literary political trick to be aware that ... with the accredited
          power of authority, tyrannical governments always have it in
          their power at a given moment to bring about a futile resistance
          to the settled order of things.
39   Feargus had earlier eaten the supper left for the Speaker in his private
     office following a refusal by that officer to issue a ruling on whether a
     root vegetable served to O'Connor and the O'Gorman Mahon (the
     MP for Ennis whom Trollope once spotted on dubious business in
     Costa Rica) was a beetroot or a manglewurzel. On 8 June 1852 Feargus
     struck another MP in the chamber, was named and apologised. On the
     9th Hansard reports,
          The Attorney General was proceeding to address the Committee,
          but was interrupted by the disorderly and offensive conduct of
          the honourable Member for Nottingham, who, on being remon-
          strated with by the honourable Member for West Riding, thrust
          a half-closed hand into the honourable Member's face.
     *Parliamentary Debates*, Third Series, CXII, p. 367.
40   O'Connor knew that local politics was not for him:
          In Tarija today there was a farce of an election for Senator, and
          it befell General Celedonio Ávila to be elected to that class of
          escort for General Belzu. The said General knows about as
          much about legislation as I do of the Chinese language, but this
          matters not at all; that is not the intended object of General
          Ávila's nomination ... These countries are ignorant of everything
          to do with sovereignty. Votes are given according to the orders of
          the leader and there's nothing more to be said of this matter.
     Diary, entry for 2 June 1850. A year earlier O'Connor's close friend
     Colonel Eustaquio ('El moto') Méndez, a guerrilla leader in the inde-
     pendence wars, had been tortured by rebels against Belzu and died in

his house whilst being nursed by Francisca. Octavio O'Connor d'Arlach, *Calendario histórico de Tarija* (La Paz, 1975), p. 114.

41   R.A. Humphreys (ed.), *The 'Detached Recollections' of General D.F. O'Leary* (London, 1969), p. 48. The final sentence of García Márquez's account is less concise but still very powerful:

> Then he crossed his arms over his chest and began to listen to the radiant voices of slaves singing the six o'clock *Salve* in the mills, and through the window he saw the diamond of Venus in the sky that was dying forever, the eternal snows, the new vine whose yellow bellflowers he would not see bloom the following Saturday in the house closed in mourning, the final brilliance of life that would never, in all eternity, be repeated again.

*The General in His Labyrinth* (London, 1991), p. 268.

42   Antonio Paredes Candia, *Anécdotas bolivianas* (La Paz, 1978), pp. 127–8.

INSTITUTE FOR THE STUDY OF THE
# AMERICAS

UNIVERSITY OF LONDON · SCHOOL OF ADVANCED STUDY

The Institute for the Study of the Americas (ISA) promotes, coordinates and provides a focus for research and postgraduate teaching on the Americas – Canada, the USA, Latin America and the Caribbean – in the University of London.

The Institute was officially established in August 2004 as a result of a merger between the Institute of Latin American Studies and the Institute of United States Studies, both of which were formed in 1965.

The Institute publishes in the disciplines of history, politics, economics, sociology, anthropology, geography and environment, development, culture and literature, and on the countries and regions of Latin America, the United States, Canada and the Caribbean.

ISA runs an active programme of events – conferences, seminars, lectures and workshops – in order to facilitate national research on the Americas in the humanities and social sciences. It also offers a range of taught master's and research degrees, allowing wide-ranging multi-disciplinary, multi-country study or a focus on disciplines such as politics or globalisation and development for specific countries or regions.

Full details about the Institute's publications, events, postgraduate courses and other activities are available on the web at www.americas.sas.ac.uk.

**Institute for the Study of the Americas**
**School of Advanced Study, University of London**
**31 Tavistock Square, London WC1H 9HA**

**Tel 020 7862 8870, Fax 020 7862 8886, Email americas@sas.ac.uk,**
**Web www.americas.sas.ac.uk**

Recent and forthcoming titles in the ISA series:

Making Institutions Work in Peru: Democracy, Development and Inequality since 1980
*edited by John Crabtree*

Right On? Political Change and Continuity in George W. Bush's America
*edited by Iwan Morgan and Philip Davies*

Francisco de Miranda: Exile and Enlightenment
*edited by John Maher*

Caciquismo in Twentieth-Century Mexico
*edited by Alan Knight and Wil Pansters*

Democracy after Pinochet: Politics, Parties and Elections in Chile
*by Alan Angell*

The Struggle for an Enlightened Republic: Buenos Aires and Rivadavia
*by Klaus Gallo*

Mexican Soundings: Essays in Honour of David A. Brading
*edited by Susan Deans-Smith and Eric Van Young*

America's Americans: Population Issues in U.S. Society and Politics
*edited by Philip Davies and Iwan Morgan*

Football in the Americas: Fútbol, Futebol, Soccer
*edited by Rory Miller*

American Civilization
*Charles A. Jones*

Printed in the United Kingdom
by Lightning Source UK Ltd.
122732UK00001B/202-216/A

9 781900 039819